£7

Astrology, Aleister & Aeon

Astrology, Aleister & Aeon

by

Charles Kipp

NEW FALCON PUBLICATIONS
TEMPE, ARIZONA, U.S.A.

International Standard Book Number: 1-56184-135-8
Library of Congress Catalog Card Number: 97-75756

First Edition 2001

Cover art by Amanda Fisher

The paper used in this publication meets the minimum requirements of the American National Standard for Permanence of Paper for Printed Library Materials Z39.48-1984

Address all inquiries to:
NEW FALCON PUBLICATIONS
1739 East Broadway Road #1-277
Tempe, AZ 85282 U.S.A.

(or)
320 East Charleston Blvd. #204-286
Las Vegas, NV 89104 U.S.A.

website: http://www.newfalcon.com
email: info@newfalcon.com

To an observer standing outside of its generating-causes, novelty can only appear as so much 'chance,' to one who stands inside it, it is the expression of 'free creative activity.'
— William James, *A Pluralistic Universe*

FOR
PAMELA

ACKNOWLEDGMENTS

I thank my father, Harry Kipp, for his love and his example through which he instilled in me values that have contributed enormously to the ideas expressed in this book.

I thank my wife, Mary Catherine Carson Kipp, for her devoted support for my efforts toward the writing of this book and her unfailing confidence in the prospect of its success.

I also wish to thank my grandmother Rebecca Ann Clinton, my Aunt Joan and Uncle Max Scoggins and Aunt Mary and Uncle Rusty Smitherman who have shown me how authentically traditional values may be upheld in the spirit of love and freedom.

I offer a special thanks to DeltaLee Bilderback who opened my mind to the galactic elements of humanity's historical evolution.

I wish to express profoundest appreciation to Hilyn Brooke who brought me into direct contact with the deepest mystery and animating current of life.

I want to issue my undying gratitude to Vivian Carlisle who has assisisted my efforts in ways that she only knows best.

I thank William Tell Gifford, Ph.D. for his painstaking review of the manuscript and his numerous valuable suggestions for improving its expression.

I thank Michael Miller for his intuitive insight into the content of the manuscript and his confirmation that its intent was fulfilled.

I wish to thank David Wodis Powers for his exemplification of actual processes of personal evolvement that go beyond mere refinement of existing patterns.

I also wish to thank Vincent P.T. Benoit d'Etiveaux for his long friendship and mutual appreciation for pushing the limits of philosophical investigation.

I express my acknowledgment of and appreciation for the genius of all the philosophers, scholars and evolutionary change agents who have carried the Great Work forward in the course of history. In addition to Aleister Crowley, those who have influenced me most directly are, in the order of their births, William James, Dane Rudhyar, Timothy Leary and Robert Anton Wilson.

Finally, I wish to thank Nicholas Tharcher of New Falcon Publications for his assistance and counsel in the preparation of this book.

TABLE OF CONTENTS

Foreword: The Hidden Heritage
by Robert Anton Wilson

> I believe in one secret and ineffable LORD, and in one
> Star in the company of Stars of whose fire we are
> created, and to which we shall return; and in one Father
> of Life, Mystery of Mystery, in His name CHAOS...
> — *Gnostic Catholic Mass,* by Aleister Crowley

Something Wicked This Way Comes

When I first heard of Aleister Crowley, in some 1950s tabloid, they called him "the Wickedest Man in the World." I wondered what Crowley had done to deserve that title in a century overcrowded with such strong rivals as Hitler, Stalin, Mao, Mussolini, and the galoot who makes up the IRS forms. I therefore read the article avidly. To my intense disappointment, I found that Crowley's "wickedness" consisted merely of having unconventional ideas and leading an unconventional sex life. I forgot about him. Lots of other people had unconventional ideas and/or led unconventional sex lives (e.g., Oscar Wilde, Ludwig Wittgenstein, James Joyce, D.H. Lawrence, Charles Fort, Wilhelm Reich, Ezra Pound, President John F. Kennedy, President Bill Clinton et al.).

Around 1970, Alan Watts recommended a book to me, called *The Eye in the Triangle* by Dr. Israel Regardie. Alan was almost a guru to me in those days, so I rushed out and bought the book that very day. To my astonishment, it was about the "wicked" Aleister Crowley and revealed that he was even more egregious, and a hell of a lot more interesting, than tabloid journalism had suggested. The title of the book, however, was never explained therein and I was left wondering what the hell Crowley had to do with the Great Seal of the United States... (I still wonder about that.)

Since then, I have read virtually all of Uncle Aleister's books and about a dozen other biographies or "interpretations" of him, and have even written introductions to three books about him, including a new printing of Regardie's *The Eye in the Triangle.*

As a result of this 28 years of study I know a great deal more about The Wickedest Man In The World and understand a great deal less. I learned, for instance, that he was a Bishop of the Gnostic Catholic Church, an author of reams of poetry (some of it excellent), a member of the now-forgotten Carlist conspiracy (which attempted to replace Queen Victoria with a surviving member of the Stuart dynasty), a mountain climber of great accomplishment, a devilishly clever prankster and practical joker, an early recruit to the Irish Republican Army, an intelligence agent for both England and Germany in World War I, and a man who, either out of perverse humor or for even stranger reasons, did as much as his most hostile critics to blacken his own reputation.

To prepare you for what you will encounter in the body of this text, let me offer a different perspective on the very gnomic, very mysterious, and actually very funny man who has become, to more and more people, the Magus of the New Aeon.

On the exoteric level, Aleister Crowley was raised in the Plymouth Brethren, a Christian Fundamentalist sect of very puritanical orientation. He once described that early training as "A Boyhood in Hell." After attaining the age of reason and rejecting all superstitions of that ilk, he majored in organic chemistry at Cambridge, which lingered in his mind for life and provided the impetus to his efforts to synthesize the insights of mysticism and the methods of modern science. "Thank God I'm an atheist," he once wrote piously—and that's not anywhere near the peaks of paradox he employed to both reveal and conceal the meanings of his very hermetic books.

On the more esoteric level, Crowley joined several very secretive secret societies, and all of them influenced his own unique visionary experiences. To look into these groups, even briefly, will give us some insight into why this man Crowley remains a mystery inside a puzzle within a controversy cloaked in uncertainty.

Hold onto to your hats. We are about to plunge into matters about which no two academic historians agree totally, and non-academic theorists who go fishing here generally accuse each other of being fools, charlatans or crackpots.

To begin with, Aleister was a Freemason. He belonged to the Ancient and Accepted Craft. He held the 33rd degree in the Scotch Rite, among other titles. What the deuce does that mean, really? What distinguishes the Freemasons from the Lions, the Oddfellows or the Elks? Why has masonry appeared so conspicuously in so many right-wing conspiracy theories?

THE ANCIENT AND ACCEPTED CRAFT

The symbol of the Craft of Freemasonry. The square and compass symbolize the rationality of the universe, as a work of Great Craft and G simply abbreviates the usual English name of that master builder, God, also known to masons as GAOTU, the Great Architect of the Universe.

Freemasonry has an extremely obscure history. Depending on which "authority" you believe, it either originated in the Garden of Eden, taught to Adam by God Himself...or else among the priests of ancient Egypt...or perhaps the builders of Solomon's temple...or possibly in the 14th century...or maybe the 17th. It certainly existed by the early 18th Century, where we read of such competing masonic traditions as the Grand Orient Lodge of Egyptian Freemasonry, the Strict Observance lodge, the Grand United Lodge of England, the Grand Orange Lodge of Ireland etc. As Ambrose Bierce wrote in *The Devil's Dictionary*:

> Freemasons, n. An order with secret rites, grotesque ceremonies and fantastic costumes, which, originating in the reign of Charles II among working artisans in London, has been joined successively by the dead of past centuries in unbroken retrogression until now it embraces all the generations of man on the hither side of Adam and is drumming up distinguished recruits among the pre-Creational inhabitants of Chaos and the Formless Void.

Or as a popular witticism puts it:

> How many masons does it take to change a light bulb?
> That's a Craft secret.

To look at masonry in some kind of perspective we must remember that many tribal peoples have both all-male and all-female secret societies, which help maintain the "cultural values"—i.e., the local reality-tunnel. Freemasonry is certainly the largest, quite probably the oldest and still the most controversial of the all-male secret societies surviving in our world, and that is about all we can say about it for sure or for certain. No two scholars can even agree on how old it is, much less on how "good" or "evil" it is. (See *Born In Blood* by John J. Robinson, Evans & Company, New York, 1989, for one book tracing it back to the Knights Templar, an allegedly Christian order, allegedly heretical, destroyed or almost destroyed by the Holy Inquisition early in the 14th Century; masonic works of the last century traced it back much, much further, inspiring Bierce's sarcasm above.)

Although masonry is often denounced as either a political or religious "conspiracy," freemasons are forbidden to discuss either politics or religion within the lodge. Gary Dryfoos of Massachusetts Institute of Technology, who maintains the best masonic site on the World Wide Web:

http://web.mit.edu/afs/athena.mit.edu/user/d/r/dryfoo/www/Masonry

always stresses these points and also offers personal testimony that after many years as a mason[1], including high ranks, he has not yet been asked to engage in pagan or Satanic rituals or to plot for or against any political party. The only values taught in all masonic lodges, Dryfoos and other masons say, are charity, tolerance and brotherhood.

The more rabid Anti-masons, of course, dismiss such testimony as flat lies.

The enemies of masonry, who are usually Roman Catholics or Fundamentalist Protestants, insist that the rites of the order contain "pagan" elements. This is probably true, but only to the extent that these religions themselves contain "pagan" elements, e.g., the Yule festival, the Spring Equinox festival, the dead-and-resurrected martyr (Jesus, allegedly historical, to Christians; Hiram, admittedly allegorical, to Masons.) All these and many other elements in Christianity and masonry have a long prehistory in paganism, as documented in the 12 volumes of Frazer's *Golden Bough,* which argues at length that everything we call "religion," whether "higher" (like our own) or "primitive" (not like our own) derives from worship of sexuality

---

[1] Both "freemason" and "mason" are correct usages. Members often refer to masonic mysteries simply as "the Craft."

and from associated rituals to ensure the fertility of nature—human, animal and plant.

For instance, the dead and resurrected god/hero (Jesus, Hiram, Osiris, Dionysus, Attis, John Barleycorn, etc.) represents the death and rebirth of nature each year, which explains why the winter solstice and spring equinox are surrounded by so much associated ritual even today in such "higher" religions (as judged by themselves) as Judaism and Christianity.

Freemasonry, then, seems one of the more rationalistic and less sectarian of the solar-phallic cults. Like its Oriental cousins, Taoism and Buddhism, it almost never remembers its origin in fertility-worship.

But Crowley was not just a masonic initiate. He began his search for scientific mysticism with an odd offshoot of freemasonry and Rosicrucianism called the Hermetic Order of the Golden Dawn.

(Rosicrucianism? That's another secret society about which those who know the least speak the most and those who know the most speak the least. It either began in ancient Egypt, or in 1414 e.v., or around 1610-1620. The founders were either high priests of Osiris, or friends of Martin Luther—whose coat of arms contained the Rose and Cross after which this order is named—or somebody actually named Christian Rosycross, if you can believe that, or Giordano Bruno[2], or maybe somebody else. There are now several Rosicrucian orders ahoof on this planet, all of them denouncing the others as frauds.)

LIGHT IN EXTENSION

The Hermetic Order of the Golden Dawn, a freemasonic order with heavy Rosicrucian symbolism, possibly came into existence in 1881 due to some combination of mysterious events involving three

---

[2] Bruno, burned at the stake by the Papist heresy in 1600, is generally regarded as a martyr to scientific rationalism for espousing the Copernican system of astronomy. Actually, the Inquisition also charged him with 17 other counts of heresy, including the practise of Magick and forming secret societies to oppose the Vatican. Historian Francis Yates believes he was somehow involved in the creation of both Rosicrucianism and Freemasonry.

See Yates, *Giordano Bruno and the Hermetic Tradition,* University of Chicago Press, 1964.

freemasons named S.L. Mathers, William Wynn Westcott, William Woodman and a mysterious Bavarian woman, Anna Sprengel. Either (1) Westcott found some ciphered papers in Freemason's Hall, London, which put him in touch with Fraulein Sprengel, or (2) he found the papers in a bookstall, or (3) he and Woodman and Mathers made up the whole story or (4) Westcott made it all up alone and deceived Woodman and Mathers.

Or maybe all the above is deliberately misleading legend. Other sources trace the Golden Dawn to (1) the *Loge zur augehenden Morgenrothe,* a Masonic lodge in Frankfurt which established a branch in France called *Aurore naissante* (both titles mean "Rising Dawn") and a branch in London and/or (2) the *Chabrath Zerek Auor Bokher,* or Society of the Shining Light of Dawn, a Cabalistic college in London, founded by one Johannes Falk from Hamburg, Germany.

However created, the Golden Dawn became the most influential occult society of the turn of the century, numbering among its members such influential persons as Irish poet and Nobel laureate William Butler Yeats; fantasy writers Algernon Blackwood and Arthur Machen (who both influenced H.P. Lovecraft); famous actress Florence Farr, who at various times was a mistress of Crowley, of Yeats and even of Bernard Shaw; Arthur Waite, creator of the best-known modern Tarot cards; and Israel Regardie, the psychotherapist and Magician whose book on Crowley first got me involved in these murky matters.

Like ordinary freemasonry, the Golden Dawn had a system of grades, each one marked by an initiatory ritual intended to make a lasting impression on the consciousness of the candidate—to bring him *or her* closer and closer to Illumination in the mystical sense. (Unlike mainstream masonry, the Golden Dawn included women as well as men.) This was combined with profound study of Christian Cabala, a derivative of the original Jewish Cabala, a science or art which provides a religious language and numerology to discuss and clarify various altered states of consciousness.

The influence of the Golden Dawn extended far beyond conventional occultism. Much of modern literary culture owes its symbolism and themes to this group; not only Yeats' poetry, but even that of Ezra Pound and T.S. Eliot, and the novels of James Joyce, show Golden Dawn elements, which were common currency in the London of 1900-1914, where all these writers met. Modern horror fiction is replete with themes Lovecraft acquired at second hand from Blackwood and Machen. Bernard Shaw's *Back to Methuselah* owes much to syncretic Golden Dawn ideas he probably learned from Florence Farr, as does his synthesis of the Salvation Army and Dionysianism in *Major Barbara*. The Tarot deck, virtually forgotten by all but gypsy fortunetellers a century ago, is now widely studied for both mystic and psychological meanings, due to the Waite and Crowley Tarot decks, both based on the Golden Dawn deck.

The Golden Dawn fell into dissension and acrimony in 1898 and has continued to remain disunited. In the late 1980s when the present author lived in Los Angeles that city alone rejoiced in three Outer Heads of three Golden Dawns, each claiming to have been appointed by Israel Regardie.

The possible connection of the Golden Dawn with the shadowy Anna Sprengel of Bavaria brings up the spectre of the Bavarian Illuminati, the most colorful of all secret societies and a perpetual source of conspiratorial theorizing by many pious persons. Was Fraulein Sprengel an Illuminatus? I don't know, but after 1914, Crowley began to use the title Epopt of the Illuminati, and his magazine, *The Equinox*, bore the masthead, "The Journal of Scientific Illuminism"...

Ignotium per Ignotius

Although the really hard-core conspiracy buffs want to trace it further back, the Illuminati known to most historians was founded on May 1, 1776, in Ingolstadt, Bavaria, by a *freemason* (and former Jesuit) named Adam Weishaupt. According to the *Encyclopedia Britannica*, the Illuminati managed to influence many masonic lodges and gained "a commanding position" in the movement of "republican free thought," i.e., anti-royalist and pro-democratic secularism. They attracted such literary men as Goethe and Herder but the whole movement came to an end when the Illuminati were banned by the Bavarian government in 1785. Or so the *Britannica* claims...

Many conspiracy hunters following the decidedly paranoid Abbe Augustin Barruel believe the Illuminati merely regrouped under other front names after 1785 and still continues to the present, although they often disagree as to whether the Illuminati is promoting democracy, communism, fascism, anarchism, Satanism, international banking, or some combination thereof.

According to masonic historian Albert G. Mackey, the Illuminati was very popular and had at least 2000 members in masonic lodges in France, Belgium, Holland, Denmark, Sweden, Poland, Hungary, and Italy. Mackey emphasizes that Baron Knigge, one of the most powerful and active members of the Illuminati, was a devout Christian and would not have worked so hard for the order if its aim had been, as Abbe Barruel and others claim, the abolition of Christianity. He concludes that it exercised no "favorable" or "unfavorable" effect on the history of freemasonry.

On the other hand, the Abbe Barruel linked the Illuminati positively to the Order of Assassins, the Knights Templar (condemned by the Inquisition for sorcery, sodomy and heresy) and a worldwide Jewish plot, an idea which later gave birth to a notorious forgery called *The Protocols of the Learned Elders of Zion*.

Both Daraul's non-hostile *History of Secret Societies* and Nesta Webster's very hostile *World Revolution* document the existence of a revived Illuminati group in Paris in the 1880s; but Daraul regards it as a copy of Weishaupt's original order with no lasting influence, while Webster thinks it was the original order coming out in the open again and heavily influencing the modern labor and socialist movements.

More intriguing and complex was the Order of the Illuminati founded by freemasonic druggist Theodore Reuss in Munich in 1880. This was joined by actor Leopold Engel who founded his own World League of Illuminati in Berlin in 1893.

In 1896 Reuss, Engel and occultist Franz Hartmann co-founded the Theosophical Society of Germany, and in 1901 Engel and Reuss produced or forged a charter giving them authority over the re-established Illuminati of Weishaupt. In 1901, Reuss, Hartmann and metallurgist Karl Kellner founded the Ordo Templi Orientis and appointed William Wynn Westcott—of the *Hermetic Order of the Golden Dawn*—Regent of England.

In or about 1912 Reuss conferred the 9th degree of the Ordo Templi Orientis upon our man Crowley claiming that Crowley already knew the occult secret of that degree. He later appointed Crowley his successor as Outer Head of the order.

In 1934 the Gestapo forcibly suppressed both the Order of the Illuminati and the Ordo Templi Orientis in Germany—along with all other freemasonic orders and lodges, and schools of Esperanto to boot. The Ordo Templi Orientis survived elsewhere, but the Illuminati as an occult order only seems to exist in Switzerland at present. (As far as I know…)

Crowley includes Adam Weishaupt, the founder of the 18th Century Illuminati, among the Gnostic Saints in his Gnostic Catholic Mass, performed regularly in all Ordo Templi Orientis lodges. But that list includes also such odd birds as King Arthur, Parsifal, Pope Alexander Borgia, John Dee, Goethe, Wagner, Nietzsche, King Ludwig ("the mad") and painter Paul Gauguin…

But where did the Ordo Templi Orientis come from?

ORDO TEMPLI ORIENTIS

THE GREAT SEAL OF THE O.T.O.

According to one interpretation, the eye-in-triangle represents God the Father, the dove represents the Holy Spirit descending and the chalice represents the "Holy Grail" or Earth transfigured by the Spirit. Alternately, the eye represents the "eye" of the penis, the dove represents the ejaculation of sperm and the chalice represents the womb: the miracle of creation, on another level. A third interpretation combines both, in a sense: the eye represents the ego of the magician, the dove represents both sperm and soul ejaculating/exploding in orgasm and the chalice represents the "body of Nuit" or the universe into which the soul disappears at the height of Tantric sex magick.

The Ordo Templi Orientis is a freemasonic-style ritualistic occult order which traces itself back to the Knights Templar. Although several groups have claimed to be the real O.T.O., and there were 1005 competing Outer Heads at one time, the U.S. federal courts have ruled that the order represented on the World Wide Web (see http://www.crl.com/~thelema/oto.html) is the "true" O.T.O. and have granted it tax-exempt status as a charitable corporation and religious entity.

The O.T.O. has eleven degrees, the first nine and the eleventh involving freemasonic-style "initiations" in which the candidate is tested and, hopefully, illuminated by deeper insight into the world and his/her/self. The tenth degree represents the Outer Head of the Order, a post currently held by one Hymenaeus Beta.

As we mentioned, Aleister Crowley became an initiate of the O.T.O. in 1912. This happened because he had published a mystic treatise and/or book of dirty jokes titled *The Book of Lies*. The Outer Head at that time, Theodore Reuss (mentionned above for his alleged link to the Illuminati) came to Crowley and said that, since he knew the secret of the 9th degree, he had to accept that rank in the O.T.O. and its attendant obligations. Crowley protested that he knew no such secret but Reuss showed him a copy of *The Book of Lies* and pointed to a chapter which revealed the secret clearly. Crowley looked at his own words and "It instantly flashed upon me. The entire symbolism not only of Free Masonry but of many other traditions blazed upon my spiritual vision... I understood that I held in my hands the key to the future progress of humanity." Crowley, of course, does not tell us which chapter contains the secret. You can spend many happy hours, days, maybe even months or years, pouring over that cryptic volume seeking the right chapter and the final secret.

Crowley succeeded Reuss as Outer Head and was succeeded by one Karl Germer who died without appointing a successor, leading to the long struggle among various factions. Charlie Manson once belonged to an alleged Ordo Templi Orientis, but not to the one currently recognized by U.S. courts as a legitimate charitable and religious organization.

We should remember at this point that Aleister Crowley also received training, sometimes briefly and sometimes lasting much longer, in such traditions as Taoism, Buddhism, Hinduism and Sufism; and we should recall his training in organic chemistry. He never abandoned his commitment to "the method of science, the aim of religion."

THE WIDOW'S SON

Two recent books that shed some light on all these murky matters deserve some attention at this point—*The Hiram Key* and *The Second Messiah*.[3] The authors of both books, Knight and Lomas, are both Freemasons and claim that they have received "support and congratulations" from "hundreds" of other masons—although they admit that their research has been greeted with hostile silence by the United Grand Lodge of England, one of the more conservative masonic bodies.

Basically, Knight and Lomas try to prove that masonry not only dates back to ancient Egypt—as only the most Romantic masons have hitherto claimed—but that it also served as a major influence on "Jerusalem Christianity," the earliest form of the Christian faith, which was persecuted and driven underground when the official Romish Christianity became dominant. Primordial or "Jerusalem" Christianity survived through various "heresies," they say, and became a major force again when rediscovered and accepted as their own secret inner doctrine by the Knights Templar. When the Templars were condemned by the Inquisition, the survivors used various other names until emerging again as Freemasons in the 17th or 18th Centuries.

Parts of this thesis have been argued in other books—the underground survival of primordial Christianity, for instance, appears in the famous *Holy Blood, Holy Grail* by Baigent, Lincoln and Leigh—but Knight and Lomas have put the puzzle together in a more convincing way than any of their precursors.

But what was the original Egyptian "mystery" out of which this underground tradition emerged? Do Knight and Lomas attempt to delve that far back and claim to find a convincing answer?

Indeed they do.

---

[3] *The Hiram Key* by Christopher Knight and Robert Lomas, Century, 1996; *The Second Messiah* by Christopher Knight and Robert Lomas, Element Books, 1997.

The masonic "myth" of the widow's son, Hiram, who was murdered for refusing to reveal "the mason word," derives from actual events in Egypt, they aver. The "word" is not a "word" but a coded euphemism indicating a secret. (How could a "word" have the magick power implied in the masonic legend?) The secret is this: every new pharaoh, before ascending the throne, had to visit heaven and become accepted among the gods. Only after this other-worldly journey could the pharaoh be accepted by the priests, *and by himself*, as one fit to fulfill the divine, as well as political, functions of kingship, as conceived in those days. This voyage to the highest stars, where the gods live, was accomplished, Knight and Lomas claim, with a ritual employing a "narcotic." When the last pharaoh of the native dynasty refused to reveal the secrets of this ritual to the new Hyskos dynasty, he was killed in the manner of the widow's son. The lost "word" = the details of the Ritual of Illumination and the name of the "narcotic" used.

It seems to me that Knight and Lomas have this last detail wrong, due to their ignorance of psycho-pharmacology. Narcotics do not allow you to walk among the stars and communicate with gods. They kill pain, they numb anxiety, and they knock you unconscious; that's all they do. Almost certainly, the magick potion used in the ritual was not a narcotic but an entheogen—the type of drug also called a psychedelic. Entheogens produce "mystic" and godly experiences, and at least one of them and perhaps two were widely used among the Indo-European peoples from ancient times, *amanita muscaria* definitely and *psylocibin* possibly, both of them members of the "magic mushroom" family.

Data to support this interpretation is now widely available. See especially Pujarich's *The Sacred Mushroom,* Allegro's *The Sacred Mushroom and the Cross,* Wasson's *Soma: Divine Mushroom of Immortality,* Wasson et al., *Persephone's Quest: Entheogens and the Origins of Religion,* McKenna's *Food of the Gods,* LeBarre's *Ghost Dance: Origins of Religion,* Peter Lamborn Wilson, *Ploughing the Clouds: The Search for Irish Soma,* Robert Anton Wilson, *Sex, Drugs and Magick.*

Crowley claimed, in his *Confessions,* Chapter 72, that he knew the lost mason "word." He had majored in organic chemistry, studied in many mystic traditions, and definitely served an entheogen (mescaline, from the peyote cactus) to the audience at his Rites of Eleusis in London, 1914. He was the one man most likely to have deduced the lost secret before Gordon Wasson "pioneered" the study of magic mushrooms in the 1950s and showed their role in religious history.

All over northern Europe traditional art shows the fairy-people and sorcerers surrounded by mushrooms, usually the "liberty cap" mushroom, now identified as psilocybin, the same used by American shamans for around 4000 years. The Irish Gaelic name for this fabulous fungus is *pookeen,* little god. ("Little fairy" in modern Gaelic, but *pook* is related to *bog*, the Indo-European root for "god.")

"Success shall be your proof," says *The Book of the Law (Liber Al),* Crowley's holy book. He never openly or explicitly revealed any of the lost secrets he had uncovered, but the lost "word" has gotten out anyway: millions all over the globe now know about the entheogens, where before Aleister Crowley the knowledge scarcely existed outside of tribal shamans, i.e., allegedly "backward" peoples. Despite continued persecution by the conservative religious bodies that control Western governments, the secret of the gods is now known on every street...

ON THE OTHER HAND

> Doubt.
> Doubt thyself.
> Doubt even that thou doubtest thyself.
> Doubt all.
> Doubt even if thou doubtest all.
> — Aleister Crowley, *The Book of Lies*

Of course, most recent books on Crowley and the O.T.O. suggest that the lost secret was Tantric sex-yoga.

And a witty Frenchman named Gerard de Sede has examined most of these mysteries in a book titled *La Race Fabuleuse* (Editions J'ai Lui, Paris, 1973). M. de Sede concludes that the real secret is that some ancient Israelis intermarried with extraterrestrials from Sirius *and their descendants still walk among us passing as human...*

Kenneth Grant, one of the 1004 other Outer Heads of the Ordo Templi Orientis not recognized by the American courts, claims that Crowley was in communication with advanced intellects from Sirius starting in 1904 and continuing.

And Robert Morning Sky, an American Indian student of linguistics, claims that invaders from Sirius heavily influenced early human religions and left traces still visible in surviving god-names.

But then Robert Wood, in his book *GenIsis,* also claims that humanity was created by extraterrestrials from Sirius but adds that the most advanced adepts of all the Mystery Schools amputate their penises as a sign of total faith. (Uncle Aleister was obviously not an advanced adept of the Schools known to Mr. Wood.)

Some mysteries, perhaps, do not allow themselves to be known in simple either/or logical terms. They remain, forever, a mystery inside a puzzle within a controversy cloaked in uncertainty, revealed to all and yet still strangely concealed...

And of these mysteries Aleister Crowley certainly ranks as the Magus of our Aeon and true prophet of one Star in the company of Stars, Mystery of Mystery, CHAOS...

Robert Anton Wilson
23 October 1998

INTRODUCTION

Astrology tends not to be taken seriously these days. As a matter of fact it has never enjoyed universal acceptance among the intellectual community of any historical period. Yet among its supporters throughout history are some of the most intelligent and illustrious thinkers of their respective periods, including our own. Why is astrology both so appealing and so maligned in the historical arena of public debate? Orthodox religion objects to it on authoritarian grounds, proclaiming it heretical and demonic. Philosophers object to it as being superstitious and uncritical. Scientists object to it as being presumably unverifiable. All these objections, however, are self-serving on the parts of their advocates. That is not to say such objections should be disregarded, but the mental attitudes from which they emanate ought to be evaluated within the context of the larger debate to which they contribute. If, as much personal experience attests, there is really something to astrology, then we are challenged to determine what that something is. All the available data must be considered first, then viable opinions may be formulated. This book contributes both to the body of available data and to the manner in which such data may be evaluated.

As its title implies, astrology *per se* is not the only concern addressed in this book. It is, however, a supporting pillar of the entire edifice. If the astrological hypotheses hold up, then the more extended personal and social perspectives that are developed in accordance with them are provided with some measure of objective verification. Therefore, by way of introduction, I would like to address what I consider to be the central problem with the standard objections to astrology.

The approach to knowledge that has dominated Western civilization, at least since Descartes, has been predicated upon the distinction between subject and object, that is, the *separation* of the knower from that which is known. Although earlier seeds of this theory of knowledge can be found in ancient Greek philosophy, it has reached its apotheosis in the methodology of modern science. This has been a fruitful development from an historical perspective. It is even argued in this book that the emergence of modern science is fundamental to the advent of the "new age" upon which we are currently embarking. This being the case, however, it may be assumed that the scientific spirit is yet in its infancy as characterized by the boastful and arrogant attitude of its most vociferous supporters. The classic formulation of this theory of knowledge is shown by the following diagram in which 'S' represents subject, 'O' object, and the arrow the phenomenon of knowing:

$$S \longrightarrow O$$

The crux of the enterprise is to eliminate subjectivity by an absolute focus upon objectivity. Subjectivity involves false notions grounded in a history of spurious beliefs, desires, appearances, and all manner of untested assumptions that must be purged by the refining fire of scientific method. The final proof for scientific truth is its ability to predict with reliable accuracy the outcome of experiments that can be replicated at will producing always the same result. Any claim to knowledge that fails to satisfy this all important criterion is said to be *unscientific* and therefore unworthy of serious intellectual consideration. Despite the philosophical debunking of the supremacy of this attitude, going back in modern times perhaps most notably to Kierkegaard, the hard-core scientific community continues to preach to us about what is patently true and false by the presumed standard of absolute objectivity. Of course, the power and prestige of this paradigm is rooted in the kinds of virtual certainty and functional efficiency that it generates *within the scope of its applicability*—predominantly the realm of industrial technology—which has undeniably benefited humankind both in our mental development and the enhancement of our material accouterments.

The philosophies of humanism, pragmatism, existentialism, and phenomenology, however, all proclaim that *subjectivity* is an extremely important, or rather, the more important component of meaning and truth. Subjectivity is the *source* of consciousness and the *root* of human experience. Attempts to develop objective approaches to subjectivity have produced the "soft" sciences, such as psychology and sociology, as opposed to the "hard" sciences such as physics and chemistry. The softer that the soft sciences become, however, the more spurious and unverifiable they appear from the perspective of the hard sciences. Ultimately, the soft sciences appear to become lost in a muddle of poetic nonsense for which the hard scientist has little or no tolerance. Astrology provides a potential resolution for the dilemma of the soft sciences by assuming a standpoint of observation that addresses *both* subjectivity and objectivity in a most ingenious and inclusive manner. Astrology is able, by virtue of its unique methodology, to observe the subject-object relationship itself as it occurs in our common experience and thereby take account of the whole phenomenon of consciousness. This perspective may be characterized by the following diagram:

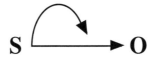

$$S \longrightarrow O$$

The ultimate ground of astrological analysis is the hard science of astronomy. This ground is as objective as any knowledge can be and is fully verifiable by collective standards of observation. The interpretive aspect of astrology, however, addresses matters of subjective human experience. The more subjective the interpretation, the more valuable it is in relation to its objective referents. It is objected, however, that there is no way to account for any linkage between the observed astronomical phenomena and their presumed subjective associations. The response to this objection is that subjective experience is by definition *self-validating*. Subjective experience rings true, as it were, beyond the grasp of objective proof. Subjective experience is the very essence of what it means to be human, to be *alive*. Human life experience is essentially *anecdotal* and therefore beyond the purview of scientific objectification. Despite the many wonderful things that it can do, science is impotent to account for the actual experience of meaning, because meaning is subjective. This accounts for the persistence of the practice of astrology, and other so-called pseudo-sciences, even after centuries of rigorous scientific development which one might suppose, in accordance with its attitude of superiority, should long ago have banished the pestilence of superstition from the face of the earth. As a matter of fact, in recent decades science has worked its way into some rather perplexing difficulties for the presumed certainties upon which its own methodology was originally thought to be grounded. These, however, are matters addressed more thoroughly in the book proper. The point here is that the so-called scientific objections to astrology are premature. It is hoped that this book will contribute to the debate that will ultimately vindicate the fundamental claims of astrology and also purge those claims of their extraneous accretions that have accumulated through unqualified presumptions and practice.

The issue is further complicated by the fact that astrological associations are not limited to experience of subjective phenomena alone. They also often apply in remarkable and uncanny ways to objective phenomena that tend to reinforce their subjective import. Such objective verification, however, is not consistent enough in terms of specific material events to be relied upon for purposes of scientific prediction. It does happen frequently enough, however, to generate a strong sense of synchronicity and thereby raises the issue of a mystery that would appear to transcend the subject-object distinction itself. Such observations inevitably result from the serious study of astrology. This may have something to do with why many scientists wish to denounce it on *a priori* grounds without conducting such a study in a manner that would be appropriate to the subtler aspects of the practice of astrology. They do not want the presumed hegemony of their realm to be challenged. In short, modern science *fits within* the context of human subjectivity, but human subjectivity *does not fit within* the positivistic context of modern science, that is, subjectivity is *inclusive* of and therefore *bigger than* science. Astrology is unique in its ability to address the manner in which science operates *within* the context of human subjectivity. The relation between astrology and science, therefore, can be shown to be mutually enhancing. Their respective purviews, however, must be rightly defined and respected.

From our present historical perspective, there is no more significant social context for the general apprehension of astrological meaning than the ubiquitous observation that our civilization is entering a new age of millennial proportion. Indeed, since the sixties, the term "new age," like so many other fads, has become prosaic as a result of its absorption into popular culture. This book is not intended to perpetuate the new age *fad* but rather to make a serious examination of the underlying structural changes that have been taking place in our civilization over the past two hundred plus years. The more recent popularization, and therefore trivialization, of these changes does little more than signal the fact that the transformative process has reached a critical juncture and is therefore producing more noticeable surface phenomena. The intensity of this process, however, renders historical perspective more difficult. This accounts for the fact that, despite much of the popular ranting, there is yet a significant lack of effectual comprehension of what is happening. A great deal of what has been included under the broad heading of "new age" in recent years is often more of a *regression* into the past than an anticipation of the fulfillment of our present needs. One of the great benefits of astrology is that it provides an *objective frame of reference* by which such personal and collective perspectives may be assessed and analyzed.

Given, therefore, the significance of Astrology and Aeon, what then is the significance of Aleister? How might the study of Aleister Crowley's birthchart help to achieve the objectives stated above? I will begin to answer that question by stating that the only way to really get down to the business of learning astrology is by doing natal case studies. The belief that personality is the most fundamental category of existence seems to be born out by the fact that, however profound astrological theory may be, such conceptualization remains vacuous and safe, as it were, until it is applied to the lives of real persons. This axiom holds true for *all* knowledge and accounts for the vast disinterest in many areas of otherwise dry inquiry by all save those who have some sense of its relevance to them personally. It is the application of astrology to the lives of real persons that makes it interesting. It is my intent to develop in this book a tightly interwoven tapestry of astrological theory and practical application to the person of Aleister Crowley in order to demonstrate, among other things, the potential for such application to all people. Although the presentation of several cases facilitates a wider range of examples for purposes of comparison and contrast, such *width* is gained at the expense of the *depth* that may be developed through the extended interpretation of one case study. To experience this benefit is, in my opinion, more instructive than the approach of considering several cases in a less comprehensive manner.

An important factor in selecting case studies for instructive purposes is the quantity and quality of biographical information available about the native. It is not only important that information be available concerning the external facts of the native's life, but it is of utmost value that as much as possible be known about the person's inner life as well. The best source for information about a person's inner life is direct testimony from that person. This criterion makes Aleister Crowley a prime candidate for astrological analysis, for not only is there available a great deal of biographical material about him but, in addition, the autobiographical material is replete with descriptions of his inner life. As far as his outer worldly activities and exploits are concerned, one could hardly find a more interesting character to work with. His many notable accomplishments and the calamitous reputation that he managed to create for himself provide a bountiful cache of material for study.

There is, however, another more important reason for selecting this man as the subject of a thoroughgoing astrological analysis in relation to the above stated concerns. Aleister Crowley claimed to be the prophet for the New Aeon. What relevance might this claim have with regard to the changes that have been taking place in our world in recent times? Surely the world has its share of crazed fanatics proclaiming themselves prophets and messiahs as we continue to experience the radical and unprecedented changes of our times. How quickly and by what criteria may we dismiss these multifarious claims? Do they all bear the mark of insanity? I personally think that in most, if not all cases they do, especially if sanity is defined in terms of conformity to the norms of one's social milieu. The phenomenon of what may be characterized broadly as charismatic spiritual leadership needs to be more thoroughly examined from psychological and social perspectives in order to raise some penetrating issues that remain inadequately addressed in the interest of preserving prevailing contemporary attitudes and mores. Lest anyone think that by participation in one of the more well established religious movements one has no need to be concerned about such matters, it must be understood that *all* religious activity is rooted in these kinds of manifestations.

Must there be a prophet of any kind for the new age? Many would say no, that what we need is simply to expand consciousness collectively and learn how to get along with one another. And yet, how far we are, in our humanity, from that! How helpful or necessary might be the appearance of a revealer, an exemplar, a *focus* of some kind for the collective need of humanity as we negotiate the difficult challenges that confront our world? How may this collective need be fulfilled? Are needs fulfilled? Is there purpose and direction in life? These questions and others like them are important, but it seems they can only be approached in ways that tend to be platitudinous at worst or divisive at best, given the current state of affairs for the concerns of religion.

Through the course of this book those kinds of questions are addressed, and Aleister Crowley's claim of prophecy is significant and challenging in that regard. Of course, that claim cannot possibly be examined fully in this book. It is rather my intent to consider it primarily from a particular perspective, that of an astrological analysis of the man himself in relation to the structure of his personality, the facts of his life, and what bearing these may have upon our changing times. Furthermore, if there is any credence to his claim of prophecy, demonstrable by empirical evaluation, then his life takes on added significance as a vehicle for cosmic forces having a direct bearing upon humanity as a whole.

The only extant astrological commentary on the personality and life of Aleister Crowley that I am aware of, except for a few occasional observations made by Crowley himself at various places in his voluminous writings, appears in an Appendix to Israel Regardie's *The Eye in the Triangle* (New Falcon Publications). Regardie's book, perhaps more than any other biography of Crowley, provides an indispensable perspective on Crowley's enigmatic and paradoxical personality. Regardie's personal knowledge of Crowley and his extensive research and astute observations are invaluable. Astrology, however, by Regardie's own admission, is outside the realm of his personal expertise. Furthermore, the tradition of astrology of which Regardie had cursory knowledge was encumbered with antiquated conceptions that precluded the approach to interpretation that has subsequently been pioneered most notably by Dane Rudhyar, which facilitates a much wider range of perspectives. Regardie was aware of Rudhyar's contribution to the discipline of astrology, but his own astrological comments reflect an unfamiliarity with Rudhyar's fundamental hypotheses. The opening paragraphs of Appendix I in *The Eye in the Triangle* are worth quoting here, because they illustrate a need to address more thoroughly the astrological interpretation of Aleister Crowley's birthchart:

> In his book *The Great Beast,* John Symonds included an appendix which gave a horoscope of Aleister Crowley with a brief reading by Robert [sic] Gleadow. This chart and reading delineated a rather fatuous and insignificant person of no outstanding ability, one doomed to failure and poor choices. This chart is based upon his birth at Leamington, at 11:16 p.m., October 12, 1875.
>
> Feeling that this genethliacal chart in no way did justice to Crowley, and certainly did not coincide with what I knew about the man and his work, I consulted a friend of mine who is, among other things, a shrewd student of Astrology. After discussing the above concepts, we agreed that the above-mentioned chart seemed to invalidate the empirical validity we felt was inherent in astrology.

My friend, Louis T. Culling, then outlined for me the thesis laid down many years ago by E.H. Bailey that it is possible to erect a so-called "lunar epoch" chart, for the probable moment of conception, and that this chart might delineate more accurately the potentialities and destiny of the individual. A chart is erected for approximately 273 days before birth, following well defined rules and regulations with which I am not at all familiar, and so will not describe at second hand. But on the basis of these rules, Culling erected a prenatal chart, which I give on the next page. [p. 511]

The rest of the appendix consists of five more paragraphs in which Regardie presents Culling's interpretation, all too brief in my opinion, of his so-called "lunar epoch" chart of Aleister Crowley. Interested readers may consult *The Eye in the Triangle*. The distinction between chart and reading made in the first paragraph of the appendix appears to be omitted from Regardie's further considerations. It is quite clear that it is in fact the *reading* by Rupert Gleadow, presented by Symonds, that Regardie finds objectionable. It is an entirely different matter to presume that such a reading could in any way "invalidate the empirical validity inherent in astrology."

There are about as many unique approaches to the practice of astrology as there are practicing astrologers. Not only are there many contending schools of thought concerning the theoretical basis for astrology, but each participant within those various schools brings one's own unique perspective to bear. The inherent ambiguity of astrology itself calls for extremely fine discernment and discrimination with regard to method that is often lacking on the part of practitioners. Being an empirical study, as Regardie correctly observes, it is of utmost importance for astrology that standards of consensual validation be employed to the fullest possible extent in its practice. This challenge is intensified by the holistic character of its study. Astrological correspondences cannot be surgically removed from the whole in which they operate, and the possibility of clear and distinct observation is thereby diminished. Therefore, whatever precision can be brought to bear must be emphasized and adhered to unfailingly as a stronghold of verifiability. Otherwise, the entire enterprise tends to become lost in a quagmire of unqualified subjective indulgence which characterizes astrology at its worst. This is the greatest vulnerability of astrology to criticism as a body of collective knowledge.

This problem lies at the heart of the theoretical formulation of what is termed "natal astrology," that is, the study of astronomical configurations calculated for the precise spacio-temporal coordinates of a person's birth as relating specifically to the structure of one's personality. The empirical validity inherent in astrology to which Israel Regardie attests must be reflected in the viability of birthcharts *in all cases*, or it has no empirical validity at all. One extremely important reason for this is that the moment of birth can be accurately documented. Indeed, it is not always known, but the point is that it *can be known* by direct observation of the birth and in a great many cases *is known*, and that provides an objective basis for the study of natal astrology. If a birthchart is found to be inconsistent with the structure of the native's personality *in any case,* providing the birth data used is correct, then the study of natal astrology is invalidated, and trying to seek out alternative horoscopes based on rationalized hypotheses and probabilities only further muddies the water.

This matter of birthcharts being viable tools for the analysis of the structure of personalities raises a host of important questions, some of which are appropriate to address at this juncture. I had been doing charts of individuals for ten years before I became fully confident in the veracity of natal astrology, and I continue to be awed by the uncanny accuracy of the method each time I work with birthcharts of individuals. For many years, it was primarily the incontrovertible value of insights provided by my own birthchart as applied to my life that sustained my efforts to expand my study so as to encompass the general principles necessary to venture forth into interpretation for others. Such is the power of the method that it survived my skepticism.

I have little doubt that the reason for my initial reluctance to accept the viability of astrology, even after much verification by practice, was the lack of an adequate explanation for how and why it works in terms of energetic processes. I believe that this also largely accounts for the widespread disrespect for astrology within our present social milieu, the hallmark of which is energy-oriented technology. It is true that there is a certain amount of talk among many apologists for astrology of gravitational attraction, magnetic fields, radio waves, and other such energy-oriented phenomena as somehow vindicating the fundamental hypothesis that there is a meaningful link between human personality and the relative positions and movements of celestial phenomena. I find such approaches to be incomplete for several reasons. That is not to say that energetic processes within our solar system and beyond are irrelevant to astrology, but that there needs to be a *non-energetic* explanation for the astrological hypothesis in order to account for the observed phenomena of its practice. There is a great deal that can be said about this matter from a philosophical perspective, however the subtleties of philosophic understanding are *not* the hallmark of our social milieu, and the value of such considerations is therefore generally lost for practical purposes. Science, however, *is* rightfully respected, and quantum physics *has* penetrated the conceptual wall of confinement by local (i.e., energy-oriented) reality constructs. These matters will be addressed in some detail at various places in this book.

To return, however, to my original theme, if in fact the birth data of 11:16 p.m., October 12, 1875, at Leamington, England is correct, or nearly correct, then the chart erected for those coordinates *must* accurately address the structure of Aleister Crowley's personality, or else the empirical study of natal astrology is invalidated. It may be that the alternate "lunar epoch" chart proposed by Culling has some value, but if it does it has no bearing on *natal* astrology. As an astrologer, I am not comfortable with such an abstract method of attempting to ascertain a moment in time that clearly cannot be practicably determined, no matter how rigorous are the "well defined rules and regulations" of the method employed. If moments of conception could be practicably determined, then certainly a branch of astrology could be built upon such data, and I for one would feel obliged and eager to incorporate it. However, for the time being, natal astrology is of sufficient value to warrant my continued study and application.

I have no knowledge of how the determination of 11:16 p.m. was reached for the construction of the chart given in Symonds' *The Great Beast.* The first chapter of Crowley's autobiography, *The Confessions of Aleister Crowley,* written in the early twenties, opens with the following statements:

> Edward Crowley, the wealthy scion of a race of Quakers, was the father of a son born at 30 Clarendon Square, Leamington, Warwickshire, on the 12th day of October, 1875 EV between eleven and twelve at night. Leo was just rising at the time, as nearly as can be ascertained. [p. 35]

A later book of Crowley's, *The Equinox of the Gods* (New Falcon Publications), first published in 1936, begins its autobiographical section thusly:

> At 36 Clarendon Square, Leamington, Warwickshire, England, at 10.50 p.m., on the twelfth day of October, in the Eighteen Hundred

and Seventy-Fifth Year of the vulgar era, was born the person whose history is to be recounted. [p. 41]

The Equinox of the Gods also contains a birthchart of Aleister Crowley, calculated for 10:50 p.m., showing 0 degrees and 3 minutes of the sign Leo on the Ascendant. From these statements it may be surmised that, during the interim between the writing of these two books, Crowley had calculated a "rectification" of his birthchart in order to bring his Ascendant as close as possible to the precise opening cusp of Leo, thus accentuating the characterization of Leonine prowess for his personality. This would account for the new time specification. It is worth noting that rectification is a common practice in astrology when only an approximate time of birth is known.

I am aware of no other information that would shed additional light upon the exact time of Crowley's birth. It seems likely that the approximation given in *Confessions* was derived from the memories of those nearby when Crowley was born. I have elected to use the 11:16 p.m. birth time for the birthchart of Crowley presented in this book. Its differences from the one presented by Crowley in *The Equinox of the Gods* are negligible. Furthermore, this selection will serve to instruct with regard to the potential for differences in *reading technique* insofar as my interpretation for these coordinates may differ in respects from that of Rupert Gleadow as recounted by Israel Regardie.

PART I

CHAPTER I

BACKGROUND

One of the major criticisms of astrology is the claim that advancing knowledge has left behind and discredited the world-view upon which astrology is presumed to be based. It is becoming increasingly evident that this criticism is an expression of the prejudice of a scientific paradigm that is itself being supplanted. The primary hypothesis of astrology is that a meaningful correspondence is discernible between celestial phenomena and structures of terrestrial and human activity. Applications of this hypothesis are *adapted* to prevailing philosophical conceptions. In recent centuries, we are witness to a remarkable evolution of astrological understanding associated with the progress of science. An extended evolutionary perspective involving the zodiac bears significantly upon this modern historical development.

The way that most people in today's world become aware of the zodiac is through the popular knowledge of Sun signs. It is a general belief among many that this is what astrology is all about. Despite the naiveté of such limited knowledge, most would agree that there does appear to be *something* significant about Sun signs in relation to personalities. This level of astrological understanding is fairly widespread and accounts for the popularity of horoscope columns in newspapers and the like. The importance of this level of interest in astrology is that it introduces one to the intuitive conceptualization of the zodiac in relation to personality. It is very common, however, to find among people with only a casual interest in Sun signs a serious misunderstanding about the nature of the zodiac, and this misunderstanding creates a barrier to grasping the real significance of astrology.

It is common knowledge that there are constellations of stars that bear the names of the signs of the zodiac. This band of constellations constitutes what is properly called the *sidereal* zodiac, because the word "sidereal" refers to stars. Most people who have little knowledge of astrology think that this band of constellations is *the* zodiac. In accordance with this belief, one thinks that for a person to have a particular Sun sign means that the Sun was aligned with that constellation at the time the person was born. This is not the case. A closer examination of the dates for the beginnings of the signs of the zodiac as they appear in the popular literature shows that they correspond to the yearly cycle of seasonal changes and *not* to the position of the Sun in relation to the constellations of the sidereal zodiac. The beginnings of the four "Cardinal" signs, Aries, Cancer, Libra, and Capricorn, are always the first days of spring, summer, autumn, and winter respectively. They are determined by the two equinoxes and the two solstices which comprise the four cardinal points of the *tropical* zodiac. This has nothing to do with stars. It is strictly a function of the relationship between Earth and the Sun determined by the tilt of Earth's rotational axis and its revolution around the Sun.

Understanding the significance of the tropical zodiac *reverses* the usual conception of what astrology is about. If we think in terms of constellations of stars, the implication is that some determining factor imposes itself upon us from the distant cosmos. If, however, we think in terms of seasonal change, we are addressing *the response of life to an existential cycle on Earth,* that is, the activity of the *biosphere,* which, according to the Gaia theory of evolution (first proposed as such by John Lovelock and Lynn Margulis in 1978) is vigorously regulated by the molecular activity of DNA, the master designer of the human body. Therefore, the difference between thinking in terms of the sidereal and the tropical zodiacs is the difference between thinking in terms of *out there* or *in here.* Considering the enormous importance of this distinction, it is quite pertinent to ask: Why are there two zodiacs? Why does a sign of the tropical zodiac occupy a *different* section of the sky than the constellation of stars bearing the same name? To find answers to these questions one must expand one's conception of astrology.

Western astrology is derived from the ancient Middle Eastern world as recorded and perpetuated by the Greeks. The ancient world view was rooted in a *vitalistic* orientation to life, and the astrological formulations of knowledge that we have inherited from those times are expressions of an extremely well developed and refined attunement to the cosmos as a *living being.* We have been separated from that world view by the evolutionary development of Western civilization, founded upon the orientation of Greek philosophy, which has interposed a rationalistic and subsequently a technological, that is, a mechanistic, perspective in its place. This largely accounts for the barrier that we encounter in the study of astrology. It seems to work *somehow,* yet it remains impervious to technological explication in terms of modern energy-based science, despite some major theoretical advancements along those lines such as the theorizing of Percy Seymour in his *Astrology: The Evidence of Science.* It seems to many that we must therefore throw out one or the other of these perspectives in order to avoid what is thought to be a contradiction between points of view. It may well be that the historical fact of the two zodiacs, combined with modern and postmodern social and scientific perspectives, may provide a means for resolving this difficulty.

The creators of our tradition of astrology did not face the dilemma of two zodiacs. The symbolism of astrology clearly indicates that its ancient authors were addressing the *tropical* zodiac as an index of the ebb and flow of the life force in accordance with the annual cycle of seasonal change. Of particular concern was the bearing this cycle had upon the organization of human society, which was obliged to plan its activities and operations around the growing season and the need to secure itself against the adversities of winter and other forces. These fundamental concerns extend back into time immemorial, and archeological artifacts show that the astrology we inherited from the ancients was a product of thousands of years of careful observations and recordings of celestial phenomena in relation to human activities. It is also worth noting that these thousands of years would naturally have entailed a considerable amount of *intentional structuring*, through customs and rituals, of social and personal life in accordance with the regularities of observed celestial phenomena. In short, observed celestial phenomena were not necessarily perceived only as *causing* human activity, but rather were used as a means of measuring, sorting out, and *planning* various aspects of human activity.

Surely, this perspective needs to be qualified. I do not doubt that many or probably most people who accepted astrology then (as now) thought in terms of a causal connection. This idea will be considered more extensively as we proceed. The point is that the ancient authors of astrology had much more immediate concerns to attend to than the notion of "influences" being somehow exerted upon humankind from arbitrary groupings of stars into patterns resembling animals and such. Such a conception by moderns only confirms a certain prejudice about the mentality of the ancients that bespeaks an

Oedipal component at work in *our own* civilization. The accomplishments of the ancients, the remaining testimonials of which continue to baffle the modern mind, attest to their being just as pragmatic within their historical context as we moderns and postmoderns are within ours. The business at hand was life on Earth within the context of natural cycles of development; night and day, seasonal changes, human life-spans, interpersonal activities, conflicts among social groups, properties and durabilities of material substances, observations of flora and fauna, agricultural productivity, structural engineering, and tendencies of societies to flourish and deteriorate, etc. Furthermore, history and legend attest to the ancients' interest in the latent human potential for experiencing very subtle forces of nature that baffle our modern conception of reality and are thought of in terms of extrasensory perception.

This being the case, then, what is the significance of the *sidereal* zodiac? It would appear to be obvious that the backdrop of "fixed" stars, referred to as such due to their *relative* stability in relation to the dynamics of our solar system, provided a convenient measuring-board, as it were, for the observations of planetary movements *within* our solar system. The pictorial images that were superimposed upon the field of the stars were in no way suggested by the actual arrangements of those randomly distributed points of flickering light, nor were they predominantly related to energies or influences coming from outside the solar system. Rather, the images of the zodiac were *adapted* to those stars found along the plane of the ecliptic, that is, the plane of Earth's orbit along which eclipses occur, so that they could be used as *symbolic references* for segments of the relative positioning of the Sun (as observed from Earth) through the course of the yearly cycle of seasonal variation.

The segments of the ecliptic designated by the signs of the tropical zodiac do not currently occupy the same space as their corresponding constellations due to a relative astronomical motion called the "precession of the equinoxes." This motion refers to the fact that each year the position of the Sun in relation to the stars in the background, as it crosses the equatorial plane of Earth, is a very little bit short (just over 50 seconds of arc) of where it was the year before, covering one degree of arc in 72 years. Although the equinoxes have been used as reference points, this motion applies, of course, to the whole tropical zodiac. Over extended periods of time this motion becomes noticeable. Even without the aid of telescopes, very careful observations over a period of a hundred years or so would be sufficient to establish knowledge of this motion. The crediting of its discovery to Hipparchus in the second century BC only reflects the recorded knowledge that is available to modern scholarship and does not preclude such knowledge on the part of the priesthoods of the ancient mystery traditions, yet it is early enough to raise a very important question.

The precession of the equinoxes takes some 26,000 years to make one complete cycle in relation to the stellar backdrop. Dividing this number by twelve shows that it takes roughly 2,160 years for the tropical zodiac to shift back one complete sign, 30 degrees of arc, in relation to the backdrop of stars. This measurement is the basis for the determination of what are referred to as astrological ages, or "months" in the Great Sidereal Year (sometimes referred to as the Platonic Year), of one complete cycle of the precession of the equinoxes. The astrological theory supporting the idea that we are currently entering the Age of Aquarius is that each age is characterized by a particular developmental theme in the historical evolution of humankind. The difference, now approximately 30 degrees, between the tropical and sidereal zodiacs is accounted for by the fact that the naming of the constellations took place over 2,000 years ago, at a time when they were in alignment with their corresponding signs of the tropical zodiac. It is generally assumed that the ancients considered that the constellations, *or regions thereof,* actually bestowed some kind of influences on humankind and the world. In any event the inherent logic of the situation is rarely explored beyond this point, and some critics even propose that the "discrepancy" between the two zodiacs is evidence of ignorance and confusion among astrologers. Unfortunately, this criticism is not completely unfounded.

In considering this matter more thoroughly, however, certain implications are inescapable. Since astrology was developed over thousands of years and the internal evidence of its formulation bespeaks considerable intelligence, it is reasonable to assume that knowledge of the precession of the equinoxes was established long before the alignment of the tropical and sidereal zodiacs as we now know them (although we have no academic means at present for documenting such knowledge). Such an assumption would imply that the development of astronomy by the ancient Greeks was rather a new beginning, as it were, based on previously lost or concealed knowledge from a yet earlier epoch. However, even dating the discovery of the precessional movement to the second century BC is sufficient to suggest that it was known by astrologers of that time that the designation of constellations in alignment with the signs of the tropical zodiac was not a permanent arrangement but rather characterized a particular *moment* in time. From an historical perspective it is clearly evident that a radically new orientation of human culture and civilization was emerging throughout the world at that time. The great civilizations remaining then had long been in decline, and the trend would not reach bottom until the Dark Age centuries later. The only permanent scroll upon which the ancient sources of superior knowledge could bequeath the essence of their wisdom unto posterity, beyond the reach of the corrupting hands of a disintegrating world order resulting from the *withdrawal* of their direct involvement, was the very sky itself.

The existence of the sidereal zodiac bears the earmarks of a *message* sent to us across time from the ancients, and the nature of this message is such as to be *self-corroborating*. This message tells us in graphic terms that there is a form of intelligence at work that encompasses the development of long-term historical processes affecting the evolution of humankind, and it demonstrates by its own example that the intentions of this greater intelligence are revealed to us through symbolic forms and images *that we find in our cultural traditions*.

Many present day scientists have taken the position that it is reasonable to assume that we are not alone in the universe; that "intelligent life" far more evolved than us humans is likely to exist within our galaxy and beyond. Some are so convinced of this likelihood that they are scanning space with radio telescopes in hopes of detecting electromagnetic signals from other sources similar to those that we currently generate on Earth. Most scientists, however, appear to be unwilling to consider (at least publicly) that messages from sources of superior intelligence may be implicit in the mythological and religious traditions of humankind. I am suggesting that we consider the possibility that the present orientation of the tropical and sidereal zodiacs constitutes such a message.

The key for us to be able to read this message is the present level of scientific knowledge and social organization reached within our own civilization. There is a certain irony here, but this is inherent in the situation and serves to account for both the self-corroborating nature of the message as well as our need to decipher it. The development of the material sciences in our civilization has been predicated upon the debunking of all so-called "pre-scientific" knowledge and the conviction that the rigor of scientific method that emerged from modern philosophy is unique in the history of humankind. This conviction appears to be confirmed by unprecedented advances in science and technology, and surely those advances would *not* have been made without the extreme tenacity of that conviction. Indeed, modern science has set the stage for a new epoch in the evolution of humankind.

Throughout the history of science certain theoretical problems have persisted in the study of biology. These problems continue to be addressed in favor of a hard-core *non-teleological* interpretation within the tradition of science, despite the blatant evidence of life itself to the contrary. This example serves to illustrate the extreme analytical bias of modern science. It *cannot* open the door to the idea of purposeful existence, because to do so shifts thought from a positivistic to a vitalistic or animistic rationale. Positivism assumes the position that "truth" must be completely represented by measurable phenomena and scientifically verified facts. Vitalism, on the other hand, assigns significance to *intentionality* which cannot be accounted for in strictly scientific terms. The source of intentions cannot be described or measured. To the traditional scientist, the idea of purposeful evolution implies a *regression* into pre-scientific modes of thought, which would be tantamount to a return to medieval flatulence.

I think, however, that despite the admirable and motherly concern of a major and dominant segment of the scientific community, we can be confident that science and technology have reached a level of sophistication sufficient to sustain the preservation of the scientific world view—that is as long as we don't wipe out our ecological niche with the "by-products" of our industrial technology. Although the general public is not yet effectually aware of it, and the priesthood of science appears less than eager to advertise the point, the discoveries in physics over the last hundred years have blown the philosophy of positivism out the window. If anything is significant about the popular new age phenomenon, it is the growling realization that there are forces and purposes at work in the world that transcend the frame of reference imposed by traditional science. It is, however, a progeny of traditional science, namely quantum mechanics, that provides a working metaphor for the advancement of knowledge and understanding of those forces and purposes as we move into a future in which the philosophical implications of the "new physics" will become more fully developed and assimilated. What the priesthoods of the ancient mysteries appear to have known *subjectively*, through the potential inward focus of the central nervous system upon itself and its molecular and atomic constituents, modern scientists have learned *objectively* through the outward focus of the central nervous system upon material substances and processes. The common pre-rational and post-rational ground of this knowledge is found within the atom.

Very briefly, the relationship of the tropical and sidereal zodiacs say, from roughly two thousand years ago, that a new beginning for humankind was at hand. It says that there was going to be an unconscious struggle between antithetical forces for roughly two thousand years, out of which humankind would emerge into a conscious knowledge and application of beneficent truth. The new beginning was indicated by the postulation of an alignment of the tropical zodiac in relation to a sidereal frame of reference *at the time deemed by the ancients* to be that new beginning. The 2,000-plus year period was indicated by the division of the zodiac into twelve segments, which is a tradition dating back to Sumer, the earliest civilization of recorded history. The struggle and emergence motif is inherent in the pictorial symbolism applied to the respective time periods indicated by the precession of the vernal equinox.

It is highly significant that the precession of the equinoxes moves *backwards* through the sidereal zodiac. While the Sun, Moon, and planets of the solar system, and the horizon of Earth all move in one relative direction, the precession of the equinoxes moves in the *opposite* direction in relation to the space established by the firmament of the stars. Therefore, the vernal equinox, taken as the key reference point for the tropical zodiac, moves through the constellations of the sidereal zodiac in *reverse order* to that of our *natural* temporal orientation codified by the tropical zodiac. While Aries, as a referent for the time of year at which life springs forth from Earth, is the first of the twelve signs from the perspective of the experience of time through the annual cycle of seasonal change, Pisces is the first stellar constellation through which the vernal equinox moves in its precession through the Great Sidereal Year. This means that the designation of the sidereal zodiac originally indicated the beginning of a roughly 2,000-plus year "age" thematically characterized by the symbolic image for Pisces. This image is that of two fishes swimming in opposite directions, their mouths joined by a chord. It also indicated that the Piscean Age would be followed by the Aquarian Age, symbolized by a man kneeling in the act of pouring water from an urn.

There has been a great deal of varied speculation about the exact times for the beginnings of the Piscean and Aquarian Ages. It is also possible to speculate along various lines with regard to the significance of the Great Sidereal Year taken as a whole. For the purposes of this book, however, these speculations are not of paramount importance. To gain an immediate perspective upon the times in which we are now living it is sufficient to work within the approximate frame of reference provided above. My fundamental assumptions are that the wisdom of the civilizations of antiquity culminated in the anticipation of a new beginning of major significance for all humankind, that they had a sense of its meaning, and that they laid the groundwork for and actually participated in the launching of that new beginning. When I refer to the civilizations of antiquity, I am, of course, referring to a knowledgeable element, undoubtedly very small and exclusive, within those civilizations. It is also reasonable to assume that the project, once initiated, was not totally abandoned by that knowledgeable element, although history attests to the fact that humankind in general has been largely left to its own resources. It is in fact inherent in the logic of my assumptions, based on historical records and observations, that it was the ultimate intention of those ancient seers to bring humankind to a greater level of *independence* and *self-determination*.

The Piscean Age has indeed been a period of great mystery. One of the major themes of this book is the elucidation of the basic elements of my perspective upon that mystery. For the purposes of this chapter, however, it is sufficient to observe that the Piscean Age has been characterized by a host of dualistic themes, the most fundamental of these involving the notions of "good" and "evil." Some others are, to name a few, heaven and hell, heaven and earth, God and Satan, male and female, and spirit and matter. The Piscean Age has been characterized by the idea and enactment of *antagonism* between the opposing factors involved, and it may be observed that this theme of dualistic antagonism is directly indicated by the pictorial symbolic image for Pisces.

The vernal equinox is currently oriented to a point near the division between the constellations of Pisces and Aquarius, although *exactly* where that division might be drawn can only be approximately determined. Even this lack of exactitude may be considered appropriate, because such a large scale and complex global transvaluation does not happen in the twinkling of an eye, despite the potential usefulness for some viable notion of a critical turning-point—a tipping of the balance, as it were. The fundamental issue, however, is that the pictorial image for Aquarius is appropriately suggestive of the historical developments characteristic of the advancement of Western civilization and the world in recent centuries. The image of a man pouring water out of an urn clearly indicates the *new orientation* that is demonstrably taking place in the world in relation to the Piscean image that it replaces.

There are many ways to compare and contrast the two symbolic images for Pisces and Aquarius. A few cursory observations will suffice to corroborate the perspective being developed in this chapter. These constellations will be interpreted to have fundamentally similar symbolic meanings as their corresponding astrological signs. This appears to be inherent in the fact of their being named accordingly. The development of the Western astrological tradition has codified a number of ways of conceptualizing structural relationships among astrological factors of analysis. This system can be understood as a group of theoretical formulations applied within the context of historical philosophical perspectives constituting a repository of applied knowledge. It is from that perspective that such codifications will be referred to throughout the course of this book. If one is able to think beyond anachronistic prejudices, the traditional schematization of astrology proves remarkably cogent and profound. Furthermore, any student of astrology is obliged to understand it, if for no other reason than to have the historical frame of reference necessary to grasp the progressive evolution of Western astrology that continues to be developed from modern and postmodern perspectives.

Alternating "polarities" have been attributed successively to the signs of the zodiac beginning with a "positive" attribution for Aries, appropriate to the emergence of the sprout from its seed encasement in early spring, followed by a "negative" attribution for Taurus, appropriate to the relative stabilization and substantiation of the original thrust of power, followed in turn by a positive attribution for Gemini, appropriate to the activation and proliferation of "mental" processes in response to the bipolarity of the two previous signs, etc. These alternating polarities are suggestive of a *dialectical* process inherent in nature. One may even draw an analogy between this process and the enhanced potential for the applications of electrical power resulting from the development of alternating current. The movement of any astrological referent from one sign to another involves a reversal of polarity with regard to its corresponding spacio-temporal field of operation. The movement of the vernal equinox from the constellation of Pisces (negative polarity) into that of Aquarius (positive polarity) therefore indicates a shift of the *initiating impulse* of natural life from a negative to a positive field of operation.

In discussing this shift of polarity it is helpful to avoid making value judgments, even though personal and social values are inherently and significantly involved in this reorientation. For purposes of analysis, a neutral approach allows for a better understanding of what is going on and may potentially facilitate the *transvaluation of values* appropriate to the contingencies of the present world situation. There is a long standing historical controversy regarding what may be considered the correct approach toward the fertility of life and the encouragement of ever greater potentialities for human nature. One view holds the idea that fertility is a stimulating and enhancing aspect of human nature that assists in the raising of humankind to more profound levels of emotional, mental, and spiritual development. The opposing view holds that fertility is an expression of the instinctual aspect of human nature from which humankind is struggling to be liberated in order to transcend the state of subservience to compulsive biological impulses. Hopefully, the thoughtful reader may consider that there is an element of truth on each side of this controversy.

The relevant point here is that the vernal equinox, the very index of fertility, which itself is characterized as a positive force within the tradition of astrology, has been moving through a negative field of operation in its precession through the Piscean Age. This seems not to be in conflict with the prevailing positions and attitudes of the major cultural institutions of the world, and Western civilization in particular, for the corresponding time period. This thematic orientation is particularly characteristic of the dominant social institution of the Piscean Age, namely Christian religion. The struggle over this issue, in fact, serves as a fundamental example of the symbolic representation of the two fishes swimming in opposite directions, joined at their mouths by a chord, insofar as the spiritual and material loves are presumed to be in conflict.

It follows that, as we enter the Aquarian Age and the vernal equinox moves into a positive field of operation, the prevailing attitude toward sexuality is being reversed, and the other side of the controversy is coming into ascendancy. We can see this process transpiring within our cultural milieu, although there are varying interpretations and beliefs about what such changes mean. Because we are yet deeply involved in the process of transition, neither has the old Piscean orientation fully lost its hold nor has the new Aquarian orientation found its stride. Contemporary social values in this regard are therefore somewhat chaotic. The process of transition, however, continues. The emphasis in this regard is shifting from the pursuit of transcendental fulfillment through the suppression of sexual urges to a sympathetic attitude toward the human body and the full expression of its inherent potentialities. The humanistic implication of the Aquarian pictorial image is blatant, and recent historical developments serve to confirm the ascendancy of this theme both in terms of a more positive and inclusive appraisal of humanity itself and through the establishment and proliferation of democratically oriented systems of government.

The comparison and contrast of the pictorial images for Pisces and Aquarius may be given a more or less inclusive perspective by considering the direct implication of the manner in which water is represented in the two images. It should first be noted that, in terms of the astrological tradition of "elemental" attributions for the signs of the zodiac, Pisces is a *Water* sign and Aquarius is an *Air* sign. (More on "elements" will come later. For the time being one may note that Water has to do with feeling and Air with thinking.) In the pictorial image for Pisces water is implied to be ubiquitous as the medium in which the fishes swim. It may also be inferred that, although the fishes *feel* the water, they are not conscious of its existence as such. The *containment* by the water is utterly inclusive of the fishes' natural existence. In the image for Aquarius water is represented in an entirely different context. It is consciously contained and directed by humanity. The contrast of these images, and the change of orientation from Pisces to Aquarius, is remarkably appropriate for the changing orientation of humankind at the present juncture of our historical and evolutionary development. A significant example of this change is the more or less successful challenge to the dogmatic conception of the primacy of *faith* inherent in the methodological development of modern science which requires *empirical verification* as the touchstone of truth.

It is important to be aware that the interpretation of symbols is always multidimensional and that many meanings can always be brought to bear upon any one symbolic image. It may be observed that perhaps the ultimate significance that we can currently give to the symbolic meaning of water, as it is represented in the above images, is that of the *realm* that we have found to be inherent within the interior of the atom. What was ubiquitous and unknown throughout the Age of Pisces has become known and directed as we enter the Age of Aquarius. It follows from this line of reasoning that the theories of relativity and quantum mechanics, at their present stage of development, are only the initial breakthroughs of a new conception of reality. This accounts for the conservatism on the part of the scientists who have most commendably been developing these theories through applications of experimental method. The lack of assimilation as yet by humanity in general of this new conception of reality is also characteristic of the fact that this knowledge is only in its budding stage of development.

The relevance of quantum mechanics to our understanding of reality has a direct bearing upon astrological theory. This observation can be made even by non-specialists in the fields of physics and mathematics, thanks to an increasingly prolific genre of publications that proffer explanations of the significance of quantum theory in terms somewhat graspable by reasonably educated lay people. The relevance to astrology of what has been termed "nonlocality" or "nonlocal effects" should be immediately obvious. This concept implies the possibility of *instantaneous interaction* at the quantum level of reality, that is, the transference or concomitance of information without any kind of energetic signal or transmission. Such "superluminal," that is, faster-than-light informational interaction is one of many theoretical ways to account for the observed data of quantum mechanics and provides a viable context for scientific research that would have been considered preposterous only a few decades ago. Some research has already been done that supports the theory of nonlocal effects occurring in the learning process of biological organisms, and that research has served as a starting point for the proposal of a radical new hypothesis by Rupert Sheldrake in his ground-breaking book, *A New Science of Life: The Hypothesis of Formative Causation*. The following passage from Sheldrake's introduction to that book summarizes that hypothesis which may be extended to encompass a theoretical approach to astrology, because it postulates a virtually magical tendency of structural patterns and processes to replicate themselves. Although the astrological implication is clearly inherent in Sheldrake's formulation, it should be noted that nowhere in his book docs he apply it in the manner that I am suggesting. He states:

The organismic or holistic philosophy provides a context for what could be a yet more radical revision of the mechanistic theory. This philosophy denies that everything in the universe can be explained from the bottom up, as it were, in terms of the properties of atoms, or indeed of any hypothetical ultimate particles of matter. Rather, it recognizes the existence of hierarchically organized systems which, at each level of complexity, possess properties which cannot be fully understood in terms of the properties exhibited by their parts in isolation from each other; at each level the whole is more than the sum of its parts. These wholes can be thought of as *organisms*, using this term in a deliberately wide sense to include not only animals and plants, organs, tissues, and cells, but also crystals, molecules, atoms, and sub-atomic particles. In effect this philosophy proposes a change from the paradigm of the machine to the paradigm of the organism in the biological *and* in the physical sciences. In A.N. Whitehead's well-known phrase: 'Biology is the study of the larger organisms, whereas physics is the study of the smaller organisms.'

Various versions of this organismic philosophy have been advanced by many writers, including biologists, for over 50 years. But if organicism is to have more than a superficial influence on the natural sciences, it must be able to give rise to testable predictions. It has not yet done so.

The reasons for this failure are illustrated most clearly in the areas of biology where the organismic philosophy has been most influential, namely embryology and developmental biology. The most important organismic concept put forth so far is that of *morphogenetic fields*. These fields are supposed to help account for, or describe, the coming-into-being of the characteristic forms of embryos and other developing systems. The trouble is that this concept is used ambiguously. The term itself seems to imply the existence of a new type of physical field which plays a role in the development of form. But some organismic theoreticians deny that they are suggesting the existence of any new type of field, entity or factor at present unrecognized by physics; rather, they use this organismic terminology to provide a new way of *talking about* complex physico-chemical systems. This approach seems unlikely to lead very far. The concept of morphogenetic fields can be of practical scientific value only if it leads to testable predictions which differ from those of the conventional mechanistic theory. And such predictions cannot be made unless morphogenetic fields are considered to have measurable effects.

The hypothesis put forward in this book is based on the idea that morphogenetic fields do indeed have measurable physical effects. It proposes that specific morphogenetic fields are responsible for the characteristic form and organization of systems at all levels of complexity, not only in the realm of biology, but also in the realms of chemistry and physics. These fields order the systems with which they are associated by affecting events which, from an energetic point of view, appear to be indeterminate or probabilistic; they impose patterned restrictions on the energetically possible outcomes of physical processes.

If morphogenetic fields are responsible for the organization and form of material systems, they must themselves have characteristic structures. So where do these field-structures come from? The answer suggested is that they are derived from the morphogenetic fields associated with previous similar systems: the morphogenetic fields of all past systems become *present* to any subsequent similar system; the structures of past systems affect subsequent similar systems by a cumulative influence which acts across both space *and time.* [pp. 12-13]

Sheldrake's hypothesis provides a viable theoretical basis for astrology, if we think of the solar system as having an integrated system of interacting morphogenetic fields associated with the dynamic components of its physical structure. Such a conception is inherent in our knowledge of the solar system as a gravitationally bound group of regularly moving bodies. It follows that the cyclic repetitions of the movements within the solar system would continuously sustain and reinforce relatively invariable patterns of such morphogenetic fields, and that our lives as humans on Earth would be *affected* in accordance with our positional orientations *within* those morphogenetic fields.

If Sheldrake's hypothesis is viable, then the effects of morphogenetic fields establishes a realm of activity that is qualitatively distinct from (although intimately involved in) energetic phenomena and is yet approachable within the context of scientific investigation. This approach requires considerable revision of the assumptions and descriptive techniques of traditional science. Such revisions would contribute to the resolution of many conflicts that have heretofore been sources of contention in the pursuit of truth and the understanding of the existential parameters of human consciousness.

In recent years other approaches have been taken toward working out a viable theoretical basis for astrology within the context of electromagnetic fields within the solar system. My experience with the practice of astrology, however, and my desire to conceptualize its workings within as broad a context as possible suggests that nonlocal effects must be included within a fully developed theory of astrology. Since Sheldrake's Hypothesis of Formative Causation takes into account nonlocal effects, I have found it to be the most *comprehensive* theory to support the practice of astrology, although it was not developed for that purpose. I have therefore structured my approach to astrological interpretation accordingly.

For the sake of linguistic simplicity, I assume Sheldrake's Hypothesis of Formative Causation to be true, even though I am aware that it is a scientific theory in the process of being tested by empirical investigation. Throughout the course of this book I make references to morphological factors and relationships as a means of supporting astrological interpretations that are advanced in association with general astronomical observations. Such references are intended to preserve a strict adherence to the theoretical perspective suggested above, which, as I attempt to demonstrate in chapter 3 and elsewhere, is also inherent in the practice of astrology as we have inherited it from its original authors. This perspective brings the practice of astrology into relation with the progressive interests of the scientific community. Although I suspect very few academicians will consider this work scientifically relevant, the morphological perspective yet provides an *objective frame of reference* as a basis for critique of my astrological interpretations.

CHAPTER 2

HORIZON

The contemporary popularity of Sun sign astrology is itself a significant phenomenon when considered from the perspective of the historical development of Western astrology. It actually suggests a most intriguing irony. It has not always been the case that the sign in which Sol is placed in a birthchart has been given primary significance. In traditional astrology, the personality was thought to be most aptly characterized by the sign found on the eastern horizon. In order to know what that sign is, however, one must know not only the date of one's birth but the time and place as well, and a calculation must be made with reference to a table of houses. This accounts for the shift of orientation in recent times.

The birth of Popular Culture as we currently know it may be thought to have occurred in the early 1890's. Since that time the proliferation of "labor saving devices" in every aspect of our lives, *including our thinking*, has been phenomenal. The hallmark of modernity became characterized by such terms as "at the push of a button" and "quicker than instant." Naturally, this ubiquitous trend was mirrored in the popular approach to astrology, and Sun signs became the rave because they are so easy to know. Herein lies the irony. As compared with the sign on the eastern horizon of a birthchart, the sign occupied by Sol represents the orientation of a deeper, more inclusive spiritual potential for the personality. By opening up the morning newspaper to the horoscope column and reading about one's Sun sign, despite the superficiality of the information there to be gleaned, one symbolically attunes *not* to the surface phenomena of personal life that such an enterprise would appear to suggest but to the *latent spirituality* of one's personality or, rather, what is called in Jungian terminology, the Self as distinguished from the persona or conscious ego. This distinction can be clarified through the application of the technique of morphological analysis suggested in chapter 1.

The observation of celestial phenomena is of course fundamental to astrology. We usually think of celestial phenomena as that which is *up* in the sky. From the modern astronomical perspective, however, we are aware that Earth is just as much *in* the sky, or space as it were, as any other celestial phenomenon that we observe. Yet even our modernistic term "outer space" suggests a distinction between the space immediately surrounding Earth and all other space in the universe. This is a valid distinction for us to make because of the radically different ways in which we *experience* those different spaces. From a morphological perspective, however, the difference involved is one of *proximity.* If we accept the fact that Earth is no less a celestial phenomenon than any other body in space, then the radical difference of our experience of Earth space from all other space serves to illustrate the morphological significance of Earth to us for purposes of astrological analysis. One may consider this fact to be so blatantly obvious as to be unworthy of mention, however, it is that very obviousness that tends to obscure the issue at hand, that is, that our experience of substances and situations *on Earth* is no less germane to the astrological paradigm than is the contemplation of the more distant cosmos. In fact, it is *more* germane due to its *morphological proximity.* This perspective forms the basis for understanding the significance of the "rising sign" found on the eastern horizon of a birthchart.

The tropical zodiac is a complex morphogenetic field relative to Earth's biosphere that is determined by dynamic interaction between Earth and Sol, which we experience as the annual cycle of seasonal change. Although that field immediately surrounds and is intimately interpenetrant with Earth, its positional orientation is *locked into the orbital movement* of Earth around Sol. On the other hand, Earth's *rotational movement*, its spinning upon its axis, occurs *within* the field of the zodiac, bringing a new sign to the horizon every two hours. This rotational movement is morphologically *Earth-specific,* whereas Earth's orbital movement is a function of the morphological *relationship* between Earth and Sol.

For astrological purposes, Earth's rotational movement is experienced most significantly at the *horizon*, which is nothing other than Earth itself. Some of the morphological factors to be considered in this regard include Earth's spherical shape, its size relative to the human body, solidity, gravity, opacity, surface variation, chemical composition, coloration, and life sustaining properties. Our human experience of life is such that the horizon of Earth is the most fundamental morphological determinant of our existence. The horizon is quite literally the *basis* of human consciousness. The visual apparatus of the human body and of the entire animal kingdom is oriented to perceive *horizontally,* as are the delicate sense of equilibrium and the auditory and olfactory organs. The entire human anatomy has evolved as an organism adapted to existence upon the horizontal surface of Earth.

Due to Earth's rotational movement, a special significance is imparted to the east-west directional orientation of the horizon, because Earth's eastward rotation causes celestial phenomena to *appear* on the eastern horizon and to *disappear* on the western horizon. The most conspicuous of these are Sol and Luna and, although these "Luminaries" are magnificent in their celestial splendor and magnitude, the horizon *exercises power* over them. It gives us Sol in the morning and it takes him away in the evening. Furthermore, in taking away Sol, the horizon gives us the firmament of the stars of the night sky and articulates the drama of the lunation cycle. The east-west horizon, as the author of this dynamic complex of phenomena, is represented in a birthchart, which is essentially a map, by the horizontal line that divides the circle of the birthchart into upper and lower halves.

In looking at a birthchart, one is assumed to be facing southward because, from our vantage point in the northern hemisphere, the path of the ecliptic along which Sol, Luna, and the planets transit is to our south. Therefore, the eastern horizon is on the left, the western horizon is on the right, and the bottom of the birthchart, the ground itself as it were, is the point of northern orientation. The eastern horizon on the left side of the birthchart is called the "Ascendant," and the zodiacal sign found on the Ascendant at any given time is therefore called the "rising sign." It is possible to gain some perspective upon the primordial significance of the rising sign, at any particular moment in time, simply by standing upon Earth and looking eastward to the horizon and imagining the symbolic image of the sign upon the horizon at that time. If one does not know what the rising sign is at a particular time, one may simply look upon the eastern horizon and imagine the significance of the greater cosmos ascending therefrom. This simple volitional act is often sufficient to generate a sense of resonance with the cosmos that is akin to the manner in which the ancient authors of our astrological tradition may be assumed to have attuned themselves with the cosmic rhythms of nature.

There is a symbolic correspondence between the emergence of celestial phenomena *from Earth*, at the Ascendant, and the emergence of new sprouts from Earth in the early spring. It is therefore appropriate that the Ascendant be given a corresponding symbolic significance as a component of the diurnal cycle to that given to the vernal equinox as a component of the annual cycle. Taking these two points as the respective beginnings of these two fundamental cycles of our experience of life, a series of correspondences is implied which carries through the wholes of both cycles, indicating a correspondence between the *microcosm* of the individual person or ego, symbolized by Earth, and the *macrocosm* of humanity as a whole, symbolized by Earth's relation to Sol which is experienced in terms of collective adaptation to seasonal change. From this perspective, Sol is comprehended to symbolize the integrating principle of humanity that lives within the *heart* of every individual, as Sol is the heart of Earth's orbit. It is worth noting here that this symbolic association suggests a heliocentric conception. This historical observation reiterates the theme that a relatively sophisticated cosmic conception is discernible within ancient cultural traditions, the origins of which are shrouded in legend and mystery.

The division of space surrounding Earth relative to the horizon provides the astrological frame of reference known as the twelve "houses" of a birthchart as distinguished from the twelve "signs" of the zodiac. The vertical axis or "Meridian" of a birthchart characterizes the verticality of the erect human stature and establishes a quadrature in relation to the Horizon. The further division of each quadrant into three houses completes the correspondence to the zodiacal division into twelve signs. The division of the heavens into *both* houses *and* signs therefore establishes a particular relationship between the *microcosm* of personality and the *macrocosm* of humanity relative to the time and place of one's birth. It is the orientation of houses to signs that *distinguishes* a particular person from the collective determination of humanity as a whole, yet that distinction is effected *within* and *in relation to* that greater human context.

The relations of houses to signs will be developed more extensively as we proceed, however enough of a theoretical foundation has thus far been established to warrant the introduction of some practical applications to the interpretation of the birthchart of the selected subject of this narrative. As stated above, the birthchart of an individual is a map of the solar system in its specific spatial and temporal orientation to the birth of that individual. The theoretical implication is that the formative essence of the person is *imprinted* by the impact of the birth experience. The most common approach advanced with regard to the manner in which this imprint is taken holds that the intake of the first gasp of air brings atmospheric conditions into the body of the infant and that his or her first crying out establishes an individual response to the environment. The theoretical perspective taken in this book is that a momentary hyper-sensitivity to the nonlocal reality of morphogenetic fields as a "wave function" at the quantum level of organic functioning is "collapsed" by sensory bombardment into the organic memory of the native as a fundamental cosmic orientation to which all subsequent changes in the morphogenetic field structure are referred. This theory is consistent with a feature of quantum mechanics addressed more thoroughly in chapter 9.

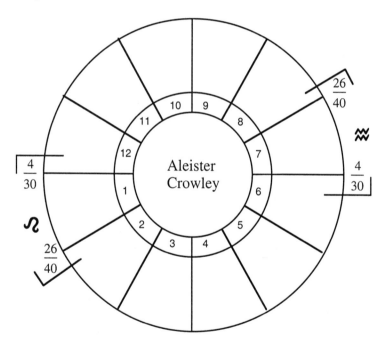

FIGURE I
Placements of Leo and Aquarius in relation to
the Horizon of Aleister Crowley's birthchart

Young Edward Alexander Crowley is reported to have committed this act at 11:16 p.m. on October 12, 1875, in Leamington, England. Figure 1 illustrates the placements of the signs found on the Horizon of Crowley's birthchart as calculated for those coordinates showing Leo at the Ascendant.

The rising sign refers most specifically to what the Swiss psychologist Carl Jung termed the *persona*, the image of personality assumed by an individual in adaptation to the outside world. The term is derived from the Latin word for actor's mask. Even a superficial knowledge of Aleister (having adopted that name as a young man) Crowley is sufficient to confirm the suitability of the image of the lion for his persona. It is hardly conceivable that anyone could act out such flamboyance and bravado as did Aleister Crowley through the course of his life without the benefit of the Leo Ascendant. His adoption of the self-proclaimed image of himself as the Beast 666 is certainly apropos, the lion being well known as the "king of beasts," and the number 6 having a symbolic association in Qabalistic philosophy with Sol, the planetary ruler of Leo.

Such a consideration of the Ascendant as a single factor, however, is incomplete, because, as the astrologer Dane Rudhyar emphasized, *the horizon is a whole phenomenon.* Rudhyar introduced the term "axis of consciousness" as pertaining to the Horizon of a birthchart. Consciousness implies both subject and object, knower and known, and the Ascendant at the eastern horizon refers only to the *subjective* aspect of this relation. The *objective* aspect of consciousness is referred to by the *western horizon*, the Descendant. In traditional astrology the Descendant is said to refer to relationships, partners, enemies and marriage. The implication in relation to the above observations is that one may go through life for an extended period of time in a relatively subjective, *unconscious* (or we could say oblivious) state, provided one were not to become directly involved with another person in a meaningfully involved relationship of some kind. Once such a relationship is initiated, however, one finds oneself challenged by *otherness* in a manner that must continuously be accommodated to oneself. This challenge creates tension, and this tension generates *consciousness.*

In accordance with the geometry of a birthchart, the sign on the Descendant is always the opposite to the one found on the Ascendant. The term "opposite" as used here refers to the 180° angular relationship that pertains to opposite sides of a circle. The sign opposite Leo is Aquarius and that sign is therefore found on the Descendant of Crowley's birthchart. The sign on the Descendant refers to the native's *approach to relationships*, that is, how the native tends to *experience* relationships. Naturally this is significant with regard to the kinds of people that one will form relationships with, but it must be kept in mind that the Descendant refers to an aspect of the *native's* personality. It must also be kept in mind that the Descendant is always involved in an interactive relation with the Ascendant.

The meaning of Aquarius is most specifically that of individual freedom and responsibility within a social context. Having Aquarius on his Descendant, Crowley assumed a characteristically Aquarian approach to relationships. The social significance of relationships was of paramount concern to him, however he considered the need for individual self-determination in relationships to be fundamental. Furthermore, Crowley's actual experience of relationships as a tension-producing phenomenon in relation to his Leonian persona was the primary *consciousness-producing* factor of his personality. This put great demands upon anyone with whom he became involved to any significant degree.

Due to angular variations of the plane of the ecliptic in relation to any particular point on the surface of Earth at any particular moment in time, the geometric divisions of houses and signs in a birthchart do not correspond to each other exactly in terms of the measurement of degrees of arc, depending upon which of the several systems of house division is used by a particular astrologer. Consequently, the 30 degrees of arc defining any given house of a birthchart will usu-ally encompass somewhat more or less than 30 degrees of arc along the ecliptical plane of the zodiac. These variations are exaggerated in proportion to the time of the year and the latitudinal distance from the equator at the native's place of birth. This circumstance produces interesting variations in the placements of "house cusps" in relation to the zodiacal signs. One such variation occurs when one zodiacal sign extends to include two successive house cusps. This is the case for the signs Leo and Aquarius in Crowley's birthchart. Not only are these two signs found on his Ascendant and Descendant, that is, his First and Seventh House cusps respectively, but they extend to cover his Second and Eighth House cusps as well (See Figure 1).

The sign found on a house cusp in a birthchart is said to "rule" that house. Likewise, the planet (or Luminary) that is the "ruling planet" of the sign found on a house cusp is said to be the ruling planet of that house in the birthchart. When a sign is found to extend over two successive house cusps, the symbolic indication is that the exercise of that sign's rulership *carries over* from one house to the next, thereby linking the successive houses involved into an extended or reiterated process. This morphologically implicit interpretation would appear to corroborate both the very near exactitude of the above time used for Crowley's birthchart as well as the system of house division employed in this study (the Birthplace system developed by Dr. Walter Koch) for the following reasons.

In a most inclusive interpretation, the Second House refers to the *substantiation* of the persona in material terms, and the Eighth House refers to the *transformation* of consciousness that results from processing relationship issues. In traditional astrology, however, which we may assume is a corrupted form of its original source, interpretation has been developed in mundane terms. The Second and Eighth Houses are therefore said to refer to personal finances and inheritance or legacy respectively. Despite the difference in the scope of application, there is a thematic continuity to these interpretations. For the present purpose of demonstrating the applicability of standard interpretive technique to Aleister Crowley's birthchart, the traditional attributions are quite adequate.

Crowley's father, a wealthy retired brewer, provided an atmosphere of financial well-being for Alick's (Crowley's boyhood nickname) childhood and, upon his death, left a sizable inheritance for his only son. Although there were prudent restrictions upon Crowley's access to the family fortune in his years as a minor, it nevertheless strongly conditioned his self-image and sense of values as a child and later afforded him the privilege of financial self-indulgence as a young man. Crowley took full advantage of this resource to the extent that he eventually depleted it. Before he was able to exhaust it completely, however, he managed to do a rather thorough job of substantiating his persona in material terms. It is also relevant to observe that, although his lavish expenditures of his inheritance may be considered by some to have been mere frolic, a more thorough examination of Crowley's attitudes and actions confirms the pursuance of a *transformative ideal* which applied not only to himself personally through the energetic exploitation of an ostentatious and adventuresome lifestyle, but also to the world at large through extravagant private publications of his acclaimed works of iconoclastic poetry and religious philosophy.

The carry-over of Leo's rulership from Crowley's First to his Second House is significant as an indicator of the manner in which his persona extended into the conducting of his financial affairs. This characteristic is illustrated by a passage from Gerald Suster's biography of Crowley, *The Legacy of the Beast.* The passage refers to Crowley's college years at Cambridge.

> As for social life, 'I [Crowley] was surrounded by a more or less happy, healthy, prosperous set of parasites.' In an economic sense, Crowley was a parasite too. He spent freely on whatever took his fancy, and as he later admitted, his upbringing had left him hopelessly ill-educated in matters of sensible money-management. He had been taught to expect every possible material comfort as a right for which his family paid, yet until now had been kept very short of pocket money for his own use. As a result, his attitude to money remained unbalanced throughout his life. Extremely generous with whatever he had, he nevertheless quarreled with tradesmen over petty sums: a proverbial case of 'penny wise, pound foolish.' Yet as his friend Louis Wilkinson would write: 'He treated his fortune as a toy. If you fit out mountaineering expeditions and are continually printing sumptuous private editions of your poems and plays and magical works, and buying places in Scotland, and living everywhere like a prince and entertaining like a Maharajah, even a large fortune won't last very long. But what *panache,* what *élan* and *brio* while it does last!' [pp. 22-23]

The "penny wise, pound foolish" attitude reflects the fact that Virgo spans the greater part of Crowley's Second House, but the house is nevertheless *ruled* by Leo. The shift of orientation toward frugality occurred *too late* for him to compensate in any meaningful way for his lavishness. The usual case for the Leo rising personality is to have Virgo on the Second House cusp which enables the native to catch hold of oneself in time to apply the acumen of Mercury, the planetary ruler of Virgo, to one's financial affairs.

The fact of this *not* being the case for Crowley, however, demonstrates another significant meaning of the extension of a sign to cover two house cusps. He not only had Leo on his Ascendant, but his entire First House, the whole of his persona, was inordinately dominated by Leo. The compensating restraint that usually comes into play as a secondary feature of the Leonian persona was absent from Crowley's personality. This lack of restraint is invariably emphasized by Crowley's detractors, and it is unanimously attested to and largely disapproved of even by his supporters. At this early stage of interpreting Crowley's birthchart it is sufficient simply to point out that these observations are relevant. It yet remains for them to be placed within the larger context of the birthchart as a whole and a more fully developed perspective upon Crowley's personality.

The first step toward the illumination of that context, as stated above, is the consideration of the house and sign interaction that opposes Crowley's Leo Ascendant, that is, the placement of Aquarius on his Descendant and its extension over the entirety of his Seventh and part of his Eighth House. Concerning Crowley's financial situation, the extension of Aquarius from his Seventh into his Eighth House indicates the significance of the fact that his wealth was not directly earned but rather inherited from his father. This significance is more specifically indicated by the placement of Saturn in Aquarius in Crowley's Seventh House, but the significance of planetary placements will not be addressed until after a theoretical foundation for their interpretation is developed in chapter 3.

A preliminary observation concerning the extension of Aquarius over the entirety of Crowley's Seventh and into his Eighth House is that this placement not only characterizes his approach to relationships, as is the case for any Aquarius descending native, but that the shift to Pisces which normally occurs in the Seventh House for the Aquarius descending native, thus facilitating the experience of personal reorientation toward transformation *within* the context of an existing relationship, was not the case for Crowley. The most blatant effect of this configuration upon Crowley's personality is reflected in the apparent need that he had to *terminate* relationships as a function of his own Eighth House experience of personal transformation. This theme may be considered to have been initiated in experiential terms by the death of Crowley's father, which had a profound effect upon his childhood development. The need for self-determination in relationships, so acutely felt by the Leo rising-Aquarius descending personality, carried over for Crowley into the death-rebirth experience that characterizes the Eighth House. The need for self-determination could not simply be affirmed by Crowley but had to be *proven* for himself by the death *of* relationships. This theme was enacted time and again through the course of his life and was certainly the source of a great deal more anguish for him than his sense of manliness would allow him openly to express in normal discourse although it is evident in much of his poetry, perhaps most notably in his *Rosa Decidua*, an ode to the death of his love for his first wife. This feature of Crowley's personality was also one of the major contributing factors to his reputation as a scoundrel.

In order further to explore the significance of the Horizon in Crowley's birthchart it is necessary to examine the placements of the planets found in the houses initiated thereby, that is, his First and Seventh Houses, but, as suggested above, such an examination cannot be conducted without first addressing the meanings of the planets for purposes of interpretation. It is therefore necessary to return to a theoretical perspective upon the meanings of the various planets and their relationships to the signs of the zodiac. In order to do this we must first examine the relation that obtains between the zodiac and the structure of the solar-planetary system from a morphological perspective. This is a major undertaking and the next chapter will therefore be devoted exclusively to that purpose.

CHAPTER 3

SCHEMA

There is a remarkable cogency to the manner in which the tropical zodiac and the solar-planetary system as a whole are integrated within the context of astrological symbolism from a morphological perspective. Although the term "morphology" is usually thought of as a fundamentally *spatial* concept, it naturally entails *temporal* components as well. For example, the length of the digestive tract of an animal has a direct relationship to the amount of time required for that organism to digest food. All morphological phenomena can be seen to have both spatial *and* temporal components.

One difference between spatial and temporal components is that spatial components constitute a whole system at any given *moment* in time, whereas temporal components can only be studied by extended observation *through* time. It follows that whole systems in space are perceptible in terms of *containment* and relative functional independence, whereas whole systems in time are perceptible in terms of beginnings and endings of processes which entail the coming into being and the going out of being of spatial systems. The tropical zodiac, although it has spatial components contributing to its structural form, is fundamentally a *temporal* phenomenon and therefore provides a perspective upon humankind in relation to *rhythmic oscillation within a living environment.* A *spatial* perspective upon human existence is provided by a morphological analysis of the solar-planetary system *as a whole* at *any* particular moment in time in relation to Earth.

There is no anachronism implicit in the geocentricity of the astrological perspective. Indeed, a heliocentric conception is fundamental to modern astrological theorizing. The significance of our geocentric perspective is simply a matter of proximity. If you happen to be living in Evanston, Wyoming, then you need to have, either on paper or in your head, a map of Evanston, Wyoming. We happen to be living on Earth. Indeed, Sol is the life-giving *center* of this cosmic organism of which Earth is but a part. From its position at the heart of the system, Sol is both the author of the zodiac and the illuminator of the planets and therefore symbolically represents, and in a real sense *is,* the *source* of both our temporal *and* our spatial wholeness. This realization forms the basis of our astrological understanding of Sol and Luna (known together as the "Luminaries"), the planets of the solar system (including Earth), and the tropical zodiac. It is the job of astrology to comprehend these components as an interrelated whole bestowing life, light, and meaning to all humankind and to that of each individual person.

A systemization of certain relations involving the Luminaries, the planets, and the signs of the zodiac is expressed in terms of what are called "dignities." (From this point on, the usual astrological practice of using the generic term "planets" to include Sol and Luna will usually be adopted. This practice is etymologically correct because the term "planet" means "wanderer," and Sol and Luna, as much as the other planets, are perceived from Earth as moving in relation to the backdrop of the stars.) Dignities assign special significances to planets in relation to the signs of the zodiac. The most important dignity is that of "rulership" in which particular planets are said to rule or govern particular signs. To adapt one of the terms employed by Rupert Sheldrake in his Hypothesis of Formative Causation, rulership of a sign by a planet implies a special *"morphic resonance"* involving them such that their respective meanings are linked to one another. In terms which have been suggested above, planets have meanings *spatially* comparable to the *temporal* meanings of the signs they are said to rule. In order to develop this hypothesis, it is necessary to elaborate the structural understanding of the zodiac.

The fundamental structure of the tropical zodiac is defined by four morphologically determined points of Earth's orbital motion, the two equinoxes and the two solstices. The equinoxes are the two points along Earth's orbit at which Sol crosses Earth's equatorial plane. They are called equinoxes (equal-night), because at those times the periods of light and darkness are equal in relation to the diurnal cycle of day and night. The vernal and autumnal equinoxes mark the beginnings of spring and autumn respectively. The solstices are the two points along Earth's orbit at which the poles of its rotational axis reach their most extreme orientations toward and away from Sol, initiating the summer and winter seasons. At those times the differences of the periods of light and darkness in relation to the daily cycle are most pronounced, the more so the farther one is north or south of the equator.

An observation may be made in this regard that is conspicuously neglected in most popular astrological literature. The seasonal cycles in the northern and southern hemispheres are temporally *opposite* to one another. When it is summer in Egypt, it is winter in Botswana. It must therefore follow that the tropical zodiac of the northern hemisphere *does not apply* concurrently in the southern hemisphere. This fact suggests a host of intriguing theoretical factors involving the relationship of the northern and southern hemispheres for astrological purposes. Let it suffice here to acknowledge its importance and to keep in mind that the system we are using has been developed fully within the context of the temperate zone of the northern hemisphere and therefore necessarily imposes certain limitations of perspective determined by such factors as the magnetic field of Earth, the continuity and distribution of land masses and the respective orientations of human experience and activity in the "upper" and "lower" hemispheres, etc.

Although there is a clear and distinct morphological basis for the division of the tropical zodiac into four segments, its further division into the traditional twelve signs would appear more arbitrary. The most fundamental morphological basis for the division of the annual cycle into twelve segments is the fact that twelve lunation cycles are completed in approximately 355 days. Therefore, there is a rough equivalence between the period of one seasonal cycle (one orbit of Earth around Sol) and twelve complete lunation cycles, thus the etymological relation of the word "month" to "moon." It follows that the division of the annual cycle into twelve segments implies a *conceptual integration* of the dynamic interrelationship involving the three most dominant celestial bodies for human experience, namely Earth, Luna, and Sol.

There are additional implications in the division of each season of the year into three stages. The two equinoxes and the two solstices signify critical turning points that *initiate* changes in the seasonal cycle. For this reason they are referred to as the "Cardinal" points of the tropical zodiac and the four signs they initiate, namely Aries, Cancer, Libra, and Capricorn, are therefore called Cardinal signs. These signs are correspondingly associated with taking initiative, connoting styles of *leadership* appropriate to their respective seasonal orientations. Extending this interpretive approach, it follows that the central period of each season is characterized by the relative *stabilization* of that season's fundamental meaning to the collective life process. Accordingly, the middle signs for each season, namely Taurus, Leo, Scorpio, and Aquarius, are called Fixed signs, connoting stable, fully actualized expressions of the life force associated with their respective seasons. At length, a *loosening up* of the characteristic expression of each season is appropriate to its final stage in order both to articulate the experience of that season and to cultivate a suitable susceptibility to the initiating impulse of the season to follow. The last signs of each season, namely Gemini, Virgo, Sagittarius, and Pisces, are therefore called Mutable signs, and are characterized by qualities of articulation and adaptability appropriate to the assimilation of lessons and the making of modifications associated with their respective seasonal orientations. Thus we inherit the astrological tradition of classifying the signs of the zodiac into three "characteristics," namely Cardinal, Fixed, and Mutable.

There is an additional system in traditional astrology for classifying the signs of the zodiac that may seem at first to be more arbitrary yet which proves to be remarkably insightful for purposes of interpretation. That system classifies the signs into four groups of "elements." These four elements of Fire, Earth, Air, and Water are found throughout all branches of occult lore and philosophy that extend back into time immemorial, and they are always employed in various ways as a means of working with conceptual quaternions— that is, thinking in fours as it were. The first four signs of the zodiac are assigned elements in the respective order listed above, and the sequence is repeated twice more to complete the series of twelve. This produces a pattern whereby signs of like elements occupy equilateral triangular relationships among themselves within the circular geometrical context of the zodiac. Aries, Leo, and Sagittarius are the Fire signs; Taurus, Virgo, and Capricorn the Earth signs; Gemini, Libra, and Aquarius the Air signs; and Cancer, Scorpio, and Pisces the Water signs. More of the rationale for this particular division of elemental attributions for the signs will be developed as we proceed.

It follows from these two systems of sign classification that there are twelve possible combinations of characteristics and elements and that each sign of the zodiac fulfills one such possible combination. This systemization provides a succinct method for ascertaining the structural meanings and relationships that obtain among the twelve zodiacal signs, and its remarkable cogency attests to the profound cosmological insights traceable to the ancient sources of the tradition.

Based upon these preliminary considerations, a general synthesis of the traditional schema of astrology in terms of planetary rulerships of the zodiacal signs may be set forth. This schema is usually presented in such a dissected manner, through lists and columns and such, that its inherent logic gets lost in the process of rote memorization, and often it would seem that one must simply accept the whole system on the basis of some seemingly arbitrary authority which may be assumed to have some mysteriously divine source. Although such considerations are not without some relevance to the matters at hand, it is yet to our advantage to find as much common ground as we can with the wellsprings of wisdom that tradition has bequeathed unto us, if we are to pursue the implicit revelation of a cooperative intent on the part of its sources. The traditional system of planetary rulerships inherited from the ancient authors of astrology is represented in Figure 2.

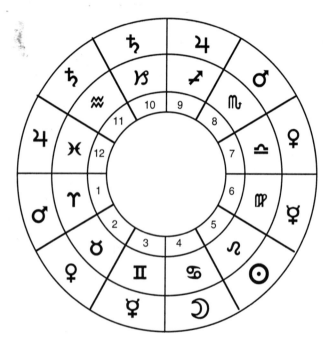

FIGURE 2
Traditional planetary rulers (outer circle)
of the zodiacal signs (inner circle)

The most fundamental frame of reference imposed upon human-kind by the cycle of seasonal variation is the need to work together for the good of all in order that as many people as possible may survive the adversity of winter and the relative freedom from that need resulting from nature's bestowal of the warmth and bounty of summer. The development of technology has significantly lessened the extremes of our experience of the changing seasons, but its reality is nevertheless fundamental to human existence so long as we continue to live on Earth. The meanings of the signs of the zodiac derive from this frame of reference and are most eloquently expressed accordingly by Dane Rudhyar in his book, *Astrological Signs: The Pulse of Life.*

It follows that the signs of summer have meanings associated with individual uniqueness and personality and the signs of winter have meanings associated with the integration of personalities in society. The signs of spring and autumn have meanings associated respectively with the *transitions* from a collective to an individual perspective and vice versa. Understanding this fundamental *temporal* frame of reference for the structure of the zodiacal cycle facilitates the comprehension of its integration with the *spatial* frame of reference provided by a morphological analysis of the solar-planetary system taken as a whole from our perspective on Earth. This integration is implicit in the traditional pattern of planetary rulerships.

Other than Earth, the two morphologically dominant celestial bodies in terms of human experience are Sol and Luna, due to the magnitude of their light-bearing properties and gravitational attractions. Although the entire solar-planetary system is involved in a network of energetic interaction, the significance for Earth of the Luminaries in terms of energetic processes is overwhelming in relation to that of the other planets. The importance of this observation is the *degree* of energetic involvement of the Luminaries into the complex of morphogenetic fields associated with the system taken as a whole. The effects of the Luminaries are fully *tangible* to human experience. We *feel* them. They appear *bigger*. They are therefore the most *personal* of all celestial bodies. We find them conventionally represented with *faces*. It is only natural that they would be assigned as rulers of the two most personal of all the signs of the zodiac, namely Luna as the ruler of Cancer and Sol as the ruler of Leo. It is worth noting that the elemental attributions listed above may seem somewhat less arbitrary by observing that Cancer, ruled by Luna, is a Water sign, and Leo, ruled by Sol, is a Fire sign.

In looking to the opposing end of the solstitial axis, we find both Capricorn and Aquarius ruled by Saturn. We may observe that Saturn dominates the difficult collective aspect of human existence; namely the making of hard decisions about how to ration limited food supplies and other resources necessary to the preservation of life through the cold, bleak season of winter. Saturn is the farthest planet from Earth that is visible to the naked eye. It is relatively dim and much slower moving compared with its companion, Jupiter. Indeed, Saturn is the most *impersonal* of all planets. Its role as the *boundary* of the visible solar-planetary system is morphologically reiterated by its pronounced ring formation. The invention of the telescope which made possible the discovery of planets beyond Saturn also enabled us to see Saturn's rings, as if to secure our understanding of its traditional function of defining our limitation to sense-bound experience. Saturn is the only planet in the traditional symbolic system to rule two successive signs, thus reiterating its association with *time*.

An elegant mathematical resolution for the integration of seven planetary rulers for twelve zodiacal signs is affected in the traditional system by the assignments of single rulerships for the two Luminaries, appropriate to their relatively greater energetic effects, and dual rulerships for each of the remaining five planets. This system is elegant not only mathematically but morphologically and conceptually as well. The planetary rulerships are assigned in a symmetrical outward pattern from those of the Luminaries in the sequence of their orbital distances from Sol at the heart of the system, closing the circle with the sequential dual rulerships of Saturn mentioned above.

In order to appreciate more of the symbolic cogency of the system of rulerships it is helpful to consider certain other morphological correspondences pertaining to the physical characteristics of the solar-planetary system. There is a fundamental morphological distinction between the group of planets including Mercury, Venus, and Mars, and the group including Jupiter and Saturn. The former are relatively small and occupy orbits in close proximity to Sol. They are also faster moving and thus have relatively shorter orbital periods. Mercury, Venus and Mars are therefore considered "personal" planets for purposes of astrological symbolism. Their interpretive meanings refer primarily to the basic functions of personal reality, namely thought, desire, and action respectively. The latter are assigned to the family known to modern astronomy as "gas giants." They are enormous and their orbits are much farther out and significantly slower in comparison to the personal planets. They *include* the personal planets, both spatially and temporally, as society includes individuals. Jupiter and Saturn are therefore appropriately called "social" planets. Another fundamental morphological distinction is that between *inner* and *outer* planets from the perspective of Earth's orbit. Mercury and Venus, having orbits *within* that of Earth, symbolize the inner dichotomy of thought and desire. In this regard, Venus puts on a rather impressive display as both the Morning Star and the Evening Star as she moves in her orb about Sol, whereas Mercury makes his analogous transitions rather swiftly and requires greater attentiveness to be observed due to its closer proximity to Sol's brightness. These characteristics reiterate a relative dominance of desire over thought as a natural tendency of personal reality (not without exceptions, of course). Mars, also a personal planet, is yet *outside* of Earth's orbit and is therefore appropriate as the symbolic referent for *action*, propelling the personality outward into the social arena. Jupiter and Saturn, the social planets, represent respectively the expansive benefits and defining limitations that naturally ensue as functions of social interaction.

The alternately opposing rulerships of the Cardinal and Fixed signs of the equinoctial seasons by Mars and Venus is particularly appropriate for the outer and inner planetary orbits adjacent to Earth. They are most suitable as symbolic representations of masculine and feminine expressions respectively, especially within the context of personal relationships and sexuality. The relatively balanced interaction of the equinoctial seasons is fully appropriate for these rulerships. The dynamic interaction of personal relationships operates *between* the extreme differentiation of the individual person and the collective state in relation to the solstitial axis. A symbolic analysis of the interrelations implicit in the polarities, oppositions, elements and characteristics of the signs ruled by Mars and Venus can be helpful for unraveling many of the complexities and ambiguities inherent in interpersonal relationships and sex roles.

The remaining planetary rulerships are those of the Mutable signs: Gemini, Virgo, Sagittarius, and Pisces. As mentioned earlier, these signs are characterized by articulation and adaptability and are therefore associated with matters such as communication, knowledge, education, technique, movement, and reorientation. They deal specifically with the refinement and expansion of *perspective*. The rulerships of the Mutable signs by the planets Mercury and Jupiter are appropriate for a host of morphologically demonstrable reasons.

Mercury's association with thought is obviously germane to the concerns of the Mutable signs cited above. Being a personal planet, we find Mercury ruling the two Mutable signs Gemini and Virgo, both belonging to the personal half of the zodiac, whose concerns are characteristically specific and logical, pertaining to language, science, technology and personal refinement. Jupiter as a social planet is correspondingly appropriate as the ruler of Sagittarius and Pisces, the two Mutable signs in the collective half of the zodiac. Although Jupiter's orbit is within that of Saturn, it is yet the larger of the two bodies and therefore characterizes a striving for extended scope and expansion *within Saturnian bounds*. Thus we find the concerns of philosophy, religion, and even mysticism, as well as voyaging, social expansion, proliferation, and commerce to be proper dominions for Jupiterian rulership.

The interrelated structure of polarities and elements of the signs of the zodiac further illustrates the cogency and facility of the system as a whole. There is a potential for confusion regarding the use of the terms "polarity" and "opposition" in astrology due to the fact that the successive alternation of positive and negative polarities of signs is not the same concept as the "polarization" that obtains between signs in diametric opposition to one another. For that reason the use of terms deriving from the root "pole" will be generally avoided when referring to factors of diametric opposition throughout this book, except for the clarification of a specific matter which will be explained presently so as to avoid any confusion in this regard.

As mentioned in chapter 1 in relation to the transition from the Piscean to the Aquarian Ages, the successive signs of the zodiac have been assigned alternating positive and negative polarities. This systemization indicates a dialectical process inherent in nature and the need for variation and differentiation through time. It is instructive to consider these polarities in terms of the elemental attributions mentioned above. From this perspective the elements may be thought of in terms of their morphological stratification in relation to gravity. We naturally think of gravity in terms of up and down relations. Gravity is experienced as a pulling downward. This frame of reference is quite workable in itself. However, the significance of polarity may be grasped more effectively in terms of movement outward and inward, or better still, as *expansion* and *contraction*. Gravity stratifies the four elements according to their relative tendencies to expand and contract in space. Of course the word "gravity" is simply a convenient term used for the contractive tendency of matter. We observe this stratification in terms of each element's tendency to rise or settle in relation to one another. The stratification therefore assumes the natural order, from the most expansive to the most contractive, of Fire, Air, Water, and Earth.

In modern scientific terms, one may think of these distinctions as between combustive, gaseous, liquid, and solid states of energy matrices. The use of the term "elements" with reference to these states is rooted in concepts that predate by millennia our modern usage of the word, and it is therefore anachronistic to attribute a lack of sophistication to its application in this manner. Furthermore, there are philosophical implications inherent in the characterization of the four traditional elements that involve a completely different frame of reference from that of modern material science, involving qualitative attributes of subjective experience. For astrological purposes the positive polarity is assigned to the expansive tendency and the negative polarity to the contractive tendency. It may therefore be observed that the attribution of elements to the signs of the zodiac is such that the two more expansive elements (Fire and Air) are said to be positive, and the two more contractive elements (Water and Earth) are said to be negative. A further differentiation is that, although both Fire and Air are positive, Fire is positive in relation to Air, and, although both Water and Earth are negative, Water is positive in relation to Earth.

With this pattern of polarities and elements in mind, some more elaborate observations about the relations and interactions among the zodiacal signs can be made. As mentioned above, the sequence of the elemental attributions of the signs is Fire, Earth, Air, and Water repeated three times to include all twelve signs. Aside from the fact that these attributions seem to work remarkably well for purposes of interpretation, one may wonder what the sense might be for that particular sequence. After all, the successive alternation of polarities could have been worked out in other ways.

The logic of the sequence would appear to be that the first Cardinal sign Aries, being associated with the burst of life initiating the spring season, is appropriately associated with the most expansive, that is, the most positive of the elements, namely Fire. Then the shift to the second sign, connoting the most primordial of polarities, is appropriately associated with the *other extreme* of the spectrum of polarity to establish the fullest possible temporal equilibrium. Thus we observe the elemental attribution of Earth to Taurus. The third and fourth signs must therefore follow in the sequence of Air and

Water to preserve the pattern of alternating polarities. This completed pattern produces an alternation between the *extremes* and the
means of elemental attributions through the overall sequence of zodiacal signs. The fact that the successive transitions from one element
to another always make the greatest possible differential leap shows
the dynamic perspective of the vitalistic experience of meaning.
Vitalistic philosophy exemplifies nature's most dynamic and pronounced manifestations more clearly to instill the understanding of
her fundamental principles. The rationale for elemental attribution
developed above exemplifies this characteristic. The initiating polarization of Aries and Taurus, by virtue of their respective elemental
attributions of Fire and Earth, is suggestive of the primordial experience of a lightning bolt striking the ground, which usually occurs in a
stormy setting that involves *all* the elements in dynamic interaction
and is appropriate to a mythopoetic conception of *creation* as a
bipolar interaction. After the violence of the storm there is the experience of the clearing of the Air (Gemini). Then the Water (Cancer)
flows across the land, returning to its oceanic source only to be
evaporated once again by the Fire of Sol (Leo), rain back upon the
Earth (Virgo), and so on. This is not intended to stand as a comprehensive explanation of the rationale for elemental attributions, for
there are subtleties that it hardly begins to account for, but it does at
least serve as a starting point for removing the entire matter from
abstruseness.

Additional subtleties in the relations among elemental attributions
and polarities can be found in the observation that diametrically
opposed signs are always of the same general polarity, although they
yet have a *relative* polarization in relation to each other. For example, the solstitial signs Cancer and Capricorn are Water and Earth
signs respectively. They are both of the general negative polarity
appropriate to the solstitial function of *containment,* but Water is
positive in relation to Earth, implying that Cancer is positive in relation to Capricorn. That is, the *person* is positive in relation to the
state. In this regard, the patterns of oppositional planetary rulerships
mentioned above preserve consistent correspondences in that the
rulerships of the Luminaries are always positive in relation to those
of Saturn, the rulerships of Mars are always positive in relation to
those of Venus, and the rulerships of Jupiter are always positive in
relation to those of Mercury. A thorough understanding of the morphological relationships involved in this rather complex interrelation
is suggestive of a process of *convection* within the entire system.

Such a conception accords with the dynamics of homeostasis observable in nature whereby processes of continuity and change elegantly integrate into a system of self-renewing vitality. This cosmic conception is eminently rational and yet not overly simplistic in that it accords with the dynamic interaction of complex compensatory principles.

This analysis has thus far only been applied to the *traditional* schema of planetary rulerships, that is, only to the *immediately visible* solar-planetary system. This approach has been taken not only for the sake of its conceptual but also its historical significance, which includes the very relevant fact *of* that natural visual limitation. It is imperative for the student of astrology to gain an understanding of the exquisite coherence and dynamic profundity of this philosophical conception in order to apprehend the viability of astrology as a whole working system. The more extended study of the rulerships involving the recently discovered planets beyond Saturn has yet to be introduced in the course of this book. It is important, however, first to comprehend the cosmic conception of humanity *before* the development of modern technology. The traditional conception of the cosmos constitutes the *organic basis* of human experience into which the roots of modern humanity are deeply planted. The further consideration of the newly discovered planets serves to elucidate the superstructure of modernity, but it is foolish to commit the common error of forgetting whence we come.

CHAPTER 4

URANUS

The importance of the First and Seventh Houses to the structure of personality was developed in chapter 2 in terms of persona and relationship, subject and object respectively, and the consciousness-producing tension generated thereby. Any planets that are placed in either of these houses refer to specific functions of one's personality that operate within the context of that dynamism. A planet in the First House refers to a function executed directly as a feature of one's persona. A planet in the Seventh House refers to a function that operates as a particular kind of screen upon which to project images that compensate for the specific orientation of the persona, that is, a function experienced through relationship. It is important to keep in mind that this is an arrangement of *diametric opposition.*

The approach to psychology developed by Carl Jung stresses the importance of the reconciliation of opposites. Any *whole truth* necessarily entails some kind of opposition, that is, to *know* it is not a simple matter of direct apprehension but rather the realization of a *paradox.* A paradox is an *apparent* contradiction that is actually a wholeness of truth. In astrological symbolism this condition is represented by any occurrence of, or reference to, diametrical opposition. Taking the Horizon of a birthchart as an example, the persona of an individual does not *fully* manifest, nor is it *fully* experienced, either by oneself or by anyone else, unless one is in direct interactive relationship with another person, and then it is experienced fully *only* by oneself *and* that other person. This example is one of the most fundamental oppositions found in astrological symbolism, and it provides the key for unlocking a great mystery of human existence.

Aleister Crowley had Uranus in his First House and Saturn in his Seventh House as shown in Figure 3. Not only are these two planets in opposing signs and houses, they are also in *exact-degree opposition* (180° angular relationship) in the twentieth degrees of Leo and Aquarius respectively. The implications of this planetary arrangement are extraordinary. Since the planet Uranus has thus far not been mentioned in this narrative and would appear to have no place in the neatly arranged schema of traditional planetary rulerships presented in chapter 3, an analysis of its meaning is an appropriate starting point for the study of those implications inasmuch as its placement in Crowley's First House shows it to be a fundamental component of his persona.

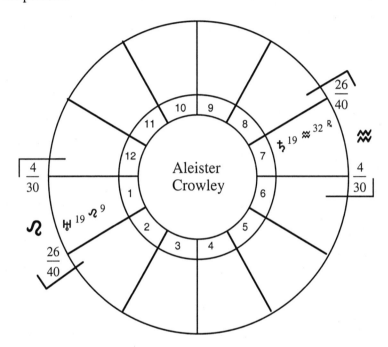

FIGURE 3
Addition of the placements of Uranus and Saturn
in Aleister Crowley's birthchart

The collective significance of the seven planets (including the Luminaries) of the traditional schema of astrology, taken as a whole within the context of the larger planetary system as we now know it, is that they are visible to the naked eye. They are *given* to the natural order of sense-bound perception. In this regard they represent a whole realm of experience. The planets beyond Saturn were not so given. They had to be *discovered.* Uranus was the first of those planets to be discovered, and the significance to humankind of its discovery, from an astrological perspective, is monumental to say the least. Before Uranus could be discovered, a particular level of scientific sophistication was required, including the material technology of the telescope and the development of specific conceptual, analytical, and mathematical models and techniques.

Uranus was discovered in 1781 by the British astronomer, Sir William Herschel, and named after him accordingly. Its name was later changed to Uranus in keeping with the tradition of naming planets after mythological deities. The scientific advancements leading to this discovery were very hard-won. Nicolaus Copernicus was forced under the threat of persecution by the Church to withhold publication of his heliocentric theory. It was published only after his death. Giordano Bruno, an Italian Renaissance philosopher who developed a naturalistic and mystical philosophy from the new Copernican astronomy, was *burned* at Rome as a heretic. Galileo was forced to recant his theories and placed under house arrest by the Church for his contributions to the emerging scientific understanding of the solar system and Earth's movements within it. Those who participated in the emergence of the scientific societies of the sixteenth and seventeenth centuries did so not only at the risk of persecution or even death, but in terms of prevailing religious dogma they stood in danger of eternal damnation as well. The pursuit of science was proclaimed contrary to the will of God by the Church in those times. Of course, the religious authorities had so diminished their power to speak on behalf of truth and morality by virtue of their personal examples that their spiritual admonitions lacked credence. Nevertheless, the courageous spirits who defied them were willing to place not only their lives but their very *souls* on the line in the name of truth as they conceived it, thus alienating themselves from their social and religious milieu. The development of the trend thus initiated by the early scientific philosophers of the sixteenth and seventeenth centuries forged the world view that has since become fully ingrained as the unconscious substratum of modern thought.

A whole new conception of humanity was inherent in the perspective leading to and accompanying the advent of the discovery of Uranus. This new perspective was one of personal freedom and independence from previously established religious and political authority. To understand the astrological meaning of Uranus it must be realized that it served as a *celestial confirmation* of the ideals of the Enlightenment that had come to fruition at the time of its discovery. Only five years earlier had the American colonies under British rule rocked the world with their Declaration of Independence, directly challenging the age-old tradition of European monarchy. In that same year of 1776, Adam Smith published his monumental treatise, *An Inquiry into the Nature and Causes of the Wealth of Nations,* the classic formulation of the economic theory of free enterprise which introduced the term "invisible hand" to connote an ordering principle of society that is superior to and beyond the reach of autocratic political authority. Also at that time the steam engine was invented as well as the means for harnessing electricity which, coupled with Smith's economics, set the stage for the Industrial Revolution.

More poignantly, in the year of Uranus' discovery, 1781, came the turning point of the American Revolution with Cornwallis' surrender at Yorktown. Only then for the first time in recorded history had a *nation* come into being and won the right to exist through force of arms that was ostensibly and explicitly founded upon the sovereignty of the individual human being. Though the ideal remains unfulfilled as a political reality, the prototypal mechanism for its fulfillment was nonetheless established as a system of government that has survived the test of time and continues to evolve as a struggling model of freedom and democracy in a world plagued with the mentality of authoritarian despotism, bigotry and corruption.

There was yet another phenomenal event that synchronously signaled the significance of the discovery of Uranus to the rarefied air of metaphysical philosophy: the appearance of Immanuel Kant's *Critique of Pure Reason.* Through his treatment therein of the inescapable observation that all we can ever perceive are mental phenomena, and never things in themselves, Kant laid the foundation for all subsequent transcendental philosophy. Appearing in the same year as the discovery of Uranus, Kant's *Critique* served a similar function as a stepping-stone toward the greater heavens.

We have several morphological determinants to guide us toward ascertaining the meaning of Uranus for purposes of astrological interpretation. Among them are its size, composition and the position and period of its orbit in relation to the whole planetary system. Its size and composition clearly place it in the group of gas giants with Jupiter and Saturn, however it is smaller than both of them. These features identify Uranus as a social planet but with a more particularized meaning. The position of its orbit *outside* of and therefore *superior* to and encompassing that of Saturn clearly implies a direct challenge to the traditional authority associated with Saturn, denying him the last word, as it were.

Uranus' orbital period of 84 years indicates another meaning of this planet for the new conception of humanity that has emerged with the advancement of free scientific thought and economic incentive. That significance is the extension of the average lifetime resulting from advancements in medical technology and other fields that contribute to a healthier environment and better living conditions. An average human lifetime of 84 years, equal to that of the orbital period of Uranus, is a reasonable expectation in terms of present knowledge, whereas 200 years ago work requirements, sanitation problems, diseases, and infant mortality, etc., held the average lifetime much closer to Saturn's orbital period of approximately 30 years.

The significance of the *historical context* of Uranus' discovery derives from the fact that a specific level of scientific sophistication was required before the discovery of planets beyond Saturn could become a possibility. There is a logical connection between the evolution of human mentality and the discovery of planets not visible to the naked eye. In this regard the solar system as a whole functions as a time-release capsule morphologically programmed to open at a specific time in relation to the development of latent potentialities for the expansion of human consciousness. The concept of a space-time continuum, originally developed by Einstein, is difficult to comprehend for those of us so strongly conditioned to think of space and time as absolute and distinct categories of existence. A significant contribution to a *psychological* understanding of the relation of space and time was made by Carl Jung with his coining of the term "synchronicity." This term refers to *meaningful coincidences* that appear to violate probabilistic explanations. This idea challenges the pre-quantum assumptions of science that have yet to be adequately purged of antiquated conceptions of reality. It is surely the chief duty of science to take account of *all* facts of experience, and Jung's development of the idea of synchronicity is a viable acknowledgment of a particular kind of experience that is attested to by many intelligent people, however difficult it may be to explain in scientific terms. The morphological significance of the *moment* of a planet's discovery, for purposes of astrological interpretation, comes under the broad rubric of synchronicity.

A further significance of Uranus' discovery is it's disruption of the pristine astrological conception codified by the traditional system of planetary rulerships. What had been conceived as a self-evident revelation of natural order would appear to have been thrown seriously out of kilter by the intrusion of this newcomer. Not only were the dogmas of church and state challenged by the knowledge of Uranus' existence, but also the dogmas of esoteric philosophy. As reference to any present day text on astrology will show, Uranus has been assimilated into astrological theory as the new ruler of Aquarius. This assignment is conventionally presented in the popular literature as a matter of fact with little or no consideration given to how such a determination was made (other than the inherent implication that it works out that way for purposes of interpretation). There is often no mention that Saturn was the traditional ruler of Aquarius before it was displaced by Uranus. These concerns, however, are of paramount importance to the astrological understanding of both of these planets, to the sign Aquarius, and to the evolution of humankind, not to mention to the study of astrology itself.

By the rationale for the traditional system of planetary rulerships, the assignment of Uranus as the new ruler of Aquarius was as logically consistent as a ball falling into a slot. It must first be observed that each of the four traditional planets, other than Sol, Luna and Saturn, holds consistent patterns of oppositional rulerships. Mars and Venus rule two sets of opposing signs as do Mercury and Jupiter. Saturn was therefore not only unique in ruling two successive signs, but also in functioning in two different oppositional rulership arrangements, one with Luna through the Cancer-Capricorn opposition, and one with Sol through the Leo-Aquarius opposition. There was therefore a logically indicated "opening" for a planetary rulership displacement of one of the signs traditionally ruled by Saturn. The determination of which of those two signs was to receive the new benediction was also clearly indicated by the astrological meanings of the factors involved in the arrangement, rooted as they are in their inherent morphological pattern. Each of the five planets having two sign rulerships in the traditional system accordingly had two distinct roles to play as such. The respective natures of these roles are ascertainable in terms of the polarities, elements, and characteristics of the signs involved, as well as a consideration of their seasonal orientations. For Saturn, there was an additional important distinction inherent in its rulership opposition to each of the two Luminaries.

As the ruler of Capricorn, Saturn participates in an oppositional orientation to the lunar principle of personal *containment,* morphologically implicit in Luna's direct orbit of Earth as her primary. This principle of containment is reiterated at the social level by Saturn's function as the *boundary* of the immediately visible solar system, symbolically reinforced by Saturn's pronounced ring formation. The solstices embody the *containment* of the annual cycle of time within the seasonal extremes of summer and winter. As the rulers of the solstitial signs Cancer and Capricorn respectively, Luna and Saturn embody the planetary principles of personal and social containment in space. Accordingly, as the ruler of Capricorn, Saturn embodies the function of social *authority,* that is, the principle of administrative decree and governmental power that is secured by the ability to incarcerate (confine) noncompliant citizens. The Saturnian conception of social authority found its consummate expression in the civil philosophy of Thomas Hobbes. His famous treatise, *Leviathan,* published in 1651, remains to this day the bedrock of justification for authoritarian social institutions.

As the traditional ruler of Aquarius, Saturn performed a significantly different function from that of governmental administration. Naturally, it remained associated with social organization, since collective management characterizes the entire winter season. However, whereas Capricorn, a Cardinal sign, focuses the need for initiating and defining the administration of social containment, Aquarius, a Fixed sign, pertains to the *stabilization* of society. Social stabilization is *not* produced by executive decree but can only result from the proliferation of *interpersonal cooperation.* The transition from Capricorn to Aquarius represents the need, well known by wise politicians and statespersons, for a shift from executive power to allowance for *natural* stability within society. This function of Saturn in the traditional system operated in opposition to Leo, ruled by Sol. In this role Saturn symbolized the social complement of personal *actualization* as differentiated from its role as the social complement of personal *containment* that it fulfills as the ruler of Capricorn. The ordering principle shifts from being externally imposed by authority to being internally felt as *conscience.*

Saturn's successive rulership of Capricorn and Aquarius in the traditional system was indicative of the feeling on the part of the people that the governing elite were an extension of their own persons through an unconscious participation mystique, much the same as currently occurs in relation to "stars" in the field of entertainment. The responsibility of the governing elite to *restrain themselves* in the exercise of power over their subjects was necessary to secure the benefits of social cooperation. This was not just a matter of honor and moral discretion but one of practical necessity. Even in an absolute monarchy, royal prerogatives may be extended only so far before repercussions endanger the stability of the state. Such repercussions manifest in the formation of cooperative groups that challenge the authority of the sovereign. Naturally, such groups must operate secretly until their objective of removing the abuse of authority is accomplished, and this accounts for the symbolic association of Aquarius with secret societies and "subversive" organizations, as well as the more benign activities of fraternal associations and voluntary social groups.

Due to its symbolic association with enhanced social responsibility and political activism, Uranus was an obvious candidate for displacement of Saturn's traditional rulership of Aquarius. This displacement witnessed a major shift in the social orientation of humanity from relying upon responsibility on the part of government to *direct assumption* of responsibility on the part of citizens. It is indeed remarkable that the discovery of Uranus occurred at such a critical time in the transition from the Piscean to the Aquarian Age, bringing this manifestly new and revolutionary perspective to bear upon the meaning of Aquarius.

With these considerations in mind, the significance of Uranus' placement in Aleister Crowley's First House is readily apparent. The very function of responsibility on the part of individuals for the well being of the community was an inherent component of Crowley's persona. But in order fully to grasp the manner in which his First House Uranus manifested through Crowley's personality it must be analyzed in terms of its sign placement and a host of other factors, the most striking of which is its exact-degree opposition to Saturn.

The manner in which Crowley's First House Uranus manifested as a component of his persona is significantly characterized by its placement in Leo. Earlier mention was made about the system of dignities whereby the nature of a planet's performance in various signs is assessed in terms of its efficacy, or lack thereof. In addition to the dignity of rulership, the other dignities are those of "detriment," "exaltation," and "fall." The sign of a planet's exaltation is one in which that planet functions especially well. When a planet is placed in the sign diametrically opposite to one of its rulership it is said to be in its detriment. When a planet is placed in the sign diametrically opposite to its exaltation it is said to be in its fall. A planet in its detriment or in its fall is traditionally held to be unfavorably placed and therefore a source of difficulty for the native. The reasons for this will be analyzed with reference to the example currently under consideration, that is, Crowley's placement of Uranus in Leo where it is in its detriment, because Leo is diametrically opposed to Aquarius.

As stated before, any instance of diametrical opposition in astrological symbolism indicates a paradoxical wholeness of truth, whereby an apparent contradiction stands in need of reconciliation such that each opposing term must be modified by the other to be consciously realized as a working truth. Otherwise it is experienced as a conundrum that plagues the native. Such natural paradoxes are inherent in each of the six pairs of diametrically opposed signs. These paradoxes are difficult enough to reconcile as they naturally appear in life, however, when a planet is placed in a sign opposite to one of its rulership it engenders an *inverted paradox,* that is, it compounds and exacerbates the already existing paradox of the signs' opposition. Such a placement poignantly complicates and increases the difficulty of reconciling the paradox inherent in the opposing signs involved. The language of traditional astrology, however, can be misleading in this regard. What have been termed "unfortunate" planetary placements may be better understood as posing challenging opportunities for engaging in more complex and profound forms and patterns of human activity. It is the failure to accept and profit from such challenges that is unfortunate, not the challenges themselves.

The implication of Uranus' natal placement in Leo, especially in one's First House, is that of a tendency toward imbalance, an over-emphasis on the acting out of personal individuality, and indeed, many of those who knew Aleister Crowley personally testify that he exercised his individuality seemingly to a fault. This aspect of Crowley's personality is unquestionably a dominant recurring theme in the course of his life, and for many it appears to be sufficient grounds for dismissing him as a person of little consequence in keeping with the usually correct observation that anyone who goes around blowing one's own horn tends to have little worth blowing about. It is important to keep in mind at this early stage of interpreting Crowley's birthchart, however, what has already been said about the First House referring to one's persona, that is, one's *mask.* The actual implications of such a placement can easily be misconstrued by uncritical observations of the resulting phenomena. It is not only the native that is challenged by difficult planetary placements but also those with whom the native interacts. This would appear to be the case for the personality of Aleister Crowley. In fact, any reflective study of Crowley's life soon reveals that he continuously *played upon the theme of his own egotism* in ways that defy conventional analysis. The close examination of Crowley's birthchart, juxtaposed with the known facts of his life, tends to support the assessment that the personal failings of his persona may have been employed largely as a blind for the manner in which he conducted his activities and interactions with other people. It is easy to see how such a method would be effective toward encouraging independence on the part of over-zealous devotees as well as preserving his own.

The foremost indicator of an exceptional circumstance for the exaggerated self-dramatization inherent in Crowley's Uranus placement is its exact-degree opposition to Saturn in Aquarius in his Seventh House. Certain angular relationships called "aspects" between planets, as a function of their various orbital periods, have special meanings for purposes of interpreting their mutual effect on one another. Naturally, the closer an aspect is to being exact the more intense is its effect. The opposition aspect of 180° is one of the more difficult to handle. It generates a great deal of tension between the planets involved by accentuating their functions in terms of a paradox characterized by their respective sign and house placements. The opposition of Saturn to Uranus in Crowley's birthchart indicates a most profound example of such a paradox.

Saturn having been the traditional ruler of Aquarius implies that its placement therein is one of natural harmony of function and field of expression. This placement accentuates Saturn's role as the facilitator of cooperative stability as differentiated from imposer of autocratic authority. In a birthchart, Saturn refers to one's *sense of identity* in that it defines the bounds of the ego in relation to society. It determines the "ring pass not," the line not to be crossed, as it were, by the actual experience of social consciousness. It is the *natural limit* of one's conscious orientation to social reality. In Aquarius, Saturn bestows magnanimity to the personality through a fundamental appreciation for social propriety and cooperative interaction. Despite his displays of Leonian ego, this feature of Crowley's personality is readily apparent if one takes the time to read his works at any length. He makes continual references to what is appropriate in the way of social interactions, and such references consistently stress a healthy respect for individual differences and predilections. When he brings his Leonian wrath to bear toward others, it invariably involves their failure to exercise that same respect, or their failure to *demand* it.

Having this placement of Saturn in his Seventh House indicates Crowley's *objectification* of this principle through relationships.

These observations are substantiated by Crowley's relationship with his father. The Saturn placement in a birthchart is usually the most significant indicator of one's perception and experience of one's father through the traditional association (primarily as a function of patriarchal society) of the father with the principle of authority as derived from the greater world outside the home. Crowley's Saturn placement in the Seventh House indicates the significance of his father to him in his childhood. His father served as a *partner* specifically suited to counterbalance the excessively individualistic tendencies of the boy's persona, exhibited in accordance with his Uranus placement. Through his *relationship* with his father Crowley was able to find his own limits as a conscious entity and define himself as a person. This astrological perspective, taken as a factor in attempting to understand what is known of the man, Aleister Crowley, is particularly revealing with regard to many of the subtle perplexities and apparent contradictions to be found in his life and work. The significance of his inherited wealth which enabled him to substantiate his Leonian persona as a young man (commented upon in chapter 2) may now be placed in a clearer perspective. Saturn's placement in Aquarius, which extends to cover the cusp of his Eighth House, connotes the theme of inheritance from his father. Such inheritance, however, should not be interpreted exclusively in material terms. Certainly an inheritance of temperament is indicated as well. It is therefore instructive to consider the influence of the elder Crowley upon his son, so strongly indicated by these factors.

Most significantly, Crowley's father was a religious man. He was a prominent and articulate evangelist for the Plymouth Brethren sect of fundamentalist Christianity. Considering the attitude that Crowley would develop toward Christianity as he grew into manhood, and the scorn that he would heap upon those who exemplified its practice, it is remarkable and deeply revealing that he would preserve a very positive and compassionate assessment of his father. In *Confessions* Crowley writes, "My father, wrong-headed as he was, had humanity and a certain degree of common-sense; he had a logical mind and never confused spiritual with material issues." [p. 55] Another very revealing passage states:

> But I feel so profoundly the urgency of doing my will that it is practically impossible for me to write on Shakespeare and the Musical Glasses without introducing the spiritual and moral princi-

ples which are the only things in myself that I can identify with
myself.
    This characteristic is evidently inherited from my father. His
integrity was absolute. He lived entirely by his theological convic-
tions. [p. 60, emphasis added]

Much can be gained toward an understanding of Crowley's spiritual philosophy from thoughtful consideration of his characterization
of his father's religious beliefs and attitudes, particularly in regard to
the elder's dealings with others in general and "sinners" in particular.
Despite exercising a high-handed and somewhat overbearing manner,
Crowley's father demonstrated a remarkable tolerance of others'
weaknesses, stressing only the importance of one's need for Jesus. It
may be observed that Crowley's father embodied a very high standard of the *traditional* Aquarian quality of social conscience which
served as the focus for Crowley's perception of him. Furthermore,
due to his Seventh House placement of Saturn, Crowley was able to
take the experience of his father not so much as coming from on high
but as a coequal partner in the advocacy of Aquarian principles.

Certainly there is a definite tension implicit in this relationship
inherent in the opposition between Aquarius' new ruler and its old
one, and it is from this tension that Crowley was able, as he matured,
to comprehend and articulate with remarkable insight what constitutes the specific issues that distinguish the new conception of
humanity from the traditional orientation of the past. The key issue
can be clearly identified in terms of the astrological symbolism for
the factors involved and the relationship between the religious attitude of the mature Aleister Crowley and that of his father. Despite
the libertarian elements characteristic of the elder's position, he
nonetheless accepted the concept of an exterior God who exercised
authority over the lives of individuals. That very idea Aleister would
fight to eradicate in order to fulfill the requirements of humankind in
its present stage of evolutionary development. The conception of
divinity, particularly in the form of its responsibility for collective
stability, must be shifted from the *outer* to the *inner* realm of individual conscience as the very fulfillment of the meaning of human
existence. This is precisely the significance that is properly attributed
to Uranus as the new ruler of Aquarius in contrast to the traditional
establishment of and obedience to Saturnian authority.

This theme is essential to the understanding of Crowley's life and
work, and it provides a fundamental perspective upon the Horizon in

his birthchart as referring to the orientation of his *consciousness*, and, by virtue of his natal Uranus in Leo in his First House, his exaggerated yet undeniably heart-felt social *conscience*.

CHAPTER 5

SOL

In traditional astrology the Ascendant and the sign in which it is placed is taken as the starting point for interpretation due to its reference to the persona as the *interface* of the personality with the world in which one lives. The first order of business for the program of spiritual development employed by various schools and disciplines of religious philosophy, as distinguished from the doctrinaire approach of societal religion, has been to foster the realization on the part of a candidate that one's persona or ego, as the focus of consciousness, is not the whole of one's person; that there is a deeper spiritual entity that animates the personality and participates in a greater order of being than that given to the perception of the bodily senses and taken as the material world that one inhabits. The traditional method employed for the development of this realization is that of initiation through progressive degrees of inner awareness leading to ever greater insight into the nature of one's whole being. Disciplines of this sort have been practiced from time immemorial, and such practice is the true and serious meaning of the word "magic." From a contemporary perspective, however, such practices may be thought of as systems of psychotherapy that can best be applied through the enactment of symbolic ritual as an objectified catalyst to assist the development of an aspirant's subjectivity.

The Hermetic Order of the Golden Dawn was a school of religious philosophy that practiced ceremonial magic for this purpose. This school is mentioned here both because it serves as an example of an advanced and well developed system of religious philosophy and because it was the school through which Aleister Crowley was initiated into the levels of spiritual awareness that will be addressed to some extent through the course of this book. Due to its extreme importance in Crowley's life, The Golden Dawn will be considered at some length as this narrative proceeds. In this chapter, a particular feature of it's teachings will serve to clarify, through a brief introduction to the planetary symbolism associated with its system of grades, the meaning of Sol's placement in a birthchart.

Although the Golden Dawn tradition still exists, that is, its original format and teachings have been preserved and continue to be practiced, the original Order that was formed in 1887 underwent an irrevocable fragmentation in 1900 resulting from a revolt in its ranks involving disputes over leadership. My references to the Golden Dawn apply to the original organization as it existed prior to the breakup in which Crowley played a significant role.

As a system of progressive realization of the inherent human potential for ever greater levels of self-actualization, the Golden Dawn school employed a sequence of grades through which an initiate was able to progress. Each of these grades was associated with a particular spiritual principle for which there was attributed a planetary correspondence. The grades of the First Order of the Golden Dawn, or the "Outer Order" as it was also called, were associated with the planetary principles of Earth, Luna, Mercury, and Venus. The next grade brought one into participation in the Second or Inner "Rosicrucian" Order, the nature of which was kept completely secret from those in the Outer Order. There was a special and very exalted ceremony that was performed to initiate one into the Inner Order whereby one attained the status of Adeptship. The planetary attribution for the grade of Adeptus Minor, identified qabalistically as the 5=6 grade (see Appendix II), that confirmed one's entry into the Inner Order, was that of Sol. It was the object of this grade to bring one into conscious experience of one's divine nature, referred to by Crowley as one's Holy Guardian Angel, and the state of equilibrium requisite for the proper assimilation of that nature by the incarnate personality. There were further grades to be attained within the complete initiatory system, but the Adeptus Minor grade had a very special significance in the total scheme of magical development. This brief account of that significance serves to illustrate the profound implications of the symbolism associated with Sol within the context of the planetary system as a whole.

The morphological significance of Sol as the heart of the solar system and the source of light and life-giving energy for Earth is sufficient to account for the exalted spiritual status it commands for purposes of religious symbolism. It is indeed appropriate, within the historical context of Western mysticism, that it is symbolically associated with the Christ principle. The tradition of this association, however, is not to be found in conventional Christian religious doctrine which stresses its opposition to naturalistic forms of spiritual philosophy and emphasizes the exclusivity that can be drawn among various philosophical and religious perspectives. The esoteric philosophical tradition that does recognize this association, however, also bespeaks an historical continuity that pervades the Egyptian, Hebrew, and Christian traditions of religion in particular, as well as an over-arching continuity that encompasses the spiritual aspirations of all humankind. One of the primary differences between the approach of conventional Christianity and its esoteric tradition, both of which find a source of inspiration in the teachings of Jesus, is that the orthodox approach insists upon the *worship* of Jesus as the *one and only* human manifestation of divinity within the historical process, whereas the esoteric tradition maintains, also in accordance with the teachings of Jesus (as represented in the Christian Bible), that the divinity made manifest through his humanity is a latent potentiality within each and every person and is in fact the fullness of what it means to be human. It is in accordance with this esoteric tradition that the placement of Sol in one's birthchart is interpreted to correspond to that latent potentiality within the native.

In nearly all major religions, and particularly for Christianity, the exoteric and esoteric schools of thought and belief have endured severe antagonism toward one another, even to the extent of each considering the other satanic and therefore inherently evil. Such is not the perspective taken in this book. It is rather my intention to demonstrate the significance of that antagonism as a manifestation of the dominant theme of the Piscean Age as symbolized by the zodiacal image of two fishes swimming in opposite directions, joined at their mouths by a chord. The chord issuing from the fishes mouths may be likened to the *Word* of Scripture profoundly lending itself to two distinct and antagonistic interpretations. Furthermore, a perspective will be developed in this book that acknowledges the viability and necessity of *both* traditions in working out the evolutionary strategy inherent in the struggle between them. This perspective, however, can best be taken now in the light of ideas developing in relation to the advent of a new age in which the antagonisms that characterized the Piscean Age are susceptible to resolution through the benefit of hindsight.

In terms of Jungian psychology, Sol may be considered the primary referent for the Self of the native's personality, as differentiated from the persona indicated by the Ascendant. The Self is the expression of the *integration* of the whole personality and therefore manifests the potential for the reconciliation of divine nature with earthly existence through conscious experience. The word *potential* must be stressed in this regard, however, because there are no guarantees that such a reconciliation will be affected. Such attainment would appear to be exceptional outside the context of initiation through a mystery school such as that uniquely exemplified and parodied for modern society (ever so briefly) by the Hermetic Order of the Golden Dawn. The emergence of popular interest in Sun sign astrology in recent decades, however, suggests an evolutionary movement toward a larger scale of Self-actualization and adeptship within the context of contemporary civilization and the increasing potential and opportunity for independent individual initiative toward such attainment. Such a large scale movement is certainly appropriate to the ongoing early development of the Aquarian Age, and Crowley's contribution to that development has been, and continues to be, considerable.

In Crowley's birthchart Sol is placed in Libra in the early degrees of his Fourth House, and is conjoined by Venus. Libra, as an equinoctial sign, has a special significance in the philosophy of magic that is fundamental to the meanings of both equinoctial signs Aries and Libra. At the equinoxes the "day force" and the "night force," to use terms developed by Dane Rudhyar, are in perfect balance. These moments of equilibrium therefore resonate to the equilibrium of all the forces and activities of nature and the cosmos that is required to preserve the order of being. The equinoxes are therefore recognized to hold special "magical" power. This power can be illustrated by the fact that a pair of scales set at a point of perfect balance, regardless of how much weight is held on either side, can be tipped, in principle, one way or the other by the smallest of feathers. Crowley's definition of the word magic, which he spelled "magick" in order to distinguish it from previous usages in his reformed approach, as "the science and art of causing change to occur in conformity with will," accents the importance of equilibrium for the achievement of greater results in proportion to the effort exerted toward any magickal enterprise.

The vernal equinox (initiating Aries) and the autumnal equinox (initiating Libra) share in the principle of equilibrium but differ in the *dynamics* of that equilibrium. For Aries, in spring, the day force is *overtaking* the night force, and for Libra, in autumn, the night force is *overtaking* the day force. The pictorial images and planetary rulers for these two signs may be considered in the light of these observations. The pictorial image for Aries is the ram, and its planetary ruler is Mars. The corresponding action in nature for this time of the year is the sprouting of seeds. The life force having been contained in a dormant state within the seed through winter breaks through its confining shell and reaches out toward the warmth and light of Sol. This is the very emergence of individualized existence. Although the sprout is actually quite fragile, it *feels* infinitely strong and vital and partakes of the qualities of Mars, the god of war. The magickal act of *creation* occurs. The action of the sprout is comparable to that of the feather tipping the entire balance of nature toward a new realm of existence.

The pictorial image for Libra is the scales, and its planetary ruler is Venus. Although the *fact* of balance is inherent in both equinoxes, the autumnal equinox, marking the end of the predominance of personalized experience, emphasizes the potential for *consciousness* of that balance implied by the symbol of the scales. The corresponding action in nature for this time of year is the withdrawal of life-sustaining fluids from the leaves of trees, such leaves being symbolic of individual personalities on the great tree of humanity. Those once green and vibrant leaves eventually fall to the ground and become reincorporated into the humus of Earth leaving behind only the skeleton of the tree, but only after giving their testimonies of transcendence through colorific transformations of reds and yellows that reflect the colors of force and fire. As such, light as feathers, they tip the balanced scales of nature toward the realization of immortality. During autumn the concerns of humanity shift from the actualization of individual personalities to the survival of collective humanity, and that survival ultimately depends upon the yielding over of personal impulses to the integration of the community. The most potent force of such integration is love, thus the rulership of the equinoctial sign Libra by Venus, the goddess of love.

Due to the strong positive force of personal emergence associated with Aries, Sol, as a symbol for fully actualized personality, is in his "exaltation" when in Aries. It follows that Sol in Libra is in his "fall." This interpretation holds that Libra does not provide an expression of the life force that is well suited to the function manifested by Sol. This must indeed be the case when the solar function is conceived in terms of its rulership of Leo. The inherent meaning of Libra is irrevocably severed by the autumnal equinox from the self-fulfilling Leonian strength of personality that is the domain of Sol. In Libra, Sol must be given over to the power of love. For a person with one's natal Sol in Libra the integration of the Self can only be achieved through sacrifice, and no false sacrifice will do. The appearance of sacrifice means nothing without the utter anguish that true sacrifice necessarily entails, and that anguish can be felt when few if any would suspect that a sacrifice is being made. The appearance, moreover, is usually that of failure. In this regard, one's very Self becomes the feather that tips the cosmic scales. And, *if* the Sol in Libra individual achieves the integration of Self, then that achievement alone must be sufficient unto one in the way of reward.

A thorough study of the life and work of Aleister Crowley shows that the aspect of his character symbolized by the placement of Sol in Libra (along with Venus and the South Lunar Node) is central to the understanding of his deep-rooted (Fourth House) motivational structure. He was truly driven by the depth of his love, and he continuously found himself cast in the role of sacrificer, although there is nothing to indicate that he consciously sought to sacrifice himself. This is one of the fundamental paradoxes of Crowley's personality. His conscious attitude, or at least the image of himself that he projected in terms of his Leo Ascendant, exacerbated by his Uranus placement, was rather that of self-aggrandizement. His solar placement, however, suggests that his love came from such a depth of pain that he could hardly tolerate its conscious emergence.

The conjunction of Sol and Venus strongly reinforces this theme, because Venus, as the ruler of Libra, intensifies the strength of the Libran qualities imparted to his natal Sol. Crowley's South Lunar Node in Libra indicates a *spiritual inheritance* of the Libran attitude. The significance of this factor, however, will be elaborated in another chapter. The placements of Sol and Venus, however, are sufficient in themselves to connote the theme of painful sacrificial love. His mask of bravado, as an *adaptation* to the outside world, was a necessary defense against that pain. When the bravado was consciously felt, the pain could be repressed. This dynamic is perceptible in terms of the events and actions of his life, and the effulgent content of his poetic writings, without the need for astrological elucidation. An examination of these features in his birthchart, however, facilitates a look beneath the surface into the processes of his internal functioning so as to corroborate what should be obvious to the discerning researcher into Crowley's life.

Crowley was born in the depth of night, less than an hour before midnight. Therefore Sol is placed far below the horizon of his birthchart, very near the *Imum Coeli* (bottom of a birthchart) just inside his Fourth House, the deepest and most private region of the entire configuration. The Fourth House corresponds to the experience of the home and one's sense of rootedness. This realm naturally extends to include one's homeland and the sustenance one draws from the living Earth. The homeland aspect of this field of experience is not to be confused with one's public life in the world at large which corresponds to the Tenth House, keyed to the *Medium Coeli* (Midheaven) of the birthchart, the highest point of the ecliptic above the Horizon and directly *opposite* the Fourth House. The *feeling* for the homeland, however, associated with the Fourth House, provides the sense of patriotism and belonging to a culture and a nation, and, for one capable of transcending cultural and national barriers, to the *world* as a *support* for one's personal existence. The Imum Coeli of a birthchart, when extended downward, refers to the symbolic center of Earth at which all Meridians converge. In this sense it symbolizes the taproot of personality into the collective unconscious mind of humanity.

In addition to connoting a potential access to the evolutionary heritage of humanity, this placement of Crowley's natal Sol speaks very strongly of his tendency to feel a deep, abiding love for his family as a child, for his native land of England, and for the world in which he lived. This of course is not the kind of man one would expect to be portrayed in the press of his native country as "The King of Depravity," "The Wickedest Man in the World" and "A Man We'd Like to Hang." [*The Legend of Aleister Crowley*, p. 152] One would not expect this kind of child to be identified by his own mother as the Beast of the Apocalypse. However, if we consider the possibility that, with the exception of his father, this young boy's family and later his homeland and the world at large may have been incapable of accepting his love, and that his natural impulse for defense against such rejection, his only means of emotional survival under those circumstances, was to throw up a mask of nasty bravado as the only remaining testimony of his manhood, then perhaps we can make some sense of the apparent contradiction. Such an explanation would also shed some light on Crowley's adoption of the motto of *Perdurabo* for his Neophyte initiation into the Hermetic Order of the Golden Dawn in 1898 at the age of twenty-three. The meaning of *Perdurabo* is "I will endure to the end." [*The Equinox of the Gods*, p. 50]

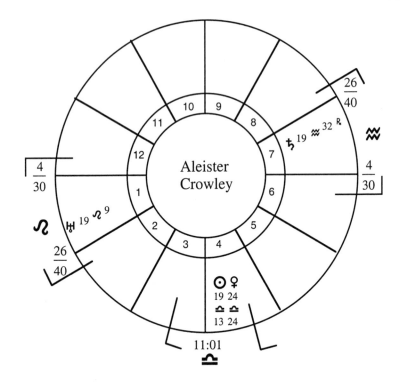

FIGURE 4
Addition of the placements of Sol and Venus
in Libra in Aleister Crowley's birthchart

Figure 4 includes the addition of Sol and Venus in Libra in Crowley's Fourth House. A very significant aspect configuration may be observed involving the placements of Sol, Uranus, and Saturn in the arrangement thus far developed. Sol forms exact-degree aspects to both Uranus and Saturn, thereby uniting all three in an intensely accentuated exact-degree aspect configuration. Sol's placement in the twentieth degree of Libra forms an exact trine (120°) to Saturn and an exact sextile (60°) to Uranus and is thus significantly related to the opposition between Uranus and Saturn. It is therefore appropriate to emphasize the *archetypal* significance of the degree of arc as a unit of angular measurement in order to elucidate the meaning and importance of this phenomenal arrangement.

The degree of arc is to the understanding of the circular zodiac what the atom is to the understanding of the nature of matter as represented by the Periodical Table of Elements. Even though modern physics has gone far beyond the earlier hypothesis that atoms are the irreducible building blocks of matter, it is yet the case that atoms are the fundamental determinants of the *qualitative distinctiveness* of the various elements that combine to form all material substances. Just such a significance has been held within the tradition of astrology to apply to the 360 degrees of the zodiac. Various systems have been developed that assign particular meanings for each of the 360 degrees. Such systems embody the understanding that the degree of arc is not merely an arbitrary unit of measurement but rather has a profound morphological significance. In order to account for the rationale that supports this understanding it is helpful to review an ancient philosophical perspective developed by Plato that suggests the conception of a realm of being that transcends the physical universe as it is given to the experience of our bodily senses.

Plato taught that ultimate reality resides in the realm of concepts as opposed to the percepts directly apprehended by the bodily senses, and that the world of material objects was composed of imperfect, corrupted copies of the true "Forms" of ultimate and eternal reality. Material perception was thereby considered an obstruction or impediment to the acquisition of true knowledge, as opposed to the modern scientific view that material perception is the very avenue to reliable knowledge. My sympathy is with the modern perspective, but not without the acknowledgment that there is indeed a paradox involved and that it is both possible and necessary to reconcile these two perspectives. The discipline of astrology is in fact the common ground of that reconciliation in that the structural components and dynamics of the solar system are sufficiently simple, regular, and *encompassing* to accommodate archetypal significance, and yet they are fully material and therefore subject to collectively verifiable empirical investigation.

So what does this have to do with the degree of arc as a unit of measurement for the zodiac? Precisely this: Astrology necessarily applies mathematical concepts to material phenomena. This is a fundamental characteristic of all science, and any scientist who is at all versed in the philosophy of one's work will attest to the fact that it is indeed a profound mystery that there is any correspondence at all between physical processes and the purely conceptual enterprise of mathematics. *Numbers do not exist.* They are pure concepts. And yet for some *unknown reason* they prove to be remarkably useful instruments for the measurement, analysis, and prediction of material processes. The elegant conceptual structure of mathematics would be considered nonsense were it not for its remarkable *pragmatic* value.

The concept of the sphere, for example, is a mathematical object. For a hard-core materialist there is no such *thing* as a sphere. It is *only* an idea. But for purposes of mathematical analysis of the material universe the *idea* of the sphere proves to be very *useful*. Therefore the idea of the sphere must be granted *some* status of reality. According to Plato, the true and perfect idea of the sphere is in actuality one of the "Forms" of eternal reality, and the various material objects that more or less closely approximate that Form, such as oranges, planets, and ping-pong balls, all "participate" in the Form of Sphereness. No material object, however, ever fully manifests the true and perfect Form. A true sphere is nowhere to be found in the perceived world of material reality. There are always *irregularities* in sphere-like material objects. What such material objects do for us, according to Plato, is *remind* us of the Form of Sphereness and, to that extent, of the realm of true Reality *from which we come* into this imperfect and ephemeral world of illusory phenomena. Moreover, this view claims that the very fact of our capacity at all for apprehending the idea of the sphere, which, we must remember, does not exist, is evidence of the derivation of some aspect of our nature from the World of Forms, which is for the most part forgotten during our sojourn in the imperfect material world.

I think it can generally be agreed that it would be downright silly to attempt to apply a literal interpretation to Platonic philosophy. A host of *reductio ad absurdums* can be shown to follow. However, the perspective must be given its due consideration for its pedagogic value within the historical context of its development. Its main difference from present day academic philosophy is that it attempts to solve a problem that subsequently has been dispensed with as meaningless. I agree that there is no *a priori* way to solve the problem, but I do not agree that it is therefore meaningless.

Interestingly, some confirmation of Plato's philosophy of Forms has emerged from what might appear at first to be an unlikely source, namely, the very recently developed field of scientific inquiry into chaos. Phenomena that was previously thought to be beyond the scope of mathematical analysis by virtue of its vast complexity, such as the movement of rising smoke, the behavior of weather, the way that water flows through a pipe, etc., has been shown, with the help of computer analysis, to assume hitherto unsuspected patterns of uniformity that pose staggering implications from the standpoint of earlier science. No conventional cause for such patterns can be ascribed. They appear, like Plato's Forms, to be *inherent* within the structure of existence.

The degree of arc for purposes of angular measurement is an *approximate* expression of the relationship between the daily and yearly cycles in nature. A closer approximation of that relationship is expressed in the ratio 1:365.25 rather than 1:360 which is used both for astrological and mathematical purposes. The simple reason for the adoption of the 1:360 ratio is the mathematical elegance of the number 360. Not only is it divisible by 4, facilitating the exact measurement of the existential quadrature of the seasonal cycle, but it is also divisible by 12, facilitating the measurement of the *approximate* relationship between the lunation and seasonal cycles. (In this regard it is interesting to observe that the number 360 splits the difference between the number of days in the annual cycle (365) and the number of days in twelve lunations (355), thus mediating the solar and lunar disparity.) Furthermore, the number 360 is exactly divisible by no less than 24 whole numbers. From the standpoint of reconciling the perfect realm of mathematical *conceptual* experience with the imperfect realm of existential *perceptual* experience, the adoption of the division of the zodiac into 360 equal degrees of angular measurement, *as an approximation of the relationship of the day to the year*, is very reasonable and useful. Furthermore, from a Platonic perspective, it would be said that the relationship of the day to the year *approximates* the elegant conceptual relationship of the 1:360 mathematical ratio.

This matter is addressed in a very interesting manner in Egyptian mythology. As a result of a dispute over the sky goddess Nut's marriage to her twin brother, the Earth god Geb, the Sun god Ra had Nut separated from Geb by their father Shu and decreed that Nut should be delivered of a child in no month in no year. Thoth, god of counting, writing, and magic, subsequently won five days from the Moon in a game of draughts. These days became the five epagomenal days added to the original 360 days of the year, and, as such, were immune to the curse of Ra. Nut was therefore able to use them to bring forth children, whereby she gave birth in sequence to Osiris, Haroeris (Horus the Elder), Set, Isis, and Nephthys.

This myth is suggestive of a profound cosmological conception that addresses both the pre-formation of a more orderly archetypal realm of being and the motivational and interactive circumstances involved in the *generation*, as it were, of an imperfect existence which harbored a strongly disruptive and inherently antagonistic combination of principles. The disruption and antagonism involved is elucidated in terms of the subsequent interactions of the five epagomenal offspring of Geb and Nut, with a particular emphasis upon Set, who was known for his capacity for evil but was worshipped for his power and ferocity which was often useful for political purposes. These developments will be considered at greater length in the concluding chapters of this book, as they have a direct bearing on the mythological motif of Crowley's magickal formulation for the historical succession of the Aeons. They have been introduced here for the purpose of elucidating a viable perspective on transcendental conceptualisms and more specifically to reinforce the archetypal significance of the division of the zodiac into 360 degrees. *That division reconciles archetypal order with existential cycle.*

This understanding serves to clarify the exceptional significance of the exact-degree aspects involving Uranus, Saturn, and Sol in Crowley's birthchart. An aspect that is close, that is, within "orb" but not exact by degree, is sufficient to *approximate* the archetypal meaning of that aspect. An aspect that is exact by degree, however, *manifests* the very archetypal meaning of that aspect in a most specific manner. The significance of this becomes yet more apparent upon consideration of a system of symbolism which specifies a unique pictorial image for each of the 360 degrees. Such a system *characterizes* each zodiacal degree much as the signs themselves are characterized by pictorial images. It follows that exact-degree angular aspects among planets specify very intensely focused archetypal themes of dynamic interaction. A brief introduction to the above mentioned system of degree symbols which illustrates this principle as it pertains to the aspects currently under consideration, as well as other particular features of Crowley's birthchart, is presented in Appendix III of this book. It is important, however, first to understand the basic structure of a birthchart before venturing into the consideration of such strongly focused symbolism with regard to the degree placements of particular factors found therein.

The interpretation of the opposition between Uranus and Saturn in Crowley's birthchart has already been introduced in chapter 4. By way of brief review, it refers to an extreme tension between Crowley's subjective persona, involving an impetuous impulse to dramatize the principle of individualism, and his projection of the image of an antiquated system of social authority, derived significantly from his childhood experience of his father, onto his experience of relationships with other people. Ultimately, this carries the potential for generating *consciousness* in relation to the factors involved, but only through experiencing the inherent tension.

Due to Sol's participation in this exact-degree aspect arrangement, as delineated above, its placement provides the most significant key for the potential resolution of the above mentioned tension. In fact, that arrangement virtually guarantees a remarkable facility for such resolution. The trine (120°) and sextile (60°) aspects are held to be the most harmonious of all aspects. The trine produces understanding and the sextile stimulates opportunity. The morphological rationale for the meanings of various aspect relations among planets and other astrological factors requires a rather extensive explanation, however it proceeds along lines of analysis already initiated in earlier chapters of this book. Briefly, the significance of angular geometrical relationships involves the interaction between numerical, spatial and temporal concepts as they apply to material structures and life situations. The qualitative interpretations for various angles are rooted in actual morphological participation of those concepts in the world of our experience. A very thorough analysis of the meanings of angular relationships in astrology is developed in one of the best available books on this subject, *Astrological Aspects: A Process Oriented Approach*, by Leyla Rael and Dane Rudhyar.

Sol's basic function as the integrator of the whole personality is superbly enhanced in Crowley's birthchart by its harmonious angular relation to the opposition between Uranus and Saturn along his Horizon. This aspect pattern fundamentally assures his ability to understand the dynamics of his relationships with other people (Sol trine Seventh House Saturn in Aquarius) and to instinctively organize his base of operations (Fourth House Solar placement) in such a manner as to create opportunities for the exercise of his self-expression (Sol sextile First House Uranus in Leo). It must be noted, however, that this function operated from the private depths of his personality and was therefore not readily apparent to the casual observer.

Further light may be shed on these dynamics of Crowley's personality by noting the placement of Sol in his birthchart in terms of its role as the ruler of the Ascendant and dispositor of Uranus in the First House. The planet that rules a sign or house is said to "dispose" of any other planet placed in that sign or house, which actually means that the ruling planet superimposes its own influence upon that other planet. The idea is similar to that of one person visiting the home of another. In such a circumstance one is more or less obliged to conform to the ambiance of the host's domain. I think the term "predispose" would be more appropriate to modern understanding, however, for the sake of terminological consistency I will continue to use the traditional term. Such an interaction has already been alluded to above in reference to Sol's placement in Libra, ruled by Venus. Venus is therefore the dispositor of Sol. As the ruler of Leo, and therefore the First House of Crowley's birthchart, Sol in turn is the dispositor of Uranus. This dispositional pattern supports the hypothesis advanced above that Crowley's impetuous and often antagonistic temperament, displayed by his Leonian persona, was fundamentally a mask shielding a more benign intent. The dispositional continuity from Venus to Sol to Uranus, as developed above, also extends from Uranus to Saturn by virtue of Uranus' designation as the new ruler of Aquarius in which Saturn is placed. The direct implication of this is that Crowley's mask of bravado tended to ride roughshod over his relationships with others (Seventh House) and *dispose* of conventional notions of social conformity by virtue of Saturn's placement therein.

Despite the fact that we have already begun to unravel some of the fascinating complexity of Crowley's personality by virtue of the consideration of features directly associated with his Horizon and Solar placement, it would be premature to venture too much interpretation stemming from these perspectives before expanding the preliminary phase of the analysis to include all of the three morphologically dominant factors conventionally recognized as the major components of personality, namely the Ascendant (Horizon/Earth), Sol and Luna. It is therefore appropriate to move directly from this point to the consideration of the significance of Luna, both in general terms and in terms of her placement in Crowley's birthchart.

CHAPTER 6

LUNA

In the jargon of a popular convention that simplifies natal astrology by juxtaposing the three most prominent features of a birthchart, Aleister Crowley would be characterized as "a Libra (meaning Sol in Libra) with Leo rising and Moon in Pisces." The analysis presented in this book has largely adhered to this basic approach, except that the rising sign (Horizon) was addressed first, as is proper to the roots of astrological tradition, and the placements of Uranus and Saturn were also introduced due to their strong associations to the Horizon in Crowley's birthchart. Sol was considered in turn along with his conjunction with Venus, and Luna was saved for introduction at this point due to the great subtlety involved with her influence. Ironically, this subtlety is a function of her overwhelming sway.

The association of Luna with the feminine principle of life is universally acknowledged in connection with her orbital period of 28 days, corresponding to the menstrual cycle of women. It is also usually the case that Sol is associated with the masculine principle by virtue of his energetic penetration of Earth's biosphere. It is true that some systems of mystical thought have evolved attributions of gender for the Sun and Moon contrariwise. The Sun has been likened to an ovum, for example, and mythology is replete with male Moon gods. The human psyche is infinitely varied and proliferated along all possible lines of conceivability, and such proliferation contributes to the richness of the spiritual heritage of humanity. Furthermore, confusion sometimes results from the fact that any one personality necessarily involves an amalgamation of both feminine and masculine attributes, whether one's biological morphology is predominantly male or female. The obvious morphological correspondence between Luna and the childbearing function of woman is not herein presented as the last or only word on the matter, but is rather taken as an implicit association at the simplest level of interpretation upon which this book focuses attention as a foundation for objective analysis.

This significance of Luna demonstrates the assessment of astrological meaning in terms of *morphogenetic fields* for which the planets themselves are dynamic focal points of establishment. One may consider an analogy to a ball point pen. The repeated retracing of a circle with a ball point pen would establish a circumstance whereby the ball of the pen is analogous to a planet, in this case Luna, and the circle to the morphogenetic field formed by the planet's orbital motion. Both the planet and the field are essential components of the whole phenomenon. Even though the field itself is not directly visible, as is the circle for the purposes of this analogy, it must be considered as *existing*. The fact that Luna directly orbits Earth, and that she does so completely within the movements of all other bodies of the solar system, establishes the primacy of her envelope as a field of containment for humankind on Earth and, by symbolic interpretation, for each individual personality. In this regard the association of the temporal period of her orbit with the menstrual cycle is reinforced by the spatial fact of her maintenance of a womb-like field of containment for Earth.

These observations provide a morphological basis for assigning greater priority to Luna than to Sol for purposes of interpretation, both in terms of proximity and *levels of wholeness*. Other factors, of course, such as heat, light, and dominance within the solar system as a whole, weigh in on the side of Sol's priority. The fact that both of their *apparent* sizes as viewed from Earth are nearly exactly the same, being a function of the *ratios* of their actual sizes to their respective distances from Earth, provides a basis for assigning balanced or equally significant values to each of the two Luminaries. Although the issue of the relative importance of Luna and Sol is debatable, it is only necessary to assess the astrological meanings of each in terms of their respective morphological characteristics.

The two fundamental components of Luna's whole phenomenon mentioned above, namely the physical body of Luna herself and her field of womb-like containment of Earth, that is, her orbit, will be considered in turn, as each of these components is given a separate astrological referent. The significance of her orbit *per se*, however, will be presented in the next chapter. The interpretation of the placement of Luna herself in a birthchart requires the combining of several factors in association. The sign and house in which she is placed are two of these factors and, as such, are common to the interpretation of any other planet or astrological referent in a birthchart. For Luna, however, it is also of utmost importance to consider her *phase*, that is, what aspect of the lunation cycle she occupies in relation to the Solar placement. The lunation cycle is a function of the relationship that obtains among the three bodies, Luna, Sol and Earth, and it proceeds from New Moon to New Moon taking approximately twenty-nine and a half days to complete. The first half of the cycle brings Luna from invisibility through increasing illumination or "waxing," beginning with the thinnest crescent on the western horizon just after sunset, to her total illumination, the Full Moon, which rises above the eastern horizon at sunset, spans the full arch of darkened sky throughout the night, and sets in the west at sunrise the following morning. The second half of the cycle brings Luna through decreasing illumination or "waning," concluding with the thinnest crescent on the eastern horizon just before sunrise, back to her complete disappearance into another New Moon. This cyclic drama has been performed for humankind since the dawn of consciousness and has constituted the most primordial reckoning of extended time. The symbolic significance of this cycle can hardly be overestimated. It must be assumed in accordance with the most scientifically sophisticated conception of human evolution that its relevance, like that of the seasonal cycle, is inherent in the very structure of the human nervous system and genetic code, responsive as they are to environmental parameters.

Dane Rudhyar has developed a thorough interpretation of this cycle and its successive phases in his book, *The Lunation Cycle*. For the more condensed perspective developed in this chapter, the meaning of Luna is considered in its broadest sense as *the subjective experience of the feminine presence*, and her phase at the time of birth refers both to the strength of that perceptual experience and its tendency to become objectified; that is, manifest to the consciousness of the native.

Although the experience of the feminine presence has an inherent tendency to be projected upon correspondingly appropriate images in one's field of perception, the most obvious being, of course, women, it must be understood that the feminine presence ultimately extends to encompass *the entire field of perception*. This may be a difficult concept to grasp because, by definition, it is impossible for one to differentiate one's entire field of perception. To do so would require some comparative frame of reference. Any comparison of perceptions, however, can only be made *within* a given field of perception, therefore the field itself, although objectively oriented, cannot be *objectified,* that is, it cannot be considered apart from its own inclusive totality. Therefore, the influence of Luna is experienced in terms of an overall *cast* or *mood* of one's personality that is so pervasive as to be largely taken for granted. It is also virtually impossible to communicate the associated feelings intelligibly from one person to another. In this regard we directly encounter the thorny philosophical problem of *solipsism.* If this idea is unfamiliar to the reader, not to worry. We will make some sense of it presently.

All we need to do is consider the association of the lunar envelope with a womb. A person, symbolized by Earth, lives within the lunar envelope as an embryo or fetus lives within a womb. The womb is the *world* of the embryo or fetus, but the embryo or fetus does not *know* that it is *in* a womb. The embryo or fetus necessarily *takes* its existence in the womb as the only conceivable way of experiencing. Such is the case for the subjective experience of a person. One's field of perception effectively determines a womb of experience and, as such, constitutes an ubiquitous feminine presence. The nature of that subjective experience for a particular person, as it obtains within an entire zodiacal and planetary configuration, is symbolized in the birthchart by the placement of Luna in terms of her house and sign position, her phase, the house she rules by virtue of her sign Cancer on its cusp, her aspects to other planets, and by the orientation of the lunar envelope indicated by the lunar nodal axis. This last referent is introduced at this juncture in the interest of completeness for the present discussion, however, as mentioned above, its significance as a referent for the lunar orbit is addressed in the next chapter.

The time of a New Moon is a time during which the subjective experience of the feminine presence is virtually unconscious and connotes a sense of the absence of the feminine presence. Indeed she is there but she is *not experienced* as being there (except, of course, in the dramatic instance of a solar eclipse at which time she unashamedly consumes her consort, thus darkening the world of their child with an indelible experience of abandonment). For a person born at the time of a New Moon there is a feeling of *openness* that characterizes one's personality, an outreaching toward an unknown infinitude. Such a person may seem abstruse and difficult to understand, perhaps even vacuous. The time of a Full Moon, on the other hand, is a time during which the subjective experience of the feminine presence is strongly felt in association with the perceptual field and engenders a sense of involvement with the images of experience.

For a person born close to a Full Moon, especially for one born at night, there is a feeling of involvement with the world in which one lives that induces a tendency to experience what has been called a *participation mystique* with images in the field of one's perception. Such a person tends to manifest a charismatic presence associated with that sense of involvement.

The periods of Luna's waxing and waning connote respectively the advancing and withdrawing of the subjective sense of the feminine presence as an experiential component of the perceptual field, and her waxing or waning phase in a birthchart is therefore suggestive of such a *tendency* of the native. A waxing Luna personality tends to experience a condition of *being drawn into* perceptual experience, and a waning Luna personality tends to experience a condition of *being drawn out of* perceptual experience.

The house and sign in which Luna is placed in a birthchart indicate the orientation of individual experience to collective humanity that characterizes the perceptual field of the native. The world appears to be naturally suited for conducting certain kinds of activities in a particular manner. The native, however, especially during one's youth, is not likely to be aware that such a taking of the world is characteristically one's own and therefore *unique to oneself.* Once again, the lunar influence is one of experiential cast or mood that colors the entire field of perception and is largely taken for granted.

A fuller perspective upon Luna's influence may be gained in terms of her traditional rulership of the zodiacal sign Cancer. Taking the vernal equinox as the starting point of the zodiacal cycle, Cancer is the first of the three Water signs, the remaining two being Scorpio and Pisces. Naturally, all these signs have traditional associations with oceanic aspects of experience. Luna's most notable influence upon Earth is her gravitational attraction which articulates the tidal rhythms of large bodies of water. The life form most adapted and attuned to tidal variation is the crab, which is therefore appropriate as a symbolic referent for Cancer. There is also an association that can be made to the crab-like movement of Sol, *turning back* as it were in relation to the summer solstice.

We find in the crab a particular tenacity in the preservation of her perspective. She is attuned to an ever changing environmental matrix to which she must continuously adapt, and she has no proclivity whatsoever to be disturbed in her particular mode of adaptation. Of all creatures the crab is one of maximum subjectivity, appropriate to her close association with water. As the sign initiated by the summer solstice, Cancer is the most personal sign, summer being the season when the individual can best afford to go one's own way and disregard the demands of society as a whole. The fact that the Cancerian expression tends to be socially conservative is complimentary to the collective requirements of its opposing sign Capricorn, but for Cancer the rationale is rather that of the enjoyment of a relatively predictable and cozy matrix of activity, which, along with the shell of her body, is suggestive of a life of adaptation to and, by extension, maintenance of womb-like conditions.

Naturally, the womb function of Luna extends to the mother image in its entirety and is reflected in the virtually total responsibility that nature has assigned to the mother for the nurturing and care of infants and young children. Certainly an advanced technological society is capable of relieving women of a great deal of that responsibility, much to the benefit of all concerned, but the primordial image of the mother yet remains firmly established in the biological roots of humanity. The liberation of particular mothers from the inordinate task of bearing the full burden of childcare can only make possible the refinement and enhancement of the archetypal dimensions of motherhood and, accordingly, all other feminine *and masculine* roles as well.

One significant morphological feature of Luna that reinforces her association with motherhood is that, due to her gravitational interlock with Earth, her heaviest side is *always* oriented toward Earth, such that her far side, her lighter side as it were, is never seen from Earth. This intriguing feature is suggestive of a deep mystery of the mother archetype. The most obvious connotation is that, due to a child's need of constant attention, the face of the mother is always turned toward it, both to observe and to reassure. Another, more subtle truth implicit in this morphological arrangement, however, is that there is a side of the mother that the child may never know, and, although that distant, hidden side of the mother becomes illumined on a regular basis, this occurs only in exact proportion to the withdrawal of her direct attention and visibility to the child. This feature is suggestive of an added dimension to the interpretation of the lunation cycle and is pregnant with mystery for the discerning reader to ascertain. One may be aided in doing so by assuming the perspective of Sol.

These observations may now be applied to Luna's placement in Aleister Crowley's birthchart. Crowley was born shortly before midnight, just two days before a Full Moon. That is, Luna had a very full appearance and was high in the night sky, just inside the Ninth

House, in Pisces. It may well have been foggy or cloudy on that particular autumn night in Leamington, England. However, if the sky were clear she would have exhibited a commanding presence, large and beaming as she waxed toward fullness. In traditional astrology the Ninth House is said to pertain to philosophy and religion. It is the house of *archetypal knowledge* most appropriately applied to social understanding and the experience of *images* that are exhibited for the inspiration and integration of collective humanity, fulfilling the need for social cohesion and continuity. The sign Pisces addresses the concern of humanity for ultimate transcendence, the reality of the unseen, and the quest for immortality in the *real* sense of surviving biological death.

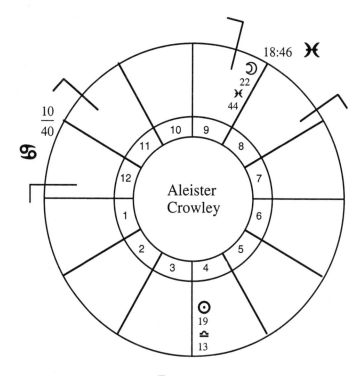

FIGURE 5
Placements of the planet Luna and the signs Pisces and Cancer in Aleister Crowley's birthchart. (The planetary symbol for Sol is included to show the nearly full phase of Luna in Crowley's natal configuration.)

Pisces on the Ninth House cusp indicates a most exalted conception of religious meaning. For such a native the transcendental aspect, as differentiated from other potential concerns such as social structuring (as per a Capricornian Ninth House) or self-actualization (as per a Leonian Ninth House), is felt to be the essential component of religious meaning. Luna's placement in Crowley's Piscean Ninth House indicates that his fundamental experience of being, that is, the cast or mood of his very perceptual field, was pervaded with a strongly manifested sense of the archetypal meaning of spiritual transcendence. This, of course, is obvious upon consideration of his life and work, but the extreme importance of this particular astrological referent is its value for the purpose of sorting out and delineating how this powerful component of Crowley's personality figures into the totality of his natal configuration.

The lunar influence is completely unconscious in early childhood, and for some people it would appear to remain so for their entire lives. The first inklings of becoming conscious of the lunar influence in one's life come as a sense of uniqueness about oneself that differentiates one from other people. This uniqueness can generally be inferred from reflecting upon a continuous pattern of responses from other people that involve an *inability to empathize*. The understanding of such patterns forms the basis for truly meaningful interpersonal rapport, but it requires a level of maturity, sensitivity, and sophistication that even highly cultured or otherwise markedly developed people find ever challenging. As a rule women are more naturally endowed with such understanding than men. The subtleties involved in such interpersonal relations are hardly ever expressed verbally but are communicated indirectly and spontaneously. A word or two may follow, but only to confirm. A knowing look or glance, suggesting a tinge of unspoken mystery, is often more appropriate. Ultimately, the difficulties that arise in association with Luna's function of limiting perception (along with Saturn's function of limiting social consciousness, corresponding to the solstitial opposition of Cancer and Capricorn) are associated with the Trance of Sorrow that plays such an important part in the evolvement of profound spiritual understanding. These rather extended ramifications of the Lunar influence are essential to a thorough understanding of her meaning and are necessary for interpreting her placement in Aleister Crowley's birthchart, due to the highly exalted spiritual realization he attained by virtue of his intense pursuit of this natural endowment.

The significance of the earlier specification of *both* the embryonic and fetal stages of intrauterine development will now be elaborated in order to make a relevant distinction between contrasting perceptual orientations. The most fundamental antagonistic dualism that characterized the Piscean Age was that of the postulated categories of "good" and "evil," which are, in their simplest forms, projections of psychological attraction and repulsion. This distinction found its most extreme historical expression in the Persian religious doctrine of Manichaeism, initiated by Mani in the Third Century E.V. Manichaeism had a significant influence on the early development of Christian theology as articulated by St. Augustine in *The City of God,* which he began writing in 413 E.V. The influence of Manichaeism on Augustine, who was himself a Manichee for nine years prior to his conversion to Christianity, is readily apparent. He postulated the division of humankind into the city of God and the earthly city in such a manner that human souls and angels occupy a plane of reality below the immutable and unique being of God but above the mutable and transitory nature of bodies. Their respective memberships in the two cities are determined by their tendencies to love God or to love the bodily realm. The love of God tends toward the presumed greater values of perfect order and harmonious communion, and the love of the bodily realm tends toward the presumed lesser values emphasizing individuality, lust and conflict.

Many variations and subtle distinctions fed into and continue to characterize this fundamental perspective, which is in fact common to all major religious doctrines of the Piscean Age throughout the world. The historical pervasiveness of this idea is such that it generally affects all spiritual philosophy. For this reason, the new spiritual perspective that characterizes the emerging Aquarian Age is largely not recognized as being spiritual at all. From the ingrained Piscean Age perspective, the modern view is rather taken to be the *antithesis* of spirituality, either in the form of materialism or diabolism. The concessions that are made by apologists for the passing age may be likened to the advancement of a one-way mirror reflecting backwards in time, whereby the old guard continues to yield more and more ground to increased understanding of and respect for material processes while bewailing the decline of traditional values and behavioral standards. This shifting orientation has reached the point of requiring a new paradigm by which to assess the traditional notions of good and evil. This distinction, which tended to be conceived as an absolute dichotomy during the Piscean Age, can now be subsumed within a larger context of spiritual understanding. A new paradigm may be constructed in terms analogous to the process of intrauterine development.

A natural perspective upon physical existence implies beginnings and endings to all processes, which is suggestive in turn of an initiating phase and a culminating phase of any whole process. In terms of intrauterine gestation we identify these two phases as *embryonic* and *fetal*, or, to extend the analogy to personal existence on Earth within the lunar envelope, as *childhood* and *adulthood*. It is instructive to consider these stages for the purpose of getting to the root of the problems abounding in ideas of good and evil. In both cases we are confronted with fundamental differences in attitude toward the experience of sensory reality.

Both the embryo and the child perceive their respective matrices of sensory experience as virtually infinite oceans of potentiality. The womb for the embryo, and the material world for the child, are *more than sufficient* to accommodate any possible anticipation of need or desire. Nourishment flows in automatically, and the only thing to do is grow and expand into ever greater realms of a seemingly inexhaustible plenitude and to *take from* that plenitude in accordance with one's desires. Both the fetus and the adult, on the other hand, perceive their respective matrices of sensory experience as being limited and, as the completing phases of their respective cycles proceed, increasingly debilitated. As the fetus grows, the womb imposes ever greater pressure upon it, intensifying its sense of confinement and constraint. The adult personality comes to realize that the world of opportunities into which one was born turns out to be considerably more resistant to exploitation than one had imagined and had been encouraged to believe during childhood. One comes to understand the conditions that *deny* the fulfillment of desire. Furthermore, the inevitable *end* looms ever more eminently on the horizon.

The intrauterine development of the human organism provides a virtually pristine symbolic representation of the cosmic evolution of human existence, both physiologically and, as suggested above, spiritually. Our experience of the world itself, on the other hand, is chock full of the burly involvements of articulated experience in all its complexity and variety. The intrauterine experience, although completely subsumed *within*, is by that very fact sealed away *from* the parental mode of being which protects and sustains it. It therefore entails no direct knowledge of the parental mode *as such*. In the "outer" world of our postnatal experience, however, we are afforded, through the magic of the hard constructs of space, time, and matter, a realm of experience whereby the distinction between parent and child, as a representation of the principle of cosmic self-perpetuation, may be perceived as an object of consciousness.

One of the fundamental characteristics of the species *homo sapiens* is the prolongation of dependency of offspring upon the adult community. Such prolongation exacerbates the distinction between childhood and adulthood. For other animals, the earliest possible attainment of self-sufficiency by newborns is generally fundamental to survival. For humankind, however, this evolutionary law has been reversed, thus supporting the traditional religious contention that humans occupy a special place in the scheme of life on Earth. From this perspective, that special place may be understood to involve confrontation with the *problem of childhood*, that is, the need to address, in extended terms, conscious devotion to perpetuity, which implies transcendence of our temporal frame of reference. We may therefore recognize human existence, whether conceived in terms of creation or evolution or both, as occupying a unique cosmic status of mediation between transitory and eternal realms of being. The recognition of this cosmic status forms the basis for the perspective taken by Augustine in *The City of God* involving the mutual exclusion of the concerns of the transitory and eternal realms of being that has characterized historical Christianity in particular, as well as all of what are referred to as the World's Great Religions.

The exaggerated antagonism inherent in the idea of a cosmic distinction between good and evil, however, *is not a necessary corollary* to the recognition of the human role of mediation between the transitory and eternal realms of being. This distinction can be understood as one between an embryonic and a fetal perspective toward the "womb" of human perceptual experience. What has been conceived as a struggle between good and evil during the Piscean Age may now be envisioned as analogous to antagonisms inherent in relations between parents and children. The entire enterprise is ultimately pedagogical. The category of evil may now be viewed as the psychological projection, to a cosmic scale, of the unpleasantness of the conflict characteristic of a critical weaning stage of child rearing. It is clearly evident in the mythic imagery from antiquity to modern times that the fundamental issue has been that of the ability to control the libidinal impulse within the context of interpersonal relations as an adjunct to the need for acceptance of self-reliance and responsibility on the part of individuals. The distinguishing challenge is that of the ability to maintain a clear and balanced perspective within the context of highly charged circumstances so as to optimize the concomitant benefits inherent in any interpersonal situation. It follows that one who is unable to maintain such a balanced perspective in a given circumstance will have to resort to an uncontrolled response that mimics the assumption of authority as a justification for the violent emotions that are experienced. This is suggestive of the pedagogical formula of controlled submission to abusive behavior, that is, assuming a *parental* role, as the hallmark of spiritual responsibility that underlies the religious doctrine of personal sacrifice most poignantly codified by the crucifixion motif.

The interpretation of Luna's placement in a birthchart suggests that such an experiential cast or mood is appropriate to the particular mode of gestation inherent in the life development of the native. Luna is the *mother* of the soul of the individual for whom the purpose of life is to be brought to term. Even a cursory knowledge of Aleister Crowley's life and work is sufficient to determine that the primary realm of his experience of life was that of religion, using this term in the broad sense appropriate to the meaning of the Ninth House. It would be fair to say that Crowley was *overwhelmed* by a sense of the religious significance of all experience. Indeed, at various times and in various ways he struggled against this ubiquitous determining force in his life, but, alas, ever in vain. He aspired to, and achieved greatness as a poet and mountain climber. He harbored ambition to hold office in the Diplomatic Service of his native England. He demonstrated a remarkable proficiency as a chess player. He also delighted in simply playing the role of a man of the world, a big game hunter and provocateur. But despite the ardor he poured into such a variety of endeavors, he ultimately succumbed to a calling he found least desirable, namely, that of religious prophet.

We may infer that Crowley's waxing Full Moon generated a very strong feeling of involvement with the images of his perceptual field and that he tended to be drawn into that field. Perceptual experience for the Full Moon personality serves as a ready screen for projections from the inner spiritual Self, as Luna reflects light from Sol. The fact that Crowley's natal Luna, although very full in appearance, was yet in the culminating days of her waxing phase is indicative of a *hyperanticipatory* tendency toward perceptual experience as an ever present feature of his personality. A circumstance that occurred in Crowley's life exemplifies this perceptual tendency. In 1920, shortly after acquiring the villa at Cefalu in northern Sicily where he established his Abbey of Thelema, Crowley was awaiting the arrival of Jane Wolfe, who was to be his first student at the abbey. Jane Wolfe was a film star in Hollywood when she heard about Crowley and read his *Collected Works* [Roberts, p. 219]. She contacted him, and they maintained correspondence for several months. When Crowley wrote her of his intentions to establish the abbey she elected to join him and his entourage there. Of Crowley's anticipation of her arrival Colin Wilson writes in *The Nature of the Beast*:

> Crowley spent a great deal of time daydreaming about Jane Wolfe, who was now on her way to meet him... In his magical diary, Crowley frequently mentions his love for her. 'I adore her name. I hope she is hungry and cruel as a wolf.' On 18 June there is a long entry in which he vows total obedience to her. 'I am hers... I die that She may live... I drown in delight at the thought that I who have been Master of the Universe should lie beneath her feet, Her slave, Her victim, eager to be abased...' [pp. 120-121]

The contrast of Crowley's anticipation to the reality of her arrival illustrates the point made above regarding the lunar phase in his birthchart. Wilson writes of Jane Wolfe's arrival: "She was a shattering disappointment. Crowley seems to have assumed that, because she had been a film star, she would be beautiful; in fact, she was a battered, tough looking lady of about his own age." [*ibid.*] Nevertheless, Jane Wolfe became a solid student and a valuable assistant for Crowley during the very difficult period when the forces of opposition to his movement viciously attacked him in the press resulting in his expulsion from Italy by Mussolini in 1923.

Crowley's Lunar placement is perhaps most aptly characterized by his involvement in the practice of ceremonial magic. Indeed, despite his significant accomplishments in other fields, Aleister Crowley's reputation is primarily and inextricably associated with the tradition of ceremonial magic as a means for reaching the depths and heights of the human potential for transcending ordinary consciousness and precipitating direct experience of what are often called supernatural or occult phenomena. Any attempt to assess Crowley's life and work that fails adequately to account for the primacy of his involvement in the tradition of ceremonial magic would lack the essential element of the context of his life. Such matters, however, often entail an aura of obscurity that the general reader may find difficult to penetrate. Not only is the subject of ceremonial magic obscure to the general reader in and of itself, but, for reasons elaborated above concerning the problem of solipsism as it pertains to the influence of Luna, there is the problem of attempting to convey the nature of Crowley's particular subjective experience as a person, that is, *what it was like to be Aleister Crowley* and why it was that ceremonial magic was so effective *for him* as a perceptual vehicle. It is hoped that the technique of astrological analysis as applied to his lunar placement will prove effective toward making this perspective more accessible to the general reader.

A good account of this peculiarity of Crowley's is provided by the man himself in a passage from *Confessions* in which he describes the events leading to and including his initiation into the Golden Dawn order at age twenty-three.

> I took the Order with absolute seriousness. I was not even put off by the fact of its ceremonies taking place at Mark Mason's Hall. I remember asking Baker whether people often died during the ceremony. I had no idea that it was a flat formality and that the members were for the most part muddled middle-class mediocrities. I saw myself entering the Hidden Church of the Holy Grail. This state of my soul served me well. My initiation was in fact a sacrament. [p. 176]

Ceremonial magic *amplifies* the experience of religious symbolism. It serves essentially the same purpose as any religious ritual but is carried to the extreme of excluding all other phenomena in order to create an encompassing cosmic apparition. Also, where conventional religious ritual is limited to a few central images presented in a simple format, ceremonial magic endeavors to incorporate more complex arrangements and to develop their presentation through stages of increasing intensity so as to orchestrate and raise the power of the subjective experience of participants. It was highly fortuitous that the brief period of the efficacy of the Golden Dawn coincided with Crowley's need for formal magical training at such a crucial juncture of his personal development.

The interpretation of Crowley's lunar placement would not be complete without the inclusion of another fundamental association. In keeping with the maternal connotations of Luna, it is natural that her natal placement should indicate the primary focus of the native's experience of one's mother and particularly her formative influence during the early years of one's psychological development. It is therefore to be expected that significant insights pertaining to Crowley's relationship with his mother are implicit in his lunar placement.

Crowley provides us with some, although not much, information about his mother and his relationship with her. The most widely known and sensationalized tidbit of lore in this regard is, of course, Crowley's claim that it was his mother who initially identified him in his much beloved role as the Beast 666 of the Apocalypse. A fairly subtle understanding of the man and his teachings is required to bring any viable perspective to bear upon both his identification with this image and his crediting of his mother for identifying him as such. Israel Regardie, who knew and worked with Crowley personally, speculates that this attribution may have been initially rooted in the more or less innocuous banter of his mother, subsequently to be expanded by Crowley himself into the monumental proportions he would eventually bring to it. This may possibly be the case. The details of the matter simply cannot be known. However, the matter certainly warrants some further consideration from a psychoanalytic perspective.

One passage from *Confessions* is particularly interesting in this regard. Crowley writes, "When I went to Russia to learn the language for the Diplomatic Service, my mother half believed that I had 'gone to see Gog and Magog' (who were supposed to be Russian giants) in order to arrange the date of the Battle of Armageddon." [p. 387] I may be accused of over-interpreting, but I think that his use of the phrase "half believed" indicates a tacit, albeit unconscious complicity on the part of Crowley and his mother in this matter, at least in Crowley's mind. A little further along he writes, "But my mother believed that I was actually Anti-christ of the Apocalypse and also her poor lost erring son who might yet repent and be redeemed by the Precious Blood." [pp. 387-388]

Regardie made a unique contribution to the literature about Crowley by introducing psychoanalytic perspectives to the assessment of his personality in *The Eye in the Triangle*. Dr. Regardie's well founded insights go a long way toward reconciling many of the complexities and paradoxes of Crowley's personality, particularly the enigma involving the strong current of negative force as an aspect of his personality and the sublime mystical attainments that characterize his personal genius. Other writers have been critical of the psychoanalytic approach as taking too wide a departure from a simpler, more direct assessment of Crowley's motives, such as that presented by Colin Wilson in *The Nature of the Beast*. This kind of assessment, however, tends to reduce the significance of any potential contribution Crowley may have made to "nothing but" the product of a disturbed personality, explaining the higher in terms of the lower. It is my opinion that Israel Regardie's claim that Crowley's psychological complexes were instrumental in his accomplishments by virtue of his spiritual discipline are vindicated by the growing power of Crowley's legacy.

Crowley's identification with the image of the Beast of the Apocalypse—taken directly from the Christian Book of Revelation—is a fundamental indication of the nature of his personality. The fact that it was his mother who in effect christened him with this accolade is highly relevant by virtue of the manner in which it weds religious and sexual imagery through the discrete levels of the personal and collective unconscious. Crowley's identification with the image of the Beast 666 completes a linkage from the collective unconscious, through his personal unconscious, to the conscious activity of his life in the world. Such linkage is not only appropriate but *essential* to the personality of a true prophet. Therefore Crowley's identification with this archetypal image is of central significance for any assessment of his claim to be the focal prophet for the New Aeon.

This entire theme is somewhat complex and is expanded upon more comprehensively in later chapters, but some important groundwork for those extended considerations can be laid here by establishing a perspective about Crowley's attitudes toward his mother in relation to the lunar placement in his birthchart. The idealization of the feminine is a fundamental component of Crowley's mystical philosophy, and such an orientation is fully appropriate to his natal lunar placement as delineated above. In many of his less exalted utterances, however, Crowley expressed a host of derogatory attitudes toward women in general, and his mother in particular, that would appear to run contrary to such an idealization. This conundrum may be assessed with the help of psychoanalytic perspectives provided by Dr. Regardie:

> [Crowley's] memories, ample though they may have been in the supposed recollection of several previous incarnations, never were adequate to provide much material of his early life. There is very little he can say about his mother. This is very significant, and is the sign *par excellence* of repression.
>
> I can only regard as evidences of defense his statements that he treated her as a servant, and that she was physically repulsive to him. Clinically, one could hardly develop a better or more effective armoring against incestuous feelings than to find the love-object

repulsive. The very affirmation of the latter set of feelings can only indicate the opposite. With Crowley's fine appreciation of symbols and their opposites, as indicated in his Tarot book, he would have been the first to appreciate the validity of this line of interpretation.

In the process of breaking the moulds and shackles of parental sexual inhibition, Crowley loved to narrate his seduction of the family maid on his own mother's bed. This was his gesture of defiance, the hoisting of the emblem of revolt, the winning of his freedom. It was all of that—and something more. What is concealed in the details of the defiant act is the incestuous factor of his lifetime. Through the maid, he was not only defying his mother but in addition seducing her. So far as the unconscious elements of his psyche were concerned, this was incest pure and simple. He has confessed in his autobiography to treating his mother like a servant. One servant can therefore be substituted for another so far as the unconscious psyche is concerned; this is the meaning of symbolism. [p. 441]

Although Crowley stated that he hated and despised his mother, a thorough study of his writings reveals that his experience of her was not entirely negative. For example, at one point he refers to her as "the best of all possible mothers, only marred beyond belief by the religious monomania which perhaps started in what one may call 'Hysteria of Widowhood'" [*Crowley on Christ,* p. 137]. This passage is revealing in regard to the Oedipal significance of Crowley's attitude toward his mother in relation to the death of his father. In keeping with a further development of this theme, there is an observation that consistently appears in his references to her. Crowley wrote in the opening paragraphs of *Confessions*:

He [Crowley's father] married (in 1874, one may assume) Emily Bertha Bishop, of a Devon and Somerset family. Her father had died and her brother Tom Bond Bishop had come to London to work in the Civil Service. The important points about the woman are that her schoolmates called her 'the little Chinese girl', that she painted in water-colour with admirable taste destroyed by academic training, and that her *powerful natural instincts* [emphasis added] were suppressed by religion to the point that she became, after her husband's death, a brainless bigot of the most narrow, logical and inhuman type. Yet there was always a struggle; she was really distressed, almost daily, at finding herself obliged by her religion to perform acts of the most senseless atrocity. [pp. 35-36]

Further along we find Crowley's account of his mother's outrage in response to the reading aloud after dinner of "The Ancient Mariner" by one of his many tutors. The passage that set her off involved the blessing of snakes. Crowley concludes the account by saying, "My mother was naturally a *rather sensual type of woman* [again, emphasis added] and there is no doubt that sexual repression had driven her as nearly as possible to the borders of insanity." [p. 78] Not a great deal of acumen is required to surmise from these remarks that Crowley's antagonism toward his mother, and by extension toward women in general, was not directed at essential femininity but more at the *distortion* of femininity by the social conditioning of the puritanical Judeo-Christian religious tradition.

In accordance with the Freudian theory of male personality development as applied to the childhood of Aleister Crowley, it is axiomatic that his own strongly accentuated sexual orientation *had* to be developed in relation to the central nexus of imagery surrounding his childhood perception of his mother. It can also be surmised that, even in his mature years, Crowley was by no means fully conscious of the dynamics of the Oedipal complex as it functioned within the structure of his own personality. His identification with the image of the Beast 666, however, and his crediting of his mother for identifying him as such, is a symbolically tacit acknowledgment of a subconscious libidinal attunement with her which held the potential for resolving the conflicts inherent in the patriarchal conditioning of the Piscean Age. The psychoanalytic perspective is essential to the understanding of these dynamics; because, of necessity, they operated at unconscious levels. To attempt to understand the greater meaning of the life of Aleister Crowley, the magician and religious prophet, without the benefit of the perspectives afforded by depth psychology would be utterly futile. This is the root of the difficulty with those of Crowley's biographies that attempt to assess his personality in superficial terms. One must conclude that the writers of such biographies are unable to get beyond the very unconscious assumptions of our Piscean Age heritage that Crowley took it upon himself to break apart.

PART II

CHAPTER 7

SOLAR GESTALT

In order to further develop the interpretation of Aleister Crowley's birthchart, it is necessary to take the step of making a general assessment of the entire configuration. In doing this, it may be observed that there are two distinct "gestalts" indicated by patterns of planetary disposition that together encompass the entire configuration. These two gestalts clearly indicate two operative themes in Crowley's personality. One of these gestalts includes Sol and is rather masculine (yang) in its composition. The other includes Luna and is rather feminine (yin) in its composition. Such clear and thematically consistent and comprehensive groupings of planets in a birthchart is a rare phenomenon. This observation alone indicates an exceptional character for the subject of our analysis. Several features of the first of these groupings, the "solar gestalt," have already been introduced in previous chapters. This chapter will complete the delineation of the solar gestalt and the manner of its operation as a functional system in Crowley's personality. The features of the solar gestalt not yet introduced are Mars, the Lunar Nodes, and the Meridian.

There is a special significance for the planet Mars in Crowley's life and work due to its correspondence to the ruling archetype of the New Aeon as it is characterized in his most important writing, *The Book of the Law*. That book constitutes the central nexus of Crowley's message to the world, and the Egyptian hawk-headed god Horus is identified therein as the ruling archetype of the New Aeon, which, based upon a pivotal event leading to the writing of *The Book of the Law,* is said to have been initiated on March 20, 1904. In the Egyptian pantheon, Horus is a god of war, and his planetary attribution is Mars. This special significance brings considerable importance to the matter of Mars' placement in Crowley's birthchart. It will be helpful to begin with an assessment of the meaning of Mars in general terms and how Crowley's conception of Mars as the ruling planet of the New Aeon can be reconciled with the rulership of

Aquarius (which characterizes the new age from an astrological perspective) by Uranus as presented in chapter 4. In a nutshell, the fundamental issue is that of personal relevance.

A prophetic message is more effective the more personally relevant it is to the individual human being at the gut level. Grand principles and abstract concepts have their place, but they are not the most fundamental driving components of human experience. The most important component of religion is *not* the cosmic conception it provides but rather the sense of personal meaning it bestows in terms of day to day life experience. There is no escaping the fact that the study of astrology is a rather lofty enterprise, and the understanding of the astrological meaning of Uranus, although it has a particular interpretive value as an indicator of personal genius, is largely suggestive of an abstract philosophical and social *concept*. Mars, on the other hand, is an intensely *personal* planet. Its significance is visceral and can be ignored only at one's peril, however poorly articulated may be its meaning in the abstract. This aspect of Mars' significance is reinforced by its high-profile status to the skyward observer. Some very pertinent associations can be drawn to support the viability of *both* Uranus and Mars as appropriate referents for the emerging concerns of human existence in today's world.

As the farthest immediately visible planet in the solar system, Saturn symbolizes the boundary of sensory reality that we experience of the "world" in which we live. In its most fundamental existential and personal sense, however, that world is limited to Earth as the place of our inhabitance. This association is inherent in Saturn's rulership of the *Earth*-sign Capricorn. As such, Saturn is concerned with the hard facts of practical reality as they pertain to the organization of society *from a traditional earth-bound perspective*. Uranus, as the next planet *out* from Saturn, symbolizes a venturing forth into hitherto uncharted territory, a daring *collective* and *extra-sensory,* that is, *abstract*, advance. Mars, as the next planet *out* from Earth, engenders a similar connotation but from a much more *personal* perspective, and fully within the context of sensory experience. Focus upon Mars suggests the *personalization* of the inherent meaning of the displacement of Saturn by Uranus as the new ruler of the social sign Aquarius. The interactive relation involving Uranus and Mars is inherent in the historical observation that the very Uranian document, the American *Declaration of Independence*, was, as everyone was well aware at the time despite its lofty tone and eloquence, a *declaration of war*. The thematic parallels between the symbolic meanings of Mars and Uranus are associated with the principle of individualism and involve the personal *courage* and *initiative* essential for effectual participation in a truly democratic society, that is, the guts to stand up for oneself, and if necessary, by oneself, as opposed to the professed virtue of obedience to authority and submission to the will of an exterior "King" or "God" which characterized the dominant mythos of the Piscean Age.

In Aleister Crowley's birthchart Mars occupies the twenty-third degree of Capricorn in his Sixth House which has Capricorn on its cusp. Mars therefore participates in the ruling impetus of Crowley's Sixth House and is solidly placed therein. Mars is said to be "exalted" in Capricorn. In Saturn-ruled Capricorn the warrior Mars is subject to rigorous discipline, and his vital energy is constrained to *greater purpose* in terms of the needs of the community as a whole. The Capricornian field mitigates Mars' impetuosity and otherwise more limited scope, providing focus and direction. The Sixth House is traditionally associated with health, work, and devotion. These associations, however, may appear arbitrary without the benefit of contextual perspective upon the whole cycle of houses. It is therefore appropriate to expand upon this greater context.

The Sixth House is the *last* of the houses of the hemisphere *below* the Horizon. Those six houses pertain to the subjective aspect of personality, the *substance* of the person so to speak. Each house represents a stage or phase of personal involvement in the process of life. Being the *final* stage of working out the subjective aspect of personality, the Sixth House completes the preparation of the personality for involvement with the world outside oneself—the objective world *above* the Horizon. The initial encounter with the objective world is experienced in terms of one-on-one interactions with *other people*; thus the significance of the Seventh House, the *first* house of the hemisphere above the Horizon, as pertaining to relationships. The Sixth House may be likened to the final preparations that one makes just prior to an important meeting with another person. This could involve getting ready for a date or preparing to meet an enemy in battle. With this more inclusive perspective in mind, the associations of health, work, and devotion with the Sixth House become logically consistent. Subjective tension reaches its peak in such circumstances thus stressing the body to its most rigorous metabolic demand. One applies diligence to one's preparatory regimen. The importance of the impending encounter engenders humility and aspiration to be the very best one can. Optimally, one experiences a purifying inner cleansing or *healing* and becomes finally *ready* to step forth and meet the challenge knowing one has done all one can prior to the fateful moment of encounter. In most general terms therefore, the Sixth House pertains to how one goes about the performance of tasks, one's *working technique*.

Crowley's stamina and ability to mobilize his personal will toward the development of *masterful technique* exemplifies his natal Mars placement in both Capricorn and the Sixth House. He typified such ability through disciplines including the regulation of his body through the practice of yoga, the performance of skillful, strenuous, and prolonged work demonstrated by his remarkable mountaineering feats, his great output of writing, his acknowledged proficiency in the practice of ceremonial magic, as well as the performance through the course of his life of his peculiar sense of duty.

Greater understanding of Mars' significance can be gained by a further consideration of its position within the morphology of the solar system as a whole. The other two personal planets, Mercury and Venus, having orbits *inside* that of Earth, have observable cycles of visibility whereby they are always within a limited angular proximity to Sol. They are seen only relatively near the horizon just before sunrise or after sunset. Mars, on the other hand, having an orbit *outside* that of Earth, ventures out on his own to span the entire arch of the nocturnal sky. Unlike Mercury and Venus, Mars can *diametrically oppose* Sol, thereby pointing directly outward to the great beyond. Being a personal planet, however, his movement is swift in relation to the social planets. His transits through signs are experienced in terms of months rather than years as are those of Jupiter and Saturn. Mars is therefore suggestive of the *mobilization of one's personal forces* toward the world outside oneself, toward participation in the greater whole of collective humanity.

Such an orientation is necessarily *challenging*. The *inner* realm of personal reality tends to be more accommodating to one's thoughts and desires (Mercury and Venus). The *outer* realm of other people and other nations, however, is often indifferent and hostile to one's personal intentions. Two morphological facts are remarkably relevant here. The most obvious of these is that Mars is red, an association implying the redness of blood. The challenging aspect of the experience of human interaction is most fully characterized by the shedding of blood in personal combat. The true martial spirit traditionally recognizes and accepts the reality and necessity of war as an essential, albeit unpleasant, component of human existence. War, of course, is destructive and requires the seemingly senseless waste of human life and resources. It is also true, however, that war has a purging and purifying effect upon humanity, discharging pent-up energy and culling out weak elements from the strain. Consequently, although the elimination of war has been espoused as a noble ideal by many who abhor its brutality, such sentiment has been sharply criticized for its weakening effect on the species in its struggle for survival. This conundrum has been poignantly addressed by William James in his monumental essay, "The Moral Equivalent of War," in which he promulgates the mobilization of martial forces toward constructive ends through meeting the challenges of natural existence in a socially cooperative manner as opposed to mutual destruction. These considerations are intensely germane to the whole gamut of social issues explored in this book. The relevant point here is the morphological basis for the association of the planet Mars with the personal characteristics and virtues of the warrior aspect of human nature, particularly as they pertain to the social and philosophical perspectives of Aleister Crowley.

The other morphological characteristic of our solar system that is remarkably germane to the challenging aspect of Mars' connotation of the outward orientation of personality is the existence of the asteroid belt concentrated between the orbits of Mars and Jupiter. There are two popular scientific theories that address the origin of the asteroid belt. Both theories find support from the formulation of Bode's Law, introduced by Johann Titius in 1766 and publicized by Johan Bode in 1772 (prior to the discovery of any asteroids) which hypothesized the existence of a planetary orbit between Mars and Jupiter based on a mathematical series that accounted for the relative distances of all known planets at that time. The most spectacular theory for the origin of the asteroid belt involves the speculation that there once may have been a planet occupying that orbital slot that was subsequently shattered by an incoming object massive enough to produce the required impact. The other prominent theory is that the original material out of which the solar system was formed was unable to coalesce into a planet in that orbital region due to the gravitational tension there between the Sun and Jupiter. The latter theory suggests that the formation of the asteroid belt was *originally inherent* in the structural dynamics of our solar system and therefore characteristic of the incipient creative process leading to the advent of humankind. The former theory suggests that the asteroid belt resulted from a *disruption* of the natural formative process of our solar system, thereby frustrating what otherwise may have evolved as a functional means of personal adaptation to social interaction, obviating the catastrophic aspects of war that have characterized humankind as we know it.

Such an event, of course, would have been a disruption only from the *internal* perspective of our solar system as an operative whole, a sort of circumcision of the solar system, as it were. If such an intrusive body disrupted our solar system from without, it would have been an action upon our solar system *from a more inclusive level of wholeness* which we may currently conceive as the *galaxy* in which we live. Whatever may be the case for the origin of the asteroid belt, its existence is symbolically appropriate to the multifarious challenges invariably encountered by the individual person as one ventures out into participation with collective humanity. It symbolizes the personal *testing ground* that either strengthens or thwarts one's efforts to function in society and thereby reinforces the need for skill and courage associated with the intrinsic astrological meaning of Mars. The autistic personality would be a primary example of failure to meet that challenge, although such a condition should not necessarily be construed to impugn the morality of the autistic individual. One has no way of knowing all the factors responsible for such a condition in a particular individual.

The asteroids will not be addressed specifically in this book, so it may be helpful to suggest here that the consideration of their positions in one's birthchart, or, for practical purposes, the positions of the four largest asteroids, Ceres, Pallas, Juno, and Vesta, would have potential value in accordance with the morphological perspective suggested above as indicators of significant *political obstacles* characteristically encountered by the native.

We may now assess two distinct features of Crowley's personality that demonstrate the value of astrology for sorting out personal characteristics. The personal qualities characterized by his Mars placement would appear to be at odds with those indicated by his Uranus placement. Indeed, these two placements together account for one of many thematic difficulties in Crowley's personality, exacerbated by the fact that both were exercised to such a marked degree. The demonstrable rancor and evident lack of discipline that characterized Crowley's persona would appear to be inconsistent with the well modulated and practically super-human exertions and achievements that he performed. The understanding of the operation of these two functions as components of Crowley's personality helps to explain certain problems that recurred throughout his life in his attempts to involve others in his personal exploits. For example, his phenomenal skill and competence as a mountain climber, a proverbial Capricornian image when taken as a symbol of social ambition, was respected and renowned by the time he became involved in two major Himalayan expeditions on Chogo-Ri in 1902 and Kanchenjunga in 1905, the second of which he led. Both expeditions, although respectable attempts in terms of their achievements, were ill-fated. There is considerable disagreement concerning Crowley's actions and attitudes on these expeditions, particularly the second which involved a mutiny against his leadership resulting in an accident that killed four men. The facts of what happened are disputed, however all accounts hinge on the personal failings of either Crowley or Jacot Guillarmod, a Swiss climber who had initially proposed the expedition. There can be no doubt, however, that Crowley's behavior was at least *perceived* as ill suited to his responsibility as leader of the expedition. There can be no doubt that his unsavory persona tainted his leadership and subverted his reputation for technical expertise as a climber.

The failure of the 1905 Kanchenjunga expedition was no doubt a bitter pill for the twenty-nine year old Aleister Crowley to swallow. What might have been his winning of a place of recognition as a man among men, his certification as a member of the adult male community, a goal he ardently pursued, rather became a scandal of humiliating proportions. His various published attempts to absolve himself from the stigma of the event only exacerbated the damage to his reputation. His history of boasting about his own prowess along with his vitriolic criticisms of other climbers had not endeared him to the community to which he appealed for vindication.

In addition to characterizing the peculiar interaction of Mars and Uranus in Crowley's personality, the Himalayan expeditions dramatized the major turning point of his life at which time his destiny as a prophet overtook him and, by the very weight of its responsibility, began to bring his conscious persona, that is, his ego, into submission. It was during the interim between the two expeditions that Crowley received *The Book of the Law*. The monumental skills and technical expertise indicated by his natal Mars placement were ultimately to be directed toward a much greater purpose than any of the various preoccupations to which he first devoted them as means for personal aggrandizement.

The astrological indication of this greater direction is found in features of Crowley's solar gestalt yet to be interpreted, namely, the

Lunar Nodes and Meridian of his birthchart. In chapter 6 I mentioned that the lunar nodal axis was an important feature of the lunar phenomenon taken as a whole. A more thorough consideration of the Lunar Nodes, however, was deferred in order to introduce it in the present context. Although the importance of the meaning of Luna is attended to by many who aspire to obtain greater astrological insights into their lives and the lives of others, the importance of the Lunar Nodes is much less understood and entails a deeper, subtler, and distinctly more profound understanding of personality than is generally obtained at the popular level of astrological discourse. Once grasped, however, the meaning of the Lunar Nodes becomes the very *key* to the interpretation of a birthchart. In order to apply this key for purposes of practical interpretation, however, one must understand certain morphological, historical, and philosophical perspectives on its general meaning.

The lunar nodal axis is the intersection of the orbital planes of Earth and Luna and results from the fact that there is a slight variation between these two planes. The point at which Luna passes through the plane of Earth's orbit *moving northward* is referred to as the ascending node or the North Lunar Node. Conversely, the point at which she passes through Earth's plane *moving southward* is referred to as the descending node or the South Lunar Node. Since none of the other planetary nodes will be considered in this book, the two lunar nodes will hereafter be referred to simply as the North Node and the South Node. The primary significance of the lunar nodes from an astronomical perspective is the fact that eclipses occur only when Sol is in near alignment with one or the other of the nodes. Only at those times do Sol, Luna, and Earth align so as to bring Earth and Luna into one another's shadows in relation to the solar illumination. Since the lunar nodes are naturally in diametrical opposition, Earth's annual orbit aligns each of them with Sol at roughly six-month intervals. These orbital relations also involve the precession or *backward* movement of the lunar nodal axis in relation to the zodiac, making one complete precessional cycle in approximately eighteen and a half years. This knowledge renders eclipses more or less predictable, depending upon the sophistication of the astronomical measurements applied. From an historical perspective, the ability to predict eclipses was a source of great political influence, due to their powerful psychological effect upon less knowledgeable members of the community.

In ancient mythological lore eclipses were accounted for in terms of a cosmic dragon that routinely devoured Sol or Luna, depending on the type of eclipse being described. Such is the basis for the traditional naming of the North and South Nodes respectively as *Caput Draconis* (Dragon's Head) and *Cauda Draconis* (Dragon's Tail), a tradition dating back through the earliest recorded knowledge of the Western astrological tradition. The dragon is a mythological image of the *life force* in its most primordial manifestation. It follows that the relation between the head and tail of the dragon connotes the orientation of the progressive *direction* of organic evolutionary development. In this regard, life on Earth may be conceived as occurring within an environmental matrix for the continuous development of the life force into ever more refined and articulated forms of organic functioning through the meeting of challenges and the resulting incorporation of ever new modes of experience.

This perspective upon the meaning of the lunar nodes is very poignantly developed by Martin Schulman in Volume I of his Karmic Astrology series entitled *The Moon's Nodes and Reincarnation*. Schulman states:

> At one level these Nodes reveal the track that your soul is running on in the current life, while the rest of the horoscope adds additional information as to how you are to make the journey. It is through the Nodes that Western astrology is now able to make its first inroads into relating this divine science to the Hindu concept of reincarnation. [p. 21]

It is not the purpose of this book necessarily to promulgate the idea of reincarnation. It is indeed a fascinating doctrine and is one largely accepted tenet of new age thought that is rooted in occult religious and philosophical tradition. Aleister Crowley accepted the idea completely and claimed to have experienced direct memories from many of his previous incarnations. It is not my intention, however, to argue that the significance of the lunar nodes must hinge on belief in reincarnation. It is certainly plausible and conceptually useful to frame one's perspective in such a manner, but the idea of karma and the role of a particular person in the continuity of vast evolutionary processes does not have to be so framed. My position, and the point of view that supports the writing of this book, is wholly existential. According to this view, both birth and death are existentially opaque. Transcendental perspectives may be implicit and intelligible, but they are *not given*. From an existential perspective they must ultimately be taken on faith, which means that we simply *do not know* what lies beyond the pale of embodied human existence.

What we *do* know is that we experience a sense of purpose (teleology) and meaning in life. Certainly, some philosophers and many scientists have attempted to deny any purposeful direction for life from a cosmic perspective, but such denial cannot negate the common experience of *striving* that characterizes human existence and all organic life. Failures of will do happen, but they cannot be held to speak for the greater experience of humanity or the driving force of life's evolvement. The unwillingness of many scientists to acknowledge purpose in nature can be understood as a necessary component of the initial development of the empirical approach to knowledge as a departure from the authoritarian institutions of the Piscean Age that claimed to hold monopolies on the administration and dissemination of purpose. The architects of the scientific world view could not hold with the notion of a Divine Will that could step in and alter, willy-nilly, their conception of the mathematical precision of the universe, and that furthermore seemed to have a propensity to do so in ignorance of and opposition to the enhanced capacity of human reason. The sentiment of meaninglessness in more recent times, however, is an indication of the *decline* of the modern world view, a matter which has yet to be addressed in this book. The interpretation of the lunar nodal axis affords an appropriate opportunity to address the decline of the modern world view, not only by virtue of its association with purpose in nature, but also due to its morphological orientation in relation to the principle of *entropy* as a function of its precessional or *backward* movement through the zodiac, that is, seemingly *against* the natural flow of universal entropy.

The precessional movement of the vernal equinox was introduced in chapter 1, but a consideration of the philosophical significance of such movement was deferred to the consideration of a theme to be developed later. The theme referred to is that of entropy, and it can now be explored in relation to the precessional movements of *both* the equinoctial *and* the lunar nodal axes. Entropy refers to the operation of the infamous second law of thermodynamics which is fundamental to a scientific understanding of the tendency of all energy and matter. The first law of thermodynamics simply states that energy (we needn't use the term "matter" here since matter *is* energy) can neither be created nor destroyed. Any *apparent* creation or destruction is actually only a change in the *form* of energy, the *quantity* never being altered. The second law, the law of entropy, states that all changes in forms of energy move progressively toward a less ordered, more diffuse and dissipated state of the total quantity.

The general purport of the entropy law in human terms, as it applies to our transition into the Aquarian Age, is a matter of utmost importance. This importance results largely from the fact that the law of entropy *does not support* the modern world view of the human potential for unlimited progress achievable through the energetic exploitation of the environment. It is rather the case that by accelerating the utilization of energy and the conversion of matter into various forms, humankind is *speeding up* the process of entropy thereby rendering the environment progressively *less useful* for continued living. We experience this loss not only through problems involving increased energy costs and pollution of the environment, but also in more subtle ways affecting our rapport with nature, the cohesiveness of societies, and the quality of our experience of life from a material perspective. Consider for example that, despite all the machines that we employ to perform labor, we yet encounter greater challenges to the maintenance of the whole economy. Indeed, we are not generally doing the same kind of work that was done prior to the development of modern technology, but we are kept busy with the greater demands, complexity, and by-products of our higher energy utilization. Rather than relieving us of the burdens of life and facilitating leisure and cultural plenitude, our industrialized economy continues to sap more and more of the life blood of humanity, despite increases in the Gross Domestic Product which we are told is the index of our prosperity.

There is an ironic correspondence between the law of entropy and the emergence of social democracy in world civilization that was expressed rather poignantly by Bertrand Russell: "Whenever there is a great deal of energy in one region and very little in a neighboring region, energy tends to travel from the one region to the other, until equality is established. This whole process may be described as a tendency towards democracy." [Quoted in Rifkin, p. 39] One of the hallmarks of conservative political thought is to resist or rather to deny the flow of entropy and therefore to resist the advance of democracy, that is, the *spreading out* of political power. Adolph Hitler was somewhat eloquent in his condemnation of democracy as the "mongrelization" of society whereby the better aspirations that characterize the self-acknowledged elite of humankind are impeded by the degrading impulses of the lowly majority of lesser humans and lesser races as it were. In contemporary American society, usually in the *name* of democracy, the conservative sentiment speaks on behalf of the "freedom" of mammoth corporations (often subsidized) to pursue the financial gain of their owners at the expense of the living conditions of those who work in their factories, or have been laid off from their factories through "downsizing" and cannot afford to buy corporate stock, or even to stock their shelves with food for their children. Of course the wealthy stockholders can afford a more affluent lifestyle amid the worsening physical and social environment, but that is only the natural right that accrues to their superior humanity which is attested to by their greater material wealth. After all, we have laws to ensure that everything is done in accordance with the highest standards of morality.

Conservatism, however, is obviously not always motivated by such dubious sentiments. Most conservatives actually believe in the moral rectitude of their position. By and large, they have worked hard and sacrificed much in the way of delayed gratification in the industrious pursuit of their material goals. They *believe in* the modern world paradigm that has failed to take entropy into account. This belief has provided the fundamental source of social optimism that has created the wonders of the present technological age. But those wonders are rapidly being overshadowed by the opposite effect to that which was supposed to follow from the deployment of free enterprise, the profit motive, and the exploitation of nonrenewable natural resources. And so we find ourselves resting precariously upon the horns of a dilemma, even as democracy advances and authoritarian structures continue to crumble under the weight of their own entropic inefficiency. We are encountering an *entropic watershed* of global proportion that will arrest the massive deployment of industrial technology as we currently know it, and this watershed will force a radical change in the organization of society in the twenty-first century. This theme is developed further in later chapters in which the advent of the New Aeon is considered from the perspective of Aleister Crowley's prophetic revelation.

There is a direct correspondence between the ideas of *entropy* and *time*. Time is comprehended only in terms of the movement of energy, and the movement of energy is inherently entropic. In the words of Sir Arthur Eddington, "Entropy is time's arrow." It only goes one way; from robust hyper-interaction (the Big Bang) to bland, uniform stasis (heat death). As a temporal frame of reference, therefore, the tropical zodiac refers to an entropic process. The planets all revolve in the same relative direction, passing through the signs of the zodiac in the same sequence as the signs themselves proceed through the annual cycle of time. Earth rotates in that same direction, bringing the signs of the zodiac to the horizon in that same sequence. Such is the whirling flow of time and the cosmic dissipation of energetic structures. *Life* appears to defy the entropic flow of time by organizing energy into ever more complex and ordered structures. This indeed is the wonder of life. It swims upstream, as it were.

It must be understood, however, that, although life *appears* to push back the direction of entropy, it does not in fact do so. Life organizes energy into orderly and purposeful structures only at the *expense* of the utilization of much greater quantities of energy, and then ultimately to relinquish its hold, whereby its structures are released back into the disintegrative flow. This point is made very clearly by chemist G. Tyler Miller in *Energetics, Kinetics and Life*. Miller states: "Three hundred trout are required to support one man for a year. The trout in turn, must consume 90,000 frogs, that must consume 27 million grasshoppers that live off of 1000 tons of grass." [Rifkin, p. 54] He further states that in the process of organic energy utilization, "about 80-90% of the energy is simply wasted and lost as heat to the environment." [*ibid.*] Rifkin makes the telling observation based on these facts: "The Entropy Law says that evolution dissipates the overall available energy for life on this planet. Our concept [i.e., the conventional notion] of evolution is the exact opposite. We believe that evolution somehow magically creates greater overall value and order on earth." [*ibid.*, p. 55] The lack of understanding of this truth about life is central to the absurdity of modern civilization.

By virtue of their precessional movements, *opposite* to the direction of the natural entropic flow of energy, the equinoctial and the lunar nodal axes refer symbolically to processes that *appear* to reverse entropy but actually register the *loss of effective potential* within the greater energetic context of existence. The connotation is that *life* and *purpose* do in fact struggle against the tendency of entropy to disorganize matter, but only through an *actual acceleration* of that tendency. This is a most sublime paradox from a philosophical perspective, and its comprehension is essential to the understanding of the spiritual principles implied by it. As a function of the tropical zodiac itself, the precession of the equinoctial axis in relation to the stellar backdrop refers to the greater purpose of life as a whole within a universal context, which proceeds nonetheless at the expense of the structural order of the universe. As a component of the lunar envelope immediately surrounding Earth, the precession of

the lunar nodal axis *through the tropical zodiac* refers to purposefulness as a function of personal existence *within* the context of life,
which also extracts a yet greater price in terms of the future usefulness of environmental resources. The ancient image of the fire-
breathing dragon attributed to the lunar nodal axis is remarkably
appropriate to the hyper-entropic, devouring and heat-dissipating
character of the life force in nature. Its orientation in a birthchart, that
is, the direction in which it is *headed*, is indicative of the *purpose* of
the native's life. The implication is that a person carries, in a particular manner, the responsibility for advancing evolutionary progress in
the direction indicated by the orientation of the dragon in one's birthchart. This responsibility is *intensified* by the fact of a person's inevitable depletion of precious resources through the course of fulfilling
that purpose. There is a job to be done and an ever-diminishing
amount of resources with which to do it. *Human purposefulness can
only be understood within the context of universal entropy.*

This responsibility can be thought of in various ways. Martin
Schulman assumes the perspective of the evolution of the soul
through the process of reincarnation into a succession of human
personalities. This conception suggests an analogy to the image of
the mighty salmon struggling against the entropic flow of water as
they swim upriver toward their spawning streams. Their leaps into
the rarefied air provide respites from the struggle, but they are drawn
immediately back into the river of life to struggle further again and
again and again. From this perspective the South Node refers to the
cumulative experience of "past lives" and therefore connotes an
orientation to life that is old and familiar to the native. Conversely,
the position of the North Node refers to an aspect of life that the soul
of the native must now incorporate, the "next lesson" needed to
counterbalance inherited karma. Schulman does a superb job of
interpreting the placements of both Lunar Nodes in each sign and
house of a birthchart from this perspective.

As already stated, however, the idea of purpose can be comprehended completely within the existential context of human experience, without the need for an explicit transcendental frame of reference. The lunar nodal axis may be interpreted to correspond to the
structural orientation of the womb-like lunar envelope such that the
North Node indicates the location of the birth canal in relation to the
personal cosmos of the native. The Dragon's Head accordingly indicates the proper positioning within the context of personality for
evolving through a progressive *birthing* toward the fulfillment of

one's true purpose for existing. If we push this metaphor to its ultimate conclusion, it may be assumed that biological death is analogous to the final uterine contraction that propels one beyond the energetic matrix of material existence into the unknown.

By applying this approach to the interpretation of the lunar nodal axis in Crowley's birthchart, a very remarkable synthesis of the factors thus far delineated becomes apparent. As shown in Figure 6, Crowley's lunar nodal axis is within 3 1/2° of alignment with his Meridian. The South Node is placed just to the Third House side of his *Imum Coeli* in Libra, and the North Node is placed just to the Ninth House side of his Midheaven in Aries. Dane Rudhyar, who referred to the Horizon as the "axis of consciousness," also referred to the Meridian as the "axis of power." The *Imum Coeli* at the Earth-centered bottom of the birthchart refers to the *foundation* of power and the roots of personality. The *Medium Coeli* or Midheaven at the top refers to the *height* of power as exercised publicly, one's *standing* in the community, whether it be considered in terms of a small community, a large city, a nation, the whole world, or (ultimately) the cosmos.

Crowley's South Node being so near his *Imum Coeli* indicates a deeply ingrained centeredness of personality and a tendency to be most comfortable in a private setting, appropriate to the ability to draw upon a deep, underlying source of personal power. The South Node in Libra also indicates a natural sense of artistic balance and an abiding experience of love that tends to yield to others in the interest of harmony. All that was said in chapter 5 about the meaning of Crowley's natal Sol and Venus in Libra can be interpreted, by virtue of his South Node placement in that sign, to mean that those characteristics constitute an inherited orientation that is rooted in the very process of human history and evolution. That grouping in Libra, at the bottom of his birthchart, represents a womb-like comfort zone for Crowley to which he could retreat at the expense of venturing forth into the harsh realities of the objective world. The Third House South Node indicates a facility with language and an aptitude for logical thinking and mental problem solving. The down side of all this, which is an essential connotation of the South Node, is that such indulgences constituted a potential weakness of his personality that could easily draw him away from the fulfillment of the ongoing purpose of his life. The initial ecstasies of succumbing to this introverted orientation would swiftly deteriorate for Crowley into a personal sense of decadence and sloth.

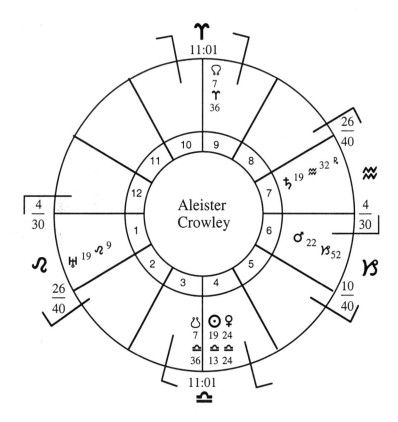

FIGURE 6
The complete "Solar Gestalt" in Aleister Crowley's birthchart (including the
planets involved and the signs occupied and ruled by those planets).

The way for Crowley to move beyond this debilitating tendency
was to focus his energy and attention into the orientation indicated
by his North Node near his Midheaven in Aries. By going public in
an aggressive manner he was able to convert his South Nodal complacency and introversion into a foundation of power for the enactment of public prominence and responsibility. The adoption of this
orientation was by no means easy for Crowley. It was rather the fundamental challenge of his life and could only be enacted through
direct confrontation with a plethora of tensions, obstacles, and fears
within his personality. Incorporating the North Node is always difficult, but for Crowley the nature of the challenge was intensified far

beyond the norm by the gauntlet of paradoxical personal struggles with himself and the world to which he was heir by virtue of the time and place of his entry into the arena of human existence.

A great deal of Crowley's personal struggles were no doubt exacerbated by his natal square (90°) aspect between Mars and Sol. This aspect contributes to the fact that, despite his phenomenal strengths and skills, he suffered with chronic asthma and considered his greatest weakness to be that of sloth. He seemed only to be able to work intermittently and was plagued by a tendency, as he wrote in *Confessions*, "to rest on my oars at the very moment when a spurt would take me past the post" [403]. As he directly acknowledged, this tendency largely accounted for his failure to sustain serious recognition for any of his rather noteworthy accomplishments in life. Once he was satisfied that he could do something, he would simply abandon the enterprise and move on to something else. He was unable, or unwilling, to sustain the necessary discipline to reap the potential harvests of his accomplishments. Indeed, Sol in his fall conflicted with Mars in his exaltation. Crowley was able to survive this aspect only by repeatedly picking himself up off the ground through dogged persistence that transcended the experience of defeat.

At the end of chapter 5, a pattern of dispositional succession was delineated involving the placements of Venus, Sol, Uranus, and Saturn in Crowley's birthchart. That dispositional succession may now be extended to include Mars, the Lunar Nodes, and the Midheaven. Picking up with Saturn, by virtue of Mars' placement in Capricorn, Saturn disposes Mars. Furthermore, since Crowley's North Node and Midheaven are both in Aries, they are both disposed by Mars. This chain of disposition indicates an *uninterrupted directional impetus* that carries from a starting point at the Libra South Node to a finishing point at the Aries North Node. This is a most unusual and fortuitous arrangement. The interactive *flow* indicated among the planets, signs, and houses involved tended naturally, despite the inherent difficulties involved, to move Crowley toward the fulfillment of his purpose in life. This tends in a manner to confirm his often made claim that his life was guided by a superior destiny which virtually compelled him to the performance of his appointed task as prophet of the New Aeon by confronting strong resistances within himself. The planetary *weight* of this gestalt is gathered around the South Node in the lower hemisphere of his birthchart, which indicates a functional emphasis on his karmic past and a great deal of spiritual inertia, as it were. Yet this chain of disposition sustained a step by step progression from the depths of his inherited sacrificial subjectivity to the heights of self-actualizing public achievement, virtually catapulting him in that direction.

The operation of Crowley's solar gestalt can best be comprehended in terms of this step by step progression of planetary disposition that in fact constitutes its cohesiveness and may be summarized as follows. The placements of Sol, Venus, and the South Node, all in Libra at the bottom of Crowley's birthchart, indicate a dominant karmic inheritance of sacrificial love and artistic sensitivity that characterized the roots of his personality. As such, they engendered a feeling of patriotism for his native land, and, when experienced to their fullest possible depth, fostered the realization of the planetary unity of humankind. This component of his personality tended to remain private, that is, cloistered from the harsh vagaries of the outer world. For Crowley to remain centered in such a perspective, however, would be to deny his potential for meaningful growth and the very impulse of life itself within him. The manner by which these factors all coalesced to mutually reinforce their dominance of Crowley's subjective perspective is remarkable to say the least. The combined factors of Sol as the center of the solar system, the Imum Coeli of the birthchart as the referent to the gravitational center of Earth, the South Node as referring to the tendency to remain within one's comfort zone, the fact that Venus was domiciled in Libra by virtue of her rulership of that sign and her disposing of Sol therein (the sign of his fall) together connote a virtually unfathomable *introversion* of personality. The richness of Crowley's inner experience was such that there was a very strong tendency for him privately to sustain himself by refraining from coming out into the world of hard facts and unpleasant conflicts. This tendency certainly had much to do with his long personal struggle with addiction to heroin, which he initially began using (legally) as a treatment for asthma.

The next link in the dispositional chain reveals what may be one of the most fundamental paradoxes of Crowley's multi-faceted personality. By virtue of his Leo Ascendant, ruled by Sol, he was immediately challenged to adopt a persona that facilitated his adaptation to the outside world by *dramatizing* the most sensitive and private component of his personality. *He had to show to the world the very aspect of his nature that the purpose of that showing was to protect.* The placement of Uranus in Leo and in his First House not only enabled him, but virtually forced him to armor his sensitive introversion behind a mask of eccentricity. Uranus being in his fall in Leo, however, this eccentric component of Crowley's persona certainly fell short of its intention in many respects, even tending to create an impression of buffoonery and apparent, if not actual, fatuity at times. In a very pathetic twist of fate, Crowley was impelled to make a mockery of his heart-felt compassion in order to negotiate his survival in the world. This mechanism, of course, set up an immediate barrier in his interactions with others and engendered considerable misunderstanding with regard to his actual feelings and motivations. The strength and immediacy of the factors involved in this conundrum suggest that this was a major source of frustration that fueled the bitterness and rancor of Crowley's persona. There was no way around it. It was a price that he had to pay for his very existence in the world.

Knowing within himself, although imperfectly, the dynamics of his facade, he would quite naturally, and not always incorrectly, project the source of his frustration upon the limited understanding on the part of other people. Such projection could not be better facilitated than by his Saturn placement in Aquarius, *thus disposed by Uranus*, in his Seventh House of relationships. The exact degree aspects involving Sol, Uranus, and Saturn should be recalled in relation to these considerations. A planetary opposition always tends to generate consciousness, but when aligned with the Horizon, as are Uranus and Saturn in Crowley's birthchart, its consciousness-generating tendency is heightened to the extreme. It is a paradox of consciousness that, as a function of the subject-object relationship, the objective component is also subjective. For example, when you look at a lamp you are not *actually* seeing the lamp. Of course, for most practical purposes you *are* seeing the lamp. But the philosophical point to be acknowledged is that what you are actually *seeing* is a picture created in your brain based on a mixture of information derived from processed photon bombardment of your retinas and a complex accumulation of stored information commonly known as memory. Critics of philosophy are forever harping on the lack of relevance of such a picayune distinction as detracting from the immediacy and therefore the vitality of experience. Not so. This distinction rather serves properly to locate the immediacy and therefore the vitality of experience *within oneself.* The qualitative reality of external objects is not denied, but consciousness *of* them is better understood in terms of this philosophical observation. The *mystery* of the interaction between oneself and the world is thereby more accurately revealed. Ultimately, one learns to *take possession* of one's projections whereby one develops the ability to impart and withdraw them with increasing appropriateness.

Crowley's Uranus-Saturn opposition accounts for the *extreme acuity* of his projection of consciousness. Saturn is a stickler for detail, definition, and distinctness and therefore served as an excellent screen for conscious articulation of experience by virtue of its remarkable placement in Crowley's birthchart. This theme is essential to the understanding of Crowley's personality and his phenomenal abilities associated with his purported role as a prophet. Were we to liken the personality of Aleister Crowley to an incandescent light, illuminating a troubled world, then the Uranus-Saturn opposition across the Horizon of his birthchart would be analogous to the filament within it, converting the heat of his personality to a most brilliant light, penetrating deeply into the experience of human relations.

By virtue of Saturn disposing Crowley's natal Mars in Capricorn in his Sixth House, this phenomenal consciousness was able to *supervise* the implementation and application of *technique* toward the performance of tasks and the accomplishment of work. This relation contributes significantly to Crowley's remarkable proficiency for whatever he became interested in and put his mind to, from his ability to assess and negotiate rock formations on mountainsides (he was acknowledged by other climbers to be virtually super-human) to his analysis of the logical implications inherent in the arrangement of pieces on a chessboard. Saturn's disposing Mars is what carried Crowley from consciousness to action, from cognizance to performance, and this is where he distinguished himself from the usual lot of philosophers. As difficult as were the ideas with which he grappled, he could not be content merely to grasp the truth of them. He had to *demonstrate* the manner in which they *worked*, and that meant that he had to challenge and instigate. He had to provoke responses. He had to get into the thick of the difficulties he was trying to resolve. He had to stir up hypocrisy from within by manipulating illusions and deceits. The requirements of his destiny were such that the mere proclamation of the Word was insufficient. Like other great teachers and prophets before him, such as Socrates and Jesus, Aleister Crowley had to show the truth of his word by *living it* in the most revelatory manner possible.

By his rulership of Aries, Mars exerted a powerful influence over Crowley's Midheaven and North Node as referents for both his temporal *and* spiritual destinies respectively. His superior working technique was inherently oriented toward the fulfillment of his purpose for existing, his standing in the world community and his religious understanding. As will be shown in later chapters, Crowley was intuitively aware of this calling even in his childhood. He was ever driven to its fulfillment. But he would have to undergo an unrelenting process of maturation into ever more difficult and profound realizations of what this calling required of him and how he was to go about fulfilling it. There were pitfalls along the way. The process had to be carried through the entire sequence indicated by the dispositional succession outlined above. His compassion served as his fundamental motivation. His persona provided the necessary ego-strength at the expense of subverting and even perverting his true intent. His objectivity ignited consciousness of the critical issues involved. His masterful technique empowered him with the means for accomplishment and the perseverance to achieve.

He exhibited many faults, as those who knew him would testify abundantly, but he also had a calling, the pursuit of which was to drag him through the anguish of private torment and the gutter of public humiliation. The example to be taken from his life is that he fulfilled that calling to the best of his formidable ability, and that forces beyond his control were at his disposal to meet him half way, as it were, in the performance of what is referred to by occult tradition as the Great Work, into which he was drawn at an early age and to which he attended, with such devotion that even his few respites were but steps along the way, unto his dying day.

CHAPTER 8

NEPTUNE

In chapter 4, a special significance for Uranus was addressed in terms of its status as a *discovered* planet, beyond the orbit of Saturn and invisible to the naked eye. The subsequent discoveries of Neptune and Pluto have expanded the number of known trans-Saturnian planets, all of which share in that special significance. As the three major discovered planets now accessible to collective consciousness only through the medium of modern scientific methods and technology, Uranus, Neptune and Pluto may all be considered harbingers of the modern and postmodern world-views, as distinguished from the age-old cosmological conception based upon the immediately visible solar-planetary system as such. Although I am in full agreement with the general consensus among astrologers regarding Uranus' rulership of Aquarius, the interpretations of Neptune and Pluto and their rulership assignments developed in this book differ from the general consensus currently found in most books and magazines on astrology. It may seem to most readers that the rulership assignments for the trans-Saturnian planets were immediately obvious and are firmly settled, however alternative perspectives on these matters have been advanced by astrologers. Such perspectives underscore the *empirical* approach that must be taken toward astrological theory. Judgments are prone to modification and subject to a variety of approaches. The incorporation of trans-Saturnian planets into the general body of astrological theory may yet be considered to be in its formative stages when compared to the millennia-old tradition to which it is being appended.

The hypothesis that the trans-Saturnian planets displace traditional rulership assignments implies that their discoveries constitute potential expansions of consciousness pertaining to the signs they are determined to rule, involving *transformations* of the meanings of those signs. The disruptive effect of such displacement upon the cogency of the traditional system of astrology cannot be denied; but then how better to characterize the historical developments of the past two hundred-plus years? Given the circumstances of today's world, it is obvious that transformations of unprecedented dimensions are underway. Such transforming power of the trans-Saturnian planets, or more specifically the phenomena associated with our consciousness of them, is very aptly characterized by Dane Rudhyar's reference to them as "ambassadors of the galaxy." The astronomical discovery that we are living in a galaxy has brought a radically new perspective to our understanding of our place in the cosmos. The vastness of interstellar and *inter-galactic* space is mind-boggling to our inherited sense of cosmic proportion. In addition to the sheer expansion of our cosmological conception, the knowledge of galaxies interposes a hitherto unsuspected *level of wholeness* within which we live and have our being. We may now envision our solar system as a functioning part of a much greater whole system that has a characteristic shape and appearance similar to a glistening, rose-centered pinwheel, and that furthermore has always been present to the out-reaching eyes of humankind as the softly illumined band stretching across the night sky that has long been called the Milky Way.

Rudhyar's characterization of the trans-Saturnians is significant in many ways. Primarily, it underscores their significance as agents of transition toward human consciousness of participation within the more encompassing galactic frame of reference. It is appropriate to our concept of civilized behavior that, if one body politic intends to establish relations with another, it initiates that process by first sending representatives to facilitate the encounter in the most amicable manner possible, even if the implications of the eventual interaction are certain to be perceived as a threat to the sovereignty of the host. No more appropriate anthropomorphic metaphor could be suggested for the expansion of human consciousness accompanying the discoveries of Uranus, Neptune and Pluto, followed immediately by Edwin Hubble's mapping of the galactic universe as we currently know it.

This theme of participation in the galactic level of wholeness is fundamental to the transformation of humankind that we associate with our transition into a new age. To shift from a primarily solar to a galactic perspective implies the incorporation of a *pluralistic* world-view. So long as our cosmic conception was overshadowed by the relative dominance of Sol, his stature was such as to virtually compel a *monistic* world-view. He was in fact the phenomenal image that supported the overwhelming dominance of monistic cultural orientations including monolatry, monarchy, monotheism, monasticism, monogamy, and other monotypical and monolithic—that is, authoritarian—patterns of social organization. Ironically, there was a twofold accentuation that resulted from the monistic orientation that generated an essential paradox for the Piscean Age. That twofold accentuation was the coexisting emphases on the unity of *both* the collective *and* the individual perspectives on human existence. Ultimately the co-development of these themes has culminated in the ideal of a universal democracy for which the galaxy serves as a most appropriate symbolic image. Since we always have been living in a galaxy, our physical discovery of this fact only serves to confirm the reality of a hitherto latent or potential comprehension of human nature that brings a fulfilling perspective to the otherwise contradictory and seemingly unworkable proscriptions of historical religions. The strategic evolutionary function of our global religious heritage may now be understood to have been designed to bring humankind to its present *material* realization *as well as* an inherently spiritual perspective upon that material realization.

A similar approach to the manner in which Uranus contributed to the modern transition may be applied to the meanings of Neptune and Pluto. Naturally, the ideas associated with these planets are effected and conditioned by the tendency to find "homes" for them among the zodiacal signs. It is not surprising that an affinity would have been conceived to obtain between the ethereal and mystical connotations of Pisces and the distant and nebulous image initially attributed to Neptune immediately following its discovery in 1846. The romantic notions of the sea associated with Neptune were, at that time, strongly suggestive of the unknown and transcendent realm of spirit appropriate to the concerns of the twelfth and final sign of the zodiac. The subsequent discovery of Pluto in 1930 understandably led to its association with reactionary feelings toward the Scorpionic current of human experience. The dark and foreboding shadows following upon the anti-sexual psychological orientation of the Piscean Age were profoundly disturbed by the economic, political, and scientific developments of that time of fear and insecurity. Both of these associations have tended to stick in the popular astrological literature. However, a good case can be argued for a reversal of those rulership assignments. Such a reversal may ultimately serve to purge a great encumbrance from the system as now popularly conceived and revitalize our understanding of the transformative impulses at work in postmodern world culture as we continue to forge our way into the future.

Neptune has come to be associated with mystery and subtlety. It is often said that Neptune tends to blur distinctions and veil its own activity, working through processes of indirection and subterfuge. The concerns of Neptune are considered distant, ethereal, and far removed from the hard facts of mundane reality. In accordance with this general conception, Neptune has come to be associated with the function of withdrawal from worldly existence as would be appropriate for departure from life as we know it and, therefore, as a referent for transcendence in accordance with the historical notion of the incompatibility of matter and spirit. This theme of "transcendence" has been considered appropriate for the rulership of a somewhat romanticized notion of Pisces. Consequently, we often find both Neptune and Pisces characterized by such terms as "escapist" and "mystical," implying a sort of wishfulness and little or no capacity for practical application or grounding. My observations do not accord with such characterizations but rather lead me to conclude that they persist as a result of a great deal of residual blockage toward the emergence of Neptune's *actual* function. That blockage is due to the deeply ingrained resistance to the full and unencumbered experience of human sexuality, which I believe is the true focus of the significance of Neptune. The prevailing characterizations outlined above may well reflect the attempt to *push away* and *sublimate* the disclosure of the powerful force of human sexuality that Neptune embodies and potentially reveals to human consciousness. The transformative implications to earthly existence in terms of psychological processes and social interactions have simply been too much as yet for modern civilization fully to assimilate and actualize, although significant changes are already underway.

Several historical developments suggest a demonstrable although subtle nexus of meaning that characterizes the significance of Neptune as reflected in the *zeitgeist* surrounding its discovery. In the realm of political economics, the Uranian capitalist industrial revolution had already proven to be less than a panacea for the social ills of humankind, and a strong counter-current of economic philosophy championing the working class had emerged. This economic philosophy was codified in the publication of *The Communist Manifesto* by Marx and Engels in 1848, just two years after Neptune's discovery. The rocky history of the communist movement and the ultimate failure of the Leninist regime should not be interpreted to discredit the holistic and humanitarian vision of a global community that is properly associated with the Neptunian cultural ideal. The lesson to be taken at this time is that Neptune serves as an ideal *compliment* to Uranus in that Neptune defines the practical limit upon the potential deployment of the Uranian ideal, comparable to the manner by which Saturn defines the limit upon Jupiterian expansion. Neither nationalism nor individualism are absolute in the political sense, and the extension of personal power through the monopolization of private resources actually thwarts the concomitant benefits that accrue within a political and economic environment of truly free enterprise. The manner by which Neptune imposes its limiting influence upon Uranian excesses, however, remains largely misunderstood due to the yet prevailing inability consciously to assimilate the full potency and subtlety of Neptune's influence, despite the visibility of its budding operation in the realms of politics, fashion, and entertainment.

Another operative component of meaning associated with Neptune, the second thermodynamic law of entropy, was introduced in chapter 7. The difficulty for modern civilization to acknowledge the significance of entropy to economic development reiterates the overall theme of resistance to the understanding of Neptunian principles. Although the term "entropy" was first coined in 1868 by the German physicist, Rudolf Clausius, the principle had been recognized some 41 years earlier in relation to the transference of heat in the operation of the steam engine. [Rifkin, p. 35] Neptune was therefore discovered during the fermenting of the understanding of entropy in modern scientific terms. One of the common astrological correspondences that is attributed to Neptune is that of *corrosive acids*. This association emphasizes the dissipative function that finds its ultimate expression in the pervasive process of universal entropy. The entropic theme also reiterates the complementary relation of Neptune to Uranus in that Neptune focuses concern for the environment and the biosphere that has been so easily disregarded by Uranian emphasis on industrial development and the exploitation of natural resources for economic purposes.

Another major historical development fermenting at the time of Neptune's discovery was the formulation of a theory of biological evolution, although Charles Darwin's landmark publication, *The Origin of Species*, would not appear for another 13 years. There is an interesting parallel in this regard between the ideas of entropy and evolution. Both emerged within the body of accepted science amidst a great deal of ambiguity as to their actual implications (although the already well established Uranian ideal was able quickly to seize upon the "survival of the fittest" concept as a rationale for the political philosophy of rugged individualism). Both entropy and evolution are assumed generally to be true, but many of the implications arising out of their operation are disputed. It is as if some strange and elusive factors are involved in these processes that science is unable to capture with its analytic methodology.

Interestingly, both the ideas of entropy and evolution were inherent in the philosophical perspectives of antiquity. It remained for modern science to *rediscover* them within its own context of scientific analysis while continuing to proclaim the intellectual inferiority of "pre-scientific" antiquity. Yet the general consensus of modern thought continues to aspire to the notion that we will somehow find a way to beat entropy and salvage our economy and environment from its ravenous flow. And, despite the debunking of the Lamarckian theory of the inheritance of physically acquired characteristics (which does *not* preclude genetic memory), the strict Darwinian theory of progressive accumulation of random micro-mutations remains inadequate to account for all observed phenomena. For example, the survival value of intermediate stages in the evolutionary development of the eye cannot be explained in strictly Darwinian terms, despite Herculean efforts to resolve this acknowledged difficulty. Furthermore, there is the major problem of accounting for the origin and *purposefulness* of life itself (teleology) in its struggle against the dissipative tendency of all energetic processes.

There was yet another important historical development that accompanied the discovery of Neptune which serves to characterize the nexus of meaning that may be attributed to this subtle and mysterious yet powerful planet, and that was the development of the process of photography. Although the first photograph (requiring an exposure time of eight hours) was produced in 1827, a camera that operates fundamentally in the manner that we are familiar with today was not introduced until 1841. This camera initiated the kind of "picture taking" that yet serves as the mainstay of family albums and modern paper and electronic journalism.

A fairly comprehensive perspective upon Neptune's influence may be ascertained by conceptually synthesizing the themes of biological evolution, entropy, political collectivism, and photography into a nexus of meaning that may ultimately be subsumed within the more focused and personally relevant context of human sexuality, properly associated with Scorpio. This perspective supports the hypothesis proposed above that Neptune may be most appropriately recognized as the new ruler of that sign, displacing Mars in the traditional scheme. These four themes may appear at first to be more or less varied and unrelated, but by finding the thread of meaning that weaves its way through them a perspective emerges that, although foreign to the cultural patterns of Western civilization as fostered by the beliefs inherited from Piscean Age religious traditions, yet helps to elucidate the inherent *telos* of those traditions that clarifies a growing trend in today's world. No less radical a reorganization of ideas is to be expected from the incorporation of an agency as significant as a major trans-Saturnian planet.

Of those four themes, the one most directly connoting the sexual focus of Neptune is biological evolution. As stated above, *life* is most significantly characterized by *purposefulness*, and the most powerful sense of purpose in life is associated with the reproductive function and experienced by humans, *physically and psychologically*, as sexual stimulation. The full significance of this fact is not so obvious in terms of the prevailing theoretical approach to biological evolution, due to the emphasis placed upon the other end of the matter by the politically dominant scientific orientation which remains preoccupied with factors required for the survival of organisms *after* they have come into existence as opposed to those factors responsible for bringing them into existence in the first place. It is largely assumed that the reproductive function is thoroughly promiscuous and determined by contests of masculine superiority. The possibility of *selectively intelligent attraction* of spermatozoa, although impossible totally to ignore, is nevertheless much less susceptible to theoretical analysis than the observation of what happens to determine the existential fate of the resulting organisms.

Stated differently, and with particular focus upon our own species, there is no way that science can get into the analysis of the magic of human love. No matter how much can be determined about anatomical features, hormonal levels, and glandular secretions, or analyzed in terms of demographics and various social and familial arrangements, the essence of the *subjective experience* of sexual attraction as a component of human love remains ever a mystery and considerably more extended in its scope of molding and shaping patterns of life than mere survival in brutal environmental conditions. And yet, nothing could be more fundamental to the process of biological evolution from which humankind has emerged, and nothing could be more fraught with the essence of *telos*, that is, purposefulness. Yet the bastion of modern science continues to deny that the evolutionary process is teleological. The dominant school of biology proceeds, *ad infinitum*, to analyze life within the absurd context of *presumed accidental* evolution. Sexual attraction is considered to be a kind of *trick* that nature plays upon herself to facilitate reproduction, having no more profound significance. It is on this fundamental point that philosophy must part company with science (as it is currently constituted) and defend itself against science's denunciation of the deeper philosophical concerns of human existence as being non-scientific, pre-scientific, and pseudo-scientific (not to mention traditional science's attempt to preempt philosophy altogether). Science has divorced itself from passion and purpose, and not without benefit to humanity, but it must not be allowed to go unchecked in its claim to superior knowledge and perspective as a result of that sterilization, *nor in its denial of an encompassing purposefulness for life*. The limited perspective of traditional science, valuable though it is as an instrument of analysis, must be exposed as a false claimant to the status of arbiter of human values. Traditional science must not be allowed to continue to disenfranchise an entire realm of human endeavor, the very pursuit of meaning itself appropriate to the concerns of religion and magic, simply because this more exalted realm does not comply with the short-sighted restrictions that would reduce meaning to the cage of a physically measurable determinism. It is claimed that the methods of traditional science are the only legitimate means for the pursuit and acquisition of true knowledge. This is the great defect of modern science, and the perpetuation of that defect is one of the major characteristics of modern world culture.

That point having been made, the case for the prosecution must also be stated. The acknowledgment of the legitimacy of the methods of religion and magic *in general terms* in no way constitutes an endorsement of any and all claims for religious and magical efficacy. One continuous theme of this book is the evaluation of what constitutes such efficacy. Matters pertaining to religion and magic stretch the potential for human understanding to its conceptual limits and venture into psychological uncertainties and paradoxical mysteries that are nonetheless vital and essential. *There is no final word on these matters*. We are driven, however, to pursue them, and such pursuit is deemed productive of real value, perhaps the greatest of all values for our lives as human beings. These kinds of philosophical investigations must be afforded their proper respect or we will only

continue to "progress" further along the road toward cultural disintegration upon which the world is currently traveling.

It is not surprising that the official scientific approach to the study
of biological evolution has taken the course cited above, due to the
fact that the tradition of science is an outgrowth of Christian civilization. Although modern science was developed as a conscious rebellion against Christian dogma, that rebellion was for the most part
confined to the realm of methodological theory versus theological
cosmology. The fundamental Judeo-Christian attitude toward sexual
morality was not directly challenged by modern science. In fact, the
emergent view of humanity as being involved in such a brutal process was largely perceived to confirm the need for the compensatory
restraints of sexual inhibition imposed by traditional religion. In
chapter 7, the point was made that the most important aspect of religion is *not* its cosmological conception but rather its application
toward day-to-day personal experience. Indeed, a very hard war was
fought over cosmological conceptions, but the real bread and butter
of the Judeo-Christian religious tradition, namely *enforced lifelong
heterosexual monogamy* as the fundamental rule of personal sexual
behavior and the primary bulwark against paganism, was never
threatened. Protestantism emerged as the new enforcer and was in
fact more fervent about the prime directive than Catholicism had
been. Cerebral types were allowed to think of themselves as being
"enlightened" as they marched side by side with the sex police. This
also accounts for the slight lag in the emergence of the official canon
of the scientific study of evolution, Darwin's *The Origin of Species*,
some thirteen years after the discovery of Neptune. Some rigorous
sorting of doctrinal priorities had to be worked out.

A great deal of antagonism persists between the evolutionist and
creationist camps, however the *real* debate over the matter has always surpassed the conventional characterizations of those two positions. The more viable philosophical perspectives, such as those of
Henri Bergson, have been largely dismissed by both simplistic
extremes, each of which lays claim to a particular kind of certitude
that denies the mystery of life in favor of scientific "fact" or revealed
"truth." The rhetoric of positivism, whether it be scientific or religious, has thus far proven superior in its ability to capture and hold
public interest and opinion. Ironically, these historically antagonistic
claims of science and religion, as classically epitomized within the
social context of modern Protestantism, are able to coexist and even
compliment one another because they are falsely conceived to

address two distinct realms. This conundrum actually reinforces the antagonistic spirit-matter dualism that has characterized the Piscean Age. Of course, the religious side of the issue gets bumped up to the status of metaphor, leaving the fundamentalists in the lurch, but the theological import of the sexual morality issue, the actual crux of the matter, is allowed to remain intact. Sexual desire may continue to be held in low esteem, necessary for reproduction and permissible as a precursor to marriage, but otherwise nasty and troublesome and most certainly *not* the very fiery essence of divinity itself.

The belief that sexual desire *is* the very root of humankind's capacity for the realization of its inherent divine nature is characteristic of the *vitalistic* orientation to life that is denied by *both* traditional science *and* traditional religion. It is precisely that philosophical and empirical orientation that lay at the heart of the ancient vitalistic wisdom from which all civilization has proceeded. The big question of the ages is why the detour into the patriarchal restriction of sexual morality was ever taken. Those who yet subscribe to the patriarchal tradition consider *it* to be the civilizing force of humanity and think of its ancient forebears as a less civilized form of humanity.

A fully developed rationale for the historical course of spiritual evolution as we may currently assess it from our contemporary perspective is developed in the concluding chapters of this book. The matter germane to this chapter is that, from an astrological perspective, the planet Neptune serves as a referent for the determining principle of *creative biological evolution* in terms comparable to the vitalistic understanding of the ancients with regard to the powerful *libidinal force* of human experience. In this regard, Neptune's association with the sea may be better understood in terms of the oceanic source of biological evolution, a Scorpionic theme, rather than the Piscean theme of the sea as an image of spiritual transcendence. Furthermore, Neptune represents the expansion of the Uranian ideal of individual sovereignty to a yet greater level of wholeness, encompassing not only the democratic ideal of social organization but extending as well to the sexual ethics and standards of society. As the Uranian ideal surpasses the authoritarian King in the realm of government, so the Neptunian ideal surpasses the authoritarian God in the realm of sexual morality.

Entropy is relevant to sexuality in that the heightened sensitivity to life that characterizes the profound experience of the sacrament of sex brings one to the realization of the consuming conflagration that is the very process of life and its ultimate culmination in death. This understanding reinforces the biological association of Neptune with Scorpio. The intuitive realizations associated with the *knowledge* of entropy that comes from a deep rapport with natural existence engenders a profound reverence for life and the *price* that is extracted for the privilege of living. In this regard one of the great mysteries of life is inherent in the realization that only through a complete willingness to *die* can the full promise of *love* be fulfilled. Such death is the absolute relinquishment of identification with existence, a complete "letting go" of the ego-persona. This perspective is brought to bear not only by the specter of biological death but is *inherent* in the experience of life as well. Love is ever elusive, beckoning unto the beyond. If entropy is the arrow of time then love is the harbinger of eternity. As such, like the rainbow, its beauty may be experienced but its actuality is ever beyond the grasp of any delimiting definition or conception that would harness or confine its essence to the entropic regime. It is free to come and go as it will, and the profundity with which it becomes manifest, endures, and then withdraws is proof of its eternal source. Such proof, however, is utterly *subjective*. When experienced, its intensity is as devastating as its departure from the degenerative world is inevitable, but the consciousness that survives it is *transformed* by the revelation of meaning and purpose. This idea is expressed most eloquently by Aleister Crowley in Part II of *A Sandal*, entitled "Of Love."

> Now in this method are many roads and ways, some simple and direct, some hidden and mysterious, even as it is with human love whereof no man hath made so much as the first sketches for a Map: for Love is infinite in diversity even as are the Stars. For this cause do I leave Love himself master in the heart of every one of you: for he shall teach you rightly if you but serve him with diligence and devotion even to abandonment. [*Gems From The Equinox,* p. 122]

Crowley's words suggest a paradox, and it is not surprising that traditional science would have a difficult time working such a perspective into its framework of analysis. Ironically, the death aspect of life is suggestive of rebirth, both in the natural sense of spring following winter and in the supernatural sense of the soul surviving the death of the body. But this suggestiveness in no way circumvents the actuality of the death experience. Even the promise of a hereafter must be *released* before it may, or may not, be realized. Perhaps it is all no more than a cruel joke. But the ennobling characteristics of sentient nature bespeak otherwise. Also in *A Sandal*, Part I entitled

"Of Liberty," we find expressed in evolutionary terms this sense of transcendent purposefulness:

> O man! behold thyself! With what pains wast thou fashioned! What ages have gone to thy shaping! The history of the planet is woven into the very substance of thy brain! Was all this for naught? Is there no purpose in thee? Wast thou made thus that thou shouldst eat, and breed, and die? Think it not so! Thou dost incorporate so many elements, thou art the fruit of so many aeons of labour, thou art fashioned thus as thou art, and not otherwise, for some colossal End. [*ibid.,* p. 119]

These expressions may be experienced psychologically to *unify* the conceptual realms of spirit and matter so as to incorporate both creation and evolution in a manner inaccessible to the orthodox approaches of both religion and science.

In relation to political collectivism, it is generally acknowledged that the proponents of communism have been motivated by a sense of compassion for their fellow humans, particularly the common man, the worker, the artist, the soldier, and all who are not necessarily favored by the capitalist profit motive, trickledown notwithstanding. The fact of communism's failure as a political ideology is a testament to the profound wisdom inherent in the distinction made by Jesus in his famous utterance, "Render...unto Caesar the things which are Caesar's; and unto God the things that are God's." [Matthew 22:21] Neptune engenders a powerful sense of the interdependency of all living beings and the dignity of the humblest among the multitudes. Neptune fosters the perception of profound beauty in the common peasant girl and indomitable courage in the simple farmer. Neptune harbors the understanding that, while the politicos enjoy the greater share of glory, the foot soldiers provide the greater share of real accomplishment. It is not surprising that the initial impulse of Neptune's discovery would spawn a naive attempt to legislate morality.

Following upon the initial abuses of capitalism and the miserable failure of communism, the prospect of a world civilization governed by a balanced perspective toward Uranian and Neptunian principles is becoming more and more plausible. The two party system that has evolved within the context of American politics, with its Uranian Republicans and Neptunian Democrats, suggests the potential for such a dynamic interaction. The Neptunian ideal of political collectivism is rooted in the global unity of humankind within the interactive biosphere of Earth. The guiding principles associated with this perspective emphasize the ideal of interdependence and inclusiveness as opposed to exclusivistic competitive struggle. Their appeal is to the heart, but are in no way antagonistic to the mind. A democratic society cannot prevail for extended periods of time without attending to its organic wholeness, its sense of *community*.

There is a very important lesson to be learned, however, from the failure of communism as a system of government. That is that *government is not an efficacious instrument for the implementation of Neptunian ideals*. What cannot be accomplished for the public domain through the Uranian principle of private enterprise must rather be addressed and administered through the *Saturnian* principle of public edict. Such administration must be *clearly defined* and *severely limited*, unlike historical communist governments. Neptunian principles are far too complex and subtle to lend themselves to any kind of *enforced* public policies. The problem thus far with governmental administration has been its tendency to *restrict* and in fact *deny* the free and full expression of Neptunian ideals within the community that it is supposed to serve. Such restriction continues to carry over from the Piscean Age tradition of sexual "morality" imposed by authoritarian standards of religion, with the cooperation of civil governments, which are nothing other than projections of the personal inability properly to control sexual impulses on the parts of individuals. There is yet an enormous amount of social difficulty for the liberation of sexual mores in today's world, but the obvious trend is toward the eventual recognition of *absolute personal freedom* in the exercise of sexual expression and behavior. Such is the necessary social context for the realization of the Neptunian ideal for humanity. That ideal, which is fundamentally *cultural*, has become politicized as a result of political incursions. Such incursions were inevitable and even necessary from an evolutionary standpoint, but humankind is in the process of shedding those old shackles of restraint. Overt sexuality is assuming its rightful place as the center of culture.

From these considerations it can readily be seen that the principles of biological evolution, entropy, and political collectivism that emerged synchronously with the discovery of Neptune in 1846 share in a common nexus of meaning that suggests a subtle yet profound focus of perspective within the modern and postmodern context of evolving humanity. The advent of photography holds a special place in that nexus of meaning due to its status as a phenomenon of hard technology. Photography is not an ideology or a scientific concept. It is a fully productive physical process that subsumes the entire Neptunian conception. The camera is for Neptune what the steam engine is for Uranus, that is, the prototypal technology of the planetary archetype.

The morphological correspondence of the process of photography to sexual reproduction is obvious. The camera as a splendid metaphor for the womb is hardly in need of elucidation. Particles of light enter through the temporary opening of the shutter and commingle with the sensitive film within to recreate an image taken from the outer world. In terms of the ideas developed in chapter 6, such a correspondence implies a strong symbolic affinity between Luna and Neptune. This affinity is accounted for by the assignment of Neptune as the ruler of a Water sign. Signs of like element always participate in trine (120°) aspect relations to one another, which indicates harmoniously related interactions among them that resolve tensions of consciousness. In the case of Luna's rulership of the solstitial sign Cancer as the first Water sign, the symbolic emphasis is on the *containment* aspect of the womb's function as pertaining to the entire matrix of material existence. The conception of Neptune as the new ruler of Scorpio, as shown by its association with the process of photography, focuses the symbolic emphasis upon the *reproductive* and *transformative* aspects of the womb's function. Whereas Cancer is associated with breasts as sources of nourishment for infants, Scorpio is associated with genitalia as organs of sexual intercourse.

In chapter 7, it was observed that the redness of the planet Mars corresponds to the blood that is shed in warfare. That association is most directly appropriate to Mars' rulership of Aries. The blood that is associated with Scorpio, however, which was also ruled by "the red planet" in the traditional system of astrology, is the blood of menstruation which is purported to possess sacred properties by the Tantric tradition of vitalistic religion. Astrology incorporates a representation of the Tantric mysteries into the symbolic associations for Scorpio in terms of the amalgamation of three images: the scorpion, the serpent, and the eagle or phoenix. This threefold image is suggestive of the transformative process associated with the Tantric mysteries. The scorpion represents the self-destructive tendencies of unregenerate sexuality. The serpent represents the process of coming to terms with one's sexuality, and, more specifically, of incorporating sexual energy into neural functioning which requires a major purging of psychological perspective. The eagle or phoenix represents the exalted and illuminated state of consciousness that culminates the transformative process initiated by the serpent. The eagle is known for the height of its flight and the acuity of its *vision*, and the organ of vision is the eye, which also figures prominently in the symbolism of the mystery cults. The eye is in effect the *camera* of the nervous system and, as such, bears a morphological correspondence to the womb. The womb and the eye are connected by the spinal column which has a morphological correspondence to the serpent and is in fact the *channel* through which the ascending *kundalini*, or serpent power, travels in the course of its awakening of the initiate to the greater mysteries of life; the fruit as it were of the Tree of Knowledge.

From these associations, the significance of the invention of the camera with regard to the deeper symbolic meaning of human sexuality becomes all the more apparent. The womb, the eye, and the camera are all instruments for the creation and reproduction of images, that is, for the process of *imagization*. (This coined word is perhaps best pronounced 'image-ization', but to pronounce it 'i-mag-i-ZAY-tion' would not be amiss in accentuating its association with 'imagination.') The camera brings to humankind the ability to control and direct that process in a profoundly powerful and creative manner for *consciousness through time*, a further transcendence of Saturnian limitation—Saturn (Chronos in the Greek cosmology) being the planet of time. Through the subsequent development of moving pictures it has become possible to create and preserve images of *processes* that engender the experience of deep catharsis that may be shared by large numbers of people within a given cultural context. The whole phenomenon of cinema has generated a *culture of charisma* that exemplifies the Neptunian ideal of transformation through the process of imagization. Such cultural power, and the ubiquitous availability of the transmission of cultural knowledge made possible thereby, characterizes the Neptunian enhancement of the scope of Scorpionic meaning for the modern world. The movie theater puts us *inside* the womb of creative imagization.

The associations of Neptune to both biology and photography can be very instructive with regard to our more complete understanding of the former. The prevailing conception of evolution *denies* the role of the Eternal Feminine and her power to create new forms of life through purposeful and preformative direction. From these observations we may conclude that, although very significant and meaningful changes have occurred within the evolution of civilization in recent centuries, we have yet fully to divest ourselves collectively of certain residual social attitudes that characterized our patriarchal heritage of the past 2,000-plus years. It follows that we are yet experiencing even *more fundamental changes* that will continue to characterize our transition into the new age. An extremely powerful indication of the nature of these changes may be ascertained from a more studied consideration of the significance of Neptune's association with the process of photography as a guiding metaphor to assist us in our understanding of the evolutionary process.

What the camera has made possible for humankind is the *selective reproduction of light images*. The *picture* that results from photography is much less determined by a contest among the photons that are allowed to enter the camera than by the manner in which they coalesce, the way the camera is handled, and the direction toward which it is aimed at the time of its opening, which implies forward vision and prefigurative formation. In terms of a symbolic correspondence to the process of sexual reproduction, or rather, *recreation*, photography emphasizes the *feminine* role in the evolutionary process, the role of selective creativity as opposed to environmental conquest. The discovery of Neptune has heralded a wholly new perspective upon the social standards of sexual behavior, one that emphasizes the beauty and power of the feminine role in determining cultural patterns of community. The Neptunian ideal of an eros-centered flowering of culture, however, remains severely inhibited in its early stages of development. There is a complex irony involved in the facts that the camera is very similar in structure and function to the eye, the organ of *vision*, and that the Darwinian theory of evolution is unable adequately to account for the evolution *of* the eye.

Perhaps the most relevant point with regard to the discoveries of Neptune and the other trans-Saturnian planets is that the social trends for which they serve as "ambassadors" have become *irrepressible* in their progressive advancement within the global consciousness of humanity. Certainly these trends are developing amidst resistance from habits and fears of residual belief systems and patterns of behavior. By now, however, it is evident that these trends will continue to develop and supplant the remaining encrustations of the dying aeon. One might even behold that these new developments are in fact *the very culmination and fulfillment* of the religious formula prophesied at the inception of the Piscean Age.

CHAPTER 9

PLUTO

During the 84 year interim between the discoveries of Neptune and Pluto, Neptune was the outermost known planet in the solar system, the most "far out" as it were. As such, and for reasons presented in chapter 8, it is understandable that Neptune was considered to be the appropriate new ruler of Pisces, displacing Jupiter in the traditional system. The prestige of science was well established by the time of Neptune's discovery, and the ideal of transcendence was in dire need of revitalization. The intuitive realization of transcendence associated with Pisces had been sufficient in and of itself, prior to the development of modern science, to accommodate the inherent need for a transcendental perspective as a component of human nature. The development of materialistic science, however, had undermined that intuitive realization, and its successes, as opposed to religious dogma, had brought the authority of religious claims into question. The authoritarian approach to securing a doctrine of transcendence, characterized by Jupiter's rulership of Pisces (Jupiter being *within* the orbit of Saturn), had been fundamentally debunked. Official sanction having been weakened, the strongest remaining testament to the transcendence of materiality and death, was life itself. Science could explain the working of machines but was unable to explain the miracle of life and the spontaneity and unruliness of the *experience* of life. And so, Romanticism was confirmed by the discovery of Neptune.

Despite scientists' attempts to preempt the transcendental implications of biology, Neptune, through its association with Pisces in the evolving tradition of astrology, helped to forge the greater dissemination of previously heretical religious perspectives that were able to fill the gap opened by the schism between science and established religious doctrines. In this regard, Neptune's stand-in duty as *acting* ruler of Pisces was indeed fortuitous. It provided an inroad for the greater proliferation of spiritual knowledge among an increasingly inquisitive public without overtly tipping off the import of that knowledge in terms of its sexual component as implicit in the association of Neptune with Scorpio. Neptune more than lived up to its reputation for subterfuge in this regard. A very powerful movement of sublimated spiritualism *(ectoplasmania)* developed accordingly as an alternative to more orthodox forms of religious doctrine and practice. It was natural to assume, after Uranus' displacement of the traditional ruler of the largely political Aquarius, associated with the coming new age, that a new planetary rulership was also appropriate for the transcendental Pisces associated with the passing age. Although that new perspective would come to be better exemplified by Pluto following its discovery in 1930, the conception of Neptune in that role had a cushioning effect for the phasing in of new formulations of transcendental imagery.

A progressive development of the theme of wombness characterizes the succession of the three Water signs. Cancer focuses the personal experience of *containment within* the material world. Scorpio actualizes the potential for *transformation within* the material world. And Pisces, as the final sign of the zodiac, suggests the potential for *transcendence of* the material world and the projection of consciousness into the ultimate *womb of the eternal*. The anatomical correspondence for Cancer is the nourishing breasts and for Scorpio the creative and transformative genitalia. This symbolic theme is completed by the anatomical correspondence for Pisces being the feet, suggesting the ability to *ambulate* through the cosmos by virtue of a mobilized grounding upon the reconciliation of opposites, that is, the fully deployed dynamic fusion of matter and spirit. Neptune's association with Pisces in most of today's astrological literature reflects the continuance of the spiritualistic movement that aspires to transcendence *without* consciously and overtly accepting the need for transformation through sexual actualization. As such, that rulership arrangement has helped to facilitate the transition from the anti-sexual orientation of traditional Piscean religion to the sex affirming perspective of the New Aeon by fostering the proliferation of transformative concepts and symbols inherited from ancient vitalistic knowledge *in sublimated form*.

Another major step of that transition was taken around the time of Pluto's discovery when the major breakthroughs in nuclear physics generated the theory of quantum mechanics. Not only the time of its discovery but the morphological fact that Pluto is a very small planet beyond the four gas giants is symbolically appropriate to its atomic and subatomic associations. Pluto's rulership assignment presented a problem, however, because the rulership of Pisces, the last and most transcendental sign of the zodiac, had already been displaced in the minds of astrologers by Neptune. There was naturally some resistance to the idea of bumping Neptune back to another sign, especially due to the cherished idealizations that had accumulated around Neptune's association with Pisces. The simple solution was to assign Pluto to the strongly cathartic Scorpio. This attribution, after all, tended to confirm the traditional association of sex with hell, Pluto being an equivalent of the Greek Hades. As such, however, this association further elucidates the naiveté of our puritanical heritage. Our civilization is yet deeply involved in a profoundly traumatic state of imbalance toward associated connotations of sex, violence (anger), degradation and death, and it appears that this is a necessary *purging phase* of our transition into the New Aeon.

The explosive power of Pluto that, in its destructive mode, tears at the very fabric of life is an understandable image for uncontrolled outbursts of long repressed sexuality. Such outbursts have traditionally been associated with the atrocities of war, the negative by-product of the expansion of civilization through conquest. With the development of nuclear weaponry, however, the spirit of warfare as practiced for millennia has been rendered obsolete. The killing function can no longer be limited by the "warrior class." Surely such a ruinous potential has thus far served as the primary deterrent to global annihilation, but it cannot be denied that a fundamental change in human nature must be affected to *relieve the tension* that has historically been discharged through outbursts of mutual destruction if we are to survive as a species. Clearly, the time has come for us to take heed of the admonition that has been made for us to love one another.

The harmful potential of nuclear physics, however, is *not* what is most significant about this newly discovered field of knowledge that emerged at the time of Pluto's discovery. It is rather due to the tendency of humankind to apply new discoveries to not-so-new preoccupations that most people's notion of the significance of nuclear physics is limited to bombs, power plants, and fallout. What is much more important about the development of nuclear physics is the radically new perspective that it brings to bear upon our conception of reality itself. With the formulation and application of the theory of quantum mechanics, the *concept* of physical substance as it was previously thought to exist has in effect been destroyed. Physics, the hardest of the hard sciences, the very bastion of anti-mystical sentiment, has actually developed the means of discovering a most strange and enigmatic conception of reality, with more transcendental and multi-dimensional implications than any other field of knowledge. In this regard the rulership potential of Pluto is obviously much more in accord with the *Mutable* sign Pisces than with the *Fixed* sign Scorpio. Furthermore, by the time of Pluto's discovery in 1930, Neptune's association with the culturally transformative significance of the *fixing* of images through photography, and particularly cinematography, bringing a new and powerfully realistic and creative dimension to the natural process of *imagization*, was sufficiently evident to establish its propriety as the new ruler of Scorpio. Despite these obvious associations, however, it is usually the case that traditions, even short lived ones, tend to die hard.

Right through the nineteenth century the science of physics remained the bedrock of common sense materialistic logic. It consistently furthered the basic belief that all observable phenomena could be boiled down to strictly determined and predictable material processes. The universe was securely thought to be made out of a complex arrangement of extremely tiny billiard ball-like particles and energy waves that behaved in accordance with simple cause and effect relations. The long and impressive chain of the successes of classical physics had dispelled many of the "childish superstitions" of bygone ages and had all but conquered the sense of the mysterious among the "enlightened" intelligentsia. Ultimately, it was believed, there was nothing mysterious about the physical world apart from our lack of obtainable knowledge. Whatever *seemed* to be mysterious was thought to appear so only because science had yet to elucidate its working. It was taken for granted that the steady progress of physics was well on its way toward, and swiftly closing in on, the goal of clarifying all apparent mysteries of the physical universe.

With the turn of the century, however, physics took a turn into a new direction. In 1900, the German physicist Max Planck announced that energy was emitted from bodies in discreet packets or bundles, which he called quanta. This led to new ideas about the properties of light and the structure of atoms involving paradoxical relationships between waves and particles. One must have *some* idea of the radical implications of quantum mechanics in order to appreciate the significance of Pluto's role in the evolving astrological schema and how that role is central to the transcendental implications associated with Pisces. Placing such considerations within the context of astrology, however, is bound to raise some eyebrows, because physics has become a highly specialized field of knowledge, and physicists do not appreciate their findings being interpreted willy-nilly by non-specialists, especially when such interpretations encompass the concerns of religion and magic. Because of this controversy, it is best to begin with statements from physicists themselves, so that the reader may more easily determine where to draw the line between approved science and speculative philosophy.

An overall perspective on the historical significance and success of the theory of quantum mechanics is given by physics professor Paul Davies in *The Ghost in the Atom.* After listing numerous scientific developments that owe their success to applications of this theory, Davies states:

> No known experiment has contradicted the predictions of quantum mechanics in the last 50 years.
>
> This catalogue of triumphs singles out quantum mechanics as a truly remarkable theory—a theory that correctly describes the world to a level of precision and detail unprecedented in science. Nowadays, the vast majority of professional physicists employ quantum mechanics, if not almost unthinkingly, then with complete confidence. Yet this magnificent theoretical edifice is founded on a profound and disturbing paradox that has led some physicists to declare that the theory is ultimately meaningless.
>
> The problem, which was already readily apparent in the late 1920's and early 1930's, concerns not the technical aspects of the theory but its interpretation. [p. 4]

How is it that such a successful scientific theory could be considered "ultimately meaningless" by some physicists? This observation alone indicates that science has entered some very strange territory. In telling us that such a conclusion has been reached because quantum mechanics is "founded on a profound and disturbing paradox," Professor Davies has in effect acknowledged that there is a strong psychological prejudice among scientists that meaning and truth are not, or *should not be*, paradoxical. It has already been mentioned in this book, however, that the renowned psychologist Carl Jung postulated in a scientific albeit psychological vein that meaning and truth *are* ultimately and inherently paradoxical. It is extremely important to grasp the fact that when we attempt to evaluate various interpretations of the theory of quantum mechanics we are dealing with *psychological attitudes on the part of physicists* as they attempt to explain the paradoxes inherent in the theory. In this regard, physics and psychology have found common ground, and the implications for humanity are staggering. What follows constitutes what I consider to be the briefest possible introduction to the implications of the theory. If the reader has had no previous exposure to these ideas, one should not be put off by the apparent illogic of the statements. They take a little getting used to. The critical issues are presented in the words of experts qualified to speak authoritatively about such matters. My own observations are based completely upon their statements.

There are two basic ideas from which most of the controversy and strange interpretations are derived. These are referred to as "the uncertainty principle" and "the collapse of the wave function." An account of "the uncertainty principle" is found in *The Matter Myth*, by Paul Davies and John Gribbin:

> The fact that electron waves are waves of *probability* is a vital component of quantum mechanics and an important element in the quantum nature of reality. It implies that we cannot be certain what any given electron will do. Only the betting odds can be given. This fundamental limitation represents a breakdown of determinism in nature. It means that identical electrons in identical experiments may do different things. There is thus an intrinsic uncertainty in the subatomic world. This uncertainty is encapsulated in the uncertainty principle of Werner Heisenberg, which tells us that all observable quantities are subject to random fluctuations in their values, of a magnitude determined by Planck's constant.
>
> ...Because of the wave-particle duality of entities such as electrons, it is impossible to attribute to them precisely certain properties, such as possessing a well defined path through space, that we are used to thinking of in connection with macroscopic objects like a bullet or a planet in its orbit. Thus when an electron goes from A to B, its trajectory is fuzzed out by quantum uncertainty, as described by Heisenberg's uncertainty principle. In one form, this principle states that you cannot know, at any instant, *both* the position and the momentum of a quantum particle. Indeed it goes deeper—it says that a quantum particle *does not possess* both a definite momentum and a definite position simultaneously. If you try to measure accurately the position, you lose information about the momentum, and vice versa. There is an irreducible trade-off between these two qualities. Either can be known as accurately as you like, but only at the expense of the other.
>
> ...This is the same uncertainty that also affects energy and time, and tells us that virtual particles can pop briefly out of nothing at

all, and vanish again. Such quantum uncertainty is not merely a result of human clumsiness. It is an intrinsic quality of nature. [pp. 208-209, 220]

The point must be made that these statements apply to the very foundation of material existence as we know it. These observations are being made about the "stuff" out of which "reality" is constructed, based upon what is currently the most successful and sophisticated scientific theory developed by empirical science, which has made possible all the technological wonders of our modern world. In order to grasp the human significance of this most profound scientific discovery it must be understood that it demonstrates a fundamental principle of the philosophy of magic, that is, the principle of *enantiodromia*. Stated simply, anything pushed hard enough will turn into its opposite. In this instance, the push for certainty has turned into the discovery of uncertainty, and how utterly devastating is the completeness with which this discovery subverts the original assumptions of its progenitors!

In order to gain more understanding of "the collapse of the wave function," it is helpful to have an idea of the wave nature of light which was the only scientific theory of electromagnetic activity prior to Planck's discovery of quanta. The wave nature of light was demonstrated as early as 1801 by the famous two-slit experiment performed by Thomas Young. In this experiment, light emitted from a single source passes through two slits in a screen onto another screen producing *bands of light*, thereby showing varying intensity resulting from wave interference. If one of the two slits is covered the bands disappear, because the interference is eliminated. This experiment graphically demonstrated that light has a wave nature. Planck's discovery of quanta, however, led to an equally viable theory that light consists of particles or *photons*. Furthermore, the measurement of radioactive particles nullifies the observation of electromagnetic waves. This process is also described in *The Matter Myth*:

The role of the observer is highlighted by what is known as the measurement paradox. Suppose, for the sake of argument, that the wave corresponding to an electron is confined to a box and the particle is equally likely to be found anywhere inside the box. Then imagine that a partition is slid into the box, dividing it into two equal halves. According to the quantum rules, the wave is still present in both halves of the box, reflecting the fact that when we look for the electron we are equally likely to find it on either side of the partition. Common sense, however, would dictate that the electron can be in either only one half of the box or the other. Suppose, now, that someone looks inside the box and finds the electron in one particular half. Clearly the probability wave must abruptly disappear from the other half of the box, because it is now known with certainty to be empty.

The oddity of this abrupt resculpturing of the wave—often called "the collapse of the wave function"—is that it seems to depend upon the activities of the observer. If nobody looks, then the wave never collapses. So the behavior of a particle such as an electron appears to vary according to whether it is being watched or not. This is deeply troubling to physicists, but may not seem of any great concern to other people—who else really cares what an electron is doing when we are not looking at it? But the issue goes beyond electrons. If macroscopic objects also have associated waves, then in principle the independent reality of *everything* seems to go into the quantum melting pot. [pp. 215-217]

The central point of the collapse of the wave function, as I understand it, is that *all* energetic/material phenomena can be examined as either waves or particles. When examined as waves, the observation encompasses the superposition of a virtually infinite number of *interacting* states. When examined as particles, however, only one of those possible states becomes manifest, and all the other possibilities cease to be observable. Furthermore, once such a particle observation is made, the wave observation *cannot be restored*, thus the meaning of the term "the collapse of the wave function." Given these circumstances, two obvious questions naturally arise: 1. Once the particle observation is made, what happens to all the other states that were manifestly evident in the wave function *before* the particle observation? and 2. What is the special significance of *consciousness* of the particle observation that causes the collapse of the wave function?

The implications of these circumstances are so bizarre that physicists were divided into two camps early on: those who accepted quantum mechanics as such, and those who believed that the theory was faulty. The most prominent among the latter group was Albert Einstein, already renowned for his development of relativity theory. Einstein, along with Nathan Rosen and Boris Podolsky, proposed a thought experiment that was designed to get around the uncertainty principle by measuring both the position and the momentum of a particle through information derived from an "accomplice" particle, thereby disclosing strict causal relations among quantum phenomena. It was proposed that, after a collision between particles A and B, information regarding A's *momentum* could be derived indirectly from the measurement of B's momentum. Then A's *position* could be measured directly, thus determining *both* the momentum *and* the position of A. This process, it was proposed, would restore total determinism to the observation of subatomic particles. Einstein reasoned that the only way quantum uncertainty could be preserved across the distance between the particles in this scenario would require some kind of "spooky action at a distance" that would violate his own theory of relativity which precluded any possibility of faster-than-light interactions. [Davies and Gribbin, pp. 222-224]

The challenge of this thought experiment sustained debate about quantum uncertainty until John Bell developed a mathematical theorem in 1965 that made possible the testing of such a two-particle interaction as proposed by Einstein, Rosen and Podolsky. Subsequent laboratory experiments, the most notable being that of Alain Aspect of the University of Paris in 1982, proved Einstein wrong. These experiments demonstrated that what Einstein called "spooky action at a distance" did in fact occur. The implications of these experimental findings are addressed in *The Matter Myth*:

> Assuming one rules out faster-than-light signaling, it implies that once two particles have interacted with one another they remain linked in some way, effectively parts of the same invisible system. This property of "nonlocality" has sweeping implications. We can think of the Universe as a vast network of interacting particles, and each linkage binds the participating particles into a single quantum system. In some sense the entire Universe can be regarded as a single quantum system. Although in practice the complexity of the cosmos is too great for us to notice this subtle connectivity except in special experiments like those devised by Aspect, nevertheless there is a strong holistic flavor to the quantum description of the Universe. [p. 224]

This "strong holistic flavor" is the basis for the observation made by some commentators that quantum mechanics tends to corroborate the holistic cosmic perspectives of Eastern religions such as Taoism, Hinduism, and Buddhism. Furthermore, the esoteric traditions underlying the major Western religions of Judaism, Christianity, and Islam (including the tradition of sympathetic magic) also partake of the fountain of holistic cosmology. Although some scientists are loath to entertain such comparisons in the interest of protecting the integrity of their own particular rigorous methodology, the cosmological similarities are undeniable.

This "strong holistic flavor" also provides some conceptual support for Rupert Sheldrake's Hypothesis of Formative Causation, which entails a causal principle that operates across space and time, that was presented in chapter 1 as a viable theoretical basis for the fundamental astrological hypothesis that there is some kind of linkage between celestial and terrestrial phenomena. Bell's theorem, however, implies a ubiquitous linkage throughout the entire universe and therefore would not appear to account for the emphasis that astrology places on the proximity of relatively nearby celestial objects. An obvious response to this criticism of astrology is that our solar-planetary system simply provides a convenient frame of reference for *monitoring* the whole gamut of quantum interconnectivity that obtains throughout the universe. However, in order to bring the significance of individual human will into the equation, it is necessary to allow for potential variations within the context of "local" effects that obtain within the perceived realm of electromagnetic forces, that is, in the material world of everyday existence. This theme has been referred to already in terms of the relative prominence of the Luminaries (Sol and Luna) in comparison with the other planets of the solar system, due to their more pronounced energetic effect on Earth. The entire solar system, however, is fully engaged in a more subtle network of gravitational and electromagnetic interactions. What must be addressed in this regard is the potential for interaction between the microscopic realm of quantum mechanics and the macroscopic realm of physical objects that we normally perceive in our daily experience of reality and which operate within the context of "locality" as defined by Einstein's theory of relativity, that is, within the bounds of the speed of light.

Such an interaction should not prove excessively difficult to conceptualize for the simple reason that the macroscopic realm of our daily existence is ultimately *made out of* atoms which are systems of quantum activity. There is an undeniable species of *oneness* involving these two qualitatively distinct realms of activity. There has to be a *threshold* of some sort that both separates *and* unifies these realms. Since the boundary that distinguishes the realm of nuclear physics from that of biology is the interface between the quantum realm of the atom and the organic realm of the molecule, it is reasonable to assume that some critical threshold of interaction obtains at that sensitive juncture. Interestingly, there is a morphological feature of Pluto's orbit that is indicative of such an interaction.

All planetary orbits are elliptical, but Pluto's orbit is by far the most elongated. This elongation is such that there is a small portion of Pluto's orbit that brings it *within the orbit of Neptune*. This fact has contributed to the astronomical theory that Pluto may be an escaped moon of Neptune. In taking Neptune as a referent for biological processes and Pluto as a referent for quantum processes, the implication of Pluto entering into Neptune's orbit is that some kind of intermittent interaction transpires at the interface of quantum and biological processes. Furthermore, the fact that Neptune and Pluto are the only two major planets that have intersecting orbits can be interpreted to imply that there is a *special significance* for the interaction of evolving macroscopic biological structures and the microscopic realm of quantum mechanics that tends to confirm the paradoxical and transcendental implications inherent in the manifestation of life-forms within the context of universal entropy.

There is more, however, that needs to be brought into this overview of the theory of quantum mechanics that may help, or perhaps render yet more confusing as the case may be, our attempt to bring perspective to the interaction between microscopic and macroscopic realms. Since the major breakthroughs in quantum theory in the late 1920's and early 1930's, there has been no fundamental change in the theory. It has thus far only proven phenomenally successful for describing and predicting experimental results and unshakable by those who would somehow like to dispense with it. In the meantime, physicists have had some time to get used to it and attempt to work out some way of reconciling the bizarre paradoxes of the theory in terms of *what it means*. As mentioned above, *the very idea of objective reality itself* has even been brought into question! Indeed, there is considerable disagreement among physicists about the interpretation of quantum mechanics.

More and more of the theorizing of various physicists has been made available to the general reader, and there is currently available a smorgasbord of authoritative commentary about the cosmological and philosophical implications of quantum mechanics taken directly from the horses' mouths, as it were. The key role of the observer in the collapse of the wave function has led to the interpretation by some that mind is the most fundamental determinant of reality. This notion, of course, is very palatable to "mind over matter" proponents in the realm of popular philosophy, religion, and, of course, magic.

There are other interpretations that play strongly upon the nonlocality theme, such as that of David Bohm who speaks of an "implicate order" of quantum potential that is enfolded throughout the universe. I find Bohm's theorizing highly intriguing, albeit almost impenetrably subtle. Then, of course, there are the more conservative interpretations that attempt to stay as much as possible within the "common sense" perspective of established reality constructs. Such approaches attempt to either write off quantum weirdness in terms of statistical probabilities or limit all dialogue to only that which is directly observed experimentally and disregard the paradoxical implications.

There is one interpretation of quantum mechanics, often referred to as the "many-universes" interpretation, first proposed by Hugh Everett in 1957, that warrants more extensive consideration for several reasons. One of those reasons is that, perhaps more than any of the other interpretations, this one dramatizes the bizarre aspect of the theory. Another reason is that the many-universes interpretation is in fact *the simplest and most direct way of conceptualizing the implications of quantum mechanics.* A third reason, for the purposes of this book, is that this interpretation of quantum theory has a very significant bearing upon the theory and practice of astrology and may actually prove to be very helpful for addressing some of the age-old difficulties concerning the predictive value of astrology and the role of free will within the context of astrological determinism.

The many-universes interpretation of quantum mechanics has been elucidated by placing it within the context of a famous thought experiment proposed by Erwin Schrödinger in 1935. Schrödinger suggested a scenario in which a cat is confined within a box that also contains a lethal device that can only be triggered by a quantum process of atomic decay. Accordingly, one could not know without looking into the box whether the cat was dead or alive. Quantum mechanics says the wave function within the box is such that the cat is *both* dead *and* alive unless someone actually looks and finds either a dead or a living cat, thereby collapsing the wave function into one of the two possibilities. Quantum theory encounters a difficult paradox with regard to the mechanism that accounts for the transition from the wave function of both a dead and a living cat to a particular observation of one or the other of the alternatives. Paul Davies explains Everett's interpretation of this conundrum in *The Ghost in the Atom*:

According to Everett the transition occurs because the universe splits into two copies, one containing a live cat and the other a dead cat. Both universes contain one copy of the experimenter too, each of whom thinks he is unique. In general, if a quantum system is in a superposition of, say *n* quantum states, then, on measurement, the universe will split into *n* copies. In most cases, *n* is infinite. Hence we must accept that there are actually an infinity of 'parallel worlds' co-existing alongside the one we see at any instant. Moreover, there are an infinity of individuals, more or less identical with each of us, inhabiting these worlds. It is a bizarre thought. [pp. 35-36]

A bizarre thought indeed! It is precisely its bizarreness that makes this interpretation unacceptable to some physicists. Its advocates may easily reply that it would not be the first idea in the history of science that at first appeared bizarre and later came to be accepted as truth. Consider, for example, the Copernican Revolution. It seemed perfectly ridiculous for the mediaeval mind to deny that the solid ground, the very earth beneath our feet, was not, as Aristotle said, the center of the universe. The Copernican theory of the solar system prevailed for one reason. It offered a simpler, more elegant description of the observed phenomena, despite the fact that it challenged the common sense notions of the day. This is precisely what the many universes interpretation does for quantum mechanics. It should therefore prove instructive to cite a few more passages from *The Matter Myth*, so that the reader may be confidently aware of its implications as expressed by recognized authorities on the subject:

An obvious objection to the many universes theory is that we experience only one reality, one Universe. Where are all the others? To understand the answer to this question we need to take on board the concept of spacetime... When the Universe divides into many copies, the splitting creates many duplicates not only of material objects but of space and time as well. That is, each "new" universe comes into being with its own space and time...

It may be difficult to picture this. But the fact that we cannot visualize many different spacetimes does not, of course, logically preclude their existence. We are still able to describe the other universes mathematically. Nevertheless, some sort of imagery is helpful. One possibility is to regard the many universes as "stacked up" like the pages of a book laid flat on a table. In this collection of two-dimensional sheets, each page represents an entire universe— that is, spacetime plus matter. The form of each universe is very slightly different from its neighbors according to the different quantum alternatives realized therein. As we move farther down the stack, away from the page chosen as our reference point, the differences accumulate. [pp. 227-228]

This conceptualization provides a rather concrete way of thinking about the actual implications of quantum mechanics. One additional observation made in *The Matter Myth* brings this conception into greater focus for the purposes of its presentation in this book: "It is possible...to conceive of a conscious individual whose sensory perception and memory operate at the quantum level." [p. 230] This speculation becomes all the more plausible by observing that the human nervous system, the very instrument of consciousness, is made out of atoms, and the very attribute of neurons that makes them conscious may well be their sensitivity to quantum processes.

In chapter 1, I speculated that the authors of the mystery traditions of antiquity may have accessed, by whatever means, the molecular (genetic script) and atomic levels of their own neurostructures thereby experiencing some kind of transcendental consciousness that surpasses the normal macroscopic frame of reference of everyday life as we know it. Such a level of consciousness may account for the superior perspective that would seem to be inherent in the magnificence evidenced by the yet remaining artifacts and remnants of their cultural attainments, not the least of which is the religious heritage that has persevered through the intervening millennia and into our own times. This speculation also jibes with the conclusion reached by modern scientists that the vastness of the universe as we now know it seems to imply that we are not alone as intelligent beings in the cosmos. Many of those scientists, however, will only entertain the possibility that our "neighbors" would be subject to detection through electronic technology, that is, the transmission of radio signals through space. What about the possibility that the human brain is a manifestation of *bio-technology* that is ultimately capable of accessing *its own* quantum potential? Such a possibility would also account for many of the unexplained phenomena of human experience that have been catalogued down through the centuries (such as *deja vu*, telepathy, telekinesis, and premonitions) that appear to defy conventional explanations and which invariably lie at the heart of humankind's noblest conceptions of meaning and spirituality that *transcend* the limitations of material reality as normally perceived. The scientific attitude has traditionally discounted the facticity of such experiences. It must be realized, however, that such assessments are rooted in the classical, that is, pre-quantum conception of the nature of reality that characterized the *infancy* of science. Surely a reassessment of human consciousness is in order in the light of our present knowledge of quantum mechanics.

A fundamental premise of this chapter is that Pluto serves as the planetary referent for the potentially conscious experience of quantum reality, and that, as such, it is clearly appropriate as the new ruler of Pisces, considering Pisces' connotations of paradox and transcendence. Before concluding the development of this premise in the light of perspectives developed above, however, some observations are in order regarding the many-universes interpretation of quantum mechanics as it pertains to general astrological theory.

The fundamental rationale of astrology is an attempt to relate the high degree of order and predictability of celestial phenomena to the relatively chaotic and spontaneous nature of human experience on Earth. This very distinction precludes the possibility of totally fulfilling that objective. And yet, there can be no doubt that *some* degree of correspondence does obtain, as in the most obvious instances of the seasonal cycle and tidal rhythms. The question has *never* been that of *whether or not* such correspondences obtain, but rather *to what extent* they do so. The truth of astrology is intuitively apparent, despite the fact that logic can be brought to bear against it. But exactly how and why it is true remains a mystery. And *to what extent* it is true is an obscure issue that invites both denial at one extreme and opportunism at the other. Indeed, this issue has always been one of the most profound philosophical concerns for astrology.

As the simplest and most direct interpretation of reality in accordance with our best science, the many-universes interpretation of quantum mechanics provides an exquisite conceptual framework for addressing the limitation of astrology's predictive value. As a corollary to this perspective, the issue of the relation between free will and determinism is also potentially resolved. If we borrow the above analogy of the many universes to the pages of a book, we may observe that the pages that are closer to one another have relatively similar content and the pages that are further removed from one another have relatively more divergent content. The totality of differences inherent in the overall proliferation of universes for this interpretation of quantum mechanics has been characterized by Robert Anton Wilson in *Cosmic Trigger: Final Secret of the Illuminati* (New Falcon Publications) with the statement that "everything that *can* happen *does* happen," [p. 193] if not in one universe then in another, or in many others. It would appear obvious, however, that there is a virtually infinite number of imaginable events that *cannot* happen. For example, I think it is fairly safe to say that I will not jump to the Moon (physically) in *any* universe. In other words, there are *ranges of possibilities* within which *all* of them are fulfilled in the quantum multiverse. It would be foolhardy to venture to say what would be the limits of such ranges in the total configuration of universes, but it would seem to be necessary to assume that such limits do apply.

It is perfectly natural that on a given day a particular individual may do something strikingly different from one's usual routine, something unexpected. People are known to do unexpected things. One may quit one's job for no apparent reason after years of reliable performance. A person known to be reasonable and consistent in one's normal mode of life may commit a bizarre act that surprises all who know her. Therefore, within the context of human events, there is a very large range of possible occurrences and interactions that spawns a continuous spewing of myriad universes, given the many-universes interpretation of quantum mechanics. It is also the case, however, that the interactive movements of the planets within the solar system *do not* deviate from their appointed courses. It is not reasonable to assume that in one particular universe Mars changes the direction of its orbit on July 29, 2003 and starts going the other way around the Sun. On the contrary, one would be hard pressed to imagine how many pages up or down the stack one would have to look in order to find *any* measurable changes in the movements of the planets within "our" solar system in some other universe. Human beings and planets are both macroscopic objects, *but they differ in regard to their relative capacity for change.* The dynamics of inter-planetary motion, due to their high level of predictability within the context of our own apparently single universe, would appear to remain relatively constant throughout an extremely wide range of multiversal divergence.

The obvious consequence of this state of affairs is that, within a relatively single astrological configuration, rather divergent occurrences of mutually exclusive events transpire. Such events could not be accurately predicted astrologically because for such a prediction to be "right" in one universe it would have to be "wrong" in countless others. It follows that an assessment of astrological configurations addresses the *wave function* of observable phenomena within the context of human experience, that is, the *range of probabilities* within a broader context of possible fulfillment. Human consciousness, by virtue of its neurological processing of quantum uncertainty, is able to *choose* its own course *within* that broader macroscopic context and in so doing to "collapse the wave function" into particular observable events. This ability to play a determining role in the *creation* of alternative possibilities may be the special significance that is attributed to humankind in some religious traditions. Furthermore, the profound adage professed by astrologer Alan Leo that "character is destiny" takes on added meaning within the context of a quantum multiverse. In this regard, character would be the determining factor of the range of possibilities for a particular person in *all* of one's multiversal manifestations. The multiverse would then effectively dramatize, in a most thorough manner, what one is capable of.

The assignment of Pluto as the appropriate new ruler of Pisces indicates that its discovery has heralded an expanded comprehension of the meaning of Pisces that is more appropriate to the times in which we currently live, as opposed to the historical perspectives associated with Jupiter's rulership in the traditional schema. This perspective becomes highly relevant and *controversial* when we consider the fact that the Age of Pisces was most significantly associated with the Christian religion. A revision and expansion of our understanding of the *sign* Pisces has a very powerful effect on how we may reassess the historical significance of the dominant institution of the *Age* of Pisces. This theme will be addressed from various angles throughout the remainder of this book.

Throughout the history of Christianity its proponents have tended to be divided into two general groups that have yet interacted within the context of the religion as a whole. These two groups can broadly be characterized as those who have responded to the more confined legalistic and authoritarian aspects of the religion and those who have responded to its greater universal implications. Clearly there is much room for jostling between these two orientations within the context of the actual scriptures of the Christian Bible. Furthermore, there are questions about the processes of the writing, compiling, and editing of the original manuscripts that were to become the official canon of the religion. Attempts to resolve such questions come under the broad heading of the scholarly enterprise of biblical hermeneutics. The point I would like to emphasize is that the *interaction* of *both* orientations of Christianity mentioned above constitute the fundamental meaning of the religion, *insofar as it is a manifestation of the Piscean Age.* It would be wrong, in my opinion, to consider that one of the two orientations has been in keeping with the truth of the religion to the exclusion of the other, despite the fact that they are clearly in conflict with one another.

Proponents of various interpretations of Christianity are wont to quote scriptures in support of their particular preoccupations. I think that such examination and analysis is healthy and profitable and, if pursued diligently, comprehensively, and in a true spirit of inquiry, leads to ever greater understanding of this profound religious tradition. I would venture to say, however, that Christianity as a whole religious system entails paradoxes and contradictions that are beyond the possibility of resolution for the purposes of future history. There is a passage in the New Testament, however, attributed to Jesus Christ, the primary spokesman for the transcendent potential of the human spirit and the founder of the dominant religious tradition of the Piscean Age, that supports the observation in this book that a quantum perspective upon reality is a *latent* characteristic of Piscean meaning, and, as such, of human consciousness. That passage reads, "In my Father's house are many mansions: If it were not so, I would have told you. I go to prepare a place for you." [John 14:2]

CHAPTER 10

LUNAR GESTALT

We may now develop an interpretation of what I have termed the lunar gestalt in Aleister Crowley's birthchart. This will complete the initial interpretation of his natal configuration. Through an analysis of this grouping of planets, a very revealing perspective may be gained upon a major component of Crowley's personality. This powerful current in Crowley's makeup was widely defamed in much of the popular literature about him. It was, however, largely misunderstood and therefore distorted by critics due to its intensity and lack of conformity to prevailing social mores. This problem was further exacerbated by Crowley's deliberate provocation which, it must be realized, was the only manner by which he was able to preserve his integrity and humor regarding such matters. It is this grouping of planets that accounts for the extreme sexual orientation of Crowley's personality and the fact that it was primarily his publicizing of unorthodox sexual attitudes, particularly in relation to their religious significance, that won for him his notorious reputation.

The complete gestalt consists of Neptune and Pluto in "intercepted" Taurus in his Tenth House, Mercury and Jupiter in "intercepted" Scorpio in his Fourth House, and Luna in Pisces in his Ninth House. Additional features of this gestalt are the rulerships of his Ninth House by Pluto, his Twelfth House by Luna, his Third and Eleventh Houses by Mercury, and his Fifth House by Jupiter. This gestalt is shown graphically in Figure 7.

As "intercepted" signs have not yet been discussed in this book, the interpretation of Crowley's lunar gestalt will therefore begin with an explanation of what intercepted signs are and what may be inferred about their meaning for purposes of interpretation. It was noted in chapter 2 that, due to the angular disparity between the ecliptical and equatorial planes and Earth's spherical shape, the angular divisions of a birthchart into signs and houses vary in relation to one another. This phenomenon was explained to account for the fact that the signs Leo and Aquarius span segments of Crowley's birthchart that completely subsume his First and Seventh Houses respectively (see Figure 1). When an opposing pair of signs is completely subsumed within an opposing pair of houses, those signs are said to be intercepted in those houses. In Crowley's birthchart, Taurus and Scorpio are intercepted in his Tenth and Fourth Houses respectively.

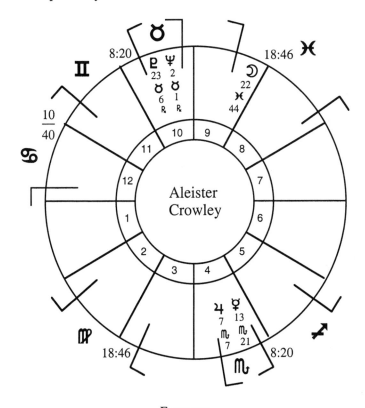

FIGURE 7
The complete "Lunar Gestalt" in Aleister Crowley's birthchart (including the planets involved and the signs occupied and ruled by those planets).

The fundamental distinction between sign and house divisions is that signs, as temporal divisions of the annual cycle, refer to seasonal orientations of *collective humanity*, and houses, as spatial divisions of the sky surrounding Earth at a particular time and place—the cosmic *moment* of a person's birth—refer to various orientations to the cosmos from the standpoint of *individual personality*. Signs refer to humanity as a whole, while *houses* refer to individual human existence *within* the context of collective humanity. The collective nature of humanity represented by the zodiac is *given* through primordial group interaction predicated upon aeonic conditions and social survival. The potential for individual personality, on the other hand, is actualized only through conscious *differentiation* of oneself from the social matrix. Whereas the collective orientation of humanity is *natural*, individual personality is *artificial*. In this context, the term "artificial" should not be construed to imply a condition of falseness or unreality, but rather a condition of being *self-created*. Individual personality is a human *artifact*.

The four "angles" of a birthchart that denote the most fundamental parameters of its house structure are determined by the Horizon and Meridian. The morphological referent for the Meridian is Earth's rotational axis (the planetary "spine" as it were) which, along with any other point on Earth's surface, determines a plane that is perpendicular to the Horizon at that point. The verticality of the Meridian corresponds to the erect stature of the human organism as differentiated from the prone stature of other vertebrates. By standing up, humankind gave rise to a new order of being, thereby *creating* the attitude of individual existence by establishing a morphological perpendicularity to the Horizon. An interesting adjunct to this observation is that the mounting activity of pre-human male vertebrates contributed to the evolutionary development of erect posture (which was of course transmitted to progeny of both genders). A further corollary is that, by standing up, humankind freed its arms and hands for purposes of personal expression and manipulation of the environment, activities which fostered the making of artifacts and the concomitant development of abstract thought. The traditional system of astrology inherited from the ancients was fully developed in terms of the divisions of signs and houses as presented above, which indicates the antiquity of this perspective on human personality. That system, therefore, has functioned as a *seed* planted within human culture that has served as a nexus for the development of individualism.

The term "house" is very appropriate because it refers to a human artifact that insulates us from our natural environment. Astrological houses refer specifically to concerns of personal individuality, and it is a direct function of that orientation to be psychologically insulated from the natural and, to a considerable degree, the social environment as characterized by the zodiac. It is the tragedy of alienation from nature and society that has become a condition of modern humanity through intensifying individualism and its concomitant technology. The tragic implications of this development, however, constitute a *rite of passage* for humankind attendant upon our attainment unto microcosmic individuation. The challenge of this rite of passage, however, is nonetheless *real,* and the phenomenon of intercepted signs, when it occurs in birthcharts of individuals, operates as a kind of safety valve for the *release of pressure* needed to maintain the dynamic equilibrium requisite for the effectual negotiation of the ordeal of individuality.

This perspective entails the notion that the zodiac refers to a condition of *primordial humanity* rooted in a previous stage of human evolution, perhaps that referred to by the ancient Greeks as the Golden Age, in which humans were more or less in communion *with,* and thereby largely controlled *by,* macrocosmic forces, as opposed to our modern condition of alienation *from* those forces. In this regard the house cusps of a birthchart may be conceived to function as bars of a prison cell of individuality, isolating the native from the experience of the flowing continuity of nature and the shared experience of humanity. It follows that intercepted signs in a birthchart, since they have no house cusp imposed upon them, afford a relatively unadulterated experience of the primordial natures of those signs. Such experience is limited to the houses in which intercepted signs are placed but, within that context, those signs are experienced with some degree of the unmolested vitality that has been lost through the process of civilization. This approach to interpreting intercepted signs, which my work has consistently confirmed, brings considerable significance to bear upon this phenomenon. Furthermore, this accentuates the importance of the various methods of house division that are employed in the practice of astrology.

With this perspective in mind, the significance of the interceptions of Taurus and Scorpio in Crowley's birthchart becomes immediately apparent. These two signs pertain most directly to human sexuality. All pairs of opposing signs represent fundamental paradoxes of human nature, that is, apparent contradictions that actually embody a complementary wholeness of truth. The paradox inherent in the opposition of Taurus and Scorpio is that involving life and death, lust and dissolution, beauty and perversion, munificence and corruption. This opposition involves the experience of sexual actualization in its respective manifestations of *stability* and *transformation.*

The symbolic meaning of Scorpio was broached in chapter 8. The manner in which Taurus represents the complementary opposition to Scorpio is inherent in its symbolic image of the bull, representing the strong lusty fertility of spring. The lust of Taurus is unencumbered by psychological subtlety. It is purely and directly *physical*. Taurus is the Fixed Earth sign and is ruled by Venus, the goddess of love and beauty. The sexual impulse associated with Taurus is completely *healthy* in that it is driven only by physically aesthetic motivation. In this regard, Taurus embodies the essence of sensuality minus the psychological complications of the Scorpionic perspective with its incumbent *knowledge* of the attendant repercussions of biological reproduction, entropic degeneration, fetishes and, of course, the sheer difficulty of controlling the sexual urge in the absence of felicitous opportunity for its immediate gratification. It is the disparity between the Taurian and Scorpionic perspectives, that is, the *lack of integration* of this wholeness of truth about human sexuality, that is referred to in the Garden of Eden story as the "knowledge of good and evil," which arises as a function of the *aftermath* of sexual gratification.

Having these opposing signs intercepted indicates that Aleister Crowley experienced sexuality in a primordial way. In one sense, this means that he had no "handle" on his sexuality. It flowed through him as a torrent along his power axis (Fourth and Tenth Houses) and was therefore *compulsive* (from the conventional viewpoint) in that it was not responsive to the civilizing constraint that one normally feels obliged to exercise in such matters. In another sense, this feature of Crowley's personality afforded him the ability to experience the primordial fullness of his sexuality without the debilitating inhibition that characterizes hyper-civilized society. Whereas nearly everyone in modern civilization has certain components of one's personality that effectively obstruct one's potential for sexual actualization, it was relatively easy and *natural* for Crowley to give full sway to his sexual impulses. Insofar as modern Western civilization is the result of an age-old process of individualization through sexual constraint, house cusps in Taurus and Scorpio serve as indexes of numbness and guilt respectively within the context of a natal configuration. Crowley had no such house cusps. There were no prison bars obstructing the flow of his lust.

Aleister Crowley's reference to himself as the Beast 666 has already been considered in relation to his Leo Ascendant in this book. That symbolic association is certainly important for the understanding of this particular feature of Crowley's self-revelation. In my opinion, however, the interceptions of Taurus and Scorpio in his Tenth and Fourth Houses, and the considerable planetary weight found therein, account for the major connotation of bestiality that characterized Crowley's personality. The bull is no less a beast than the lion, and its sexual prowess is yet more renowned. Having Taurus intercepted in his Tenth House, as differentiated from his Leo Ascendant, is indicative of Crowley's public standing in the community at large, his *office*, so to speak. His reputation as a sexual deviate is relevant in that it was in fact part and parcel of his message to the world that the sexual impulse was not to be fettered in any way by restrictive social taboos. The fact that Crowley was prone to take maximal advantage of this banishing of sexual taboos served to *demonstrate* this ideal as opposed to its mere proclamation. Furthermore, Taurus' inclusion in his Tenth House enabled him to propagate a healthy aesthetic characterization of sexuality, emphasizing the sheer physical beauty of sexual fulfillment. Within a social context long steeped in sexually repressive mores, however, the expression of such an unbridled attitude toward sexual pleasure necessarily entails a host of repercussive complications, mutually reflected in Crowley's own personality and the responses elicited from others.

Both Neptune and Pluto are found in Taurus in Crowley's Tenth House. Therefore, these two powerfully transformative agents were directly operative as functionaries of his public demonstration of unfettered lust. In keeping with the traditional rule that a planet in the sign opposite its domicile is said to be in its detriment, embodying an inverted paradox as it were, such is Neptune's placement in Taurus. This accounts for the manner in which Crowley carried his public expression of deviant sexuality to the extreme that he did, as well as the fact that certain elements of the press spared no effort to maliciously defame him for much of his alleged depravity. Those who knew him have observed—and it may easily be surmised from the reading of his own words—that he indeed provoked such hostile attacks upon himself and thereby fueled the fires of his own infamous reputation far exceeding the reality. Certainly he became known for his bisexuality and his amusement with sexual deviance, and he made allusions to secret methods of using sexual practices for magickal purposes. However, his lavishness entailed no lack of decorum or failure to respect the sanctity of others. Such a judgment is, of course, largely personal and subjective, and there are many who would disagree with this assessment. However, within the context of

Crowley's world-view, decorum and sanctity are matters of artistry and *respect for* and *insight into* the wills of others.

Pluto's placement in Taurus suggests the capacity to experience transcendental consciousness within the context of physical lust, or, as a function of quantum mechanics in relation to Pluto, the capacity to employ libidinal energy to affect multiversal divergence. Such concerns are addressed in Crowley's writings on sexual magick and his applications thereof. He considered it his public duty (Tenth House) to be the primary disseminator of this kind of knowledge. It is important to bear in mind that these trans-Saturnian planetary placements, within the context of this gestalt, help to account for the nature of Crowley's extraordinary abilities in areas beyond the normal concerns of the average person who does not consciously integrate these transformative functions. Therefore, even his more direct and overt literary expressions on such matters appear obscure to the general reader. This tends to obstruct the cultural assimilation of his ideas. For the same reason, however, his writings are a well-spring of revelation concerning the social and psychological dynamics of human sexuality and the potential for its utilization for attaining personal liberation from the repressive heritage of the passing Aeon. Exactly how Crowley's writing and publishing figures into this planetary gestalt will presently be developed in a discussion of his natal placements of Mercury and Jupiter in Scorpio.

It should first be noted, however, that both Neptune and Pluto, due to their extended orbital periods, remain in one sign long enough to characterize an entire generation with such a given association. It is therefore important to realize that it is the relatively unique positioning of their placements in Crowley's birthchart that accounts for the extreme *accentuation* of their meanings as elucidated here. Furthermore, most people are yet unwilling or unable to actualize these functions in their own lives due to the extreme *cognitive dissonance* that results in relation to conventional personal and social reality constructs. It is certainly relevant to observe, however, that another great pioneer of knowledge about the transformative and transcendental potential of human sexuality, namely the Swiss psychologist Carl Jung, was born in the same year as Crowley and therefore also had Neptune and Pluto in Taurus. In Jung's birthchart these planets are placed deep in the lower hemisphere as opposed to their placements near Crowley's Midheaven. This difference alone provides some insight into the comparative approaches of these two giants in their closely related fields of practical and theoretical expertise.

Crowley's prolific literary output and the style and content of his writing may be accounted for by his Mercury and Jupiter placements, both in intercepted Scorpio in his Fourth House, forming *opposition aspects* to Pluto and Neptune respectively. (In the case of Mercury and Pluto the technical assignment of this aspect requires the granting of a rather wide ten degree orb of variance, however, a general sense of the opposition is certainly inherent in the configuration.) The information disseminating planets, Mercury and Jupiter, were therefore positioned to activate conscious objectifications of the functions associated with Pluto and Neptune respectively. Furthermore, both of these objectifications are characterized *by* the sign Scorpio in which they are found, and are objectifications *of* the Taurian qualities imparted by Neptune and Pluto in Taurus. In this regard, Jupiter is able to *bring back* the Neptunian quality to its Scorpionic domicile from its detrimental position in Taurus, and such Jupiterian objectification may be seen to *expand* and *exaggerate* the Neptunian quality that it reflects. In a similar fashion, Mercury objectifies Pluto's impulse from Taurus in a *specifically articulated* manner characterized by Mercury's placement in Scorpio. The sardonic wit of Mercury in Scorpio found in Crowley's writings is therefore reflective of a transcendent utilization of physical lust, and the Jupiterian enterprise of disseminating those writings was devoted to the imagization of inverted psycho-sexual motives.

As the planetary ruler of Crowley's Third House through Virgo, Mercury's placement and aspects exerted a powerful influence over his particular style of communication. As the planetary ruler of his Fifth House through Sagittarius, Jupiter's placement and aspects exerted a powerful influence over his creative self-expression. The fact that many of Crowley's literary works were self- published is a direct manifestation of his Sagittarian Fifth House, and the unorthodox sexual and religious themes that invariably characterized those publications—in his earliest poetry and throughout his writing career—may be accounted for by both Mercury's and Jupiter's placements and participation in his lunar gestalt.

This planetary grouping had a profound effect upon Crowley's public destiny insofar as it involved the placements of two trans-Saturnian planets in his Tenth House of *public achievement and recognition*. Although his writing and publishing came from his own private depths (Fourth House), which helps to account for the often obscure and sometimes perverse (Scorpionic) motives exhibited therein, those efforts were *reflections* of a public destiny imposed from above (Tenth House) to exemplify the Neptunian and Plutonian agencies of transformation and transcendence through the direct incorporation of physical lust (Taurus). By accepting his spiritual destiny to go public in a singularly assertive and courageous manner (indicated as a "calling" by his North Lunar Node in Aries near his Midheaven) Crowley automatically activated an overt expression of the powerful convention-breaking forces symbolized by the trans-Saturnian planets in intercepted Taurus in his Tenth House.

As his personality matured out of boyhood, the spiritual impetus within him was such as to virtually compel him along these lines. This observation applies *both* to the solar and lunar gestalts in Crowley's birthchart and reinforces his claim to have been virtually coerced by superior forces of destiny. Although critics interpret that claim as a mere boast, characteristic of Crowley's colossal ego, this interpretation of his birthchart provides objective corroboration of his own statements. It is often the case that the greater is explained in terms of the lesser. Indeed, Aleister Crowley, the persona, exhibited a phenomenal ego, but it may be observed that such an exhibition served to screen out from the comprehension of the more profound mysteries of his revelation those who suffer less consciously and less conspicuously from a similar affliction. Rather than boasting about the manner in which his life was directed by a superior destiny, it is perhaps more consistent with the whole of his personality to grant that he openly acknowledged an awful and opprobrious truth about himself, but, in the spirit of true manliness, without undue complaint.

As with the solar gestalt, the cohesive factor that knits the lunar gestalt into a functional system is its *dispositional linkage*. Luna's placement just inside Crowley's Piscean Ninth House brings her within the dispositional governance of Pluto. Luna is therefore subject to the powerful influence of Pluto's participation in the grouping of planets in Taurus and Scorpio delineated above. This disposition can now be understood to contribute significantly to Luna's significance as elaborated in chapter 6, involving Crowley's most fundamental matrix of perception, that is, his experience of the feminine presence in terms of transcendent religious meaning, and, from the perspective of developmental psychology, his relation to his mother during the formative years of his childhood. Luna's rulership of Crowley's Cancerian Twelfth House brings the theme of personal transcendence to its apotheosis. The Twelfth House serves as a repository for one's personal unconscious, which is intimately related to its connotation of transcendence. Were one to apply the analogy of incarnate personality to the larval state of a caterpillar, the Twelfth House of a birthchart refers to the *cocoon* that one prepares for oneself in anticipation of the ultimate need to shed one's earthbound existence. The combined effect of the dispositional succession from Pluto and Luna to the Twelfth House made Crowley a rather effective "channel" for transcendental religious revelation. This connotation must extend to the transcendental impact of Crowley's work in terms of the lasting effect of his legacy, that is, the magick of the Beast as the prophet f the New Aeon.

There is another somewhat subtle feature of this planetary arrangement that contributes to Crowley's ability to bring meaningful perspective to bear upon the transition *out of* the Piscean Age. That feature is the fact that the near opposition of Mercury to Pluto, by virtue of their respective rulerships of the opposing signs Virgo and Pisces, involves a reiteration, or echo as it were, of the paradoxical wholeness of truth that has characterized the Piscean Age. The perspective inherent in this planetary opposition is suggestive of a characterization of transcendence that was virtually inconceivable at the inception and throughout the historical development of the Piscean Age, insofar as Pluto, as the future ruler of Pisces, was an unknown planet during that period. It is nonetheless the case that the *potential* for understanding that may explicitly be articulated in terms of our present perspective lay *buried within* the temporal context of the Piscean Age from its very beginning. Such a potential may even be considered, *from a trans-temporal perspective*, to have functioned as a hidden driving *telos* of the aeonic motif itself, that is, a key to the mysteries, or final cause (in the Aristotelian sense), that rendered Piscean religion so obscure and impenetrable in its orthodox manifestations. Such a perspective was suggested at the close of chapter 9 in addressing the religious implications of quantum mechanics. This particular feature of Crowley's natal configuration, therefore, would indicate his ability to objectify and articulate such a hidden driving force from an historical perspective. The fact of this planetary opposition's occurrence in the signs Scorpio and Taurus indicates, in this vein, a focusing of perspective in terms of sexual imagery, rendering Crowley's articulation nothing short of a *purging psychoanalysis* of the Piscean Age in general, and, in view of the noxious indoctrination of his own upbringing, the Christian religion in particular.

There is a special morphological feature of the metallic element mercury, naturally associated with the planet of the same name, that proves instructive in regard to the symbolic meaning of Mercury in relation to Pluto as the respective rulers of the opposing signs Virgo and Pisces. Most of us, at one time or another, have had the opportunity to hold a bit of mercury in our cupped palm and watch it roll around as a shiny ball of liquid metal. Placed upon a table, one can attempt to pick it up or touch it only to see it break into smaller balls and thereby resist any attempt to get a hold of it or pin it down. This elusive quality provides a most apt physical representation of the "mercurial" nature of human thought and the manner by which analysis, no matter how rigorously pursued, is never able to reach ultimate answers to probing questions, despite the fact that a great deal of interesting information is generated in the process.

This property bears directly on the great importance placed upon this metal in the historical enterprise of alchemy. Contrary to the popular modern belief that alchemy was nothing but a somewhat fanciful and naive precursor to today's physical science of chemistry, Carl Jung has demonstrated rather effectively that alchemy was actually, and continues to be, a very sophisticated system of spiritual philosophy, the object of which was nothing less than the realization of the human potential for an exalted psychological grasp of the divine nature of personal reality. In this regard alchemy is fundamentally associated with the historical practice of magic in its most profound philosophical sense. This association is characterized by the symbol of the caduceus as the staff carried by Mercury which has been adopted by medicine as a symbol for the healing art. Of course, the more sublime philosophical implications of the association of this image with the patron of magic have been discarded by members of the modern medical profession as nothing but the colorful but superstitious remnants of humankind's pre-scientific ignorance.

To return, however, to the significance of the dispersive property of the metal mercury, this quality may be considered to be *reflective* of the Plutonian quality of the transcendence of the normal conception of material existence insofar as Mercury's rulership of Virgo complements by opposition Pluto's rulership of Pisces. The metal's tendency to break up into multiple embodiments of its original singularity in response to pressure from without, provides a physical representation of the tendency of material existence to break up into multiple embodiments of its original singularity in response to the application of *consciousness,* as characterized by the many universes interpretation of quantum mechanics. The implication of this interpretation is that there is some elusive process by which consciousness affects the particularization of myriad potentialities within any given context of experience, and that it is the business of magick to acquire some degree of comprehension and volitional direction of that process. The key significance in this regard is the *elusiveness* of the process—its resistance to simple and consistent logical explication—which gives the appearance of irrationality. This elusiveness is dramatized by the Schrödinger's cat scenario in which the two manifestations of the one scientist who respectively observe a dead and a living cat are each *unaware* of the other's mutual multiversal existence. This suggests a conundrum in the practice of magick, which renders it forever beyond the pale of traditional science's quest for comprehensive, objective determinism. The quest of magick is rather for *subjective* determinism, that is, *to access the core of quantum potential within the human nervous system as the instrument of consciousness and volition within an objective frame of reference(s).*

These observations help to foster some understanding of the peculiar difficulties that Crowley faced in the enactment of his self-proclaimed destiny as the Magus of the New Aeon, that is, the enunciator of the Word and the initiator of the magickal current needed to transform the world in accordance with the requirements of a new stage of evolutionary progress for humankind. Acceptance or rejection of his claim is not the matter at hand. It is rather that an understanding for the reader be reached concerning Crowley's own conception of his role in this regard. Such an understanding requires not only a grasp of enhanced knowledge associated with the aeonic transition but also a recognition of the need for *historical continuity* in the evolutionary process. This necessarily includes an appreciation for the highly developed philosophical comprehension of magick and its historical roots that was central to Crowley's world-view. Without such an appreciation, his life takes on the appearance of a travesty of human nature, opaque to any attempt at conventional assessment. It must be granted that such an appearance is fundamental to the efficacy of his performance, if in fact his claims are to be taken seriously. Indeed, Crowley characterized himself in these terms, although many of his critics are wont to make light of that self-assessment as just one more example of his personal fatuity and rationalization for his own shortcomings. Crowley's critics, however, are left with the difficulty of accounting for his personal genius and phenomenal proficiency in a remarkably wide range of challenging enterprises. Aleister Crowley was certainly not a man to be taken lightly, despite his many apparent personal failings.

Another technical feature of Crowley's lunar gestalt is Mercury's rulership of his Geminian Eleventh House. Whereas Mercury's ruler- ship of Virgo (Earth) is associated with *practical* applications and techniques of actual working processes, its rulership of Gemini (Air) is associated with the more abstract manipulation of ideas through logic and rhetoric. Therefore, Mercury's rulership of Crowley's Virgoan Third House characterizes *his personal style of communica- tion* along the lines of technical proficiency in practical matters (including, of course, magick, due to its strong association with Virgo). Mercury's rulership of his Geminian Eleventh House rather characterizes his use of linguistic formulations and logical systems for purposes of furthering *his personal hopes and aspirations and his social involvements and interactions*, traditionally associated with the Eleventh House, and, more specifically, his participation in the various fraternal associations to which he belonged throughout his adult life. The meaning of the Eleventh House may be ascertained from its strategic position between the Tenth and Twelfth Houses. It connotes a very social orientation, but it is less constrained by overtly pubic institutions. This accounts for its traditional association with friendship and social activities in general. Furthermore, by immediately preceding the utterly transcendental Twelfth House, which closes the cyclic process of individual existence, the Eleventh House engenders the conception and projection of new possibilities in anticipation of the approaching new cycle which accounts for its traditional association with hopes and aspirations.

A notable example of the Geminian character of Crowley's Eleventh House was his composition and self-publication (Sagittarian Fifth House of personal self-expression *opposite* his Geminian Eleventh House) of the *Equinox* series as the official organ of his own fraternal organization (Eleventh House) which he called A∴A∴, and which embodied his hopes of reforming the religious orientation of humanity. His Geminian Eleventh House had been strongly activated by the reading, at age 22, of *The Cloud Upon the Sanctuary* by Karl von Eckartshausen, which led in an interesting manner to his association with the Hermetic Order of the Golden Dawn. That book touched upon Crowley's earliest hopes and aspira- tions for fraternal association in a manner that profoundly coincided with the impetus of his lunar gestalt. It is therefore appropriate to quote a passage from *Confessions* that illustrates not only the above observations but also reveals an aspect of Crowley's personality that bears no resemblance to the sensationalized image of wickedness and depravity that later became the hallmark of his public reputation. It is essential to the understanding of the man to know that, at the heart of his motivation, were sentiments such as these.

> *The Cloud Upon the Sanctuary* told me of a secret community of saints in possession of every spiritual grace, of the keys to the treasures of nature, and of moral emancipation such that there was no intolerance or unkindness. The members of this Church lived their secret life of sanctity in the world, radiating light and love upon all that came within their scope, yet they were free from spiritual pride. They enjoyed intimate communion with the immanent divine soul of nature. Inheritors of innocence and illumination, they were not self-seekers; and their one passion was to bring mankind into the sphere of their own sublimity, dealing with each individual as his circumstances required. To them the members of the Trinity were nearer and more real than anything else in the universe. But they were pure ideas of incorruptible integrity. The incarnation was a mystical or magical operation which took place in every man. Each was himself the Son of God who had assumed a body of flesh and blood in order to perform the work of redemption. The indwelling of the Holy Ghost was a sanctification resulting from the completion of the great work when the self had been crucified to itself and raised again in incorruptible immortality. [p. 146]

Although these words were written later in life, after much hard experience and many sobering realizations, they yet reflect the initial impetus that caused Crowley to seek and find the Golden Dawn Order, which in turn set him upon his tumultuous path of self-discovery and struggle with the deep rooted psychological and social resistances to his Self-appointed task in life. As the passage continues, Crowley subtly reflects upon perspectives that he had gleaned during the interim.

> I did not yet see that this conception reposed on metaphysical bases as untenable as those of orthodoxy. There was no attempt to explain the origin of evil and similar difficulties. But these things were mysteries which would be revealed to the saint as he advanced in the way of grace. Anyhow, I was certainly not the person to cavil. The sublimity of the idea enthralled me; it satisfied my craving for romance and poetry. I determined with my whole heart to make myself worthy to attract the notice of this mysterious brotherhood. I yearned passionately for illumination. I could imagine nothing more exquisite than to enter into communion with these holy men and to acquire the power of communicating with

the angelic and divine intelligence of the universe. I longed for perfect purity of life, for mastery of the secret forces of nature, and for a career of devoted labor on behalf of 'the Creation which groaneth and travaileth.' [*ibid.*]

In considering Crowley's subsequent career, one would not be amiss to observe that indeed he did find the labor he sought. It can fairly be said that the lunar gestalt, as delineated in this chapter, characterizes the full religious component of Crowley's personality in a manner most appropriate to his own conception of himself as well as others' conceptions of him. The differences among those conceptions may be attributed to *varying responses* to the enormously disturbing power of this astrological configuration.

Some concluding observations may now be made concerning the manner in which the solar and lunar gestalts interact in Crowley's natal configuration. Despite the fact that these gestalts are distinctly suggested by their patterns of dispositional linkage, they are yet interrelated in at least three significant ways. Perhaps the most dramatic way is that, if the wide opposition between Mercury and Pluto is taken as a meaningful aspect, which I consider to be a viable supposition within the context of the total configuration, then that opposition and the exact degree opposition between Uranus and Saturn together form the most infamous aspect configuration in astrology, namely the Grand Fixed Cross. This configuration is considered particularly stigmatic. In *The Arkana Dictionary of Astrology*, Fred Gettings says about the Grand Cross:

An aspectal pattern involving at least four planets which are so placed as to form two axes of opposition which intersect at right angles. ... The Grand Cross is an extension of the so-called COSMIC CROSS. It is said to bring considerable tension into the life of the native, often with creative results. [p. 220]

The next entry in Gettings' *Dictionary*, for the Grand Fixed Cross, is the only particular example of the Grand Cross to receive any special notation: "Name given to a MAJOR CONFIGURATION in which two pairs of oppositions are placed in all four of the Fixed quadruplicities—that is, in Taurus, Leo, Scorpio and Aquarius." [*ibid.*]

The Grand Cross is a relatively rare phenomenon, and it engenders so much conflict and struggle for the native that one must either become strong and proficient at coping with the relentless challenges of one's life or succumb to the point of incapacitation or death. The study of Crowley's life would tend to suggest that he had a Grand Cross even without the benefit of seeing his birthchart, were one prone to that kind of speculation. He always seemed to be in some kind of trouble. It certainly is the case that he was unable to realize his objectives in terms of his conscious intentions, and yet his legacy lives on in a manner that nonetheless conforms to those intentions, a manner that Crowley himself came to apprehend more clearly in his later years. That legacy also appears to be growing in a most intriguing manner, despite the assertions of his critics that his efforts were to no avail. Furthermore, it is clearly observable from our present perspective that the world is in fact headed in the direction prophesied by Crowley. For the purpose of understanding the meaning of this Grand Cross, however, one may consider that the themes developed in chapter 7 and this chapter, regarding the oppositions of Saturn to Uranus and Mercury to Pluto, are related to one another in such a manner as to generate considerable conflict among the planetary functions involved. This would imply that these two fundamental themes of Crowley's solar and lunar gestalts set up a most difficult pattern of personal obstacles that directly involved his persona, his relationships with other people, his innermost feelings, and his position in the community at large. This is due to the placements of the four planets in the angular houses, that is, in alignment with the Horizon and Meridian of his birthchart, thereby placing their indelible stamp upon the most fundamental structure of his personality.

Furthermore, the opposition of Jupiter to Neptune, also in the Fixed Quadruplicity, adds significantly to the tension and power of this configuration, especially upon consideration of the fact that it forms a solid right angle to Crowley's Horizon—suggesting a *Double* Grand Fixed Cross—and characterizing a most profoundly disturbing yet creative conflict concerning consciousness and sexuality.

Another significant manner in which Crowley's solar and lunar gestalts are interrelated is their connection, by way of the exact degree sextile (60°), between Mars and Luna. This aspect bespeaks a very fortuitous cooperation of the two functions represented by these planets. The dynamic interaction indicated by this aspect, *accentuated by its exactness*, is suggestive of Crowley's remarkable skill for mobilizing his personal efforts in relation to religious activity in general and his talent for the efficacious practice of ceremonial magic in particular. Such talent is attested to by the recognition, even on the part of many of his critics, that his magical operations did in fact produce noticeable *results* in the phenomenal world. Also, the very tight trine between Mars and Pluto, in the context of the whole chart, tells of a smoothly flowing yet powerfully charged and focused application of energy to every task at hand.

There is another connection between the solar and lunar gestalts, the observation of which is most appropriate to the forming of a whole perspective regarding the complete birthchart and, therefore, the whole personality of the man. That encompassing connection is the function of Venus is the "final dispositor" of *every other planet* in Crowley's entire configuration. It is a very rare case indeed for one planet to play such a supremely significant role in the personality of an individual. In fact, this astrologer knows of no other such case. The term "final dispositor" applies to a planet that is last in a sequence of dispositional linkage as traced back from any particular point of reference, usually another planet. In Crowley's case, this means that tracing back dispositions from any point of reference in his birthchart invariably leads back to Venus, and there it ends, because Venus is positioned in a sign that she herself rules. She is therefore not disposed. In terms of the hypothetical division of Crowley's natal configuration into the solar and lunar gestalts as proposed in this book, which together include all the planets, this means that Venus exerts ultimate rulership over both of these gestalts by way of the two routes indicated by her rulerships of Libra *and* Taurus. The fact that Venus is placed in Crowley's Fourth House near the *Imum Coeli* of his birthchart, and in conjunction with Sol, indicates that her ultimate power resided within the depths of his personality and therefore characterizes an overwhelming motivation of love that dictated the primary impetus of Crowley's life, yet in such a manner as to be largely concealed from public view. This provides a fundamental key to understanding the man.

Obviously he did everything in his considerable power to protect this sensitive core of his being. This psychological strategy was accomplished, first and foremost, by the manifestation of an irascible persona, characterized by Crowley's First House, and was elaborated by every other feature of the complex and paradoxical pattern of his natal configuration. The perspectives developed in the interpretation of this remarkable birthchart should prove helpful for resolving the controversies and disparities found throughout the many published accounts and interpretations about who Aleister Crowley was and what significance his influence may or may not have upon our world as we progress ever onward into an enormously challenging future.

CHAPTER 11

TRANSITS

Although a rather thorough interpretation of Aleister Crowley's birthchart has been developed in preceding chapters, the astrological analysis of his life is far from complete. Indeed, no astrological interpretation is *ever* complete. Furthermore, no attempt has been made thus far to provide a biographical perspective upon Crowley's life, other than a few miscellaneous facts and characterological observations appropriate for assessing his personality in relation to specific features of his birthchart. We may now begin a more thoroughgoing examination of Crowley's formative years, with the benefit of applied astrological technique, by analyzing planetary transits in relation to his natal configuration.

The interpretation of planetary transits poses a particular problem for those not familiar with astrological technique. Although natal astrology employs a somewhat comprehensible set of determinants, the analysis of transits becomes infinitely complex by virtue of myriad and continuous interactive planetary movements in relation to a particular natal configuration. The problem then becomes one of *selection*. Questions arise such as: What is the relative importance of the virtually infinite number of interactive movements that can be pointed out? How are the various factors to be integrated into a consistent frame of reference? How can the obscurity of complex and arcane terminology be avoided? And, more significantly for the potential value of astrology as a body of collective knowledge, how can the non-specialist be sure that the astrologer isn't simply selecting from an infinite pool of factors those which are specifically suited to a particular agenda or prejudice?

Those considerations constitute no small part of my penchant for emphasizing the *morphological* basis for astrological interpretation, for therein lies the only *objective* key for sorting out and resolving the above mentioned difficulties. As stated earlier, astrological factors cannot be surgically removed from the whole in which they operate. Furthermore, nearly all astrological configurations are ultimately and necessarily *unique* and therefore cannot be replicated for purposes of comparative analysis. (Exceptions to this are cases of simultaneous births at the same location which are invaluable for advanced astrological studies, provided enough information is available about the natives; a formidable challenge for this kind of research.) These conditions are obstacles to scientific understanding, but they are also particularly well suited for addressing the holistic and singular characteristics of human existence that have always and will forever defy a totally rational explanation. For these reasons, astrology is a study in which science and mystery converge. Morphology is the ground of its science, that is, the objective means by which we may significantly orient ourselves *in relation to* the mystery of life in terms of *relative proportion.*

Any focus upon the transits of various planets through a birthchart is largely determined by the nature and scope of one's inquiry. A teenager in high school, for example, may be most acutely interested in relatively short-term personal concerns in one's life and would therefore be more attuned to the swifter movements of the personal planets through one's birthchart. The understandable lack of interest in more encompassing long-term developments in the life of one so young would render the perspective provided by the much slower movement of Saturn, for example, less compelling. Conversely, an older person, having the benefit of many years of experience upon which to reflect, would find the movement of Saturn through one's birthchart of considerable interest for the perspective it can provide upon the structural context of those years of life experience. Of course, there are many other factors in addition to one's age that contribute to which planetary movements would be of greater concern to any particular person, or that would facilitate any particular line of inquiry.

Transits are the actual movements of planets in space. As such, they indicate ongoing developments of the planetary system in relation to the imprinted pattern of a birthchart, showing evolving environmental parameters for the life of an individual. The ability to focus selectively upon transits of particular planets requires holistic understanding to bring *perspective* to such observations. It is helpful to think about the transits of any particular planet as similar to a *filter* over the lens of a camera, producing a *special effect.* By focusing on the transits of one planet, one actually selects a perspective upon the life of the native that corresponds to the meaning of that planet. One must be able *both* to observe the effect of such a selective focus *and* be aware that several other foci can also be taken, all of which provide different functional perspectives and determine different sets of temporal parameters. For example, Saturn transiting through a particular region of a birthchart exerts a greater influence upon long-term structuring in one's life than does Mars transiting through the same region. This is due to Saturn's slower relative movement and other determinants of the meanings of these two planets. For each complete cycle of the zodiac made by Saturn, Mars makes some fifteen-plus cycles. Mars' transits must therefore be interpreted *within the context* of Saturn's transits, often having a *triggering* effect upon longer-term processes.

Naturally, such factors must be considered for *all* interactive movements within the whole planetary system. It is therefore advantageous to examine the more comprehensive transiting pattern of the social and trans-Saturnian planets at the beginning stages of biographical analysis in order to establish the *context* for the more frequent and repetitive cycles of the personal planets. Furthermore, due to the greater complexity of interactive movements among the personal planets, especially those of Mercury and Venus in relation to Sol, the interpretation of their effects is subject to such a wide array of potential implications that it is generally impossible to make definitive statements about their effects outside the context of extended personal consultation.

It is also necessary to consider the specific meanings of transiting planets for an individual in terms of their natal placements in one's birthchart. For example, the transits of Saturn through Aleister Crowley's birthchart refer not only to the function of character structure, social authority, and circumstantial limitations in general, but also to Crowley's *particular experience* of Saturn's function as an objectified screen of consciousness with distinct social implications that he experienced in terms of relationships with other people as a function of its Aquarius Seventh House placement in *his* birthchart. For all the above stated reasons, Saturn's movement through Crowley's birthchart provides an optimal example for the study of planetary transits.

It is difficult to determine exact dates for many specific events during Crowley's early years. Although his memories of childhood contain many vivid images, the dates of occurrences are often lacking. Due to the complexities inherent in the astrological analysis of planetary movements, however, there is no need to split hairs about the timing of every circumstance in a native's life, even though there are always notable instances when the exact timing of transits are remarkably appropriate to developments in any life. Fortunately, however, the date of the death of Crowley's father and the significance of that event for the formative development of his personality are both securely known, providing a useful fulcrum for the study of transiting Saturn through his birthchart.

Edward Crowley Sr. died on March 5, 1887. Alick (Aleister's boyhood nickname) was eleven years old. Aleister writes about this event in *Confessions*:

> From the moment of the funeral the boy's life entered on an entirely new phase. The change was radical. Within three weeks of his return to school he got into trouble for the first time. He does not remember for what offense, but only that his punishment was diminished on account of his bereavement. This was the first symptom of a complete reversal of his attitude to life in every respect. It seems obvious that his father's death must have been causally connected with it. But even so, the events remain inexplicable. The conditions of his school life, for instance, can hardly have altered, yet his reaction to them makes it almost incredible that it was the same boy.
>
> Previous to the death of Edward Crowley, the recollections of his son, however vivid or detailed, appear to him strangely impersonal. In throwing back his mind to that period, he feels, although attention constantly elicits new facts, that he is investigating the behavior of somebody else. It is only from this point that he begins to think of himself in the first person. From this point, however, he does so; and is able to continue this autobiography in a more conventional style by speaking of himself as I. [p. 53]

This passage is revealing in many respects and serves to corroborate and extend, in terms of temporal dynamics, many of the observations made earlier about Alick's relationship with his father. Before examining the corresponding Saturn transit, let us assess, from a biographical perspective, the nature of this turning point in young Alick's life. A key word used by Crowley to characterize this change is "reversal." This is a very strong word to apply to *any* change in the course of one's life and is characteristic of the extremely paradoxical nature of the man. Surely such a change would entail considerable psychological and even metabolic *disruption* for one undergoing it so abruptly.

Edward Crowley's death was not a total surprise. He had been diagnosed with cancer of the tongue nearly a year earlier, but he had appeared to be responding to treatment (electro-homeopathy), and Alick, away at boarding school since the previous Christmas, was not expecting his abrupt demise. It is reasonable to assume, however, that Alick was able to prepare psychologically for the event.

Prior to his father's death, young Alick had been a devout fundamentalist Christian of the Plymouth Brethren sect and a quite normal English lad with a lot of spunk and a sharp mind. He took the privilege of his family's wealth for granted and had an exalted sense of his social position. He was a bit of a bully and a snob. This basic disposition is very much in keeping with the natal planetary placements examined in previous chapters, particularly those of Uranus and Mars. He felt secure and well supported in his home life, as per his South Node, Sol and Venus in Libra at the Imum Coeli of his birthchart, which provided the context of his whole world as a young child. His impetuous nature (First House Uranus in Leo) was exquisitely counterbalanced by his feeling of partnership with his father (Seventh House Saturn in Aquarius), which he accepted unquestioningly in the quest of winning souls for Jesus. His father's overbearing nature tended to justify his own, and, so long as he proclaimed his faith, his father's ultimate approval was guaranteed. Despite whatever disruptive flurries may have occurred, Alick was possessed of all the ingredients for happiness and contentment.

The radical change that occurred in young Crowley's attitude immediately following the death of his father is indicative of the extreme importance the presence of his father had played as a key factor in the dynamic equilibrium of the boy's life. The removal of that factor left such a vacuum as to precipitate a psychological storm of immense proportions. The direct implication inherent in the curious observation made by Crowley in the above passage, involving his recollection of himself in the third person prior to his father's death, is suggestive of a host of interpretations. Most significantly, it indicates an unconscious *identification* with his father such that he was not confronted experientially with a sense of *his own* identity until the screen image upon which he had been projecting it was removed from his life, and, in effect, absorbed into himself. Certain implications are inherent in this scenario. First and foremost, the inherent difficulties of the boy's personality, as delineated in previous chapters, were simply *too much* for any child consciously to accommodate. He *needed* some kind of a vicarious buffer zone of personality in order to cushion the blow of coming to terms with himself. Secondly, by using the image of his father in this manner, his father had a molding effect upon Crowley's conscious orientation toward a proselytizing and evangelical temperament. In response to his father's death it remained for Crowley to develop, or be remolded by the inherent challenge of the event into a persona more appropriate to his identity as a person in his own right.

There is another extremely important component of young Alick's identification with his father, and that pertains to the formation of the Oedipus complex in early childhood for the male personality. Young Alick's identification with his father may be comprehended as a usurpation of his father's role as the consort of his mother. This allegory implies that, despite his conscious allegiance with his father, at an unconscious level he had challenged and destroyed the image of his father within himself in order to possess the image of his mother for purposes of imaginary sexual gratification. This patricidal component of the Oedipus complex naturally generates "castration anxiety" in relation to the actual experience of the father which holds the personality of the boy in check. In this sense, the death of Crowley's father removed a major constraint upon the boy's libidinal economy at the critical preadolescent stage of his development.

Despite the fact that Freudian psychoanalysis has been severely criticized in recent decades, often justifiably I believe, the phenomenal insights into the dynamics of the formation of unconscious complexes that Freud developed, *particularly as they obtain within the context of Judeo-Christian civilization*, have proven to be of great value for the understanding of personality formation and development. As stated earlier, I am in agreement with Israel Regardie's position that this kind of analysis is essential to the understanding of any personality, and particularly the personality of Aleister Crowley. Such an explanation would certainly help to account for the boy's incredible naiveté with regard to sexuality as he entered puberty and his obsessive quest to unravel the mystery of "sin" insofar as it pertained to such matters.

The reversal of attitude that young Crowley experienced as a consequence of his father's death was accompanied by an entirely different home life resulting from his mother's relocation to London to be near her brother, Tom Bishop, immediately following her husband's demise. Crowley goes to great lengths in *Confessions* to contrast the temperament of his uncle Tom, whom he utterly despised, with that of his father. Despite whatever self-serving embellishments or exaggerations that may be attributed to Crowley's characterization of Tom Bishop, it is evident that the man embodied the most detestable features of Christian hypocrisy and thereby contributed to young Crowley's emergent revulsion for the Christian religion.

There was, however, a more poignant antagonism that ensued at this time in Crowley's life with the headmaster of the school he was attending, the Reverend H. d'Arcy Champney, himself a Plymouth Brother who had started a school for the sons of the Brethren in Cambridge. A thorough account of this episode is given in *Confessions*, including a passage from Crowley's *The World's Tragedy*, entitled "A Boyhood in Hell," which contains an account of the perverse manner by which supervision and discipline were conducted by Champney. Severe corporal punishment was administered for petty crimes on the mere basis of accusations from fellow students. Long maledictions were delivered concerning the Lord's supervision of the school. "I remember one licking I got—on the legs, because flogging the buttocks excites the victim's sensuality!—fifteen minutes prayer, fifteen strokes of the cane, fifteen minutes more prayer, fifteen more strokes—and more prayer to top it!" [p. 65] About the change in his attitude toward his school life Crowley writes: "It is impossible to suppose that the character of the school had completely changed between my father's death and my return from the funeral. Yet before that I was completely happy and in sympathy with my surroundings. Not three weeks later, Ishmael was my middle name. I cannot account for it at all satisfactorily." [p. 66]

Several months later, one of Alick's classmates claimed to have found Alick drunk at the bottom of the stairs while visiting him over the holidays. The boy had visited Alick, but the story was a fabrication. With no investigation whatsoever, Champney forthwith called Alick in and demanded a confession without telling him what he had been accused of. Unable to satisfy the demand, Alick was put into "Coventry," that is, he was not allowed to speak or be spoken to by any master or boy. He was fed on bread and water, consigned to work in the schoolroom during play hours and walk the perimeter of the empty playground alone during work hours. This punishment went on for a term and a half, after which he was threatened with expulsion if he would not confess. At this point Alick's health broke down. His ailment was diagnosed by the family doctor as albuminuria, a kidney disease. The doctor warned that the boy might not see manhood. He advised private teaching, outdoor activities, and circumcision. His advice was followed on all counts.

Some reflections upon the long-term effect of this episode are in order at this juncture. One would be hard pressed to find any person in history who has been more severely slandered in the public media. It is assuredly the case that Crowley exacerbated his own defamation, but that is not to say that the allegations made against him were valid and factual. For the most part, they were false. The revaluation of Crowley made possible by the journalistic efforts of people who were close to him, as well as the study of Crowley's own writings, absolves him in no uncertain terms. Misunderstood, he surely was. Mean tempered, petty, ornery and nasty he surely was on many occasions. And, of course, he was markedly eccentric in his attitudes about sexuality and religion. But truly wicked and villainous he was not. Nor was he a Satanist in the commonly understood sense as many have accused. Furthermore, he was perhaps unequaled in his honesty about his motives and beliefs as a human being, and this trait is perhaps the single most contributing factor to the journalistic abuse he suffered at the hands of an influential element of his fellow countrymen which extended to prejudice the world against him.

It is obvious that Crowley was galvanized against Christian religion by his experience at the hands of Champney, Bishop, his mother, and the community of Plymouth Brethren which constituted his entire world well into his adolescence. The loss of his father, precipitating his initiation into manhood in the mythic sense at the tender age of eleven, jolted him from his childhood dream of Christian glory. Without the qualified magnanimity of his father to mediate the exuberance of his highly charged and insightful personality, the boy could no longer refrain from becoming himself. The challenge to traditional authority was such a latent feature of his persona that it simply *had* to manifest itself. It is pitifully ironic that Crowley was so ill prepared to undergo the ordeals of this initiation that nature and circumstance visited upon him.

It is extremely important to ascertain the admixture of conscious and unconscious motives on the part of *all* players in this drama. The inherent cruelty of Champney, inexcusable in a man of full maturity, was given a virtual free reign toward Alick by the death of his father. The duplicity of his classmates toward a formerly privileged cohort was likewise facilitated. It is reasonable to assume that young Crowley was made to pay for the relative tolerance and wealth of his father, which no doubt irked the mendacious element that dominated the boy's immediate milieu, not only at school but in his new home environment as well. It should not prove surprising that the boy responded as he did.

We find him saying in *Confessions* about his changed attitude upon returning to school: "Indeed, my falling away from grace was not occasioned by any intellectual qualms; I accepted the theology of the Plymouth Brethren. In fact, I could hardly conceive of the existence of people who might doubt it. I simply went over to Satan's side; and to this hour I cannot tell why." [pp. 66-67] It is essential to understand that Crowley is in no way speaking of a conversion to Satanism as it is commonly conceived or a proclivity for the abhorrent practices of such cults as practice ritual murder or the like, as many of his detractors, and even a host of misfits who speak of him with ignorant misguided awe, would prefer that we believe. "Satan's side" of which Crowley spoke was simply an *alternative* to the way of life dogmatically sanctioned by the religious teachings upon which he was raised. Ultimately, it meant no more than what is normally thought of as having a good time by way of indulging one's sensual nature and the instinct to freely express one's thoughts and feelings. This is the essence of what Crowley stood for through the remainder of his life. Even the tentative emergence of this attitude was sufficient to evoke the resistance of the opposition such that we find Crowley acknowledging, in a concluding assessment of this episode, a deeper significance than that of a merely behavioral dispute.

> My revolt must have manifested itself by actions which were technically not blameworthy. I cannot accuse myself of any overt crime. The battle between myself and the school was conducted on the magical plane, so to speak. It was as if I had made wax figures of the most inoffensive sort, that yet were recognized by the spiritual instinct of Champney as idols or instruments of witchcraft. I was punished with absolute injustice and stupidity, yet at the same time the mystical apprehension of Champney made no mistake. [*ibid.*, p. 68]

This passage reveals a clear understanding on the part of the mature Crowley about what had been taking place at the time of his boyhood encounter with Champney, and it provides an apt example of the manner in which unconscious forces and motives are played out at the conscious level. In short, there is no way that the conflict could have been averted. It was destined to occur by inherent aspects of character on the part of both parties. For Champney, the traits were ingrained by a lifetime of attitude formation and rigidification. For Crowley, they were yet latent and untried by conscious articulation. Yet in each case the force behind them far exceeded the conventional frame of reference that would normally be attributed to the situation at hand. It is as if on an innocuous school-yard two locomotives traveling on unseen tracks collided. More of the subsequent career of Aleister Crowley will be examined as we proceed. As for Champney, we are informed that after Crowley was removed from the school, "within a very short time the insanity of the headmaster became patent and the school was broken up in consequence." [*ibid.*, p. 70]

In accordance with the interpretation of Crowley's natal Saturn in previous chapters, it follows that its transiting motion had a significant bearing upon the emergent direction and development of his conscious orientation to life. As the objective component of his natal Uranus-Saturn opposition, Saturn served as the *screen* upon which his sense of identity was projected, as opposed to the *source* of that projection from Uranus which galvanized his persona *automatically*, that is, without Crowley's conscious awareness. This function of the projection of consciousness was facilitated early on by the presence of his father. It is therefore the case that only through Saturn's transiting back toward the ascending side of his birthchart was young Alick able slowly to assimilate his projected identity into his subjective experience of selfhood.

The period of Saturn's orbit (just under thirty years) is such that it approaches the opposition aspect to its natal position at the onset of puberty. It follows that this transit is associated with the *tension* experienced during early adolescence and is symbolically appropriate to the issue of social identity; that is, personal *definition* within the context of society that confronts one at this time. More specifically, the first opposition of Saturn to its natal position refers to a time at which the native is forced to realize, although incompletely and usually for the first time in one's life, that social existence imposes conditions of *responsibility* for one's personal existence therein. The tendency in this regard is toward disillusionment. Optimally, this is a time at which meaningful counsel from one's father, or some other figure who embodies maturity and understanding, can be helpful toward making necessary adjustments toward a mature acceptance of social constraints.

It is appropriate at this juncture to cite an additional factor closely associated with the onset of adolescence to provide a more balanced perspective upon the whole phenomenon. Jupiter has an orbital period of almost exactly twelve years, whereby its first return to its natal position is universally experienced at the age of twelve, roughly three years before Saturn's opposition to its own natal position. These two aspect formations are fundamental to the onset of adolescence. The Jupiter return produces a feeling of expansive wholeness in terms of meaningful social participation and accounts for the highly idealistic component of early adolescence, often precipitating a sense of spiritual exaltation. The *subjective* nature of this experience is a function of the *conjunction* aspect being formed by Jupiter to its natal position. The *opposition* aspect thereafter formed by Saturn to its own natal position counterbalances that subjective expansiveness with the *objective* experience of socially imposed limitations that define the realm *within which* one's social expansion is to be contained. The timing of this pattern characterizes the social awakening and adjustment generally associated with the period from age twelve to fifteen. It becomes particularized for an individual within the context of one's unique natal configuration.

In directing our focus to planetary transits in Crowley's life it is helpful to visualize them in relation to his complete birthchart presented in Figure 8.

Saturn made its first transiting contact to another planet in Crowley's birthchart upon reaching his natal Luna in the 23rd degree of Pisces at age 2 years and 5 months and made a retrograde pass returning to within 3 1/2° of his natal Luna one and a half months after his third birthday. This transit occurred at the onset of the formation of the Oedipus Complex in the male personality, that is, around age three. This indicates an *accentuated archetypal experience* for little Alick of this otherwise more generalized process. For transiting Saturn, which for Crowley carried an especially strong *identification* with his father, to reach the position of his natal Luna (naturally associated with the experience of the mother image) at the time when, through normal childhood development, the male child experiences the awakening of libidinal striving toward the mother is indicative of a peculiar *magnification* and *focusing* of this process for Crowley. In this regard, we find him singled out already as an exemplar for this archetypal motif. It will be recalled that, through her rulership of Crowley's Cancerian Twelfth House, Luna rules that house which evinces the domain of most profound mystery for the native and also implies the potential for personal transcendence. This theme is accentuated by Luna's natal placement in Pisces, the twelfth sign, which therefore bears a macrocosmic resonance with the microcosmic Twelfth House producing an exalted transcendental concep-

tion of femininity, with strong philosophical and religious connotations, due to her Ninth House placement and the fullness of her
phase. The core period of Alick's Oedipal phase was experienced as
Saturn made a retrograde pass over his Midheaven, contacting it
three times from age 3 years and 7 months through age 4 years and 3
months.

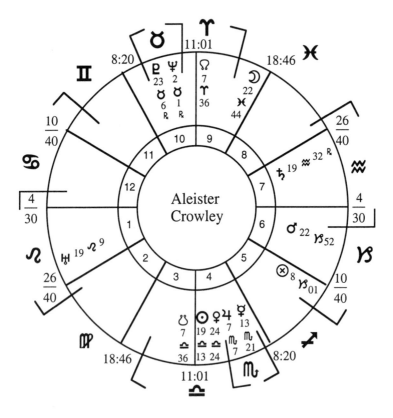

FIGURE 8
The complete birthchart of Aleister Crowley

The timing of this transit bears heavily upon the development of
Crowley's attitudes toward women insofar as issues of power and
authority are concerned. In one sense he tended to hold himself
above women as exemplified by his treating his mother "as a servant." A statement in *Confessions* in which he tells of having to

satisfy his urges during his college years with the younger women of the district exhibits this aspect of Crowley's attitude toward women: "The stupidity of having had to waste uncounted priceless hours in chasing what ought to have been brought to the back door every evening with the milk!" [p. 113] The compensatory component of masochism, however, must also be considered to have its roots firmly entrenched beneath this timely transit of Saturn as little Alick languished under its heavy advantage.

It was soon after that time that Crowley's father moved the family from Leamington to Redhill, Surrey. We are informed in *Confessions* that, "Alick lived here till 1886 and his memory of this period is of perpetual happiness." [p. 46] He says of this period that "Aristocratic feeling was extremely strong." [*ibid.*] A passage in *Confessions* characterizes Alick's sense of the roughly six-year period from the Crowley's move to Redhill until May of 1886, when he was called home from Champney's school due to his father's illness. This is the period of Saturn's transit through Alick's Tenth and Eleventh Houses, from late Aries, through Taurus and Gemini, and into early Cancer. With reference to this period Crowley writes:

> Practically all boys are born with the aristocratic spirit. In most cases they are broken down, partly by bullying, partly by experience. In the case of Alick, he was the only son of a father who was naturally a leader of men. In him, therefore, this spirit grew unchecked. He knew no superior but his father; and though that father ostentatiously avoided assuming authority over the other Brethren, it was, of course, none the less there. The boy seems to have despised from the first the absence of hierarchy among the Brethren, though at the same time they formed the most exclusive body on earth, being the only people that were going to heaven. There is thus an extreme psychological contradiction inherent in the situation. It is improbable that Alick was aware at the time of the real feelings which must have been implanted in him by this environment; but the main result was undoubtedly to stimulate his pride and ambition in a most unwholesome (?) degree. His social and financial position, the obvious envy of his associates, his undoubted personal prowess, physical and intellectual, all combined to make it impossible for him to be satisfied to take any place in the world but the top. The Plymouth Brethren refused to take any part in politics. Among them, the peer and the peasant met theoretically as equals, so that the social system of England was simply ignored. The boy could not aspire to become prime minister or even king; he was already apart from and beyond all that. It will

be seen that as soon as he arrived at an age where ambitions are
compelled to assume concrete form, his position became extremely
difficult. The earth was not big enough to hold him. [p. 52]

Matters of public ambition and social aspirations are concerns of
the Tenth and Eleventh Houses respectively. His reflections upon
these themes are very appropriate to his conception of the significance of this period of his childhood. The energetic and personalized
tone of his language befit the zodiacal signs involved, and Crowley's
positive assessment of this period indicates that this transit of Saturn
helped to establish the incorporation of energy through his North
Node in Aries near his Midheaven, despite the fact that his feelings
in this regard were being held in check by his father's religious
orientation.

The time at which Alick was called home from school to learn of
his father's illness was the time of transiting Saturn's entry into his
Twelfth House. The particular significance of this moment is characterized by Crowley in *Confessions*:

> In looking back over his life up to May 1886, he can find little con-
> secution and practically no coherence in his recollections. But from
> that month onwards there is a change. It is as if the event which
> occurred at that time created a new faculty in his mind. A new
> factor had arisen and its name was death. He was called home from
> school in the middle of the term to attend a special prayer meeting
> at Redhill. His father had been taken ill. The local doctor had sent
> him to see Sir James Paget, who had advised an immediate opera-
> tion for cancer of the tongue. Brethren from far and near had been
> summoned to help discover the Lord's will in the matter. The
> upshot was that the operation was declined; it was decided to treat
> the disease by Count Mattei's electro-homeopathy, a now dis-
> carded system of unusually outrageous quackery. No doctor
> addicted to this form of swindling being locally available, The
> Grange [at Redhill] was given up and a house called Glenburnie
> taken at Southampton. [pp. 52-53]

Several factors coalesced that corroborate the association of this
development in Crowley's life with Saturn's entry into his Twelfth
House. A transcendent pressure was brought to bear upon his
heretofore undisturbed identification with his father. The *foreshad-
owing* of an awakening to himself was brought to consciousness by
the realization of the inevitability, if not the immediacy, of his
father's death. A continuation of the Oedipal theme is also directly

implied. As transiting Saturn proceeded to move through Cancer, having conjoined natal Luna (planetary ruler of Cancer) at the initiation of Crowley's Oedipal phase, its entry into his Twelfth House brought an acute *focus* to Crowley's conception of transcendence. The *actual* prospect of his father's death dramatically struck the boy at this time, thus activating the patricidal component of the Oedipus Complex in a most remarkable manner as puberty loomed on the horizon. His natural, albeit unconscious, libidinal striving for the mother image as a developing child was being focused by the structuring power of Saturn into the realization of a transcendental ideal. Crowley was actually developing an *unconscious sense of power* in relation to this event as a function of an archetypal mystery of life that has been codified by Freud as the Oedipus Complex of male personality development. This process of normal childhood development, thus magnified and focused by the phenomenal timing of Saturn's transits in relation to natal factors, established the personal foundation from which Aleister Crowley would ultimately launch his attack upon the supreme father of Western civilization, namely the authoritarian God of Christianity, and take possession of the Eternal Feminine through his identification with the Beast of the Apocalypse and its mythological association with the Scarlet Woman, who Crowley would come to exalt, by virtue of his prophetic revelation, to the status of supreme power.

The culmination of this mysterious process of protracted initiation that characterized the entire childhood of Aleister Crowley turned upon his father's actual death some nine months later on March 5, 1887. Saturn was yet in Cancer and about to enter Leo, Crowley's rising sign, which it did the following summer, five months after his father's death. As Alick turned twelve, Saturn reached his Ascendant and, one year later, his natal Uranus, forming the exact opposition to its own natal position. Crowley informs us that the false accusation made against him to Champney occurred when he was twelve years old and that the severe punishment for his inability to confess continued for a term and a half. His conscious orientation associated with his natal Seventh House Saturn had been reconnected to the source of its projection (First House Uranus), bringing the weight of social authority in the noxious form of the putrefied residua of a dying aeon which animated the person of the shadow father figure of the headmaster Champney to bear upon the very persona of the boy who, after the loss of his father's benevolent intercession, was forced to withstand alone the extended ordeal of public humiliation and alienation that was visited upon him through the very institution of his father's religious zeal and God's will on Earth, namely the Plymouth Brethren religious sect. The complex irony of this scenario, focused within the developing personality of this most unfortunate lad, is monumental to say the least.

For the male personality, the onset of puberty has primordial associations with initiation into manhood. Such an initiation has archetypal significance because it corresponds to the awakening of the sexual impulse through the maturation of the reproductive organs and is traditionally celebrated through some form of ritual enactment of acceptance into the adult male community. No religious tradition has proven more inept at affecting the experience of initiation into manhood than Christianity (appropriate to the theme of crucifixion), and a worst case scenario of that ineptitude was mercilessly visited upon young Edward Alexander Crowley through his experience at the hands of the Plymouth Brethren. The psychological impact of such an ordeal upon the formation of Crowley's adult personality can hardly be overestimated. In one fell swoop, a fundamentally innocent, bright, and regal young lad was reduced to blind disgrace and alienation from the only world he had ever known. Later in life, Crowley would identify himself with the image of "Alastor, the Spirit of Solitude, the Wanderer of the Wastes," and, in fact, the original title for *Confessions* was *The Spirit of Solitude.* No great acumen is required to attribute the roots of this identification to lonely hours of solitary walking for months on end around an empty schoolyard at 51 Bateman Street, Cambridge, England. The manner by which the Oedipal theme (including its component of castration anxiety) was reiterated through Crowley's initiation into adolescence is indeed remarkable. This theme was punctuated in proper fashion by the perfunctory performance of the ancient mutilation ritual of purification by circumcision. For Crowley, even *that* aspect of the extended magnification of the Oedipal theme was in a manner literally fulfilled.

There was another important transit taking place during the three year period of Crowley's entry into Champney's school, his father's death, and his confrontation with Champney. That was the transit of Uranus over his natal South Node, *Imum Coeli* (Fourth House cusp), and natal Sol respectively. A great deal could be said about this transit in terms of the factors involved as interpreted in previous chapters. Perhaps the most succinct assessment would be that this transit affected a severe *disruption* of Crowley's comfort zone within the inner depths of his personality, a quickening of his greater Self and a linking of that Self to his persona through Uranus' implicit reference back to its natal placement in Crowley's First House. One interesting correspondence is that, as transiting Uranus reached his natal Sol in Libra at the culmination of his ordeal with Champney, the boy's kidneys failed. The kidney region is said to be ruled by Libra. What is remarkable about the severity of the concurrence of the transits of Saturn and Uranus at this time in Crowley's life is that, after this crisis, he was able to revitalize himself, albeit over a period of many years, and become one of the greatest physical specimens of the twentieth century, demonstrated adequately enough by his phenomenal mountaineering exploits. This accomplishment alone is a testament to the powerful inner resources of the man (largely attributable to his Sixth House Mars in Capricorn).

Crowley's removal from Champney's school marks the completed culmination of the childhood formation of his personality. Indeed, he was yet a child in many respects, but the die had been cast. Through the greater freedom of expression facilitated by the appointment of a succession of tutors, the boy slowly regained his health. It would continue to plague him even after his entry into a public school at Malvern in 1892. In the interim, however, he had been introduced to a more liberated perspective upon the world by one of his tutors that his Uncle Tom Bishop had inadvertently let slip through the crack. This was Archibald Douglas, "an Oxford man who had purged that offense by having traveled for the Bible Society across Persia" [*ibid.,* p. 75] Crowley was fifteen years old at the time (Spring of 1891) and ripe for new perspectives in the wake of his crisis with the Brethren. Douglas' influence on Crowley was appropriate to the continuing transit of Uranus through the grouping of planets in his Fourth House. Crowley writes:

> Though Douglas called himself a Christian, he proved to be both a man and a gentleman. I presume that poverty had compelled the camouflage. From the moment that we were alone together he produced a complete revolution in my outlook upon life, by showing me for the first time a sane, clean, jolly world worth living in. Smoking and drinking were natural. He warned me of the dangers of excess from the athletic standpoint. He introduced me to racing, billiards, betting, cards and women. He told me how these things might be enjoyed without damaging oneself or wronging others. He put me up to all the tricks. He showed me the meaning of honour. I immediately accepted his standpoint and began to behave

like a normal, healthy human being. The nightmare world of Christianity vanished at the dawn. [*ibid.*]

As Uranus completed its transit through the South Node and the
grouping of four planets at the Imum Coeli of his birthchart (1886-
1894), transiting Saturn had reached his South Node to follow immediately upon Uranus through that same region (1893-1896). Crowley
was appropriately coming to terms with his inner life and consolidat-
ing the ground of his personality. This was the period in which he
began seriously to develop his skill as a mountain climber. As transiting Saturn reached Jupiter and Mercury (the knowledge planets)
Crowley entered Trinity College at Cambridge and embarked upon
an enormous program of self-education, immersing himself in the
major philosophical works and literary heritage of the English language through long hours of reading late into the night and early
morning. In keeping with the Scorpionic theme of this transit, he
indulged his sexual appetite with local girls who were readily available for the purpose. He also formed a profound friendship with one
Herbert Charles Jerome Pollitt, with whom he enjoyed "that ideal
intimacy which the Greeks considered the greatest glory of manhood
and the most precious prize of life." [*ibid.*, p. 142]

There is quite a remarkable correspondence of two experiences in
Crowley's life to the transiting conjunction of Saturn to Uranus in
late Scorpio that occurred in 1897. This correspondence is most
illuminating in relation to the natal placements of those planets in
Crowley's birthchart and the temporal pattern established by their
transits thus far delineated. Saturn had finally "caught up with"
Uranus, thus completing the cycle of relationship that had been fully
extended in the opposition aspect at the time of his birth. The *subjective impact* of this conjunction upon Crowley was indeed profound.
An account of these experiences is given by Gerald Suster in *The
Legacy of the Beast*:

> It was in Stockholm on New Year's Eve 1896 that he underwent
> his first mystical experience—something of which he tells us little:
> 'I was awakened to the knowledge that I possessed a magical
> means of becoming conscious of and satisfying a part of my nature
> which had up to that moment concealed itself from me. It was an
> experience of horror and pain, combined with a certain ghostly
> terror, yet at the same time it was the key to the purist and holiest
> spiritual ecstasy that exists.' In October 1897, there occurred a
> second experience which he defined rather more clearly and it was

one which many have undergone. Its nature and its significance to Western Man have been brilliantly explored, for instance, by Colin Wilson in *The Outsider*. The Outsider is the one 'who sees too deep and too much', becoming, in consequence, alienated from the herd and its material concerns; for he is appalled by the futility of all human endeavour. Buddhists call this the Trance of Sorrow. Others might term it 'an existential crisis'. All who have experienced it agree on three points: the feeling is one of bitter agony; eventually one becomes conscious of a ravenous hunger and infinite yearning—suspected in themselves to be futile—for some secret glory which will restore essential meaning to life; and it changes one's fundamental point of view for a lifetime. [pp. 23-24]

The first transiting conjunction of Saturn to Uranus in this series occurred on January 5, 1897. Saturn had been applying within 13 minutes of arc on New Years Eve! The second (retrograde) conjunction occurred on June 1, and the third and final conjunction occurred on September 8, just before Crowley's second experience. The extreme importance of this transiting conjunction for Crowley is confirmed by these experiences and the powerful effect they had upon his life.

The next major nexus of events in Crowley's life involved his association with the Hermetic Order of the Golden Dawn and the break-up of the Order. The significance of that episode for Crowley is best accounted for astrologically in terms of his second Jupiter Return. The transit of the first Jupiter Return was mentioned above in general terms as being one of the fundamental determinants of the onset of adolescence. This occurred for Crowley as his situation worsened at school, following his father's death. Jupiter's natal opposition to Neptune must be taken into consideration in this regard. Young Alick was secretly obsessed at this time with trying to discover the mysterious essence of "sin" as it pertained to sexuality. The right angle (square) of this opposition to Crowley's Horizon (axis of consciousness) helps to account for the incredible naiveté of his pubescent development. An enormous damming of libidinal energy is implied, affecting a charging-up of the unconscious regions of personality.

It is also relevant to observe the placement of Crowley's natal Jupiter, within the grouping of the South Node, *Imum Coeli*, and three other planets, whereby the whole phenomenon of his Jupiter Return involves Jupiter's transit through this entire cluster of factors in his birthchart. Interestingly, for Crowley's first Jupiter Return this process was kicked off by a transiting conjunction of Jupiter and Uranus at his South Node right at the time he was informed of his father's illness. He attests to a radical change in his thinking at this time as recounted above in relation to transiting Saturn's entry into his Twelfth House. This powerful transiting conjunction at his South Node indicates a powerful disruption of his inner karmic orientation at that time, shaking up his tendency to acquiesce in sacrifice through complacency. In accordance with William Wordsworth's profound adage, "The child is father to the man," surely the transits of Jupiter, Saturn, and Uranus at that crucial time in young Alick's life are indicative of a shaping tendency that would come to fruition in later years.

Crowley's involvement with the Golden Dawn Order in his early to mid-twenties, the time of his *second* Jupiter Return, confirms the significance of that earlier conditioning. Transiting Jupiter reached his natal South Node and *Imum Coeli*, thus initiating its movement through his Fourth House cluster, in the spring of 1898, the time of his reading *The Cloud Upon the Sanctuary* at age 22. This helps to account for the profound effect the book had upon him in relation to the Jupiterian activation of his karmic past, through its particular characterization of a community of saints who directed the spiritual progress of humanity, at a time appropriate for him to be inspired by such an idea. He conveyed his interest in this matter to Julian Baker at the time of their first meeting by chance encounter in the Swiss Alps. Baker introduced him to George Cecil Jones, an Adept of the Order, and on November 18, Crowley undertook the Neophyte initiation into the Golden Dawn. At the time of his actual Jupiter Return in January of 1899 he was quickly working his way through the grades of the Outer Order.

Crowley was to reenact the pattern of his relation to his father image through his involvement with the Golden Dawn and the head of the Order, S.L. MacGregor Mathers. This drama developed in a fascinating manner, especially from the perspective of assigning a pivotal significance for the Order to the appearance of the young aspirant Crowley himself. Although Jones, Mathers, and Allan Bennett, another formidable magician in the Order, recognized Crowley's natural abilities, only a very few of those involved would see Crowley as anything other than an impetuous nuisance to the sanctity of the Order.

The Golden Dawn had reached a difficult impasse regarding its leadership at the time of Crowley's admission. Mathers, one of the original three co-founders of the Order, had assumed sole authority, which he exercised from his Paris Temple. His autocratic manner had begun to alienate many of the Second Order initiates of the London Temple. His authority was based on his claim to have established contact with the "Secret Chiefs" of the Order in 1892, the time of his formulation of the rituals of initiation for the Second "Rosicrucian" Order, that is, the Inner Order of Adepts who would thereafter exercise authority over the Outer Order. The Secret Chiefs presumably only betray their identities to a very few selected emissaries for the purpose of advancing the evolutionary progress of humanity. Mathers' claim of having established contact with the Secret Chiefs, as well as the claims regarding the manuscripts authorizing the original formulation of the Order in 1887, were, of course, questionable by their very nature. The only credible basis for evaluating them was the efficacy of the methods employed to affect the stated objectives of the order. In this regard, Mathers' creative genius was undisputed by those who were involved in the practical working.

In early January of 1900, Crowley had successfully completed the preparatory work, although there is some question about his fulfillment of the requisite waiting period, for him to be eligible for initiation to the Adeptus Minor grade of the Second Order. His elevation had been approved by Mathers, and he eagerly anticipated being the first twentieth century initiate into the Inner Order. His petition was refused by the London Temple, however, on the grounds of "moral turpitude." The Second Order Adepts of the London Temple did not approve of Aleister Crowley's private affairs, particularly the manner in which he conducted his sex life. One of the members, W.B. Yeats, wrote in a letter to Lady Gregory, as recounted by Colin Wilson in *Aleister Crowley, The Nature of the Beast*, that they had refused to admit Crowley into the Second Order "because we did not think a mystical society was intended to be a reformatory." [p. 55] Mathers, however, was of the opinion that a person's sex life was one's own concern, and he performed the Adeptus Minor initiation for Crowley at his Temple in Paris on January 16, 1900. [Howe, p. 206] The London Temple, however, did not recognize Crowley's initiation and refused him the instructional manuscripts to which he was entitled by virtue of his Adept status.

It would appear that it was not only Crowley's "moral turpitude" that was at issue. The London Adepts were also using Crowley's petition as an issue of contention in a power struggle with Mathers. This dispute led to an outright declaration of independence from

Mathers by the London Temple in March of 1900. Hearing of this, Crowley broke off his magical exercises at his home in Boleskine, Scotland and went immediately to Paris, placing his resources at Mathers' disposal. Mathers sent Crowley to London as his Envoy Plenipotentiary to change the locks on the London Temple. In a dramatic confrontation, Crowley, dressed in highlands kilts and calling himself Aleister MacGregor, took brief possession of the London Temple. The police, however, ordered the premises returned to the custody of the London group. The Hermetic Order of the Golden Dawn had nonetheless been irrevocably fractured.

The alliance between Crowley and Mathers can easily be interpreted as self-serving for both, however, the entire scenario, which ultimately culminated in Crowley's claim four years hence to depose Mathers as the one chosen by the Secret Chiefs to bring the Word of the New Aeon to humankind, embodies a very discernible pattern that may be comprehended by anyone who understands the purport of Crowley's prophetic revelation, *thus obviating the need to recognize any second-hand authority in matters pertaining to spiritual truth.* When viewed in this light, the events of the break-up of the Golden Dawn bespeak a greater intelligence on the part of the Secret Chiefs that fully transcends that of any participants in the parody. Both the hero-worshipping and patricidal components of Crowley's Oedipus complex can be seen in this fiasco to have served a greater purpose in the working out of his destiny, which it was his will to place at the disposal of divinity in whatever form proved strongest, as in accordance with his oath of obligation for entry into the Second Order of Adepts, which was the pivotal event of the whole dramatic episode.

By June, Jupiter had entered its own domicile of Sagittarius and Crowley's Fifth House of self-expression. Appropriate to Jupiter's association with "long journeys," Crowley sailed for New York on what would become a trip around the world. During this journey he spent time in Mexico with his mountain climbing mentor, Oscar Eckenstein, who taught Crowley a technique for developing mental concentration that would greatly enhance his magical abilities. He also spent some time with his friend from the Golden Dawn, Allan Bennett, who had moved to Ceylon. There he learned the practice of yoga and achieved the first major trance of Dhyana in which subject and object become united. After returning to England, and a disappointing visit with Mathers in Paris, Crowley was disillusioned with everything. All his pursuits and achievements had led him back to his

Trance of Sorrow. He resigned himself to the Buddhist position that Existence is Suffering.

In 1902, Crowley participated in his first Himalayan expedition to Chogo-Ri, where he established a record, reaching a height of over twenty-two thousand feet, a climb that would not be surpassed until the 1920's. The expedition, however, failed to reach the summit due to a horrendous blizzard. Saturn was transiting over Crowley's natal Mars in Capricorn at the time of this expedition. Capricorn connotes personal ambition, and mountain climbing is one of its most appropriate symbolic embodiments. Although the traditional symbol for Capricorn is a sea-goat, that is, a figure with a goat's upper body and a fish-like lower body, the goat aspect is suggestive of the renowned climbing ability of that species. Moreover, the complete symbol is a representation of the entire earth-bound animal kingdom suggesting the evolutionary drive from the depths of the ocean to the heights of the mountain tops. When the zodiac is drawn in its traditional circular pattern, Capricorn is initiated by the topmost point of the circle, appropriate to the attainment of heights. Saturn, the ruler of Capricorn, strongly accentuates the theme of ambition and all things Capricornian as it transits through its domicile.

Upon Saturn's reaching Crowley's natal Sixth House Mars in Capricorn, which in turn rules Crowley's Midheaven (the topmost point of *his* birthchart), Crowley's mountain climbing skill became the means for a thrust of ambition on his part to obtain recognition in the world for his personal prowess. The outcome of the expedition proved in fact to be prophetic of the course of Crowley's whole life. He would reach for ultimate heights and would outperform all others in his milieu, but he would fall short of his consciously intended goal. The blizzard of world folly and his own paradoxical machinations would drive him away from the summit of social recognition which he sought for his achievements.

On August 12, 1903, Aleister Crowley married Rose Kelly. Saturn was passing in retrograde motion through the *very descending degree* of his birthchart, the cusp of his Seventh House of relationships. Indeed, Crowley was embarking upon a marriage of destiny. Furthermore, transiting Jupiter was conjoined to his natal Luna, transiting Mars to his natal Jupiter, and transiting Sol to his natal Uranus with all four of these transiting planets in their traditional domiciles, bringing their dispositional pressure directly to bear upon their guests, at it were. Crowley's bases were extremely well covered. The climax of this *mysterium coniunctionis* would occur in an improvised temple in an apartment room in Cairo, Egypt on April 8, 9 and 10, 1904. The story of these events will be recounted in the next chapter.

The most significant transit at that critical moment in the life of Aleister Crowley, the time at which he penned the pivotal work of his prophetic career, is that of Saturn less than one degree from its natal position. It made exact contact on April 18. The first Saturn return is a crucial time in anyone's life. It marks the onset of the maturity that is associated with adulthood. At this time a person is brought to the realization of full responsibility for one's life in what is often called "the real world." Real life psychology is seldom this cut and dried in relation to specific dates, but the advent of the first Saturn return is nonetheless especially significant for the structuring of one's unique existence. In Crowley's case, this transit proves to be the critical turning point of his entire life, which, along with the earlier transits of Saturn elucidated above, emphasizes the archetypal power of this man's unique contribution to humanity.

Not only was this the time of Crowley's first Saturn return, bringing closure to the thematic developments of its earlier transits, but transiting Sol and Jupiter were conjoined at Crowley's Midheaven in Aries—Sol for the first time since his meeting and marrying Rose, and Jupiter for the first time since his initiation into the Golden Dawn at the time of his second Jupiter return. Transiting Mercury and Mars were also conjoined in his Tenth House, and transiting Venus was conjoined to his natal Luna in Pisces in his Ninth House. At this most auspicious moment, twenty-eight year old Aleister Crowley received *Liber AL vel Legis*, also entitled *The Book of the Law*, which purports to be the Logos of the New Aeon upon which collective humanity is now embarking. The remainder of his life would be devoted, initially at variance with his conscious wishes and intentions, to the fulfillment of his role of Prophet as specified in that book.

PART III

CHAPTER 12

PROPHET

In 1898, during his college years at Cambridge, Aleister Crowley
began his career as a poet with the publication of *Aceldama*, a poem
expressive of spiritual struggle. A fellow undergraduate, Gerald
Kelly, was so taken by the poem that he sought out its author. Crowley and Kelly thereafter developed a solid and lasting friendship. In
early August of 1903 Gerald wrote Aleister at Boleskine and invited
him to join his party at Strathpeffer. Having nothing better to do,
Crowley accepted the invitation. On August 11, Kelly and an
acquaintance named Hill were playing golf. Aleister, having no
clubs, was free to talk with Gerald's sister Rose. Finding Aleister to
be a good listener as they wandered out over the links to walk the last
few holes with Kelly and Hill, Rose told him of her difficulty at the
time.

Rose was a widow involved in an affair with a married man
named Frank Summers. She was satisfied with her situation in all
respects, but her family was attempting to force her into a marriage
with Hill as a result of a scheme in which she had received forty
pounds from her mother under the pretense of needing an abortion
only to use the money for dinners and dresses. (*Confessions* reads:
"She told me that she was being forced into the marriage with
Howell by her family," [p. 363] but there is no prior or subsequent
mention of any Howell. Furthermore, the entire context of the
account appears to suggest that Hill was the suitor. Having no better
knowledge at my disposal, I am inclined to suspect either a typo-
graphical error or a ploy on Crowley's part in the use of the name
Howell.)

Crowley took sympathy with her plight and offered to marry her
as a means of resolving her dilemma. After the wedding, he proposed, they would simply go their separate ways, and Rose would be
free from her family's machinations. The following morning they
caught an early train to Dingwall and were married by the sheriff

there. Gerald burst in immediately afterwards and took a swing at
Crowley. Mrs. Kelly and Hill were also on hand to protest the marriage. However, Crowley informs us, "Rose stuck to her guns like the
game little bitch she was. Mr. Hill made the discovery that he had
not made the law, and Mrs. Kelly and Gerald that they had not made
mankind." [p. 367] The Kellys came to accept the marriage when
Aleister agreed to follow up the ceremony with certain social formal-
ities, and Aleister's friendship with Gerald survived the ordeal.

As fate would have it, Aleister and Rose fell passionately in love
soon after their unusual wedding. Crowley writes in *Confessions* that
Rose fell in love with him as a result of his willingness to help her in
such a selfless manner, although this writer is tempted to ask who
may say why or when a woman falls in love. According to Crowley,
he experienced annoyance at the need to make adjustments in the
immediate concerns of his life.

> I had not even yet suspected the truth that the fine flight of Rose's
> rapture was carrying me away on its wings. Her love for me was
> evoking my love for her, and I had rather made a point of contract-
> ing out of any such complications. I was prepared to propitiate
> physiology, but only on the condition that the domain of psychol-
> ogy suffered no interference.
>
> However, there I was, married to one of the most beautiful and
> fascinating women in the world. The love between us grew to the
> utmost possibilities of passion without my suspecting it. [pp. 369-
> 370]

Aleister and Rose were obviously well suited for one another, and
it appears that only the abruptness of their initial meeting and impul-
sive wedding were able to precede the impact of their mutual affec-
tion. Crowley's account of the entire fantastic episode leaves room
for considerable speculation with regard to the actual motivational
factors involved on either side of the protagonists' thresholds of consciousness. Indeed, the occasion of the marriage of Aleister and Rose
suggests unconscious or superconscious machinations dovetailing
fortuitously with conscious intentions and serendipitous circumstances. The following several months would be spent traveling the
globe.

> As soon as the summer showed signs of waning, we started our
> hypertrophied honeymoon. We pretended to ourselves that we
> were going big-game shooting in Ceylon and to pay a visit to Allan
> at Rangoon..., but the real object was to adorn the celebration of

our love by setting it in a thousand suave and sparkling back-
grounds. As my poetry had petered out, so had my Magick and my
meditation. I let them go without a pang. I was supremely happy;
love filled the universe; there was no room for anything else. [*ibid.,*
p. 371]

During the course of their travels, a rather phenomenal occurrence
took place in Cairo that is indicative of the activity of supernatural
forces that played an integral part of Aleister's and Rose's intense
relationship.

It was one of the extravagances of our passion that suggested our
spending a night together in the King's Chamber of the Great
Pyramid. It was the gesture of the male showing off his plumage. I
wanted my wife to see what a great Magician I was. We went,
accordingly, after dinner, with candles. More from habit than anything else, as I imagine, I had with me a small notebook of
Japanese vellum in which were written my principal invocations,
etc. Among these was a copy of the 'Preliminary Invocation' of
The Goetia.

We reached the King's Chamber after dismissing the servants at
the foot of the Grand Gallery. By the light of a single candle placed
on the edge of the coffer I began to read the invocation. But as I
went on I noticed that I was no longer stooping to hold the page
near the light. I was standing erect. Yet the manuscript was not less
but more legible. Looking about me, I saw that the King's Chamber was glowing with a soft light that I immediately recognized as
the astral light...

The King's Chamber was aglow as if with the brightest tropical
moonlight. The pitiful dirty yellow flame of the candle was like a
blasphemy, and I put it out. The astral light remained during the
whole of the invocation and for some time afterwards, though it
lessened in intensity as we composed ourselves to sleep... In the
morning the astral light had completely disappeared and the only
sound was the flitting of the bats.

In a sort of way, I suppose I did consider myself rather a fine
fellow to have been able to produce so striking a phenomenon with
so little trouble. But it did not encourage me to go on with Magick.
My wife was all in all. [*ibid.*, pp. 372-373]

From Cairo, they continued their travel to Ceylon. Crowley had
the following to say about his wife at this time: "Physically and
morally, Rose exercised on every man she met a fascination which I
have never seen anywhere else, not a fraction of it. She was like a

character in a romantic novel, a Helen of Troy or a Cleopatra; yet, while more passionate, unhurtful. She was essentially a good woman. Her love sounded every abyss of lust, soared to every splendour of the empyraean." [*ibid.*, p. 375] While in Ceylon, Rose discovered she was pregnant, and the Crowleys thought it best to arrange their itinerary so as to be back at Boleskine for the event. They left Columbo on January 28, "intending to see a little of the season in Cairo, of which we had the most delightful memories, and then to sail for England, home and beauty. I had not the slightest idea that I was on the brink of the only event of my life which has made it worth living." [*ibid.*, p. 385]

Although *The Book of the Law* is written in terms commensurate with high magical attainment, Crowley elaborates that he was in a fallow period with regard to any spiritual discipline at the time of its writing. In the closing words of the chapter in *Confessions* that precedes Part Three, "The Advent of the Aeon of Horus," he states, "I have dwelt on the character of my life at this time in order to emphasize that the event to be recorded in the next section was an absolute bolt from the blue." [p. 389] Despite his prior accomplishments as magician and yogi, which contributed, one may surmise, to his qualification as the vehicle for the transmission of *The Book of the Law*, at the time of its reception he was not pursuing any regimen beyond that of a happily married man with an expectant wife enjoying the sporting life and the sites of the world. It would appear that he had largely purged himself of his neurotic quest for absolution from the religious perversions of his youth. His destiny, however, proved not to be so simple. It is a supreme irony that the vehicle of his grace was the instrument that induced him to perform his life's task as the prophet of the New Aeon.

Upon taking an apartment in Cairo on Wednesday, March 16, 1904, Aleister again attempted to perform a little magic for Rose.

> I had no more serious purpose than to show her the sylphs as I might have taken her to the theatre. She could not (or refused to) see them, but instead got into a strange state of mind. I had never seen her anything at all like it before. She kept on repeating dreamily, yet intensely, 'They are waiting for you.' I was annoyed at her conduct. [*ibid.*, p. 393]

This occurrence began a series of events in which Rose assumed the leading role in instructing Aleister in the formulation and performance of a ritual designed to put him in contact with the Egyptian god Horus, identified by Rose as such. Aleister was put out by the whole episode, because the formulae stipulated by Rose violated established rules of magical technique, and furthermore, Rose had no knowledge whatsoever of magic or Egyptology. She was, according to Crowley, "an empty headed woman of society." However, when he tried to trip her up with a series of technical questions regarding symbolic associations to Horus, she answered every question correctly, defying odds of many millions to one. In addition to this:

> On some day before March 23rd, Ouarda [Rose] identified the particular god with whom she was in communication from a stele in the Boulak Museum, which we had never visited. It is not the ordinary form of Horus but Ra-Hoor-Khuit. I was no doubt very much struck by the coincidence that the exhibit, a quite obscure and undistinguished stele, bore the catalogue number 666. But I dismissed it as an obvious coincidence. [*ibid.,* p. 394]

This entire development is most intriguing, and the interested reader is referred to *Confessions* and *The Equinox of the Gods* for more thorough accounts of the facts involved. The climax of the operation was the receiving of *The Book of the Law* by Aleister Crowley, from a source identified as Aiwass, at three successive sittings alone in a room of their apartment from Noon to 1:00 p.m., on April 8, 9, and 10, 1904. Crowley describes the actual experience in *The Equinox of the Gods*:

> The voice of Aiwass came apparently from over my left shoulder, from the furthest corner of the room. It seemed to echo itself in my physical heart in a very strange manner, hard to describe. I have noticed a similar phenomenon when I have been waiting for a message fraught with great hope or dread. The voice was passionately poured, as if Aiwass was alert about the time limit... I was pushed hard to keep the pace; the MS. shows it clearly enough.
> The voice was of deep timbre, musical and expressive, its tones solemn, voluptuous, tender, fierce or aught else as suited the moods of the message. Not bass—perhaps a rich tenor or baritone.
> The English was free of either native or foreign accent, perfectly clear of local or caste mannerisms, thus startling and even uncanny at first hearing.
> I had a strong impression that the speaker was actually in the corner where he seemed to be, in a body of "fine matter," transparent as a veil of gauze, or a cloud of incense-smoke. He seemed to be a tall, dark man in his thirties, well-knit, active and strong, with the face of a savage king, and eyes veiled lest their gaze should

destroy what they saw. The dress was not Arab; it suggested Assyria or Persia, but very vaguely. I took little note of it, for to me at that time Aiwass was an "angel" such as I had often seen in visions, a being purely astral. [pp. 117-118]

The Book of the Law purports to set forth spiritual truth for the New Aeon as distinguished from previous and succeeding aeons in the evolution of humanity. It is a relatively short book consisting of three chapters of 66, 79, and 75 verses respectively, the whole totaling just over 6,000 words. The first chapter is written in the feminine voice of the New Aeon, characterized as Nuit or Nu as a representation of Infinite Space, the potentiality of all possible experience. The second chapter is written in the masculine voice of the New Aeon, characterized as Hadit or Had as a representation of the driving or motive force of human nature. These two principles have been said by Crowley in his commentary to be reducible in their simplest terms to matter and motion. [*The Law Is For All*, p. 70] The third chapter addresses the meaning of the New Aeon from an historical perspective and is written directly in the voice of Horus in the form of Ra-Hoor Khuit, the presiding deity of the New Aeon.

The Book of the Law remains mysterious in many respects. Crowley and some of his associates did considerable work toward elucidating its meaning (as Crowley was instructed to do by the book itself). Yet much of its text proved impenetrable even to Crowley (as the book itself also proclaims). This is in keeping with its nature as a cipher, the meaning of which will unfold throughout the entire aeon that it purports to initiate. Ultimately *The Book of the Law* is written for each to consider privately and assimilate in accordance with one's own unique perspective. However, Crowley is designated therein and lays claim to exclusive authority as the final arbiter for interpreting the meaning of the book. This policy precludes the possibility of any claims of authority on the part of would-be priesthoods and prevents any individual from abrogating one's own responsibility to determine the meaning of the book for oneself. This much is discernible from those parts of the book that speak in simple and direct terms, and it is implied that Crowley's role as the Magus of the Aeon continues posthumously in some fashion. Crowley came to understand his primary task as that of midwife for the delivery of *The Book of the Law* into the historical current of the world.

A certain amount of commentary on the subject of *The Book of the Law* can be found in a host of books written about Crowley.

Some of this commentary is basically supportive of the authenticity of the book as a viable revelation of truth, and some is derogatory of the book as a vainglorious effulgence of Crowley's personal delusions. Such a divergence of opinions tends to corroborate the challenging nature of the book's message. This writer's opinion is that *The Book of the Law* is worthy of full consideration as one of the major religious writings currently available to humanity in its quest for spiritual truth. It is in this spirit that I have devoted attention to it in the development of this book.

The references from *The Book of the Law* that are included in this book are intended to suggest parallels between them and the astrological outlook developed thus far in relation to the Aquarian perspective upon the new age, with particular correspondences to the meanings of the trans-Saturnian planets as direct referents for the transformative functions that are operative components of the aeonic transition. I also attempt to show what I find to be a remarkable correspondence between the perspectives elucidated in *The Book of the Law* and the astrological configuration of Aleister Crowley's birthchart. This correspondence supports the hypothesis that Crowley was indeed destined to set forth the Logos of the New Aeon in accordance with the development his own inherent character. However, that very observation could also be used to argue that *The Book of the Law* is nothing more than an expression of Crowley's personality and therefore has no significant value as a revelation of truth for collective humanity. The dispute between these two assessments can only be resolved through personal judgment and the trial of experience on the part of any investigator. In the words of the book itself, "I forbid argument. Conquer! That is enough." [*AL* III:11]

There are two statements from *The Book of the Law* that Crowley selected as being most representative for purposes of conveying the general purport of the entire writing. These are: "Do what thou wilt shall be the whole of the Law," [*AL* I:40] and "Love is the law, love under will." [*AL* I:57] Crowley developed the practice of initiating social interactions, including the writing of letters, with the salutation, "Do what thou wilt shall be the whole of the Law." He also used "Love is the law, love under will," as a closing salutation. Rather than interpreting this behavior as an exercise in personal fatuity, we may take it as an indication of the literalness with which Crowley eventually came to discharge his responsibility to teach the Law as prescribed by the book which he at first had great difficulty accepting; "...and to each man and woman that thou meetest, were it but to dine or to drink at them, it is the Law to give. Then they shall chance to abide in this bliss or no; it is no odds." [*AL* III:39]

The statement, "Do what thou wilt shall be the whole of the Law," is directly reminiscent of the sixteenth century French writer and scholar Francois Rabelais' *"Fay ce que vouldras,"* (Do what you will), which, in his *Gargantua and Pantagruel,* appears inscribed above the door of an abbey that is named Theleme, similar to Crowley's Abbey of Thelema which he founded in Cefalu, Sicily in 1920. This affirmation is a most direct and emphatic expression of the principle of enlightened self interest that emerged from modern philosophy and serves as the ideological cornerstone for political democracy and economic free enterprise. This idea also forms a component of the spiritual wisdom of antiquity expressed, for example, in the words attributed to Jesus in the Christian Bible: "Neither shall they say, Lo here! or, Lo there! for behold, the kingdom of God is within you." [*Luke* 17:21]

Despite the modern world's familiarity with this fundamental principle, there has yet been a failure to fully appreciate its value even on the part of many who purport to advocate it. A recurrent criticism of the Thelemic ethic ('*Thelema,*' Greek for 'Will,' being "the word of the Law" as specified in *AL* I:39) is that, should this ethic prevail, it would presumably sanction a complete breakdown of social order whereby all manner of abusive behavior would become the order of the day. The basic truth that is generally overlooked by this criticism is that all human cooperation and social cohesiveness comes from nowhere other than the hearts and minds of individuals. Of course, there will always be conflicts of interest. But the first necessary step toward any efficacious resolution of such conflicts is the respect for the freedom of others and the demand of freedom for oneself. Any presumption of authority beyond that context can only exacerbate conflicts and make matters worse for everybody. Naturally, the full social actualization of this principle presupposes an authentic will to freedom on the part of a substantial segment of humankind powerful enough to marshal a dominant force in the world.

This fundamental principle of social reality was introduced in chapter 4 in relation to the astrological meaning of Aquarius and the amplified impetus to the principle of democracy brought to that sign by the discovery of Uranus. The placements of Uranus and Saturn in Crowley's birthchart indicate that an essential identification with and dramatization of this idea was acutely focused and projected as the characteristic theme of Crowley's conscious orientation to life. His powerfully felt uniqueness and individuality as a function of his First House Uranus in Leo projected a laser beam of consciousness to his Seventh House Saturn in Aquarius, thus bringing the old ruler of that sign to the service of explicitly articulating, with authority, the new law of freedom to the objective world, still very much ingrained with traditional authoritarian values. Crowley's experience of "receiving" the dictation of *The Book of the Law,* occurred at the time of his first Saturn return, bringing closure to the acute consciousness of this *message* through the experience of *objectified* personal revelation.

The statement, "Love is the law, love under will," is expressive of an enlargement of the theme implicit in "Do what thou wilt shall be the whole of the Law." Firstly, it is a direct acknowledgment of the exalting and guiding power of love in the affairs of humankind, a theme common to all the great religions. Secondly, it specifies the manner by which the power of love may be brought within the sphere of efficacious human activity, as distinguished from its characteristic historical manifestations which have thus far been unable to overcome the inertia of human lethargy and servility. Crowley's commentary concerning this prescription says: "Love under will—no casual pagan love; nor love under fear, as the Christians do, But love magically directed, and used as a spiritual formula." [*The Law Is For All,* p. 141]

This matter of love requires the making of a very critical differentiation affecting strongly held values that distinguish the past from the present aeon. The crux of the issue is the meaning of the word "love." Proclaiming the "Word" for a new aeon of historical evolution entails a need to affect *both* a clear departure from the established ways of the past *and* a continuous progression of the fundamental truths of human existence that encompass the full course of evolution, as far as we are able to conceive it. The truths that characterize a new period of history must be sharply distinguished from those that characterized the preceding period. The relatively new perspective must be cast, however, within the context of more comprehensive truths that would appear to be common to *all* temporal periods. We are here confronted with paradox. This observable historical process reflects the dialectical theory of historical evolution developed by the early nineteenth-century German philosopher, Georg Hegel, involving three recurrent developmental stages termed "Thesis" (the immediate grasp and incorporation of an objective idea), "Antithesis" (contradictory evidence produced by further reflection and experience), and "Synthesis" (resolution of the contradictory evidence that raises understanding to a new level) which in turn generates a new thesis, and so on. We are reminded of the alternating polarities of zodiacal signs whereby movement from one symbolic orientation or theme to another requires a *reversal* of polarity, as opposed to a smooth, continuous transition or climb, in order to affect further development. Although this dialectical process is observable for a wide range of temporal scales, from the very short to the very long, astrological ages of some two-thousand-plus years are the longest temporal periods that we can place within an historical context and therefore involve the deepest and most fundamental changes in orientation at times of transition from one to another.

This is perhaps the greatest challenge to a prophet of *any* new aeon. In this regard, we are afforded a helpful perspective by examining the manner in which this challenge has been handled by prophets from other times, because our temporal distance from them allows for a more detached and therefore objective point of view. The best example of this process for most Europeans and Americans, and for other purposes in keeping with the thematic development of this book, is that of the prophetic mission of Jesus Christ, taken as representative of the transition from the Ariean to the Piscean Age, as recorded in the Christian Bible. In order fully to apply such observations to the concerns of this book it will be necessary to probe more deeply into Aleister Crowley's attitudes toward Christianity in general and the figure of Jesus Christ in particular. It is helpful, however, first to establish some historical perspective surrounding this matter of a prophet's need to affect both change and continuity.

Jesus was a Jew. This simple historical fact proves to be the source of a great deal of controversy in that the religion he founded became fully separated from the one he proclaimed himself a representative. No more bitter historical antagonisms can be found than those between Christians and Jews, and clearly there are aspects of Jesus' teachings that were revolutionary within the context of the tradition of Judaism from which he emerged. It can be said that he "took advantage" of his religious heritage in order to initiate a radical departure from it. And yet he proclaimed as an integral aspect of his teaching: "Think not that I am come to destroy the law, or the prophets: I am not come to destroy, but to fulfil. For verily I say unto you, Till heaven and earth pass, one jot or one tittle shall in no wise pass from the law, till all be fulfilled." [Matthew 5:17-18] Such a statement could only be taken as fomenting discontent by those who officially represented the Jewish tradition of which Jesus said, only a few words further along: "For I say unto you, That except your righteousness shall exceed the righteousness of the scribes and Pharisees, ye shall in no case enter into the kingdom of heaven." [Matthew 5:20] Compare these statements of Jesus' with the following taken from *The Book of the Law*: "He that is righteous shall be righteous still; he that is filthy shall be filthy still. Yea! deem not of change: ye shall be as ye are, & not other... There is none that shall be cast down or lifted up: all is ever as it was." [*AL* II:7-58] These statements on the part of both Jesus and Aiwass are emphatic expressions of the continuity of truth that runs through the current of history from aeon to aeon, yet in both cases those truths are couched in contexts that disturb the status quo.

The essential point is that, as a prophetic writing, *The Book of the Law* must affect a sharp *antithesis* to the temporal truth of the previous aeon, and that such an antithesis must necessarily take center stage for purposes of vitalizing humanity and bringing the world out of habitual attitudes and behavior rooted in a formula of life that has dissipated into meaninglessness by virtue of its temporal exhaustion, as well as *the completed fulfillment of its purpose* from an evolutionary perspective. This explains the strong and often disturbing language of *The Book of the Law*. The *temporal* truth of the Christian faith that is now to be discarded in accordance with the social and psychological requirements of modern humanity is the idea of the efficacy of *personal sacrifice* for the benefit of others. Indeed, sacrifice was rightly identified with the principle of love in the formula of the Christian religion, which was, as proven by the dominance of Christian civilization as the spearhead of evolution through the two thousand year period associated with its history, the most profound and efficacious manifestation of truth for the Piscean Age. The theme of sacrifice, however, has come to an end. It is no longer efficacious. *The Book of the Law* announces a new ethic, the ethic of self-actualization. From the perspective of Christian values this new ethic appears to be selfish and brutal, but only because it is vital and strong, and gives no quarter to the weak. It says: Let weakness be blessed with death that strength may prosper; let love prosper in strength; let love not be sacrificed that weakness may survive. Ironically, this is a bitter pill to swallow for a world steeped in over two thousand years of a self-sacrificial ethos, the roots of which go much deeper than is even conventionally acknowledged. In the world's present stage of transition, these ideas confuse the unconscious as well as the conscious mind. Therefore, we read in *The Book of the Law*, "Behold! the rituals of the old time are black. Let the evil ones be cast away; let the good ones be purged by the prophet! Then shall this Knowledge go aright." [*AL* II:5] It may be noted that the Thelemic ethic in no way precludes a willingness to die for one's convictions, which naturally include the rights of others, but it is unlawful to sacrifice oneself *for or to one's enemies*, as did Jesus.

As mentioned above, the statement, "Do what thou wilt shall be the whole of the Law," is succinctly expressive of the interpretation of the Horizon (axis of consciousness) of Crowley's birthchart as delineated in previous chapters. The statement, "Love is the law, love under will," is equally appropriate as an expression of the interpretation of Crowley's Meridian (axis of power). Crowley's deep-rooted tendency toward sacrificial love, indicated by his placements of Sol, Venus and his South Node in Libra at the Imum Coeli or *bottom* of his birthchart had ultimately to be brought under the direction of his Martial will to stand out fearlessly in the world as a prophet of non-sacrificial self-actualization, indicated by his North Node in Aries at the Midheaven or *top* of his birthchart. Indeed, "love under will" is a literal expression of the personal need for self-actualization as indicated in Crowley's birthchart by the orientation of his lunar nodes.

Ironically, his ego *was* sacrificed in the process, but this can be understood in terms of the actualization of the total planetary configuration of his personality as an expression of a transcendent principle, that is, his True Will, that supreme aspect of his personality that governed his destiny from behind the *mask* of his ego from the mysterious realm beyond space and time. This is the age-old formula for mystical attainment and the deeper spiritual truth *behind* the orthodox religious doctrine of sacrifice. It is a process of personal transformation. It is self-fulfilling *and must be self-directed,* whereby one becomes reconciled as an individual with the greater cosmos and is thereby reborn through the experience of becoming a whole person. In so doing, Crowley *exemplified* through self-actualization the formula of "love under will" by bringing his own love to the service of the fulfillment of his will to teach a doctrine he at first found untenable. He affected the aeonic transition *within himself*, even as he taught it to the world, which was in fact his formula of power, the truth of his word. He did this without sacrificing himself *to* those whom he sought to teach, or *to* those who opposed him, thus turning the old formula inside out, actualizing an antithetical paradox by demonstrating the supremacy of will over love.

There is another statement in *The Book of the Law* that also conveys a very powerful and comprehensive sense of the book's full meaning. This statement comes early on, being the third verse of the first chapter: "Every man and every woman is a star." [*AL* I:3] This simple statement is so eloquent that to speak further about it would seem to detract rather than contribute to its poetic profundity. Yet I have found Crowley's commentary on this verse to be for me among his most powerful and thought-provoking passages. I will merely point out that the sense evoked by this statement is fully in keeping with the *galactic* perspective associated with the New Aeon. The image of the galaxy offers a new perspective upon the idea of community as distinguished from the authoritarian solar models that have dominated our historical past. Galactic structure prescribes only that every star fulfill its unique character and destiny, and that by so doing the continuity of the whole is preserved. Only by deviating from one's self-ordained course can one disturb the greater order. There is a cosmic proportion that calls for the total fulfillment of each individual.

Before proceeding to further considerations of *The Book of the Law,* I would like to venture some observations in regard to the overarching perspective that is at once explicit and implicit in the verses thus far considered. What is being addressed is not so much a radical change in human nature but rather an emerging development *of* human nature into a more actualized embodiment of what it has always ultimately been. Freedom is not new. Humanity has always been free. Humanity cannot be other than free. Every person has always made choices about how to behave and interact with other people. There has *never* been an exterior authority. There has only been the *relinquishment* of authority, largely to pacify the brutality of uncontrolled and misdirected impulses. There have been unconscious projections of the inherent sovereignty of individual human beings onto collective images of group order and meaningful existence. Such projections have been manipulated by those in positions to do so, often by those who have learned how to attract such projections onto themselves, for various purposes. Some such manipulations have been conducive to evolving awareness and human actualization, and some have been conducive to exploitation and repressive control of human resources. These unconscious projections have been characteristic of a larval, unactualized humanity, living within the bounds of Saturnian constraint. We are currently pushing the envelope of the physical resources of our planet, as a larval creature expands within its protective encasement, or as a fetus grows within the womb. We are on the brink of emerging into a level of real experience that can only be envisioned metaphorically from our larval perspective. Our neuro-structures are accessing their molecular and atomic potentials for functioning at this new level. We are a multiverse of unique cosmic beings, each with enormous creative power. We must take responsibility for ourselves. No one else is going to do it for us, and we *cannot* do it for one another.

As revolutionary as are the above perspectives taken from the context provided by *The Book of the Law,* it must be acknowledged that they are mild in comparison with the entire revelation. The full incorporation of the ideal of personal freedom, as opposed to the operative constraints of the Piscean Age, is indeed challenging beyond our present comprehension, even though implicit within our modern and postmodern conceptions of humanity. It was also impossible for the early Christians to comprehend the full significance of the forces they were setting into motion in their time. How could they possibly have anticipated the developments of recent history that are the ultimate fruition of the social and spiritual movement they in fact initiated under the spell of the masterful articulation of religious doctrine uttered by their exemplar? Yet they *did* initiate that movement through their feeling of the need for and vitality of *their* New Aeon. That was enough. That is always enough. Indeed, there are great and constant truths of human nature expressed in the Logos of the Piscean Age. *Those very truths are also expressed in the Logos of the Aquarian Age.* Such is the root source of power for all religious revelation. But there was also the *antithesis*, the challenge to *repent*, which etymologically means *to change one's mind.* We are also challenged to repent today by *The Book of the Law.*

In the introduction to a 1938 edition of *The Book of the Law,* Crowley states: "The third chapter of the Book is difficult to understand, and may be very repugnant to many people born before the date of the book (April, 1904)." [p. 11] The reader may hardly need to be advised, however, that one does not have to be born before April, 1904 to find certain aspects of *The Book of the Law* very repugnant. Abundant testimony is extant from recent years to confirm this fact. This circumstance, of course, is fully in keeping with the above observations about the historical significance of the book and the need for antithesis in the aeonic transition. The keys for resolving the antithetical perspectives of the two aeons that we are currently negotiating may be found by delving into the deeper continuity of truth that puts some ground beneath our feet below the raging torrent of temporal reorientation.

Immediately following the statement "Love is the law, love under will," in *AL* I:57 are the words, "Nor let the fools mistake love; for there are love and love. There is the dove, and there is the serpent. Choose ye well! He, my prophet, hath chosen, knowing the law of the fortress, and the great mystery of the House of God." In his commentary for that verse Crowley states, "This love, then should be the serpent love, the awakening of the Kundalini." [*The Law Is For All*, p. 141] Crowley points out that the Hebrew word for serpent is numerically equivalent to that for messiah [*Magick Without Tears*, p. 297], which implies that both of these words have the same root concept in the Qabalistic tradition of Hebrew mysticism. These references imply a continuity of meaning that extends from the ancient Hebrew tradition into the New Aeon of Horus, fully encompassing the Christian dispensation. This continuity also extends further back into Egyptian, Babylonian, and Sumerian sources, by virtue of the cognate accounts of serpent imagery found in those ancient traditions, which provided the source material for the Mosaic revelation. "And Moses was learned in the wisdom of the Egyptians, and was mighty in words and deeds." [Acts 7:22]

It follows that the mysteries of love that are addressed in *The Book of the Law* are associated with the meaning of Neptune as interpreted in chapter 8. The assignment of Neptune as the planetary ruler of Scorpio secures its association with the serpent image. In accordance with this hypothesis, a greater understanding of the theme of love in *The Book of the Law* may be obtained through astrological perspectives on Neptune as the planetary representative of the modern and postmodern current of Scorpionic power. This love cannot be considered apart from the sexual component in human physiology and psychology. Neptune challenges modern humanity to accept the fullness of sexual meaning, or, to put it more bluntly, to *grow up* amid the challenges of this much neglected and abused aspect of human nature. This attitude is expressed with poetic splendor in *The Book of the Law*. Gone are the veiled references and cryptographic avoidances. Gone are the slanders, jealousies, and condemnations. Gone are the restrictions. Nowhere in *The Book of the Law* will one find a trace of the sin complex haunting sexuality. Rather, it states: "Come forth, o children, under the stars, & take your fill of love!"

[*AL* I:12] and "The word of Sin is Restriction: O man! refuse not thy wife, if she will! O lover, if thou wilt, depart! There is no bond that can unite the divided but love: all else is a curse. Accursed! Accursed be it to the aeons! Hell," [*AL* I:41] and "Also, take your fill and will of love as ye will, when, where and with whom ye will!" [*AL* I:51]

As the cognate symbolism inherently suggests a significant degree of correspondence between the concerns of Neptune and those of Nuit, so also does it suggest an equally poignant correspondence between the concerns of Pluto and those of Hadit, the personification of the masculine principle of existence for the New Aeon, the motive force of personal reality, the *source* of consciousness and action. The relation between Nuit and Hadit in *The Book of the Law* is that between the objective and subjective aspects of consciousness respectively. The opening verses of chapter two are appropriate to these planetary correspondences:

1. Nu! the hiding of Hadit.
2. Come! all ye, and learn the secret that hath not yet been revealed. I, Hadit, am the complement of Nu, my bride. I am not extended, and Khabs is the name of my House.
3. In the sphere I am everywhere the centre, as she, the circumference, is nowhere found.
4. Yet she shall be known & I never. [*AL* II:1-4]

In exploring the philosophical implications of quantum mechanics in chapter 9, certain strange paradoxes were encountered involving the relation of consciousness to the determination of verifiable experience. These paradoxes emerged in relation to science's attempt to penetrate to the core of the atom and learn about the most fundamental constituents of matter. Rather than finding anything solid, as matter was supposed to be in accordance with our sensory perception of it, a realm of incomprehensible mystery was discovered. This means that matter itself is an incomprehensible mystery. Our relation to that mystery of matter is expressed in the marriage of Nuit and Hadit. Through these images we are provided with personifications of the most sophisticated scientific discoveries of the nuclear age. The implication is that the human nervous system is an instrument of bio-technology that has evolved through the impetus of quantum intentionality within the context of "matter," and that, as such, neuro-structures mediate "consciousness" as an intimate interaction of Hadit and Nuit. The time of the writing of *The Book of the Law* is early enough to demonstrate its *anticipation* of quantum mechanics in poetic terms that are meaningful and comprehensible to common human experience. This theme is further developed in these subsequent verses from the second chapter:

> 6. I am the flame that burns in every heart of man, and in the core of every star. I am Life, and the giver of Life, yet therefore is the knowledge of me the knowledge of death.
> 7. I am the Magician and the Exorcist. I am the axle of the wheel, and the cube in the circle. "Come unto me" is a foolish word; for it is I that go. [*AL* II:6-7]

The epistemological difficulties associated with quantum mechanics, that is, the inherent problem of the role of consciousness in the determination of perceived reality, is addressed directly in *The Book of the Law.* The formulations of quantum uncertainty and the collapse of the wave function were yet future scientific discoveries, although the initial breakthroughs into the understanding of nuclear physics were already underway. A great deal of philosophical debate was going on at that time between idealists and empiricists, monists and pluralists, positivists and pragmatists. In the midst of this debate amongst the mighty philosophers, *The Book of the Law* struck with plutonian hegemony to the very core of the matter, in full anticipation of the implications of quantum mechanics, coming down on the side of pragmatism, which is not the crass philosophy that its less reflective critics suppose, but one essential to the mystery and purposefulness of life. "Now let there be a veiling of this shrine: now let the light devour men and eat them up with blindness!" [*AL* II:14], "Also reason is a lie; for there is a factor infinite & unknown, & all their words are skew-wise." [*AL* II:32]

The significance of this matter of knowledge can hardly be overemphasized. Invariably, authoritarians who would dictate to others how to behave stake their claims upon some presumed ground of absolute knowledge, be it biblical revelation, positive logic, mystical apprehension, or even something so innocuous sounding as common sense or conventional wisdom, always backed, of course, by the threat of force. The sovereignty of every individual in the determination of truth strips away the veneer of justification from that threat and exposes it for what it really is, an attempt on the part of one particular faction to control the behavior of others, invariably to the material (or presumed spiritual) advantage of the former. Furthermore, individual sovereignty forces everyone to exercise one's brain and think for oneself, whereby one may discover one's own latent potential and make some *real* contribution to the commonweal other than the performance of mindless tasks in the service of one's corporate masters.

Having addressed the metaphysical interaction of Nuit and Hadit in the first two chapters, the third chapter of *The Book of the Law* is expressive of the fundamental attitude appropriate to the Aeon of Horus in terms particularly meaningful within an historical context. This is the chapter Crowley warned could be "very repugnant" to some readers. It includes direct assaults upon various religious traditions of the past, and it couches its admonitions in the hardest of terms, appropriate to the attitude of Uranus as the new planetary ruler of Aquarius, as we enter the astrological age characterized by that symbolic theme. Uranus has already acquired an iconoclastic reputation among astrologers, and the attitude expressed in chapter three of *The Book of the Law* is surely that. This attitude is appropriate both to the need for antithesis concerning the submissive attitude fostered within the religious formulae of the dying aeon as well as the strongly individualistic tenor of the Aquarian mode of social interaction. Chapter three of *The Book of the Law* contains such statements as: "Now let it be first understood that I am a god of War and of Vengeance. I shall deal hardly with them," [*AL* III:3] and: "Mercy let be off: damn them who pity! Kill and torture; spare not; be upon them!" [*AL* III:18] Also there is the strongly Aquarian and Uranian sentiment expressed in the verses: "But the keen and the proud, the royal and the lofty; ye are brothers! As brothers fight ye! There is no law beyond Do what thou wilt." [*AL* III:58-60]

Surely these brief comments about *The Book of the Law* leave much to be explored. If indeed that book is a revelation of spiritual truth from a praeterhuman source of knowledge, as Crowley believed and endeavored to demonstrate through the inherent structure of the book itself, then this writer has no authority to explicate its meaning. The reader can do no better than to go to Crowley's commentary for any elucidation thereof to complement one's own understanding. My observations are ideas that have occurred to me in my attempt to understand the book and assimilate its meanings within the context of *my own* understanding, particularly as they pertain to an astrological view of history. I would only hope that such perspectives may serve to stimulate thought that might help to enliven philosophical and religious investigation. If my statements about *The Book of the Law* help only to shed a modicum of light upon the historical context within which it came to be written, then my purpose for incorporat-

ing knowledge of it into this book is fulfilled. My primary intent has
been to lend support to the credibility of *The Book of the Law* as a
viable revelation of spiritual truth for our time, which in turn may
help validate the contention that Aleister Crowley was a true prophet.

A poignant perspective upon the credibility of *The Book of the
Law* may be obtained by considering the course of history since the
time of its first publication. Crowley himself made some telling
observations along these lines in his introduction to the 1938 edition:

> He [Horus, the child] rules the present period of 2,000 years,
> beginning in 1904. Everywhere his government is taking root.
> Observe for yourselves the decay of the since of sin, the growth of
> innocence and irresponsibility, the strange modifications of the
> reproductive instinct with a tendency to become bisexual or
> epicene, the childlike confidence in progress combined with
> nightmare fear of catastrophe, against which we are yet half unwill-
> ing to take precautions.
>
> Consider the outcrop of dictatorships, only possible when moral
> growth is in its earliest stages, and the prevalence of infantile cults
> like Communism, Fascism, Pacifism, Health Crazes, Occultism in
> nearly all its forms, religions sentimentalized to the point of practi-
> cal extinction.
>
> Consider the popularity of the cinema, the wireless, the football
> pools and guessing competitions, all devises for soothing fractious
> infants, no seed of purpose in them.
>
> Consider sport, the babyish enthusiasms and rages which it ex-
> cites, whole nations disturbed by disputes between boys.
>
> Consider war, the atrocities which occur daily and leave us
> unmoved and hardly worried.
>
> We are children.
>
> How this new Aeon of Horus will develop, how the Child will
> grow up. these are for us to determine, growing up ourselves in the
> way of the Law of Thelema under the enlightened guidance of the
> Master Therion. [pp. 12-13]

These observations by Crowley at that time make abundantly
clear the manner in which the prophecy is being fulfilled. How much
more so now than then!

Additional historical perspective may be gleaned from observations made by Israel Regardie in his introduction to *The Law is for
All* in 1970, some twenty-three years after Crowley's death.
Although Crowley was able to point out very clear historical developments that confirmed the emergence of the New Aeon within his

own lifetime, it is true that his prophecy won practically no overt support or agreement in the world until the phenomenal cultural developments of the 1960's, during which his ideas were incorporated into a widespread and outspoken movement calling for social revolution. It is certainly the case that that brief period was characterized by the excesses and confusion of baby-boomer adolescence that were soon exhausted, but the cultural impact of that movement upon the world cannot be denied. It has made a lasting mark which actually serves as a background and foundation for more recent cultural developments. It must be acknowledged, however, that even the attitudes of the "radical sixties" were naive in relation to what is going on now. The slogan's of peace and love come across very shallowly within the increasingly disturbing and violent context of the social and economic problems that confront us some thirty years hence. Regardie's observations were nonetheless accurate. He wrote:

> Crowley has been dead less than three decades. Who can estimate how many hundreds of people have been influenced in one way or another? Thelema may have to wait awhile before it can show, better than Christianity, its capability for transforming our society. Yet the transvaluation of values documented in this introduction suggests that Crowley has succeeded beyond his wildest dreams. What he was writing about decades ago has already begun to arrive. The young generation presently active is his enthusiastic audience and his congregation. And he has been dead less than twenty-five years! [The Law is For All, p. 40]

There is more to be addressed in the concluding two chapters of this book about more recent developments and social trends from which much of the naiveté of the 1960's has been stripped away. In closing this chapter, however, I would like to bring to the reader's attention a statement made by Crowley in the final years of his life, at which time he had the benefit of World War II to provide perspective. In a letter of instruction to an aspirant he wrote concerning atrocities fresh to the minds of all at that time: "You disagree with Aiwass—so do all of us. The trouble is that He can say: "But I'm not arguing: I'm telling you." [*Magick Without Tears,* p. 305]

CHAPTER 13

ARCHETYPES

The topic of archetypes forms a central theme in the development of this book, however they have not yet been specifically addressed as such. The psychologist Carl Jung pioneered the development of a theoretical approach to the study of archetypes as primordial images that constitute the fundamental structure of the human mind. Archetypes are studied and experienced as gods, goddesses, angels, heroic or otherwise significant mythological or fictional characters, dream images, geometric figures or arrangements, and are often associated with strong numinous feelings. Aleister Crowley's characterization of them as "aggregates of experience" is perhaps as comprehensive a reference for them as can be made. I also think that archetypes are intimately related to and may actually be the morphogenetic fields incorporated into Rupert Sheldrake's Hypothesis of Formative Causation referred to in chapter 1 as a potential theoretical basis for astrology. Archetypes assume images that embody intelligence and purposefulness in their interactions with nature and the subjective reality of human perception. Whenever any reference is made to an archetype of one cultural tradition or another, a *structural pattern* of human activity and experience is being identified. Furthermore, as Jung and others have demonstrated, there are basic archetypal images that are common to *all* cultures in various modified forms. In short, the history of mythology and religion is the history of the diversity and evolution of the human mind and the underlying structural patterns supporting the activity of human nature.

One may view comparative mythology and religion as an exploration, both geographically and temporally, of the evolution of subjective human experience to the extent that mythological images have been preserved for posterity. To do this, one must be able to *recognize* archetypes as they appear within diverse and progressive cultural developments, whereby *changes* in the expressions of various archetypes may be observed and analyzed within the context of historical evolution. This process of recognition and analysis is rather involved due to the complexity of variations represented in all the myths, legends, and stories that have accumulated throughout the world. The complexity is generated not only from intercultural diversity but also results from *intra*cultural variations of perspective with regard to any particular mythological or legendary motif. For example, an archetype may be cast in either a favorable or an unfavorable light, depending upon the *perspective* taken by any particular account of the archetype's actions and motives. Due to the peculiar logic of the mental realm in which archetypes interact, various interpretations can be applied to the *same* myth involving differing perspectives, each of which is fully cogent in terms of its own rationale.

As a result of this seemingly infinite potential for flexibility and variation of interpretation, it is not uncommon to encounter a tendency to reject the enterprise of archetypal analysis as a morass of unresolvable confusion, especially when it comes to the many variants found in the academic study of mythology. The compelling power of archetypes persists, however, not as a function of their value for determining objective facts, but rather for their value in addressing *subjective experience* and *truth.* They speak to our sense of *meaning*, which cannot be accounted for in objective terms. We perform archetypal analysis primarily because we are *seized* by archetypes. To the extent that we are not so engaged we lack a sense of vitality and meaning in life, however accurate we may be at counting beans. To be seized by an archetype, or a constellation of archetypes, is to have a profound "mystical" or "religious" anecdotal experience whereby one feels especially close to the source of vitality and meaning. The function of regular religious practices, such as attending church or performing ceremonial rituals, is to awaken and intensify a sense of participation in the vital flow and meaning of life through exposure to and re-creation of archetypal images. It is important to realize, however, that the archetypal dimension of life permeates all individual and collective human experience, regardless of whatever rituals may or may not be performed. Rituals focus and direct archetypal imagery, but *all* human thought, feeling, and, by extension, action, is actually supported by archetypal meaning, even the thought of the denial of meaning. There are many people whose experience of archetypal meaning is very private and who may therefore be wrongly assumed to have no such experience in their lives because they choose to keep it to themselves.

Archetypes provide a method of *conceptual shorthand* for analyzing human activity and getting to the heart of subjective motives involved in any situation. This accounts for the cathartic value of many forms of literature and artistic expression that reflect archetypal images in their structural forms. The "Christ image," for example, is found repeatedly in literature in the forms of characters that must die in order to effect some profound transformative process in the lives of other characters. For example, in Ken Kesey's *One Flew Over the Cuckoo's Nest*, the character Randle McMurphy suffers the role of sacrificial lamb, whereby Chief Bromden is inspired to come out of his self-imposed silence and make a break for freedom, thereby reactualizing himself as a person. If we apply this kind of archetypal understanding to the study of comparative religion, it becomes possible to ascertain the *story* of historical evolution. The very existence of religious traditions formulated around central archetypal images is evidence of the nature of the driving motivational forces operative within their associated cultural milieus. The outgrowth or *springing forth* of newer religions from older ones indicates major changes in the *arrangement* of archetypal structures within the evolutionary contexts from which they emerge. It is the new arrangement that accounts for the difference and revolutionary character of a new religion, that is, its function as an *antithesis* to its parent religion. The fact that the same archetypes, although in modified forms, are found to operate within each arrangement that characterizes any particular myth or legend accounts for the continuity that underlies *all* religions.

There is no absolutely objective criteria for determining correspondences among archetypes as represented in various pantheons. In some cases similar features and characteristics are obvious enough to establish strong correspondences as they obtain, for example, among the Egyptian Thoth, the Greek Hermes, and the Roman Mercury. Other examples are more subtle, however, such as the correspondence of Lancelot du Lac in the Arthurian legend to Jesus Christ in the Christian Bible. Furthermore, some mythological or legendary figures appear to embody combinations or mixtures of various archetypal images and motifs. As with any other field of study, there are various theoretical approaches to assessing the evolutionary development of archetypal images through the course of history. The nature of this enterprise, however, fosters a respect for variation and a certain tolerance for ambiguity. In *The Time Falling Bodies Take to Light*, William Irwin Thompson makes a poignant observation along these lines, specifically in regard to the Egyptian archetypal image of Osiris:

> To understand how a myth about the origins of the calendar can also be about the origins of the solar system, we need to understand that a myth is not a linear code, but a polyphonic fugue. One single myth can be a narrative about the formation of the solar system, the seasonal movement of planets and stars, the formation of civilization in the shift from Neolithic matriarchy to the patriarchal state, the development of consciousness in the emergence from the Great Mother to the fully individuated being, and, finally, the transformation of the central nervous system in the yogic achievement of illumination. A mythic narrative works through a system of correspondences, so a god is at once a principle of order, a number, a geometrical figure, a dancing measure, a mantram, a special planet, and a heavenly body. If one puts together the analyses of Jung, Levi Strauss, von Dechend, Neumann, and myself, one would still not have all the dimensions of the myth drawn out. [p. 213]

The Book of the Law is written from the archetypal perspective of Egyptian mythology. This is appropriate to the formal magical training and instruction of the scribe and prophet, Aleister Crowley, because the Golden Dawn system into which he was initiated was formulated around the central images of the Egyptian mystery tradition. Such a formulation is consistent with the esoteric Judeo-Christian religious tradition, even to the extent that this tradition can be documented by existing manuscripts. This implies a continuity of archetypal development that *encompasses* the Judeo-Christian tradition, because the images of Egyptian mythology both predate and contribute to the Mosaic revelation, and furthermore by the purport of *The Book of the Law* to supplant all previous religions. By virtue of the geographical and historical perspective implicit in this formulation, an inclusive conception of teleological development for Western civilization is implied.

In chapter 5, a brief account was given of the birth of the five epagomenal gods to Nut and Geb after some maneuvering between Ra, Nut, and her father Shu, involving the trickster Thoth. The five offspring were, in the order of their births, Osiris, Haroeris (Horus the Elder), Set, Isis, and Nephthys. In this group we find the three god forms associated with the historical aeons described by Crowley, although Haroeris is not specifically the form of Horus the Crowned and Conquering Child proclaimed as the governing archetype of our

New Aeon. The latter form of Horus is the Divine Child of Isis and Osiris who was conceived in the womb of Isis *after* the death of Osiris. It is essential to have a mythic perspective upon the events that transpired involving the epagomenal gods that led to the birth of Horus the Child, who later came to subsume all the diverse Horuses of Egyptian mythology, and how Isis, Osiris, and Horus became the dominant triadic configuration in Egyptian theology, in order to obtain some perspective concerning the natures of these archetypes and how they may be placed within the context of the evolution of humanity as a whole.

Even before recounting what we can about that story, however, some preliminary perspectives may be ascertained from the brief account of the origin of these deities given earlier. The fact that their births are associated with the five epagomenal or intercalary days of the year, *outside* the official 360-day year of the ancient Egyptians (the period of time that symbolically distinguishes the experience of our actual temporal world from a perfect and eternal realm of Platonic conception), specifically characterizes this group of deities as having a special relation to the worldly or existential realm of "imperfect" being—the realm of *change* as opposed to the realm of *permanence*. The group of epagomenal deities, therefore, may be interpreted to depict the very significance of the temporal world, their interactions with one another *dramatizing* the purpose of temporal existence. What, then, is that purpose? A thesis of this book is that the purpose of temporal existence is to provide a realm of *gestation* for developing spiritual processes, which ultimately implies the bringing to birth of wholly new creations of spiritually sentient beings. In this regard, an interplay is implied between the eternal and the temporal realms of being such that the temporal realm operates as laboratory for creation and change while the eternal realm operates as repository for perfected patterns and processes.

With regard to the material process of spiritual gestation symbolized by the interactions of the five epagomenal gods and goddesses, a significant perspective may be taken both from the order of their births and the peculiar manner of the birth of Set, which distinguish him as having a special significance among the group. According to the only full account of the story available to us, recorded by the Roman Plutarch, Set was born *prematurely* on the third of the five epagomenal days. Furthermore, he was not born in the natural manner. He tore himself violently from his mother's womb. He was rough and wild and finally became the incarnation of the spirit of evil who opposed the spirit of good embodied in the image of Osiris, the first born of the five. Osiris was fundamentally a great developer of culture. He taught methods of agriculture and social intercourse that brought the Egyptians out of a more primitive way of life and generated a prosperous economy. He was greatly loved by the Egyptians for his benevolence and wisdom. His sister and wife Isis was his natural mate. They were said to be married even in the womb before their birth. Isis assisted Osiris in his benevolent governance.

When Osiris left Egypt to carry his teachings to other lands throughout the world, Isis stayed in Egypt and carried on the good work there. By the time Osiris returned, his brother Set had become jealous of his accomplishments and wanted to take his place upon the throne. So Set devised a scheme in which he constructed an ornate chest to the specific dimensions of Osiris' body and brought it to a festival in celebration of Osiris' return at which Set announced that whoever best fit into the coffer could have it as a gift. After the other guests had tried and failed to fit perfectly into it, Osiris went along with the pleasantry and lay down therein, whereupon seventy-two co-conspirators of Set closed and sealed the lid of the coffer and threw it into the Nile whence it floated to the sea and ended up at Byblos. Thereafter, Osiris became the Lord of the Underworld, that is, the supreme judge of souls in the afterlife, but his governance of the material world was effectively terminated, whereby Set assumed a more powerful status among the gods. Through much travail, Isis recovered the coffer and brought it back to Egypt where she miraculously conceived a child, Horus, by the deceased body of Osiris. While hunting in the marshes by moonlight, Set rediscovered Osiris' body and cut it into fourteen pieces which he scattered far and wide. Again Isis set out to find her deceased husband and was able to recover all the pieces except the phallus, which had been devoured by fish after having been thrown into the Nile. Meanwhile, the child Horus grew to maturity through the careful guardianship of Isis and came to challenge Set as his father's avenger. The battle that ensued between Horus and Set was long and brutal, but Horus eventually prevailed and won a judgment from the council of the gods. Horus was thereafter recognized as the primary ruling deity of Egypt.

A great deal has been written about the meanings of this story that fall somewhat short of addressing the vital needs of our daily existence in today's world. This circumstance is largely due to the enormous cultural abyss that separates modern scholarship from the object of its study. Out of that tangle, however, a vital perspective may be gleaned that cuts to the heart of the matter making it relevant to our lives in today's world. This perspective incorporates theoretical elements developed in this book in relation to these five Egyptian archetypes.

The birth order of the five epagomenal deities places Set in the middle, with two male gods (Osiris and Haroeris) before him and two female goddesses (Isis and Nephthys) after him. This pattern identifies Set as the focal image of the group through his *containment* by the others—implying an embryonic condition—and therefore represents his *potential* for actualization as a spiritual entity. He comes *between* the other masculine and the feminine images and is therefore the offspring of those forces. The fact of the other two masculine images coming first, as well as Set's own masculinity, accords with the nature of temporality, which it is the essential purpose of the myth to depict, as masculine in relation to eternity. This reiterates the theme implicit in the relation between the parents of the five, namely Geb (male/earth/temporality), and Nut (female/sky/eternity). Therefore, Set represents the spiritual potential for gestation in the temporal world. Set's tearing himself out from his mother's womb indicates his inability to negotiate consciously the rigors of temporal existence. He cannot bring himself to endure the constricting passage through the birth canal. He is endowed with sufficient strength, however, to tear out of the womb and wreak havoc in the world. His great strength is his only manifest virtue and his only means of survival. He is a god, however, and is therefore possessed of the fullness of spirit. He possesses spiritual intelligence and is capable of interacting with the other gods and goddesses. His inability to discipline himself to the natural rigors of material existence, however, exposes his spiritual immaturity.

The fundamental principle symbolized by Set has become manifest to modern consciousness in the form of the nuclear explosion. In the process of natural biological evolution, the quantum potential is *mediated* through the molecular structures of living organisms, making possible the birth of living forms into the world capable of interacting in a fortuitous manner, whereby the drama of living intelligence can be enacted. In the case of the nuclear explosion, however, the quantum potential is forced to tear into the material world in an uncontrolled and utterly destructive manner. This application of nuclear power was accomplished through the knowledge of science upon reaching a particular level of technical sophistication. Hadit speaking in *The Book of the Law* says, "I am the flame that burns in every heart of man, and the core of every star. I am Life, and the giver of Life, yet therefore is the knowledge of me the knowledge of death." [*AL* II:6] Hadit is here found to represent the quantum aspect of reality. The nuclear explosion, as well as its accompanying fallout, dramatically demonstrates one possible manifestation of that reality within the material world.

Osiris, as the primary male deity and benevolent ruler, bespeaks knowledge of the relation of temporality to eternity rooted in *collective memory* of previous experience, that is, well established morphogenetic fields built up through previous rounds of experience with temporal reality. This is precisely what Set is unable to integrate into his being, because he is the prototype for a *new generation* of spiritual entities and therefore has no reservoir of experience in his nature to resonate with the wisdom and maturity that comprehends a full gamut of existence. Implicit here is a cyclo-cosmic conception of Being that is inherent in all spiritual and mystical philosophy, whereby the cycle becomes the temporal metaphor for eternity. The dualistic relationship between temporality and eternity is represented both by the figure-8 symbol for infinity (oriented horizontally like breasts) and the yin-yang mage of the Tao. The ultimate rationale for any cycle is exemplified in nature by the process of *generation*, the bringing forth of new creations of life. Temporal existence therefore implies an inherent parent-child relationship. The five epagomenal gods of the Egyptian pantheon represent an inceptional formula for the gestation of a new generation associated with the cycle of temporal existence. The implication is that it takes two images of each parental gender to facilitate the gestation of the male child in accordance with the formula derived from the eternal realm of Being.

The initial phase of the process is exemplified in the early development of the story in which Osiris acts directly in the world as the older brother of Set. At first Set more or less goes along with the rule of Osiris and Isis. He is rambunctious, but he has not yet gained sufficient coherence to envision himself as the master of the world. Osiris' departure gives him yet more space to develop and foster the desire to exercise the power to which he is destined to aspire. When Set reaches the stage of development at which he can envision himself as the ruler, Osiris returns in order to set the stage for the most difficult passage of Set's individuation, the stage at which Set assumes power and the responsibility that accompanies that power. Surely Set is not prepared properly to exercise power, but how else is he to learn except through trial and error and the *real experience* of being responsible for the functioning of the world? *This is the method of gestating the new generation.* It is a process that involves the granting of hands-on experience. Nothing else will do. This is the ultimate purpose of temporal reality. It provides a whole realm in which an embryonic humanity can exercise real power and thereby come to learn what real power means.

As a spiritual embryo, Set sees power simply as a means of directly getting what he wants without any sense of consequences. Such irresponsible exercise of power disturbs the sustaining economy of the social system, and the general welfare of the community suffers, bringing unpleasant repercussions to all, including Set, although he is unable to appreciate his own responsibility for the general malaise. Such consequences are the actual forces that can ultimately teach Set what life is really all about. It may appear unfortunate that everyone involved has to share in the suffering that results from Set's spiritual immaturity, but this condition is inherent in the process of gestation. It is characteristic of the process by which the embryo draws upon the very sustenance of the mother's body. Set simply dramatizes this basic truth of gestation at a cosmic level. As a spiritual embryo, he draws upon the resources of eternity. Why else would Osiris, a wise and experienced ruler, allow himself to be tricked into such an obvious ploy except that he willingly acquiesces to Set's need to take the reigns of power in order to learn the lessons of power? In this regard, Osiris demonstrates the understanding that a father must have in relation to the process of gestation. He imparts the seed and then withdraws.

As the Good Spirit, Osiris exemplified pure conscience, and as such he was powerless to oppose Set with coercive force. He could not demonstrate goodness by beating Set down with force. His power was rather that of example, which Set was incapable of respecting by virtue of his immaturity. Osiris understood that the only "punishment" that would have a beneficial effect on Set was the unpleasant consequences of Set's own actions. Set would have to learn the law of karma—that is, spiritual cause and effect. This truth is revealed by the symbolism inherent in the manner by which Set contrives to entrap Osiris. It is actually a sublime reflection of the very process by which Set was himself being trapped into fulfilling his own destiny. In one sense, Set felt he was getting back at Osiris for trapping him in the material world in which wish-fulfillment is not automatic. In another sense, he was trapping himself into the responsibility of power over others, which looks appealing to one who would abuse it,

but ultimately deprives the tyrant of the opportunity for self-fulfill-
ment through its many demands upon one's time and personal attention, as well as the resentment, resistance, and retaliation by those
who are unjustly governed.

As Lord of the Underworld Osiris became the judge of the
departed, thus orchestrating the karmic destinies of evolving souls.
This set the stage for the conception of Horus through Isis to function
as Osiris' representative on Earth. Thereafter, Osiris lost his phallus
which reiterates the theme of relinquishment of power. Osiris was
consigned to a passive role in the process of evolution. Horus was
born and raised for one purpose, to avenge his father—that is, to
provide a counter-balancing force in the world to Set's mischief. In
that context, Horus represents the potential for recovering power by
the Osirian principle. Therefore, he was destined to be a warrior
whose primary *modus operandi* was devotion to duty and conscience. He was raised on the sly by his mother in the kingdom of
Set. It was the duty of Isis to protect Horus and instill in him the
knowledge of the other world where his father dwelt so he could
understand his own purpose on Earth. But, as the son of Osiris, the
necessary attributes were visited upon him through his paternal
heritage as well.

After Horus reached sufficient maturity, he came forth and fought
Set in a gruesome battle of many days and was able eventually to
bring Set tied in bonds before Isis. But, rather than killing Set, Isis
freed him. Horus was not at all pleased with this action and proceeded to cut off his mother's head. Thoth then replaced Isis' head
with one of a cow, thus partially restoring her original image but also
indicating an evolutionary mutation of her functional role. Set then
continued to challenge Horus and bring against him the charge of
illegitimacy, but, although Set was not without allies, the greater
sentiments of the gods and the people remained with Horus. Nephthys as well, whom Set had taken for his wife, abandoned him and
sided with Isis, Osiris, and Horus in the continuing struggle against
Set. Clearly, however, the whole matter was left short of full resolution. The forces of "good" and "evil" both remained operative in the
world in a rather precarious balance. This myth gives expression to
the mysteries of the matriarchal world system inherited from neolithic times that in turn prepared the way for the patriarchal world
system that would follow. These are the periods of time referred to
by Crowley respectively as the Aeons of Isis and Osiris. The distur-
bance between Isis and Horus signals the imminent emergence of the

patriarchal system. By reacting with antipathy to Set's release by Isis, Horus clearly demonstrated that he was not the son-lover reminiscent of neolithic matriarchy. The seed of patriarchy would come to be exported out of Egypt through the Hebrew Exodus, thus setting the stage for the Aeon of Osiris, the Father God.

As stated earlier, the Christian religion would prove to be the dominant institution of the Piscean Age, which corresponds directly with the Aeon of Osiris from the historical perspective advanced by Aleister Crowley. The linkage of Egyptian, Hebrew, and Christian doctrine is directly expressed in the following passage from *The Book of Splendours*, written by the French Catholic magician, Alphonse Louis Constant, under the pseudonym of Eliphas Levi. Levi's words are especially relevant to the thematic development of this book, because Aleister Crowley believed himself to be his immediate reincarnation (Levi died only three months before Crowley's birth) and claimed to have direct memory of that incarnation. Whether or not one accepts Crowley's claim, the fact that he believed it has a significant bearing upon his sense of his spiritual heritage and the continuity of his soul's mission and development within the context of history. Levi argued very strongly for the continuity of the Hebrew and Christian religious traditions, which he perceived as a continuous development of spiritual truth. In *The Book of Splendours* he wrote:

Commentary

Here we can clearly see that the occult dogma of Moses, professed to by Rabbi Simeon, comes from the sanctuaries of Egypt. There, in fact, one was subjected to great trial before being admitted to initiation. These rituals took place in immense underground spaces, which those who gave way to fear were never to leave. The adept who, on the contrary, came out triumphant, received the key to all religious mysteries, and the first great revelation, whispered close to his ear in passing, was contained in this formula:

Osiris is a dark God

That is: the God worshipped by the profane is only a shadow of the true God.

We give him man's anger so that he may be dreaded by man.

For if men are not presented with a master who resembles them, the idea of divinity will so surpass their feeble intelligence that it will escape them completely, and they will fall into atheism.

When man does evil, he throws himself into disorder, he trans-
gresses the law which guards his happiness. Then he is miserable,
dissatisfied with himself, and he is told that God is angry with him,
in order to explain to him the workings of his own angered
conscience. He must placate God with expiations which, like pun-
ishments inflicted upon unreasonable, willful children, serve to
impress on the mind a horror of evil. He must above all return to
the path of goodness, and then, from the calm he experiences, he
feels that God has forgiven him. God, however, does not forgive,
for he is never angered; but if you say to the vulgar man that the
supreme judge lives in the heart of his own conscience, he will
believe that God is only a word, and he will come to argue with his
conscience, attributing his scruples or his remorse to learned prejudice. He will thus have no other guide than the self interest of his
passions which are the harbingers of death. [pp. 56-57]

As a Christian, Levi accepted the formula of Osiris as the true
religion capable of uniting the world under its banner. He taught that
Judaism, Christianity, and Freemasonry were, in their true forms, all
expressions of the one universal religion of humanity. The above
passage clearly sets forth the rationale for the Aeon of Osiris which
assumed its ultimate expression in the teaching and ministry of Jesus
Christ. For this reason, Jesus can be cast in the archetypal image of
Osiris, and, as a god who dies and is resurrected, he certainly conforms to that image. It is also manifestly clear, however, that Jesus
enacted an embodiment of Horus. Jesus' prophetic mission becomes
comprehensible through the realization that he accomplished the
actualization of Horus as a *man*, and that as such he truly affected the
advent of a new beginning for humanity of cosmic proportions
appropriate to the devotional ebullience of sincere Christians, however lacking may be their conscious understanding of what he did.
This identification will likely be considered controversial. It will
therefore be developed further in the next chapter. The fact that Jesus
acted out the image of Osiris and gave that image an historical
embodiment constitutes the essential meaning of the crucifixion. For
Osiris, as a symbol of conscience, to die in order to facilitate the
growth of the new generation was an act appropriate to his essential
purpose. But for the warrior Horus, having been victorious over Set
in battle, to *take on* the image of the Dying God, yielding power to
the abusive spirit of the undeveloped one, was a violation of his
nature. Why then was this magickal act performed? What was its
efficacy in the evolutionary scheme?

Referring back to the Egyptian scenario as a prefiguration of the Christian motif, the significance of Horus was that he remained in the world with Set and was therefore able to function as a counter-force to Set's destructive behavior. Without Horus in the material world, Set would simply have destroyed the very matrix of activity in which he was able to learn and grow. There had to be an instrument of transcendental perspective in the world with sufficient power to preserve the viability of the temporal order. At the same time, however, Set had to be given sufficient reign to utilize the temporal order for its ultimate purpose, namely his own spiritual growth and development. Therefore, it was necessary for Horus *both* to prove his superiority to Set *and* to refrain from exercising that superiority to the point of breaking Set's spirit, which would have defeated the purpose of the enterprise as surely as giving Set a completely free hand. This was the truth demonstrated by Isis when she released Set from bondage after Horus had defeated him in battle. At that time, Horus was yet unable to comprehend the full significance of his task, which he would only come to learn progressively. Horus had to incorporate the full meaning of his father's act of relinquishing power to Set before he (Horus) could realize his own full potential, which was ultimately greater than that of Osiris in that it involved his ability to manifest the realization of spiritual conscience *and yet remain in the material world*, where he could function as a force within Set's realm of activity.

Horus had evolved to this realization by the time of his animation of Jesus, which epitomized the fulfillment of all that went before in that Jesus was a *man* of flesh and blood. The true act of redemption became possible by the joining of the wisdom of eternity with the bodily realm of temporal existence through the incarnation of a man capable of incorporating that union into the enactment of a fully human life. The *concept* had been manifested before in the form of the *god* (archetype) Osiris, but the ability to *prove* it had yet to be enacted, and could only be accomplished by a *man*.

Ironically, however, the incarnation, although the fulfillment of the process of descent outlined above, signaled not the end of the work but rather its actual beginning. Jesus' mission as a man affected a victory not by overcoming evil at that time, but by playing the trump card that evil could neither match nor comprehend, thus establishing the conditions for Set's embryonic viability. The *potential* for Set's ultimate assimilation of cosmic wholeness was secured by Horus' sacrifice. The understanding of this rationale clarifies the mysteries of the Christ mythos. The nature of Jesus as Horus was concealed behind his adoption of the *image* of Osiris, the Dying God. Thereafter, he could function in such a manner as not to overwhelm Set but at the same time exert his martial force in the world as needed to *contain* Set's abusive behavior. Meanwhile, the teachings of the Christian Church maintained a visible image of the Osirian principle of spiritual conscience for Set's edification, which was yet non-threatening toward him by virtue of its doctrine of "resist not evil" which jibed with his submerged memory of deposing Osiris. Furthermore, the ascendancy of the Roman Church itself provided an institutional structure in which an essentially Caesarian papacy was contained by a self-imposed mode of operational sequestration.

Before clarifying more explicitly the archetypal transformations appropriate to the Christian motif, a few more observations are needed to bring a more focused perspective to bear upon the Egyptian deities. Due to the lack of much information concerning the many complex overlappings, generations, and transformations of the gods and goddesses of the Egyptian pantheon through the course of historical development, it is reasonable to assume that the original five epagomenals afford us the most pristine perspective upon the structural pattern that subsequently proliferated within the more chaotic and distended context of Egyptian history. That grouping is clearly suggestive of two couples separated according to gender by Set. Since we know from extant texts that Osiris and Isis were a connubial couple, it is implicit in our hypothesis that Haroeris (Horus the Elder) and Nephthys would also be paired in some significant manner. There appears to be little or no evidence to that effect, however, in the extant texts. In fact, as mentioned earlier, it is recorded that Set took Nephthys as his wife. Furthermore, there were various intrigues that ensued involving jealousies and adulterous desires and liaisons, such as Set's lust for Isis, Nephthys' seduction of Osiris producing Anubis, and Nephthys' abandonment of Set, after his act of fratricide, to join forces with Osiris' defenders.

This latter event would appear to imply an alliance of Nephthys with Horus the Child, which logically suggests her assumption of another form, even though her form of Nephthys continued as a close associate of Isis. Since Horus the Child came to subsume all other forms of Horus, which would include that of Haroeris, it is reasonable to equate the cat goddess Bast, the twin sister and therefore female counterpart of Horus, with a subsequent form of Nephthys, whereby the original implicit relationship between Haroeris and

Nephthys would be reiterated in accordance with the further development of the evolutionary motif. The Horus-Bast twin motif suggests a more complete involution of the cosmic parents into the material world, made possible in direct proportion to the progress of Set's gestation. The name Nephthys signifies "Mistress of the Palace" [*New Larousse Encyclopedia of Mythology,* p. 21] which implies a more worldly status in contrast to that of Isis as the mother goddess. This theme parallels that of Horus as the more worldly expression of the Osirian principle.

The significance of this mythological arrangement to modern times is that the archetypal images involved have continued to evolve through the course of history and have manifested within the cultural consciousness of various regional groupings transmitting them in the forms of legendary events and religious doctrines, some of which have been proclaimed heretical. This migratory pattern has determined the course of Western civilization, most eminently through the historical development of the Judeo-Christian religious tradition.

In the Christian format, the cognates of the original five epagomenal deities are, in their respective Egyptian birth-order, God the Father in Heaven, Jesus the Son of God on Earth, Caesar the Ruler of the Temporal World, Mary the Virgin Mother, and Mary Magdalene the Whore. Due to the fact that Christianity has been the dominant archetypal institution supporting the development of European and American cultures, this arrangement has a more immediate relevance to our common contemporary perspective than do the Egyptian archetypes. It would appear, however, that our understanding of both traditions may be enhanced by this analogy. Furthermore, certain implications are inherent in this configuration. As stated in Eliphas Levi's account of the theological rationale for the cult of Osiris, the purpose of the religion was to keep alive a working doctrinal system whereby *conscience* may be mediated to *consciousness*, especially for those in greatest need of such mediation. The only way these two realms of experience could be brought into meaningful relation to one another, bridging the gap in the schizoid mind of Set (Caesar), was (during the Aeon of Osiris) through the sacrifice of men for whom such an integration was already inherently affected, the prototype for whom is symbolized by the image of Horus (Jesus).

The historical context of the temporal world has been such that it has been possible to attain power through acts of treachery and deception, that is, through a dissociation from conscience. Thus unethical men have had an actual advantage in the political arena of the temporal realm at a particular stage of human evolution. This explains both Set's role as Caesar, able to conceal his unjust intentions in the shadows of materiality, and Horus' role as Christ, the bearer of the light of conscience that produces those shadows. The masculine roles are accentuated by the *patriarchal* character of the tradition, placing emphasis upon the *temporal* aspect of reality as opposed to the self-luminous realm of the Eternal Feminine.

The primary significance of the Aeon of Horus, the Crowned and Conquering Child, is that the sacrifice of Horus is no longer called for. It is implicit in the new formula that the bringing of Set to viability has been accomplished through the formula of the now completed Aeon of Osiris. This, of course, does not mean that all moral conflicts have been resolved; far from it. The *new beginning* is characterized by the condition that Set doesn't have to be coddled anymore. He has become *viable*, although not fully developed, as a spiritual entity. Horus, therefore, can come down from his cross and reassert his full power at will. It follows that Horus has also benefited from the experience of the past aeon and has accordingly established a *fully developed* ability to incorporate spiritual conscience into temporal existence, an understanding he lacked at the time of his outburst over the release of Set by Isis in the ancient context of the story. Therefore, for both of these reasons, there is no longer any need for an archetypal image of authority beyond the heart of one's own conscience.

Rather than initiating an aeon of peace and harmony, however, our present situation sets the stage for an unprecedented mode of conflict between Horus and Set. There is an enormous amount of karma left over from the past that will have to be balanced. Even though Set has taken the prodigious step of acquiescing to his own immortality (which may be considered analogous to the transition from the embryonic to the fetal stage of his gestation), he is still ingrained, by virtue of his past experience, with the habit of having his way without having to pay the full price. Responsibility is always accepted *before* one is prepared fully to comprehend its implications. Such is the nature of personal and spiritual growth. Otherwise, we would live in a perfect world, or rather the utopian conception of a "perfect" non-disruptive world which would lack the aesthetic depth inherent in the cyclo-cosmic perspective.

Set has accepted immortality because he has grown to the point of being able to comprehend its ultimate benefit to himself. He is looking forward, and this is as it should be. He has come to the realization that he must learn to control himself in the face of all the trials of temporal existence. But knowing that he must do so and actually doing it, or being able to do it, are very different things. The gradual discovery of the magnitude of his commitment, and his inability to evade it, will tend to further enrage him during moments of difficulty and strife. But his rage will serve as the fuel of his progress through the New Aeon. *The Book of the Law* seems to make little provision for the lessening of tension. His progress will be accomplished through his meeting with Horus on a *level playing field*, thus the vital significance of the notification, "Do what thou wilt shall be the whole of the Law." There is no outside authority to spell out the rules of the game. This has the effect of raising the ante for Set. Horus will follow his conscience, one may be sure, but he will have his full range of power at his disposal for the administration of his own conception of justice. Set's old tricks of taking advantage of his presently elapsed handicap will get him nowhere in the Aeon of Horus.

It is assuredly the case that Horus will do many things considered unlawful by the old standard of Christian morality, *but the old standard no longer applies*. Set is perfectly free to engage in tactics as he will, but now so is Horus, and it has already been shown through Horus' initial victory over Set in the ancient Egyptian myth that acting in accordance with spiritual conscience produces superior results on the field of battle, *when the field is level*. Set will be angered by self-acknowledgment of his true status as the prototype of a newly emergent generation. He will still want to imagine that the task of his development is already completed. But his anger will be the cause of his defeat at the hands of Horus who will fight with cool confidence grounded in spiritual knowledge and experience. Horus is now free to venture into the utilization of material principles and resources that were reserved only for Set during the period of restraint upon Horus. This will tend to obscure the superficial appearances of the world's activities. But one need not be concerned. As always, the law of karma continues to apply. Superior moral force will prove the ultimate victor for all parties concerned, and Set will be brought to yet another level of spiritual development.

It must be kept in mind that all activity in the world is primarily for the benefit of Set, who is none other than the hope of eternity, the unborn child worthy of the love of his peers and parents. It may be objected that the "evil" one will take advantage of the explication of this formula, exactly as forewarned by Eliphas Levi in the passage quoted above. Of course, such an objection is correct. Set takes advantage of everything. The point is that in this aeon he is going to get a serious whipping. Case in point: Adolph Hitler. Let him take advantage of *that*.

It remains for a greater balance to be brought to these perspectives by considering the role of Woman in the progressive development of this process. Just as the seeds of the patriarchal system of the Aeon of Osiris were discernible within the context of the development of the Aeon of Isis, so were the seeds of the juviarchal (child-ruled) system of the Aeon of Horus discernible within the context of the development of the Aeon of Osiris. Before developing an analysis of this, however, it may prove helpful to emphasize that the Aeon of Horus as prescribed in *The Book of the Law* promotes an ideal of sexual equality. It places the emphasis on the *individual person*, male *or* female. The fact that the ruling archetype is a male deity only serves to accentuate its aggressive nature and its application to the temporal aspect of reality. The masculine aspect is fully compensated in this regard by the image of the Scarlet Woman.

As the Aeon of Osiris progressed, it gave rise to a cultural development in Europe, codified in the Grail legend, that spawned the unique contribution of Western civilization to the evolution of humanity. That contribution was the emergence of a social system based upon the experience of courtly love. This kind of experience was first introduced as an actual social movement by the troubadours of Provence, France in the twelfth century and proceeded to spread throughout Europe. This development was in fact an expression of Christianity but was violently suppressed by the Roman Church as a heresy through the execution of the Albigensian Crusade of 1209. The authoritarian church could not abide this movement, because the troubadours put the personal experience of courtly love above any other rule of life. This established the actual basis of the Western ideal of individualism and clearly foreshadows the love ethic expressed in *The Book of the Law*. The significance of the role of Woman in the tradition of courtly love is directly addressed in the transcripts of a conversation between Bill Moyers and the renowned authority on mythology, Joseph Campbell, edited by Betty Sue Flowers in *The Power of Myth*:

> MOYERS: So the age of chivalry was growing up as the age of romantic love was reaching out.
> CAMPBELL: I'd say these were the same thing. It was a very strange period because it was terribly brutal. There was no central

law. Everyone was on his own, and, of course, there were great violations of everything. But within this brutality, there was a civilizing force, which the women really represented because they were the ones who established the rules for this game. And the men had to play it according to the requirements of the women.

MOYERS: How did it happen that the women had the dominant influence?

CAMPBELL: Because, if you want to make love to a woman, she's already got the drop on you. The technical term for the woman's granting of herself was "merci." Now, that might consist in her permission to kiss her on the back of the neck once every Whitsuntide, you know, something like that—or it might be a full giving in love. That would depend upon her estimation of the character of the candidate.

MOYERS: So there were rules to determine the testing?

CAMPBELL: Yes. There was an essential requirement—that one must have a gentle heart, that is, a heart capable of love, not simply lust. The woman would be testing to find whether the candidate for her love had a gentle heart, whether he was capable of love. [pp. 193-194]

One surely finds an expression of this ideal in the following verse from *The Book of the Law*:

> There is help & hope in other spells. Wisdom says: be strong! Then canst thou bear more joy. Be not animal; refine thy rapture! If thou drink, drink by the eight and ninety rules of art: if thou love, exceed by delicacy; and if thou do aught joyous, let there be subtlety therein! [*AL* II:70]

In the legend of the Holy Grail, Lancelot du Lac comes to Britain from France and clearly represents the heretical Christian development of courtly love. He may therefore be understood to represent the esoteric side of the religion. It is worth noting at this point that the transcendental figure and orchestrator of the Grail legend, namely Merlin the Magician, is associated with the astrological sign Virgo. (Interestingly, this character is superbly portrayed in the 1981 movie *Excalibur* by the actor Nicol Williamson who was born with Sol in Virgo.) Being the sign opposite Pisces, Virgo may be understood to reflect a mirror image, as it were, of the direct expression of the formula of the Piscean Age as represented in the Christian Bible. Therefore, a *reversal* of that perspective is presented in the Grail legend such that Caesar (Set), as the ruler of the temporal realm, is cast in a positive light in the form of King Arthur, the boy king who

establishes law to unify the kingdom. Conversely Christ (Horus), as
the exemplar of heart-felt virtue, is cast in a negative light in the
form of Lancelot, the superior knight who nonetheless covets and
engages carnally with Arthur's wife and queen, Guinevere.

Here we have the true gist of the matter revealed, and from this
we are able to understand what Jesus *really* gave up and what constituted the ultimate meaning of the crucifixion. Again, we have the
theme of the embryo (Set) coming between the cosmic parents, but
by this time, the parents have evolved more fully into forms fore-
shadowed by the original images of Haroeris and Nephthys. It will be
recalled that Set took Nephthys for his wife. In the story of King
Arthur, the awakening of the love between Lancelot and Guinevere
foreshadows the eventual need for Set (Arthur) to be born out of his
mother's womb, for the love between Lancelot and Guinevere is the
courtly form of love, discovered through the eyes, which therefore
takes precedence over all else—that is, such love is the undeniable
manifestation of the true and supreme power of existence. This development is appropriate to the growing realization of responsibility
on the part of Arthur that is shown in his learning through the experience of governing his kingdom. The imminent realization of the
responsibility of his power has led to his need to recognize (albeit
ever so feebly) a yet stronger power. This is the manner by which Set
is actually brought to the greater experience of conscience and
humility, virtues with which Horus had long been familiar. The end
of the Grail legend, however, remains tragic, connoting a process not
fulfilled. Thus is the inner working of the beautiful mystery of the
Aeon of Osiris, the Dying God, revealed by this legend.

As we enter the Aeon of Horus, the Crowned and Conquering
Child, as prescribed by *The Book of the Law,* we find ourselves
involved in an entirely different set of circumstances. The roles of
man as Beast and woman as Scarlet Woman invoke the full expression of material love, governed by instinctual desire. This, of course,
is accomplished through *control* of the energies involved, "love
under will," and in no way implies a promiscuous debauch. The
moral crises that ensue within this context will be resolved through
conflict, and the morally strong will be united through the realization
of personal liberty. Issues will not be obscured by false concepts of
obedience and sacrifice. Already we are able to see this attitude
taking hold in the world. Surely it is disturbing to all, and there is a
great deal of confusion and misunderstanding about the way things
are going. Enormous aggregated problems loom menacingly on the

horizon. The naive enthusiasm about the new age that has characterized recent decades is being severely tempered by the heat of persis-
tent and increased social and economic difficulties. Indeed, we are
experiencing a purge, and the preparation for a greater purge that will
to some degree resolve the tension of the aeonic transition, thereby
opening the way for the unencumbered advance of evolution in
accordance with the Law of Thelema.

CHAPTER 14

JESUS

Among the most intriguing aspects of the study of the life and teachings of Aleister Crowley are his beliefs and attitudes toward Christianity and its central figure, Jesus Christ. He is emphatic enough in his denunciations of both that there can be no doubt of his antipathy. Yet an in-depth study of Crowley's writings shows that the issue may not be resolved so simply. There are many layers to the whole matter, which are sufficient to rebuff all but the most intrepid diggers. Furthermore, such an enterprise would appear to be rendered superfluous by the simple admonition to leave the formula of the Dying God behind and move steadfastly forward into the Aeon of Horus. Is it not written: "With my Hawk's head I peck at the eyes of Jesus as he hangs upon the cross"? [*AL* III:51] To a devout Christian, or even a casual one, that verse from *The Book of the Law* would appear as strong a blasphemy as could be uttered. Considered apart from its emotional charge, however, it simply affirms that whoever persists in the ethos of self-sacrifice and self-denial will be blind to the truth of the Aeon of Horus. The fundamental admonition appears to be that if one can't figure the thing out for oneself, tough; one is left to one's own miserable resources. Surely, this is the case.

It is perhaps also the case that a fundamental criterion for an efficacious entry into the Aeon of Horus on the part of any individual is to be so fed up with the bouquet of the carcass of Osiris as to simply repudiate it altogether and be done with the matter, whereby one may proceed merrily into the light of freedom. Such an attitude surely characterizes the aspect of *antithesis* essential to the aeonic transition from a dialectical perspective. It is inherent in the process of dialectical change that antithesis must precede synthesis, and that these are two distinctly different attitudes. Furthermore, the attitude of antithesis must be extended to its fullest possible expression in order that its inherent function of defining issues and setting up a new pattern of tensions may be accomplished. Otherwise, the birth of a new synthesis would be aborted for lack of impetus, and the potential for historical change would degenerate into a mire of unresolvable chaos. Fortunately, it may be assumed that the dialectical process of evolutionary change is so well established through untold rounds of dynamic equilibrium that there is no danger of its being disturbed by any "mistakes" that may be made by any who are involved in its workings.

I can't imagine there would be any disagreement among Crowley scholars that his personality became thoroughly polarized into an antithetical mode toward Osirian doctrine in general and Christianity in particular. In so doing, however, he was continuously in need of addressing his own spiritual roots, both as a person and as an evolving soul, and those of the world he ironically considered it his duty to save. It is highly significant that Crowley's formative years were characterized by an attitude of extreme devotion to Jesus Christ and a thorough knowledge of Christian doctrine based on rigorous biblical study. His own account of his personal development tells of his change of attitude toward the particular brand of puritanical Christianity visited upon him by his parents and the Plymouth Brethren. His religious orientation, however, remained essentially Christian through his initiation into the Second Order of the Golden Dawn. His travels to the East and the influence of his friend Allan Bennett later enabled him to shift his orientation to Buddhism, whereby he came to repudiate the scourge of his childhood religion altogether. Or so it would seem, except that Buddhism is also an Osirian religion, predicated upon suffering and the relinquishment of existence.

Such was Crowley's position at the time he received *The Book of the Law,* and it was so fully ingrained that he was unable to accept the message of the new revelation for several years. Crowley had to exert a great deal of conscious effort, along with unconscious promptings, to adopt the attitude appropriate to the New Aeon for which he was the chosen prophet. An astrological perspective on Crowley's life lays bare, to an almost voyeuristic degree, the nature of his struggle in undergoing this transformation of his conscious orientation.

Crowley attempted with great resolve to fulfill the ideal of Christianity, not only as a young Plymouth Brother, but later, upon gaining freedom from his family's household, through a flirtation with the Celtic Church, and yet later through his involvement with the Golden Dawn. The fact of the unconscious struggle going on at that time in his life is revealed in an observation from *Confessions*:

But all these ideals [the Grail Quest of the Celtic Church], seriously as I entertained them, were in the nature of reverie. In practical life I was still passionately engaged in cleansing myself from the mire of Christianity by deliberate acts of sin and worldliness. I was so happy to be free from the past tyranny that I found continual joy in affirming my emancipation.

There were thus several diverse strands in the loom of my soul which had not yet been woven into a harmonious pattern. I dealt with life empirically, taking things as they came, without basing them on any fundamental principle. [p. 123]

A more comprehensive self-appraisal of Crowley's attitudes toward Christianity during the period between his rejection of his childhood religion and his involvement with the Golden Dawn, as well as during the development of his opinions at the time he wrote *Confessions*, are revealed in the following passage:

It will be seen that I had developed enormously in these years. Unfortunately, my misery was so great during this long battle with my tyrants that, while the incidents themselves stand out luminously in focus, I find it very hard to remember the order in which they occurred. There are, moreover, curious contradictions in myself against which I seem always to be stumbling. For example, as late as 1894, I think it must be, I find myself writing hymns of quite acceptable piety. One was published in *The Christian*; it began:

> I am a blind man on a helmless ship
> Without a compass on a stormy sea.
> I cannot sink, for God will hold me up, etc.

Again, I wrote a poem on the death of my Aunt Ada, which I thought good enough to include in my *Songs of the Spirit*, and it is entirely irreproachable on the score of piety. It seems as if I possessed a theology of my own which was, to all intents and purposes, Christianity. My satanism did not interfere with it at all; I was trying to take the view that the Christianity of hypocrisy and cruelty was not true Christianity. I did not hate God or Christ, but merely the God and Christ of the people whom I hated. It was only when the development of my logical faculties supplied the demonstration that the Scriptures support the theology and practice of professing Christians that I was compelled to set myself in opposition to the Bible itself. It does not matter that the literature is sometimes magnificent and that in isolated passages the philosophy and ethics are admirable. The sum of the matter is that Judaism is a savage, and Christianity a fiendish superstition. [pp. 72-73]

In Crowley's fully developed philosophical perspective he had virtually banished Christianity from his conscious outlook altogether. He found particularly reprehensible the doctrine of vicarious atonement, which he apparently did not consider essential to the formula of Osiris, but rather a carry-over from more primitive forms of worship rooted in the ego-appeasing practice of human and animal sacrifice:

It is the modern fashion to try to dismiss these barbarous absurdities as excrescences on Christianity, but they are of the essence of the religion. The whole theory of the atonement implies that man can set up his own will in opposition to God's, and thereby excites Him to anger which can only be pacified by the sacrifice of His Son. ...The tendency has, in fact, been to forget about the atonement altogether and to represent Jesus as a 'Master' whose teachings are humanitarian and enlightened. Yet the only evidence of what he actually said is that of the gospels and these not only insist upon the incredible and immoral sides of Christianity, but contain actual Logia which exhibit Jesus in the character of a superstitious fanatic who taught the doctrine of eternal punishment and many others unacceptable to modern enlightenment. General Booth and Billy Sunday preach perfectly scriptural abominations. [*ibid.*, p. 145]

Here Crowley has clearly delineated the antithetical attitudes found *within* the Christian religion that, in accordance with the hypotheses of this book, are characterized by the two fishes of the Piscean image, swimming in opposite directions and bound at their mouths by a chord, as a referent for the formula of the Christian dispensation; two opposing attitudes bound by the Word of one body of doctrine. Indeed, it is the atonement that is preached most strenuously by "fundamentalists," and their answer to those who would choose to extract only the universal and humanitarian precepts from Jesus' teachings is that one must accept the *whole* Word of God, and that includes, among others, the doctrine of vicarious atonement. Having had that doctrine stuffed down his throat through his entire childhood, culminating in his experience at the hands of the Reverend H. d'Arcy Champney, and subsequently maturing into a moral inability to acquiesce in allowing another person to have "died for *his* sins," Crowley eventually chose simply to *reject* the "whole

Word of God" and find his universal and humanitarian religion else-where, first through Buddhism, and ultimately in *The Book of the Law* which overthrows the religious attitude of suffering altogether by proclaiming: "Remember all ye that existence is pure joy; that all the sorrows are but as shadows; they pass & are done; but there is that which remains." [*AL* 2:9]

His experience with the Golden Dawn during the interim, how-ever, best elucidated by Israel Regardie in *The Eye in the Triangle*, brings a significant perspective to bear upon the importance of Jesus Christ in the life of Aleister Crowley. It may be recalled that upon being initiated into the Outer Order, Crowley adopted the motto of Perdurabo, which he translated as "I will endure to the end." The Christian implication of this motto is obvious with respect to the scripture, "And ye shall be hated of all *men* for my name's sake: but he that endureth to the end shall be saved." [Matthew 10:22] There is another motto adopted by Crowley, however, that could perhaps prove much more significant in terms of his identification with the image of Jesus, except for the fact that we do not know what that motto was. Crowley had no qualms about publishing the various mottos he adopted for each of the grades of initiation, even those of the sacrosanct Third Order, *except for one*. The special significance of the 5=6 grade of Adeptship, bringing one into the Second or Rosi-crucian Order, was alluded to in Chapter 5 in relation to its associa-tion with the symbolism of Sol. Although there are several yet higher grades, this one is the very *heart* of the system, and it has a direct correspondence to what may be called the "Christ principle" as a component of personality. The ritual of initiation through which Crowley was conducted for that grade employed predominantly Christian imagery. One actually places oneself upon a cross in one phase of the ritual.

Israel Regardie devotes an entire chapter of *The Eye in the Trian-gle*, entitled "I Am The Heart...," to the significance of this initiation for Aleister Crowley, providing an insider's account upon the very texts and ceremonial recitations of its enactment. Regardie's author-ity in this matter derives both from his personal knowledge of Crowley, for whom he worked directly as personal secretary from 1928 to 1931, and his exhaustive knowledge of the Order, the com-plete teachings, rites, and ceremonies of which he revealed in his monumental work, *The Golden Dawn*. Furthermore, he advances a most interesting hypothesis regarding the unknown motto that Crowley adopted for this portentous initiation.

Crowley's later anti-Christian fervor no doubt led him to eliminate and totally destroy any obvious clue that might lead one to discover the Christian intent of his motto for the 5=6 grade. He was not very proud of his earlier Christian zeal. He could not take the more mature view that a youth can be forgiven for every extravagance. Advancing years and maturity give one the right to take a benign stand where the excesses and extravagances of earlier life are concerned. Somehow Crowley could never attain this benign stand relative to the hated religion of his mother and the Plymouth Brethren, which was anathema to him. *Thus every reference to the Second Order name he adopted appears to be blotted out almost beyond hope of recovery.*

However, I propose that there are two or three clues that, pieced carefully together, may give us a hint as to his motto. [*The Eye in the Triangle,* p. 169]

Without presenting the development of Regardie's extensive evidence for his hypothesis, I will quote what I consider the central passage:

While he was still rebelling against mother and her distortions of Christianity, and studying Ingersoll, Bradlaugh and James G. Frazer, together with Buddhism, Hinduism and Yoga, his total rejection of Christianity had not yet been fully developed. It was an interim period. He could still use Christian words and phrases without actually becoming outraged, as later.

For the time being, I will assume that these words "I am the Heart of Jesus girt about with the swift Serpent," whatever they were when put in good Latin, became his magical motto for Adeptship. They were part of the most important magical ritual of his Adeptship, and Christian enough to conform to the Christian mysticism of the 5=6 grade. I can well imagine Mathers greeting Very Honoured Frater "Heart of Jesus" after having conferred upon him the 5=6 degree!

So our young adept, with a natural Christian bias approached the central core of the Golden Dawn initiatory system with devotion and aspiration. He was prepared for an inner rebirth. [p. 173]

The philosophy of magical attainment is based upon the continuity of human existence, personal and collective. Every level of progress is inherently grounded upon all previous experience and development. This is fundamental. Crowley proposed, after the breakup of the Golden Dawn and in accordance with the perspective of *The Book of the Law,* to reformulate the rituals of magical initiation, but he never abandoned the fundamental structure of the Golden Dawn initiatory system, based upon the Qabalistic pattern of the Tree of Life. He recognized the efficacy of his own progress through the grades of initiation in accordance with that system, the roots of which presumably extend into antiquity and beyond into the eternal wellspring of humankind's unknown spiritual origins. The central significance of the 5=6 grade is its purpose in establishing contact between the conscious personality and the divine inner Self. This contact, which Crowley referred to throughout his career as "Knowledge and Conversation of the Holy Guardian Angel," (taken from Mathers' translation of the medieval manuscript *The Sacred Magic of Abra Melin*) is, in accordance with Crowley's own teachings, the only legitimate goal of magick.

Although Crowley received *The Book of the Law* over four years after his 5=6 initiation and during a period in which he had virtually abandoned the discipline of magic altogether, the importance of that initiation for Crowley in the course of his personal development must be considered fundamental to his being the vehicle for the transmission of *The Book of the Law*. His later attitude toward Christianity is indeed critical to the understanding of his life's work, but his earlier devotion to Jesus must be considered in terms of *continuity*, as well as contrast, in the course of his development contributing to his unique status as the chosen prophet of the New Aeon. I suspect that Crowley's very understanding of this truth prompted him to obliterate all references to the Christian intent of his 5=6 motto, and not merely that "He could not take the more mature view that a youth can be forgiven for every extravagance," as Regardie surmises. This is not to say that Regardie's assessment is false. It may well be that Crowley simply could not consciously accommodate the plethora of contradictions involved with this most sensitive matter, particularly as it concerned his own personal history. This would all pertain to Crowley's maintenance of his persona. I am moreover concerned with the significance of Crowley's Christian *roots* in relation to the placement of his natal Sol within the context of the solar gestalt of his birthchart, as delineated in chapters 5 and 7.

The interpretation of this astrological configuration tends to support an hypothesis suggested by various references to Jesus made by Crowley in his writings, even *after* his virtually absolute anti-Christian position was established. This hypothesis may be summarized as follows: Crowley recognized and was willing to acknowledge that Christianity was the primary and dominant religious formulation of the Aeon of Osiris, which was fully legitimate and necessary to the evolutionary progress of humanity. He realized, however, that the inherent paradox of the religion was beyond redemption in its totality, and that, as with the case of Christianity's supplanting of traditional Judaism, so must the Thelemic perspective virtually eclipse the Christian formula in order to effect the quickening of the Aeon of Horus, thus fulfilling the requirements of the present dispensation of human evolution. Crowley therefore focused his writing and teaching upon the Thelemic perspective as elucidated in *The Book of the Law* and made no attempt to reconcile that perspective with Christian doctrine. Yet toward the end of *Confessions*, in explaining the role of the grade of Magus in the course of history, Crowley wrote:

> The Magus is thus, of course, not a person in any ordinary sense; he represents a certain nature or idea. To put it otherwise, we may say, the Magus is a word. He is the Logos of the Aeon which he brings to pass.
>
> The above is obscure. I perceive and deplore the fact. The idea may be more intelligible, examined in the light of history. Gautama Buddha was a Magus. His word was Anatta; that is, the whole of his system, which revolutionized the thought of Asia, may be considered as based upon and consecrated in that one word, which is his denial of the existence of the Atman or 'soul' of Hindu philosophy.
>
> Later, Mohammed also partially overturned an age by uttering his word, Allah. But to us, practically, the most important case of the kind is that connected with such 'gods' as Dionysus, Osiris, Baldur, Marsyas, Adonis, Jesus, and other deifications of the unknown Magus concerned. The old pagan worship of the Mother-idea was superseded by the word IAO or its equivalents, which asserted the formula of the Dying God, and made the Male, dying to himself in the act of love, the engineer of the continued life of the race. This revolution cut at the root of all previous custom. Matriarchy vanished; self-sacrifice became the cardinal virtue, and so through infinite ramifications. [p. 795]

The above reference to Jesus reiterates the overt position taken by Crowley in a writing on Christianity done in 1916, during a "Great Magical Retirement" for which he went to live in a cottage on the shores of Lake Pasquaney in New Hampshire during a five year stay in the United States. The impetus for the writing was Crowley's intention to generate a destructive critique of the preface to Bernard Shaw's play, *Androcles and the Lion*, in which Shaw set forth the theory that the actual truth of Christianity was the intent of Jesus to establish a socialist society. This Crowley did with great thoroughness, based on his exhaustive knowledge of Christian scriptures that he had learned so well as a child under the tutelage of the Plymouth Brethren. The writing, however, originally entitled *The Gospel According to St. Bernard Shaw*, exceeded Crowley's original intent such that his textual analysis of the gospels formed a theory of the mystery of their composition. Of this he later wrote in *Confessions*:

> It became clear both those who believe in the historicity of 'Jesus' and their opponents were at fault. I could not doubt that actual incidents and genuine sayings in the life of a real man formed part of the structure. The truth was that scraps of several such men, distinct from and incompatible with each other, had been pitch-forked together and labeled with a single name. It was exactly the case of the students who stuck together various parts of various insects and asked their professor, 'What kind of bug is this?' 'Gentlemen,' he replied, 'this is a humbug.' [p. 809]

Crowley's basic position was that the "Jesus" described in the Christian gospels, although based upon the life of a particular "holy man" of Eastern tradition, not unlike many other such "holy men," became a composite of a full host of pagan deities suitable to consolidate the Roman world into a synthetic unity of religious belief, thus facilitating the centralization of political power, and all its attendant abuses, under the sanction of divine authority. In the opening paragraphs of *The Gospel According to St. Bernard Shaw*, Crowley states the general hypothesis that he would develop as the dominant theme of the entire work:

> The majority of persons who have gone deeply into the fundamental question of the Bible have come to the conclusion that Jesus Christ is merely a convenient title, a kind of hatstand on which to hang the sayings and doings of a number of people, just in the same way as Zoroaster in the matter of the Chaldean Oracles, David in the matter of the collection of the Hebrew Songs which we call the Psalms, and possibly Homer as regards the Iliad and the Odyssey. Of course it is a common literary trick. [*Crowley on Christ*, p. 22]

In addition to Crowley's exhaustive biblical knowledge, he also drew extensively upon references from the works of J.G. Frazer, including *The Golden Bough*, to demonstrate that much of what came to be official Christian doctrine was directly adopted by the church from pre-existing pagan religious traditions in order to assimilate those traditions into an all-encompassing framework that became Christianity. Perhaps the most notable example of this policy was the designation of the twenty-fifth of December for the celebration of the birth of Christ, with no scriptural basis whatsoever, in order to assimilate the pagan celebrations of the winter solstice.

Damning as this analysis is to the Jesus of the gospels, which would appear on the surface to be a wholesale denunciation of Christianity, it raises some fully unresolved questions in the light of Crowley's understanding of spiritual evolution. One such question is: Who was the "unknown Magus" who initiated the fundamental formula of the Dying God that would become the dominant religion of Western civilization? Another: What was the special significance of the "actual incidents and genuine sayings in the life of a real man" that "formed part of the structure" of Christianity that would catch hold so strongly and lend itself to the accretions that would render it so effective as an instrument of power? In his further denunciation of Bernard Shaw's hypothesis, Crowley provided an excellent reason for not attempting to answer such questions:

> [Shaw] claims to have made a synthesis of his subject; in reality he has only made an extremely sectarian analysis. He has not even tried to analyse *The Bible* in an unbiased way; he has only been concerned to pick out the bits that suited him and label them "the Essence of Christianity". He has, in short, wished to found a new heresy, and to popularize his own political views by attributing them to Jesus, just as a dishonest tradesman might try to thrust his biscuits on the public by stamping them with the name of Huntley and Palmer.
>
> Here let me voice my own objection to his method. It is pernicious because his opponents will not play fair. They will misrepresent him, as they have always done to every one who has not come out against them with fire and sword as did Voltaire. Better to be damned out and out with him than to suffer what Bernard Shaw will suffer! The Christian will wipe the slate clear of all that he has said about "psychopathy and superstition", and say, "Even Bernard Shaw admitted that in Jesus lay the one hope of the whole world. In the name of Bernard Shaw, therefore, I say unto thee, Sell that thou hast and give it all to me!"
>
> Mr. Shaw knows this as well as I do. He thought (I doubt not) to make his preface a subtle sidelong thrust at Jesus; but the

weapon will turn in his hand. He had better to have trusted to the
broadsword of Bradlaugh. [*ibid.*, p. 198]

As stated above, these words were written in 1916 and the gist of
them was reiterated in *Confessions*, written in the early twenties.
They clearly set forth Crowley's fully-developed denunciation of
Christianity that he would hold to for the rest of his life.

In 1936, Crowley privately published the first edition of *The
Equinox of the Gods*, which was intended to fulfill the admonition in
The Book of the Law: "All this and a book to say how thou didst
come hither and a reproduction of this ink and paper for ever." [*AL*
III:39] In the brief closing chapter of that book, entitled "Summary
of the Case," is found another mention of Jesus Christ. Surely, it
suggests no change in Crowley's attitude toward the matter from that
already elucidated, but it does appear more clearly to set forth the
acknowledgment of the questions suggested above concerning the
initial impetus and subsequent significance of Christianity.

> Do what thou wilt shall be the whole of the Law! Refuse this, and
> fall under the curse of destiny. Divide will against itself, the result
> is impotence and strife, strife-in-vain. The Law condemns no man.
> Accept the Law, and everything is lawful. Refuse the Law, you put
> yourself beyond its pale. It is the Law that Jesus Christ, or rather
> the Gnostic tradition of which the Christ-legend is a degradation,
> attempted to teach; but nearly every word he said was misinter-
> preted and garbled by his enemies, particularly by those who called
> themselves his disciples. In any case the Aeon was not ready for a
> Law of Freedom. [pp. 135-136]

Crowley's last published work, *Magick Without Tears*, was com-
piled in the last two years of his life and written in the form of a
series of letters in response to queries from students of magick. His
first reference to Jesus Christ in that work reiterates the theme so
extensively developed in earlier years:

> When you talk of the "actual record" of the "Being called Jesus
> Christ," I don't know what you mean. I am not aware of the exis-
> tence of any such record. I know a great many legends, mostly
> borrowed from previous legends of a similar character. [p. 7]

Crowley's final reference to Jesus in *Magick Without Tears*, and
therefore the last of his published words on the matter, complements
the first by reiterating the other half of his perspective on the histo-
ricity of Jesus. That is, even though we have no reliable record of the

factual history of the man behind the legend, we may yet be confident that such a man existed and that, furthermore, we may be
instructed by the legend itself concerning certain moral principles
and magical intentions inherent in its inception. The context of this
passage also bears upon some issues addressed in the concluding two
chapters of this book in regard to politics and ethics:

> There is one other matter of incomparable importance: the wars
> which have begun the disintegration of the world have followed,
> each at an interval of nine months, the operative publications of
> *The Book of the Law.* This again seems to make it almost certain
> that "They" [the Secret Chiefs] not only know the future, at least in
> broad outline, but are at pains to arrange it. I have no doubt that the
> advance of Natural Science is in the charge of a certain group of
> "Masters." Even the spiritually and morally as well as the physi-
> cally destructive phenomena of our age must be parts of some vast
> all-comprehensive plan.
>
> Putting two and two together, and making 718, it looks as if the
> Masters acquiesced in and helped to fulfill, the formula of the
> catastrophic succession of the Aeons.
>
> An analogy. We have the secret of the Elixir of Life, and could
> carry on in the same body indefinitely; yet at least some Masters
> prefer to reincarnate in the regular way, only taking care to waste
> no time in Amennti, but to get back to the Old Bench and pick up
> the New Tools with the minimum of delay.
>
> By having attained the freedom of "Elysian, windless, fortunate
> abodes Beyond Heaven's constellated wilderness" "we are blessed;
> and bless" by refusing to linger therein, but shouldering once more
> "Atlantean the load of the too vast orb of" the Karma of Mankind.
>
> This hypothesis does at least make intelligible Their action in
> riding for a fall instead of preventing it. It may also be that They
> feel that human progress has reached its asymptote so far as the old
> Formula can take it. In fact, unless we take some such view, there
> does not seem to be much point in taking an action so fundamen-
> tally revolutionary (on the surface) as the proclamation of a New
> Word.
>
> But then (you will object, if an objection it be) people like
> Lenin, Hitler, Mussolini, the Mikado, *et hoc genus omne*, are loyal
> emissaries of the Masters, or the gods! Well, why not? An analogy,
> once more. In the Christian we find God (omnipotent, omniscient,
> omnipresent) employing Judas, Pilate, and Herod, no less than
> Jesus, as actors in the Drama which replaced Isis by Osiris in the
> Great Formula. Perfectly true; but this fact does not in any way
> exculpate the criminals. It is no excuse for the Commandants of

Belsen and Buchenwald that they were acting under orders. The Drama is not merely play-acting, in which the most virtuous man may play the vilest of parts. [pp. 457-458]

This reference to the image of Jesus is a direct acknowledgment of the legitimacy of the legend as an implementation of the Osirian formula. Putting together the whole of Crowley's attitudes toward Christianity and the life of Jesus, and the historical significance of that life, it is demonstrably the case that those attitudes involve mystery, reverence, and antipathy in a most subtle and complex combination. Clearly those attitudes are not inconsistent with the hypothetical existence of a continuous esoteric doctrine of Christianity that underlay the superstructure of the official church and the later proliferation of Protestant sects. I make no attempt to draw any conclusions beyond the direct evidence taken from the life and the pen of Aleister Crowley himself about his beliefs and attitudes, conscious or unconscious.

Now that a somewhat comprehensive perspective upon Aleister Crowley's attitude toward Christianity in general and Jesus in particular has been presented, it may fairly be asked: Whence do I derive the hypothesis presented in chapter 13 that Jesus was indeed a manifestation of Horus in the flesh? Surely it does not come from Crowley. Among all the various cultural deities listed by Crowley as cognates for the image of Jesus, or particular aspects of the composite image of Jesus, nowhere is Horus to be found, at least not to my knowledge. Furthermore, in addition to those correspondences mentioned in the above quotations taken from Crowley's works, there is an account given in *Confessions* of a magical operation conducted in early 1914 by Crowley and Victor Neuburg in Paris. Of this operation Crowley writes:

We began work on the first day of the year and continued without interruption for six weeks. We invoked the gods Mercury and Jupiter; [The reader may be reminded that these are the traditional planetary rulers for the signs Virgo and Pisces respectively, the historical relevance of which I commented upon in chapters 10 and 13.] and obtained many astonishing results of many kinds, ranging from spiritual illumination to physical phenomena. It is impossible to transcribe the entire record, and to give excerpts would only convey a most imperfect and misleading idea of the result. As an example of actual intellectual illumination, however, I may quote the very impressive identification of the Christ of the gospels with

Mercury. This came as a complete surprise, we having till then considered him as an entirely solar symbol connected especially with Dionysus, Mithras, and Osiris. [p. 720]

Crowley then proceeds to quote the actual record of the results of that aspect of the operation in which an impressive host of correspondences between the symbolic associations to Mercury and Jesus Christ are marshaled in support of the hypothesis of their identification. Such an analysis is interesting to say the least, and in effect it further supports the above-stated hypothesis of Crowley's in that it accords with the Logos aspect of the amalgamation of the Jesus image that would render it palatable to the more intellectually-oriented religious sects of the Roman world. This kind of archetypal parallel-drawing is a perfect example of what I referred to in chapter 13 as the seemingly infinite potential for flexibility and variation of interpretation that frustrates the entire enterprise of archetypal analysis. This eventuality, however, is essential to the contemplation, and more importantly, the *experience*, of the archetypal realm of mental phenomena. Strictly exclusivistic logic must be abandoned, and such a condition is surely unacceptable to the positivistic mind-set. This conundrum will always arise in the dispute between science and magic. Subjectivity, as the inherent *source* of consciousness and meaning, partakes of the quantum weirdness of ultimate reality.

These matters of archetypal identification and continuity are only partially susceptible to objective analysis. When it comes to the "inner" realm of being, we are not unlike Alice and her Adventures in Wonderland. This condition of our existence is neither to be lamented nor extolled, but it must ultimately be acknowledged. For these reasons, I will not belabor the hypothesis that a meaningful correspondence may be observed involving Horus and Jesus. After all, if the symbolic significance of Christ may be shifted from the central Solar position on the Qabalistic Tree of Life to that of Mercury as well, as per Crowley's Paris Operation, why not to Mercury's immediate superior upon the Qabalistic Pillar of Severity as well, namely Mars, *provided that the associated imagery is in fact appropriate*. I will merely state the obvious rationale and leave the rest to the subjective apprehension of the reader. Although I have seen this correspondence alluded to in various studies of mythology, I must take full responsibility for advancing it within the context of this book. It would be a serious error even subtly to suggest that such a view is in any way explicit or implicit in the teachings of Aleister

Crowley, for I find absolutely no evidence whatsoever to that effect. I must say, however, that the symbolic associations involved require no great stretch of the imagination.

Horus is the Divine Child of a transcendental father and a living mother who conceived him through a magical process. Horus is the representative of his Father in Heaven, and it is his duty to dedicate himself to the performance of the continuity of his father's intentions in this world. Furthermore, it is Horus who ushers the deceased into the presence of "the Good One" (Osiris) and often presides over the weighing of souls. Horus is a warrior, and although Jesus is often cast as a peacemaker who taught a doctrine of "resist not evil" (*in compliance with the will of his father*) he was fully able when necessary to demonstrate his wrath and is certainly depicted as capable of wielding martial power. It is hardly the image of a gentle man who drives the moneychangers out of the temple with a scourge. The warrior image is also implicit in his saying: "Think not that I am come to send peace on earth: I came not to send peace, but a sword." [Matthew 10:34] As a warrior, Horus, like Jesus, is pitted against the powers of the darkness of this world in the form of Set, and, although Horus suffers a severe disadvantage in his struggle, he ultimately prevails over his adversary. Furthermore, Horus' relinquishment of power in the form of the crucified Christ actually provides a rationale for the doctrine of atonement, albeit *not* as an appeasement of God's anger, but rather *as a necessary condition for the gestation of Set*, the offering of his body and his blood for the nourishment of the embryo. Many more parallels can be drawn, such as Jesus' aloof attitude toward his mother, his distress over the need for his sacrifice, his anguish over being "forsaken," and the obvious correspondence to the warrior motif through being cut down by his enemies in the prime of his life. But the point should be made well enough without need for further elaboration.

This theme has already been developed in chapter 13 and will be touched upon and expanded somewhat in the concluding two chapters of this book. In closing this one, however, I would like to make one additional point, lest there be any misunderstanding as to my intentions. One might surmise from the themes developed in this and the previous chapter that I am attempting to suggest a reconciliation of Crowley's outlook and teachings with Christianity. This would be a mistaken apprehension. Such an intention would be a direct violation of Crowley's own stated position. Furthermore, if *The Book of the Law* has any viable meaning at all, its claim to supplant all previous religious doctrines must be taken seriously. From this perspective, my interest in Christianity is purely academic. The central tenet of my position is that a discernible continuity runs through the history of humankind that suggests its spiritual evolution is being guided by forces of superior intelligence, and that ultimately those forces reside within our own nervous systems, composed as they are of some mysterious quantum network of proto-consciousness that we conventionally refer to as "matter." Religions, like people, come and go as they are needed, but a thread of truth runs through them. We must hold to that thread of truth which is the essence of ourselves.

Crowley concluded *The Gospel According to St. Bernard Shaw* with a rather lengthy passage from one of his (Crowley's) earlier works, a play entitled *The World's Tragedy*, in which a dialogue takes place between Jesus upon the cross and one King Alexander, "the great magician whose power is directed to turn the tragedy to final good." [*Crowley on Christ*, p. 205] I should like to close this chapter with one passage from that dialogue:

ALEXANDER: I too have died to Pan, and he
               Hath begotten upon me
               A secret wonder that must wait
               For the hour of the falling of thou fate.
               Nineteen centuries shalt thou
               Plague earth with that agonizing brow,
               And then that age of sordid strife
               Give place to the aeon of love and life.
               A lion shall rise and swallow thee,
               Bringing back life into Arcady.
               So strong shall he roar that the worlds shall quake
               And the waters under the heaven break,
               That the earth, of thy father's hate accurst,
               Shall be greener and gladder than at first. [*ibid.*,
               p. 207]

CHAPTER 15

POLITICS (ENTROPY)

In the preceding chapters a body of information has been assembled that is intended to provide meaningful perspective upon major themes and currents that have been and continue to be operative in our world and that show our *direction* in relation to the greater scheme of history and evolution. Despite the fact that a great deal of inference in terms of our actual lives is inherent in the ideas developed thus far, it remains for them to be applied specifically to actual issues that we face in today's world. Therefore, in the closing two chapters I will incorporate this body of information into a working synthesis that addresses contemporary concerns in our lives. Our present situation will be addressed from two perspectives, those of "politics" and "ethics," taking into account social and individual concerns respectively, with the full realization that these are in fact inseparable, in keeping with the great mystery of "the one and the many."

There is an inherent difficulty in attempting to deal with these matters that I would like to acknowledge at the outset. The Aquarian outlook is so pluralistic and complex that it virtually defies circumscription or delineation. So much depends upon an individual's point of view. There is always a point at which any particular person's perspective and analysis of the overall situation must give way to distinctly variant assessments. The understanding of this circumstance is itself perhaps the most significant tenet for learning how to get along in the New Aeon. We must each take account of our own subjectivity, that is, the *uniqueness* of each of our particular points of view, and realize how vast is the psychological space that separates any one of us from any other in terms of our body of experience and conceptualization of life. There is yet a very strong tendency in today's world to continue in the ingrained habit, inherited from the authoritarian tenor of the previous aeon, of attempting to delineate One Truth that determines us all. We are nevertheless being forced by evolution's relentless advance to abandon that futile quest. There is, of course, an encompassing physical fact that supports the necessity of our acceptance of interdependence as human beings, and that is our mutual *containment upon* and personal *derivation from* the substantial and environmental parameters of Earth. In point of fact, such an interdependence logically extends to encompass all sentient beings in the universe, but in this chapter I propose that we address the scope of our immediate horizon, that is, our commonality as inhabitants of Earth.

The individualistic tenor of *The Book of the Law* appears to many, upon superficial consideration, not to take account of the unity of humankind. This, however, is certainly not the case. That unity is *given* by virtue of social and physical reality, and is experienced as the manner in which we are mutually affected by each other's presence and actions, for better or for worse. The issue is how best to negotiate the life of humanity within those parameters at the present stage of our planetary evolution. It is my intent in this chapter to discuss specific contemporary facts of social reality within the context of the greater dialogue concerning vital political issues confronting the world today.

Before doing so, however, it should prove helpful to provide an account of Aleister Crowley's ultimate mystical vision of metaphysical truth in relation to human existence. That vision is relevant because it provides a paradigm for the interaction of personal and social existence. The vision was initiated in 1916, at the time of Crowley's "Great Magical Retirement" at Lake Pasquaney in New Hampshire and is credited by Crowley in *Confessions* with throwing light upon "the radix of my whole philosophical outlook" and characterizing "my inmost apprehension of the universe from this time forward." [pp. 809-810]

Crowley provides a description of this vision, which he called the Star-Sponge vision, in his commentary upon Verse 59 of Chapter 1 of *The Book of the Law* which reads, "My incense is of resinous woods & gums; and there is no blood therein: because of my hair the trees of Eternity." Being from the first chapter of the book, these words are spoken by Nuit, that is, Infinite Space as the feminine aspect of existence. In his commentary Crowley states, "It seems possible that Our Lady describes Her hair as 'the trees of Eternity' because of the tree-like structure of the cosmos." [*The Law Is For All,* p. 143] He then proceeds to give an account of the "Star-Sponge" vision including the following description.

I was on a retirement in a cottage overlooking Lake Pasquaney in New Hampshire. I lost consciousness of everything but a universal space in which were innumerable bright points, and I realized this as a physical representation of the universe, in what I may call its essential structure. I exclaimed: "Nothingness, with twinkles!" I concentrated upon this vision, with the result that the void space which had been the principle element of it diminished in importance; space appeared to be ablaze, yet the radiant points were not confused, and I thereupon completed my sentence with the exclamation, "But what Twinkles!"

The next stage of this vision led to an identification of the blazing points with the stars of the firmament, with ideas, souls, etc. I perceived also that each star was connected by a ray of light with each other star. In the world of ideas, each thought possesses a necessary relation with each other thought; each such relation is of course a thought in itself; each such ray is itself a star. It is here that logical difficulty first presents itself. The seer has a direct perception of infinite series. Logically, therefore, it would appear as if the entire space must be filled up with a homogenous blaze of light. This, however, is not the case. The space is completely full; yet the monads which fill it are perfectly distinct. The ordinary reader might well exclaim that such statements exhibit symptoms of mental confusion. The subject demands more than cursory examination. I can do no more than refer the critic to the Hon. Bertrand Russell's *Introduction to Mathematical Philosophy*, where the above position is thoroughly justified, as also certain positions which follow. At the time I had not read this book; and I regard it as a striking proof of the value of mystical attainment, that its results should have led a mind such as mine, whose mathematical training was of the most elementary character, to the immediate consciousness of some of the most profound and important mathematical truths; to the acquisition of the power to think in a manner totally foreign to the normal mind, the rare possession of the greatest thinkers of the world.

A further development of the vision brought the consciousness that the structure of the universe was highly organized, that certain stars were of greater magnitude and brilliancy than the rest. I began to seek similes to help me to explain myself...

Further developments of this vision emphasized the identity between the universe and the mind. The search for similes deepened. I had a curious impression that the thing I was looking for was somehow obvious and familiar. Ultimately it burst upon me with fulminating conviction that the simile for which I was seeking was the nervous system. I exclaimed: "The mind is the nervous system," with all the enthusiasm of Archimedes, and it only dawned on me later, with a curious burst of laughter at my naiveté, that my great discovery amounted to a platitude. [*The Law Is For All,* pp. 144-145, 147]

The philosophical implications of Crowley's "Star-Sponge" vision are legion. The aspect which I would like to emphasize for the purposes of this chapter is the extreme degree of *interrelatedness* implied with regard to the individual "stars." Rather than suggesting a state of rebellious and disjointed anarchy, it would appear that the admonitions from *The Book of the Law,* "Do what thou wilt shall be the whole of the Law," "There is no law beyond Do what thou wilt," and "Thou hast no right but to do thy will," taken within the context of Crowley's Star-Sponge vision, affirm the *responsibility* of self-directed individuals to prevent the universe from collapsing upon itself within one's particular sphere of activity. From this perspective it is our duty as individuals to actualize our uniqueness and distinctness as essential components of our interactive universe. We fulfill the greater structure of the cosmos by exerting our distinct and separate wills. As Crowley says in *Confessions*:

The physical parallel still holds. In a galaxy each star has its own magnitude, characteristics, and direction, and the celestial harmony is best maintained by its attending to its own business. Nothing could be more subversive of that harmony than if a number of stars set up in a uniform standard of conduct insisted on everyone aiming at the same goal, going at the same pace, and so on. Even a single star, by refusing to do its own will, by restricting itself in any way, would immediately produce disorder. [p. 401]

In a certain respect it is unfortunate that the term "socialism" has come to mean a system whereby virtually everything is controlled by governmental bureaucracy, because such a notion seems to preclude the kind of sensitive, intimate and responsive social interaction that is implicit in the tenets of *The Book of the Law* and Crowley's Star-Sponge vision. To juxtapose "socialism" and "individualism" as ideological adversaries sets up a no-win situation whereby there appears to be only a choice between totalitarianism and social chaos or some necessary compromise between these two extremes—as if any degree of cooperation could only be gained at the expense of personal freedom. Such a perspective is generated by the unconscious projection of the authoritarian attitude. Quite the contrary is in fact the case. Personal freedom can only be extended and enhanced

by social cooperation. But the impetus for *and direction of* cooperation must come freely from each individual. It cannot be imposed by
anyone upon another or from any source beyond the hearts and
minds of the participants. In its failure to resolve this paradoxical
truth, the political rhetoric of "socialism," which advocates increased
centralization of control, and that of "individualism," which advocates the protection of the "rights" of private aggregates of political
and economic power to determine culture in such a manner as to perpetuate and increase that power, offer no promise of liberation from
habitual forms of oppression that stifle the self-actualization of individuals and the proliferation of cultural diversity. We find that these
two ostensibly variant ideologies are but the left and right hands of
an inclusive political body of oppression and exploitation that largely
perpetuates the *modus operandi* of patriarchal authoritarianism.

The very existence of this state of affairs, however, is evidence of
the *failure of will* on the part of those whose resources are being
usurped. There is a general weakness in the body politic. There can
be no masters without slaves. We need not be dismayed, however, by
this conundrum which characterizes our present moment in the
evolution of world politics (despite the rhetoric of freedom and the
inevitable advance of democracy), for our progress into the New
Aeon is yet in its germinal phase, and the hold of oppressors will
only prevail so long as it serves to contain, like the outer shell of a
seed, the germ of our freedom.

The matter of individualism, therefore, is more subtle than political rhetoric would imply, and it is in that subtlety that true understanding gets lost in the arena of public debate. Many volumes have
been and will be written about this central issue of contemporary
political philosophy, and such pleonasm will become more meaningful only through the actualization of *real* personal liberty. By and
large, within the context of American politics, the advocates of "individualism," often termed "rugged individualism," consider themselves "conservatives," sometimes rhetorically harkening back to
better times "when things were done right." This ploy is characteristic of our yet rudimentary understanding of Aquarian and Uranian
principles (combined with residual Saturnian attitudes) generating a
tendency to deny entropy by playing on the false hope that we might
somehow recover the fresher energy potential of the past. On the
other hand, the advocates of "socialism" (or some sanitized term
likewise connoting the proliferation of bureaucracy) consider them-

selves "liberals," aspiring to innovative utilization of coercive public institutions for the betterment of humanity.

Even at this preliminary level of mainstream rhetoric we find some rather curious paradoxes. So called individualistic conservatives tend, at least publicly, to be beholden to puritanical social values that define family and sex roles in the most rigid mold of Judeo-Christian heterosexual monogamy, while so-called socialistic liberals tend to be more tolerant of a diversity of personal, sexual, and familial lifestyles. If conservatives believe in free enterprise, why don't they apply it to personal lifestyles as well? And if liberals are more tolerant of freedom in the personal sphere, why do they advocate the growth of governmental bureaucracy with its tendency to hamstring individual initiative in the economic sphere? Many complexly developed arguments are marshaled by political theorists of both persuasions to justify their respective positions, and it is not the purpose of this book to wade into the mire of contemporary partisan political analysis. What is germane to the matter at hand is that *there is no political system that can compensate for the moral and intellectual inadequacies of the people that administer it and that it purports to benefit.* As Joseph de Maistre observed in 1811, "Every nation has the government it deserves."

I think it is possible to assess current trends so as to foresee the manner by which the free spirit of the New Aeon will manifest and come to dominate the world in coming centuries. To do so, however, requires both courage and faith, as well as rigorous logic and an understanding of science. When I say faith, I mean primarily faith in ourselves *confirmed by experience* which must be the source of the "certainty" spoken of in the following verse from *The Book of the Law*: "I give unimaginable joys on earth: certainty, not faith, while in life, upon death; peace unutterable, rest, ecstasy; nor do I demand aught in sacrifice." [*AL* I:58] The word "certainty" in this context would appear to imply a direct involvement in *self-fulfilling* and *self-validating* processes, as opposed to having to rely on someone else's definition of what is and what ought to be, or on promises of fulfillment in the hereafter to compensate for the experience of worldly deprivation. In the more general sense, however, there is always a need for faith in relation to the potential for transcending the temporal frame of reference that characterizes the religious attitude toward the limitations of the material world. Crowley directly acknowledges this need in *Confessions* where he writes about the claim of *The Book of the Law* in respect of religion. He says, "Religion is justified in demanding faith, since the evidence of the senses and the mind cannot confirm its statements." [p. 395]

The issue of religious faith is critical to our understanding of history and politics, because it involves the idea of a greater purpose and direction in life that transcends the common material frame of reference. Perhaps the most fundamental issue in this regard is the belief in the survival of the soul after the death of the physical body. There is an inherent opacity of physical existence that precludes the scientific proof of such a theory, at least at the present level of general neurological evolution. Any testimony on the part of people who have had near-death experiences of "seeing the light" or who claim to have memories of previous incarnations are anecdotal from the perspective of a rigorous approach to material science, and are therefore generally indistinguishable from the categories of hallucination and subjective wish fulfillment. Yet, to borrow a term from William James, we are confronted with a *"forced option"* regarding the life after death issue. Even if we cannot objectively be certain about it, it nevertheless makes an enormous *difference* whether we think of it one way or the other. Furthermore, either option in our thinking involves a *risk of error*. It makes a great deal of difference in how we view our political stake in the world if we believe that the principle of cause and effect continues to operate in the destinies of our souls beyond the pale of our physical deaths. If we do not so believe, then the ideals of morality and justice are pure bunk, and the ludicrous adage, "Whoever dies with the most toys wins," is patently true from a purely material standpoint, regardless of any moral satisfaction that may be associated with poverty. If, however, morality and justice are not mere delusions and there is some form of continuity to our eternal destinies, then our political situation affords opportunities for self-edification and strategic maneuvering beyond the lottery of gross material acquisition.

In keeping with his own inherent social attitude *and* the tenets of *The Book of the Law,* Aleister Crowley was an advocate of a political philosophy closely resembling social Darwinism. This attitude, however, entails a subtlety that may easily be lost to some theorists. Obviously, considering Crowley's philosophy of magick, his perspective on evolution differed in some respects from that of traditional science. In *Confessions* he writes:

> We have a sentimental idea of self-sacrifice, the kind which is most esteemed by the vulgar and is the essence of popular Christianity.

It is the sacrifice of the strong to the weak. This is wholly against the principles of evolution. Any nation which does this systematically on a sufficiently large scale, simply destroys itself. The sacrifice is in vain; the weak are not even saved. [p. 401]

A little further along, however, he writes: *"The Book of the Law* regards pity as despicable..., to pity another man is to insult him. He also is a star, 'one, individual and eternal'. The Book does not condemn fighting—'If he be a King, thou canst not hurt him.'" [*ibid.*] This second reference addresses a critical distinction between the position of *The Book of the Law* and that of strict Darwinism. This distinction, subtle as it may appear, forms the crux of the entire matter of politics.

The historical development of social Darwinism has been characterized by the materialist perspective of nineteenth century science. The attempt is to explain all phenomena so as to preclude the requirement of "supernatural forces," thereby conforming to a simple material logic that denies an inclusive directing intelligence to the evolutionary process. The survival of species is therefore thought to be subject to brutality as an ultimate principle, despite the fortuitous benefits of interactive cooperation. Crowley's notion of natural selection, however, was not confined to the materialist conception. He recognized an encompassing principle of evolutionary direction, an actual force, that manifests in accordance with principles of morality. The working of that force, which may be characterized by the adage that "right makes might," became perverted during the Christian era by the vulgar notion that "might makes right." This perversion could only have resulted from the willing relinquishment of "might" on the part of "right," which is demonstrably the working rationale of Christianity. That doctrine exemplifies the existential paradox suggested in the Piscean symbolic image. As we enter the Aquarian Age, that is, the Aeon of Horus, the Crowned and Conquering Child, that fundamental perversion stands in need of rectification. The freeing up of the world situation will result in the forceful establishment of a true moral order. "Behold! the rituals of the old time are black. Let the evil ones be cast away; let the good ones be purged by the prophet! Then shall this Knowledge go aright." [*AL* II:5]

It is possible to speculate about the future direction of the New Aeon along rather definite lines of causation by recognizing as a guiding principle the fundamental law of *entropy* as a political determinant. One is immediately confronted, however, with two difficulties. The first is the unpopularity of the idea that entropy raises the awful specter of unwholesome limits and a downward and depressing trend in the affairs of humanity, which actually tends toward rejection of life itself as characterized by the philosophy of Arthur Schopenhauer. This does not make for good press or good politics. Such a Neptunian perspective appears to fly in the face of the Uranian ideal of infinite economic deployment and opportunity. The second difficulty is that inevitable conclusions from a comprehensive assessment of how entropy applies to the world situation run contrary to the attitudes of those most prone to popularize the matter. Consequently, Crowley's perspective tends to alienate both camps of contemporary dialogue about environmentalism and population growth in recent decades. It is therefore appropriate to frame an analysis in terms of the contemporary debate between Malthusians and developmentalists.

The term "Malthusian" is derived from the economic theory of Thomas Malthus, which became a public issue in 1803 with the publication of his *Essay on Population*. Malthus predicted that the rapid increase of population accompanying industrial development would lead to horrific conditions of overcrowding that would reduce humanity to a state of brutal competition for the limited resources necessary for survival. It was this line of reasoning that caused economics to become known as "the dismal science." Malthus' immediate predictions, however, were proven wrong. Humankind showed itself to be much more innovative in developing ways of exploiting material resources and coping with the problems of swelling numbers than could have been imagined in Malthus' time. The miraculous improvements of the standard of living in industrialized nations fostered an enthusiastic counter-philosophy that extolled a virtually infinite potential for economic expansion resulting from the unleashed power of human resourcefulness. This counter-philosophy has come to be known as "developmentalism."

In terms of astrological perspectives developed in previous chapters, the developmentalist position is associated with Uranus and the present day Malthusian position with Neptune. There are certain qualifications, however, that must be addressed regarding the latter correspondence. Malthus published his essay twenty-two years after the discovery of Uranus. The trend of industrialism was clearly evident at that time. His essay, however, preceded the discovery of Neptune by forty-three years. Thus Malthus' perspective may be considered to have been somewhat prophetic. However, it may be more appropriate to characterize Malthus' theory as a reactionary regression to a *Saturnian* perspective, with its emphasis on the more restrictive principle of limitation to the perception of immediate physical conditions, that is, the *denial* of the potential for innovation. The Saturnian sentiment, firmly established through the course of history, would have nipped the Uranian impetus in the bud through reactionary applications of authoritarian edict, had it been able to do so. Present day Malthusians, in fact, continue to echo Saturnian responses to the proliferation of Uranian economic development. In support of their authoritarian prescriptions, however, they now marshal the more sophisticated knowledge of entropy and ecology associated with Neptune, of which Malthus can be assumed to have had at best only a faint intuitive apprehension. The fact remains, however, that the orbit of Neptune does *contain* that of Uranus and therefore embodies an *actual* limitation of the potential deployment of Uranian industrial development within the biospheric context of human existence. That limitation, however, has become evident to the common understanding of humanity only in recent decades, and it is yet typical for political activists to revert to the advocacy of Saturnian methods of social control in response to perceived Uranian abuses. Such a confusion of the principles of Saturnian and Neptunian limitations is reminiscent of the Communist fiasco.

Present day Malthusians and developmentalists have published impressive bodies of literature that assemble many facts, theories, and convictions in support of their respective positions. Invariably, both camps advocate recommendations for public policy, that is, the allocation of public monies, the enactment of laws and the implementation of governmental policies, to accomplish various objectives. Malthusians ultimately seek to curtail the growth of population, particularly in developing nations, and rigorously police the effect of industrial technology on the environment with the hope of reaching optimum levels of ecological balance within the biosphere. Developmentalists ultimately seek to expand population as the ultimate resource of human innovation and encourage further development of technological approaches to solving problems that arise with the hope that such solutions will be adequate to propitiate ever greater satisfaction for an ever greater number of people. Both camps make powerful arguments for their respective positions, and we may have been worse off than we are today should either of them have decisively prevailed over the other at some juncture of recent history. If the Malthusian extremists had their way we would be living in a socialistic quagmire of fear and resignation, and if the developmentalist extremists had their way we would be fighting among ourselves for survival and choking in our own garbage while a few corporate potentates and their consorts play happily in atmospherically sealed luxury palaces. In fact, these two eventualities are not mutually exclusive and may yet be realized as one brief shining moment along the course of our continuous evolutionary development as a species.

It is a fair assessment of world conditions to say that the economic prosperity of our civilization has already peaked. It appears to have done so during the post World War II period, culminating around the decade of the 1960's. Of course, technology has continued to advance remarkably since that period, as has population growth, gross productivity and energy utilization, but those increases have not been reflected in the actual improvement of the *quality of life* for humanity on the planet. Even affluent societies have been under increasing strain since that time. By now it is clearly evident that entropy is manifestly overtaking us, despite the burst of naive optimism that accompanied that most remarkable decade, and there are no feasible governmental policies that can reverse that trend. The present world population is supported by an enormous expenditure of energy that is ravaging the remaining nonrenewable resources of our closed environment. Furthermore, the proliferation of information through the mass media is exacerbating the situation by making it more apparent to all classes of people that our social systems are failing, from the most affluent societies to the poorest developing nations of the world. This increased awareness contributes to social tensions despite the tendency toward wholesale denial of the horrible truth. This is not a pretty picture by any conventional standards. The poor are reaching out for a piece of the pie, and the rich are fortifying their positions in defense against the onslaught of the impoverished multitudes. Political rhetoric abounds, but only naive, habitually ingrained dullards believe it at face value. There is no one who is not directly effected by the downward trend of our present economic situation. We continue to mass produce more and more items and generate optimistic rhetoric about "economic growth," but our collective standard of living is worsening at an accelerated pace. Many of our institutions are already at the breaking point, and we do not have any viable political alternatives.

It would appear that Malthusians are now vindicated on a larger scale than developmentalists were earlier, however they hold no more promise of averting the impending crisis than do their ideological adversaries, despite their admirable quixotic efforts. It is true that some remedial measures are being taken that would appear encouraging for environmental conditions. Some rivers are being allowed to revitalize themselves, car owners are required to have their vehicles smog certified, and bureaucratic regulations are curbing some of the more blatant intrusions upon the sensitive ecosystems in the more nominally progressive nations of the world. Any meaningful gains that are made in these areas, however, have an inhibiting effect on the economy that displaces industry and employment. Furthermore, we have reached a point at which short-term solutions for immediate problems are becoming so commonplace that they override the perspective required for the development of long-term solutions for the even greater problems out of which the immediate crises arise. A network of band-aids will hold our systems together longer than would be the case without it, but it cannot affect the fundamental structural changes that would be required to establish long-term homeostatic balance in the world's economy.

We are headed for a global crisis that will significantly reduce the world's population and drastically alter the system of human values and political structures that yet remain in place, despite their deterioration in recent decades. The most significant question about this trend is how humanity as a whole will respond to the inevitability of the crisis as it accelerates. A radical shift in human values will occur when the threshold is reached at which a sufficient number of productive people will no longer be able to secure a tolerable existence. From an astrological perspective, this will be the historical moment when the actual Neptunian limit to Uranian expansion is reached and collective humanity is confronted directly with the dire consequences of actual environmental saturation. Only then will we encounter the fully manifested experience of Neptune's significance as the planetary ruler of Scorpio, and will an appropriate global transformation of humanity be affected, turning toward a truly workable balance between Uranian and Neptunian principles of social interaction.

The phenomenon of industrial expansion and urbanization over the past two centuries has been a natural outgrowth of the evolutionary process of human development that was initiated some two thousand years ago by the authors of our present philosophical and religious traditions inherited from antiquity. Furthermore, the mushrooming effect of the rapid acceleration of population growth, energy utilization, and the more recent massive dissemination of informational imagery through photographic and electronic media is suggestive of an evolutionary *orgasm* of collective human experience on the planet. This historical analogy is appropriate in many respects, and the sexual connotation is significant in terms of the nexus of factors associated with Neptune as developed in chapter 8. As this global orgasm continues, matters of *collective* import increasingly impinge upon individual concerns by virtue of sheer numbers within a closed environment. A sense of an *evolving process* becomes more strongly suggestive of inevitability. The ravages of *entropy* become more and more consuming, whereby the environment becomes more threatening. And, perhaps most significantly, the proliferation of *imagization*, as manifested through the mass media and currently conceptualized as the "information revolution," increasingly dominates world culture. However catastrophic are the dimensions of this veritable explosion of human activity, the resulting phenomena of imagery in terms of the actual products of material technology as well as the development of cultural artistry are magnificent. It is very easy, however, to be distracted from an appreciation of this perspective by the entropic context of events. The tragic aspect of economic hardship and environmental deterioration tends increasingly to obscure the collective burst of consciousness that is also occurring. We harken back to the freshness of nature before it was molested by knowledge, but in so doing we tend to overlook the ineffectual naiveté of our heritage as a species.

Malthusians want to reverse this process while developmentalists want to continue the plunge headlong into it. Herein lies a most intriguing irony that frustrates conventional political analysis. The Malthusian attitude is characteristic of political "liberalism," and the developmentalist attitude of political "conservatism." That is, the sexually tolerant liberals tend to be devoted to a course of global *coitus interruptus*, while the sexually restrictive conservatives tend to be bent upon a course of orgiastic frenzy. These comparative attitudes effectively illustrate the psychological principle of unconscious *compensation* for conscious attitudes, and, so long as the members of either camp fail to integrate these opposites within the context of their own psyches, this rather comical conundrum will continue to plague conventional wisdom. Such attitudes articulate the paradoxical relationship of love and death, as well as that of matter and spirit. In life we continuously observe the process of entropic transformation as, for example, in the hatching of an egg. The chick within the egg undergoes a condition of severe depletion of natural resources and immersion within its own waste just prior to its pecking out a hole in its universe. One wonders if the thought may occur to the chick in its increasingly traumatic condition, "If only I could stop growing." The manner in which this situation applies to philosophical attitudes is clearly expressed by Jeremy Rifkin in his powerfully informative book, *Entropy*. He writes:

> There are those among us who are willing to accept the finiteness of the physical world but who believe that the entropic flow is counterbalanced by an ever-expanding stream of psychic order. To these people, the becoming process of life is synonymous with the notion of an ever-growing consciousness. In the Newtonian scheme, human consciousness is perceived as moving on an uphill grade against the downward journey of the entropy flow. Eventually, it is believed, humanity's collective consciousness will expand to a point where it will escape the physical plane altogether, overcoming the Entropy Law in a kind of cosmic metamorphosis. Piercing through the physical veil of existence, the collective human consciousness will then begin a steady ascent into the ethereal world of spiritual enlightenment.
>
> It is not hard to understand, then, why people also harbor the unstated belief that in a nongrowth or low-energy flow-through environment, consciousness will atrophy or be prevented from developing. The idea lingers on that consciousness must be constantly watered and cultivated by accelerated physical activity if it is to grow. Taken to its logical conclusion, this line of reasoning would suggest that greater energy flow-through and greater disorder and dissipation in the world create a more conducive environment for the nourishing of consciousness. [p. 253]

Here Rifkin has expressed the essence of the meaning of Scorpio in its cyclo-cosmic function within the context of astrology, that is, the very formula of sexual magick as a means of expanding consciousness through the orgasmic surrender of the material frame of reference around which ego-consciousness is formed. As he continues, however, Rifkin expresses his own denial that this may be a global truth for evolving humanity at the present stage of our development. He continues:

> This just isn't so. Speeding up the physical flow doesn't insure greater spiritual development; quite the contrary. Transcendence comes out of quietude and the recognition of the beauty of "being," not out of discord and the travails of "doing." Hermann Hesse's *Siddhartha* had to sit down by the river and listen quietly to the flow in order to become one with it and to reach enlightenment.

> Human development up to now, however, has been bound up with resistance to the natural flow of things. The hallmark of the colonizing mode is the attempt to conquer and subdue. We continue to think of enlightenment as something to "achieve" when it's really something to "experience." As long as we frantically struggle for enlightenment, we will continue to resist the natural rhythm of the unfolding process and slide further from the enlightenment we seek. [pp. 253-254]

Indeed, Rifkin has something profound to say about contemporary civilization, but there is irony in his position in that he actually advocates the very resistance he purports to repudiate to the natural rhythm of the unfolding process. This is not, however, an uncommon error. It is quite a natural response on the part of many to want to try to clean up the mess humanity is making of the world, and this attitude may well have its proper place in the present configuration of humanity as an inhibitor of premature climax for the building collective planetary orgasm. Quietude, however, is a state of mind that can be maintained *in the face of* adversity but cannot be attained through the attempted *denial* of life's inherent challenges. The natural rhythm of life cannot be turned back for the sake of our peace of mind. It is inherent in Rifkin's position, which characterizes the entire camp that travels under the banner of "environmentalism," that the evolution of Western civilization has somewhere taken a wrong turn; that the development of modern science and industrial technology somehow should not have happened. Developmentalists, on the other hand, continue to cling to the false hope that the material world itself can somehow accommodate a transformation that will negate the entropic flow, whereby the living conditions on Earth will actually be enhanced by accelerated energy utilization by ever greater numbers of people, in keeping with the admonition of the tribal god Jehovah for the creatures of the earth to "be fruitful and multiply." [Genesis 1:22] Both factions, the Malthusians and the developmentalists, are seeking in their own ways to avoid our inevitable global appointment with the grim reaper. From a political standpoint, however, both their positions are justifiable. The governance of the material world is the proper concern of the political sphere, and the attempt to insure the best possible material conditions for ourselves and our posterity is the legitimate objective of political machinations. Everyone is trying to survive and prosper.

Surely as individuals we each have a responsibility to our communities, local, national, and global, and we must form our political associations accordingly. We are better off, however, not to delude ourselves about our ability to influence the affairs of the world through political action. Aleister Crowley states this realization quite succinctly in *Magick Without Tears*:

> So, whichever way you vote, you are asking for trouble; or would do, if the vote had any meaning. The result of any election, or for the matter of that any revolution, is an almost wholly insignificant component of those stupendous and inscrutable Magical Forces which determine the destinies of the planet. [p. 463]

Such an attitude toward the affairs of the world may appear both defeatist and fatalistic to the advocate of political responsibility. This, however, is surely not the case. The general direction of the world situation is quite discernible in terms of entropy and observable historical trends. It is not fatalistic to believe that the world will continue to turn. The escalation of crime and violence throughout the world, the increasingly obvious mockery of traditional values and the rule of law on the part of all classes of society despite the fact that most of us yet subscribe to their stabilizing effect, the lowering of the effective wage of the worker who bears the actual burden of the economy, the blatant prevalence of unvarnished scamming for political and economic advantages, these and many other undeniable trends bespeak the impending crisis.

The inevitability of the situation can be dramatically emphasized by contrasting the social and economic opportunities that obtained for our three most recent generations in American society at the times of their reaching adulthood. The young adults at the end of World War II surely faced a greater opportunity for attaining "the American dream" than did their children who reached maturity in the wake of the much different Vietnam War, despite the fact that the baby-boomers were largely raised to believe that the same opportunity that had awaited their parents was also there for them. Now, the baby-boomers' children, popularly referred to as Generation X, are confronted with an almost hopeless world of increasing social chaos and diminished expectations, despite the continuing political rhetoric of potential prosperity mindlessly reiterated in the ghostly form of their grandparents mentality, as if saying it is what made it true. To see the crisis coming, however, does not mean that we are impotent in the face of it. Our power, however, is not the power to avert the crisis but rather to position ourselves favorably in relation to the furtherance of the evolutionary progress of humanity. We can exert our personal force, *as it is required by our individual destinies*, to activate the principles of morality that will sustain the course of humanity *through* the crisis.

In this capacity, the realm of politics becomes subsumed within the realm of ethics (more specifically addressed in the next chapter) leaving the political arena to the direction of the renowned Uranian "invisible hand." This, of course, in no way obviates the necessity for administrative systems and the performance of administrative duties by civil servants essential to the body politic, but it does remove the mystique of "the state" as a manifestation of some kind of presumed paternal authority over the citizenry of any nation or territorial realm with the power to "take care of" *its* people. Some concluding remarks about politics are therefore in order to address the necessary change of attitude that is appropriate to our entry into the Aeon of Horus.

Perhaps the most definitive characterization of the attitude toward politics associated with the now defunct Aeon of Osiris has been that of the Christian prescription to "Render...unto Caesar the things which are Caesar's; and unto God the things that are God's." [Matthew 22:21] In a universal sense, that doctrine is suggestive of the qualitative differentiation of the transitory concerns of material reality from the realm of Eternal Spirit. More specifically, however, in terms of the Osirian formula as presented in chapter 13, that differentiation was exacerbated and actually dissociated through the relinquishment of material power by Osiris—as imagized by the sacrifice of Horus (Jesus)—and his acquiescence to the administration of the earthly kingdom by Set (Caesar). Such an evolutionary stage was necessary for the binding of the destinies of the godhead among themselves and to the destinies of evolving humanity, and, more specifically, the gestation of the embryonic Set unto a condition of spiritual viability. Upon the culmination of the Osirian formula, however, and the establishment of a new world order as "Ra-Hoor-Khuit hath taken his seat in the East at the Equinox of the Gods," [*AL* I:49] it is no longer the case that the affairs of the world and the affairs of the spirit are dissociated. The actualization of their unity is now called for within the personal sphere of every individual human being. From an institutional perspective, the problem of the relation of "church" and "state" is resolved by the formula, "Do what thou wilt shall be the whole of the Law." Institutions are nothing other than amalgamations of individual wills and therefore have no sovereignty of their own. They come and go as a function of voluntaristic cooperation. Only individuals are sovereign.

One may therefore ask: How does the fulfillment of collective purpose come to pass? Wherein lies the power of direction and articulation that insures continuity and order in the affairs of the world? The answer to such questions is obviously that collective purpose will continue to be achieved *as it always has been,* through the maintenance of cooperative institutions. There is nothing about the Law of Thelema that stands in the way of human cooperation. The ingredient that is perverting our present world system, which is yet a direct carry-over from the Aeon of Osiris despite the infusion of the Horian current, is the *lack of respect* people have for one another. We continue to interact in terms of servile personal debasement, and this social condition illustrates how politics is subsumed within the context of ethics. This is why the present political institutions must be further transformed by the continuing encroachment of entropy. Humanity is undergoing a *rite of passage* into the New Aeon. Although the Osirian formula has been terminated on the spiritual plane, its *residua* remains to be purged from the arena of world politics. The impending world crisis will affect that purge. Each of us is being and will continue to be called upon to make choices in our lives about what we *stand for* within the community of humanity, and those choices will determine our personal destinies and the destiny of the world. The greatest sense of responsibility that can be applied by anyone within this context is to act *as if* one has a vested personal stake in the outcome, not only for the duration of one's own particular lifetime, *but also as a participant in the destinies of future generations.* Obviously, such an orientation is best facilitated by the actual belief in its literal truth. It must therefore *be* true. This is both a moral and a pragmatic argument and therefore requires faith. No faith, however, is required to demonstrate that each individual must decide for oneself how to act in the face of this possibility, or inevitability, as the case may be.

The themes thus far developed in this chapter will be continued in the next as the emphasis continues to shift from politics to ethics. In keeping with the astrological theme of this book, however, an overview of political trends may be facilitated by the consideration of some specific astrological factors involved. By looking at the manner in which historical trends and developments in the past have corresponded to the dynamics of planetary transits through the zodiac, a structural perspective may be obtained which not only contributes to the understanding of those trends and developments but also provides a basis for anticipating their projection into the future in terms of the predictable continuation of those transits. Since the trans-Saturnian planets are not only the slowest and most encompassing of all the planets, but are also those which pertain most significantly to *transformative processes*, the analysis of their transits and interactions are most instructive for understanding the greater context of change in the development of world affairs. The remainder of this chapter will therefore be devoted to a brief analysis of some of the "highlights" of the transits of Uranus, Neptune, and Pluto in relation to each other and through the zodiac in recent history and into the immediate future.

In his writings about the trans-Saturnian planets, Dane Rudhyar placed considerable emphasis upon the "cycles of relationship" among them. [*Astrological Timing*, 1969] Rudhyar observes that the times at which Uranus, Neptune, and Pluto form conjunctions with one another mark critical moments in history at which powerful transformative impulses are introduced into the evolutionary process. The working out of those impulses continues to unfold throughout the entire cycle during which the faster moving of the two planets involved proceeds on around ultimately to complete the cycle by forming another conjunction of the same two planets. Since Uranus, Neptune, and Pluto have relatively lengthy orbital periods of 84, 165, and 248 years respectively, their cycles of relationship involve rather extended periods of time. Successive conjunctions of Neptune and Pluto occur at intervals of some 493 years. Successive conjunctions of Uranus and Neptune occur at intervals of some 171 years. The interval for successive conjunctions of Uranus and Pluto is less regular, due primarily to variations in the speed of Pluto's orbital motion, but it is always well over a century. The twentieth century has been strongly characterized by the occurrences of all three possible trans-Saturnian conjunctions, which connotes an enormous closing of accounts, as it were, and initiations of new transformative processes appropriate to the aeonic transition.

In chapter 2 we noted that Popular Culture, as we know it today, had its major inception in the early 1890's. That inception may now be associated with the conjunction of Neptune and Pluto in Gemini in 1892. The phenomenal burst of progressive attitudes that characterized the "gay nineties" may be likened to the "radical sixties" of more recent memory in terms of its revolutionary implications. A direct sense of the period, of course, is completely lost to nearly everyone alive today, but a review of history confirms this assessment. What we *can* directly appreciate, however, in regard to the

1890's, is the legacy of culture-transforming knowledge and technology that emerged at that time that we currently take for granted as the mainstays of our existence. To name a few: automobiles, airplanes, moving pictures, four-function calculators, fingerprint identification, radio, mass-circulation magazines, relativity theory, and depth psychology. The emergence of these phenomena alone has been sufficient to utterly transform the face of modern human existence in a most remarkable manner. Our present historical perspective confirms that the evolutionary impulse associated with the 1892 Neptune-Pluto conjunction spawned the cultural context that has characterized the phenomenal uniqueness of global civilization in the twentieth century as compared to all previous history.

Interestingly, the 1892 Neptune-Pluto conjunction occurred in the seventeenth year of Aleister Crowley's life (on the cusp of his Eleventh House, thereby affecting his social involvements and his aspirations for the future) and was the only conjunction of trans-Saturnian planets to occur in his lifetime. That was the critical period during which he was liberating himself from the religious indoctrination of his childhood, and we may assume that his efforts were facilitated considerably by the social ferment associated with this transiting conjunction. It was also at the time of this conjunction that MacGregor Mathers allegedly experienced his contact with the Secret Chiefs and formulated the rituals of initiation for the Second or Rosicrucian Order of the Golden Dawn to which Crowley was attracted like a magnet six years later. As recounted in chapter 11, Mathers would personally officiate the performance of the most notable of these rituals for Aleister Crowley, who was the first twentieth century candidate for entry into the Second Order.

The next transiting conjunction of trans-Saturnian planets was that of Uranus and Pluto in Virgo in 1965-66. Many of us who are alive today, namely the baby-boomers and their parents, can directly appreciate the significance of that conjunction by reflecting upon our memories of that tumultuous decade. Furthermore, by virtue of the development of electronic media then, even those who were born during and after that time have been exposed to an enormous barrage of imagery taken directly from the explosive cultural developments associated with the social changes of that period. The proliferation of electronic media itself was a major manifestation of the 1965-66 Uranus-Pluto conjunction. As mentioned above, the spirit of optimism that animated the sixties is appropriate to the fact that, from an economic standpoint, our industrial and technological development still appeared to hold great promise for future humanity. The *quality of life* yet seemed to be improving in a manner that engendered hope for all the world. But the idealism was also tempered by deep foreboding. There was an intuitive realization of social and spiritual strife that accompanied the celebratory spirit of optimism. This foreboding manifested itself in the form of protest, and the most fundamental values of Western civilization were challenged by a vocal element of the cultural intelligentsia. Racism, concern for the environment, women's rights, sexual freedom, and the use of mind altering drugs became major social issues. The authority of government to wage war and impose its edicts upon common citizens was questioned. (This particular feature of the times is directly associated with the opposition by transiting Saturn in Pisces to the position of the Uranus-Pluto conjunction.) Such challenges found sympathetic ears among the youth of that period, and a full scale cultural revolution resulted. The fact that the 1965-66 Uranus-Pluto conjunction occurred in Virgo accounts for the *"magical"* connotation that characterized the social upheaval as well as its emphasis upon common humanity and personal issues.

The strong sexual current that pervaded the social orientation of that period is more appropriately attributed to the transit of Neptune through Scorpio from 1956 (the time of Elvis Presley's sudden and controversial rise to super-stardom) through 1970. The major shift of social orientation from the gritty hard-core attitude of the late sixties to the more spiritual easy-going attitude of the early seventies can be attributed directly to the transit of Neptune out of Scorpio and into Sagittarius. The breakup of the Beatles and the Manson murder trail characterized the culmination of a brief yet profoundly disturbing chapter of cultural history, as John Lennon so announced with his characteristic poignancy and succinctness by the simple phrase, "The dream is over." With Neptune's entry into Sagittarius, the cultural mood shifted from the emotional turmoil of the streets to the spiritual liberation of the ashrams. Suddenly it was yoga, health food, and religious cults. The "anti-establishment" political admonitions of the sixties were abandoned for the more palatable strategy of "working within the system." The seeds of transcendental consciousness had been planted, or rather "broadcast," and the "New Age" movement gained popular ascendancy over magickal activism.

The third and final conjunction of trans-Saturnian planets to lend its impulse to the historical developments of the twentieth century was that of Uranus and Neptune in Capricorn in 1993. Capricorn is the sign most directly associated with governmental and corporate administration. Therefore, the transits of Uranus and Neptune through Capricorn necessarily imply profound transformations in governmental and corporate systems and structures throughout the world (insofar as the world is dominated by political institutions rooted in the northern hemisphere). It is particularly noteworthy that Neptune's entry into Capricorn in 1984 was accompanied by Jupiter, and Uranus' entry into Capricorn in 1988 was accompanied by Saturn. In each of these transiting conjunctions at the winter solstice point, the conventional planet involved provided a vehicle of mediation and implementation for the transformative influence associated with the unconventional (trans-Saturnian) planet, thereby facilitating optimal patterns of meaningful change concerning matters of governmental administration. The fundamental themes of those changes include a greater appreciation for the role of government in matters pertaining to culture and increased political awareness on the part of individual citizens as applied both within and without official institutions.

The subsequent conjunction of Uranus and Neptune in Capricorn in 1993 connotes a major redefining of political factions and organizational systems that incorporates the strong transforming power of those planets. This process of transformation is underway, most notably characterized on a global scale by the effect of the breakup of the Soviet Union and the communist block. Neptune's involvement in this process, however, suggests that the driving impetus for change involves a high degree of subtlety and a great deal of behind-the-scenes negotiations. Since, by their very nature, governments continue to be more directly responsive to the interests of the moneyed elite than to the productive multitude, it is virtually impossible (through conventional sources of information) to ascertain the actual intentions and machinations that are being worked out in association with this most intriguing conjunction of trans-Saturnian planets. This fundamental truth, however, is not grounds for bringing a cynical interpretation to bear upon the matter. Certain factions of the moneyed elite are capable of operating in the best interests of the world as a whole and, whenever such powerful planetary agents as these are involved, no faction or combination of factions is able to thwart the evolutionary impetus inherent in the situation.

The national elections of both 1992 and 1994 in the United States were galvanized by a strong desire for change on the part of the American people, although the drastic swing from Democratic to

Republican sentiment evidenced the lack of effectual alternatives available to the electorate. The central issue of those campaigns, government deficit spending, is the political focus of the increasingly entropic context of our social existence. Deficit spending is the manner by which governments preempt the future in their attempts to accommodate the ever-mounting entropic residua from massive energy deployment, not to mention the largely camouflaged mystery of the nature of legal tender itself that governments "borrow," and the question of why bankers should profit from collective misfortune. It must be understood that the entropic trend refers not only to the actual physical pollution of the environment but also to the social deterioration of our communities. Furthermore, this is far from being only a domestic concern. It is a global situation in which the United States, since the collapse of the Soviet Union, has become the central player. Changes are occurring so quickly that as soon as something is recorded in print it becomes subsumed by the mighty wave of historical transformation that is engulfing the world.

Interestingly, we may derive some measure of perspective upon the unfoldment of emerging impulses associated with the barrage of conjunctions among the massive social and transformational planets in Capricorn from the national episode of the liaison involving President Bill Clinton and White House Intern Monica Lewinsky. This occurred in association with a transiting square formed by Saturn to Neptune in 1998 and 1999. A square aspect between these two planets is suggestive of a political scandal such as that exemplified by the Clinton-Lewinsky affair.

Being the opening square of Saturn to Neptune, this transiting aspect connotes the outbreaking crisis of the unfoldment of the cycle initiated by the previous conjunction of Saturn and Neptune in Capricorn throughout 1989. Since this was the year following the 1988 presidential election, it is reasonable to assume that 1989 was the time at which the deepest political machinery went into motion toward the selection and grooming of candidates for the 1992 election which brought the dark horse, Bill Clinton, to the presidency, despite a political scandal early in the primaries involving his extramarital affair with Jennifer Flowers. It would appear that the Neptunian impulse imparted to Saturn was strong in overcoming traditional prejudice against what is commonly thought of as infidelity.

The Clinton-Lewinsky story broke in the month of Neptune's first entry into Aquarius, January 1998, and reached a peak of intensity as Saturn formed its first square to Neptune from Taurus the following

June. The final activation of this transiting square in April, 1999, with both Saturn and Neptune having made their completed entries into Taurus and Aquarius respectively, brought closure to this political episode. Neptune thereby joined Uranus in Aquarius from which they were squared by a major constellation of planets (including a Jupiter-Saturn conjunction) in Taurus, focused at the New Moon on May 3, 2000. It may therefore be surmised that the Clinton-Lewinsky epiphany solidified a significant shift in the national psyche as a preparation for new policy agendas of a highly practical nature.

Since this much of the current Saturn-Neptune cycle has already been briefly delineated, it might also be mentioned that Saturn will form its opposition to Neptune, delivering the fully developed and objectified manifestation of the meaning of the cycle, with two colliding and a final surpassing opposition in 2006 and 2007.

From our perspective as these words are written, it can be hoped that the transits of Uranus and Neptune through Aquarius herald some new and innovative strategies for adjusting to the apocalyptic dimensions of our world situation as we enter the third millennium. As these two transformational planets move through Aquarius, it is to be expected that new and innovative patterns of *interpersonal grouping* that will displace long entrenched and increasingly dysfunctional social and familial arrangements of the past. The proliferation of gang activity may be an actual precursor to a new approach to social organization. Already gangs are *negotiating* with official governmental institutions. The spreading activity of "militia" type groups is also suggestive of an increased dispersal of political autonomy. As unwholesome as we may consider the activities of groups like gangs and militias, it must be observed that their emergence is occurring in direct proportion to the disenfranchisement of the common people of the world. It should not be surprising that the entropic residua of our civilization is taking negative forms.

In a more positive and responsible vein pertaining to political organization *per se*, a reasonable prediction in light of the imminent transits of Uranus and Neptune through Aquarius is that the Libertarian Party, or one with a similar philosophical orientation, may well emerge from the pack of "third parties" as a truly viable alternative to the traditional two-party system in American politics. It may be assumed that the recent conjunction of Uranus and Neptune in Capricorn will have loosened up long-entrenched structures of traditional political alliances enough to render them vulnerable to a groundswell of populist sentiment, even if such sentiment is incapable of uniting under any ideological banner other than that of liberation from bureaucratic encroachment and incapacitation. The Libertarian Party is the only extant political vehicle that provides that particular focus of attraction for concerned voters (although both major parties proffer rhetorical appeals designed to pull from that pool). The emergence of such a groundswell, however, would require a spontaneous collective orchestration of cooperative volunteerism on the part of capable leaders from all walks of life. In any event, the valuable contribution that government can make toward joining the entropic watershed is to serve as a negotiating forum for the diverse factions of the body politic. Government will not be able to centralize the management of resources. If an attempt at centralization precedes the inevitable dispersal of power, the transition would likely be more violent and destructive than would a natural breaking-up of existing political structures. Uranus and Neptune transiting through Aquarius bode well for the spirit of freedom during the all-important opening years of the twenty-first century.

Pluto's entry into Sagittarius in 1995 initiated a large-scale transformation of popular philosophical and religious conceptions that will accommodate the quantum outlook toward conscious transcendence of linear perspectives on time and space. This transit signaled a shift of Pluto's direct involvement from matters Scorpionic, which began with his (and Saturn's!) entry into Scorpio in the fall of 1982 (the breaking of the AIDS epidemic), to Sagittarian concerns of Archetypal Formulations suitable to accommodate Pluto's multi-level perspectives. Since archetypal knowledge is, by nature, rooted in morphogenetic field structures (quantum phenomena), Pluto's transit through Sagittarius can only bring fundamental enhancements to conscious participation in archetypal motifs; even to the point of the application of occult technology toward the development of healing powers or "mind cures" as a dialectical response to the AIDS epidemic, inherited from Pluto's transit through Scorpio. From a strictly materialistic biological perspective, however, the *results* of such a deployment of "mind power" would be indistinguishable from the emergence of a particularly resistant strain of human beings as a mutational adaptation to adverse conditions. Either way, such an academic distinction is a moot point from the perspective of practical survival at this critical stage of planetary evolution, the pattern for which has already been largely determined.

Another transiting phenomenon that should prove extremely significant for the global transformation of humanity currently under-way is the passage of Pluto through that segment of its orbit just before and after its perihelion (the point at which it is closest to the Sun), during which it actually passes *within* the orbit of Neptune. Pluto made this passage from 1978 to 2000 [*Astrological Timing* 67], the very closing of the twentieth century and the second millennium. According to the symbolism developed in this book, during such a passage the quantum substratum of matter itself is able to traverse the threshold of molecular biological processes to effect significant mutations in organisms (and human neuro-structures) that *bypass* the normal mode of evolutionary development through an accelerated or apparently "supernatural" mutation of genetic patterns that produce organic interactions that would normally be considered impossible, or at least extremely unlikely, *within existing organisms.* It is also significant that this is the first occurrence of such a passage at which time either of the planets involved has been consciously known to exist by common humanity (the last such passage having occurred during the 1730's and 1740's). This suggests the possibility of *con-scious imagization* of transforming patterns of personal experience at the archetypal level of human evolution. In relation to Sheldrake's Hypothesis of Formative Causation, such phenomena may be thought of as the infusion of actual creative impulses of *conscious evolutionary change* into the otherwise predominantly repetitive patterns of life activity that are normally sustained by established morphogenetic fields—that is, deeply ingrained patterns of habitu-ated cultural responses. Pluto reached perihelion in 1988 at Scorpio 12° 43´ [*ibid.*], at which time the intensity of such imagization may be assumed to have been most portentous. Certainly a major reorien-tation in the affairs of the world transpired at that time, most conspic-uously associated with the unraveling of the Soviet Union. The implicit symbolism of this transit, however, particularly in view of Pluto's perihelion occurring in Scorpio, is suggestive of a more fun-damental change in the sexual ethos of humanity; that is, the enact-ment of a new archetypal configuration of sexual bonding and imprinting.

From a broader social perspective, the focus of politics is being placed more and more upon our individual existences as human beings, that is, as Laws unto our individual selves. The social context of our lives remains pervasive, but our sense of identity and meaning is becoming less and less susceptible to being subsumed within the social institutions that have dominated our past. Political parties, churches, and even nations and families are not the solid bastions of meaning they once were. Humanity is becoming increasingly global and increasingly individualized. Our experience of our relation to eternity (*a la* Pluto), is taking widely variant forms from those of traditional religions, although we may come to realize that these "new" forms, which of necessity must incorporate the acutely felt need for independent self-determination, are actually continuations and further developments of the spiritual potential for humanity that traditional religions have helped to foster as a preparation for the changes currently at hand. This shift toward individualism is pushing the development of human potential to a new level by *forcing* personal independence and abolishing the kinds of *evasion of personal responsibility* that have been so prevalent in the past. Herein lies our hope as a species. Ironically, this hope is actually enhanced by the deterioration of the old world order.

CHAPTER 16

ETHICS (LIBERTY)

In earlier stages of human evolution, the well-being of each person was perceived as more directly dependent upon the cohesion of the local or regional group to which one belonged. The fundamental meaning of being a person was defined in terms of one's participation in the survival matrix of the community. The tribe, and in more recent times, the nation, came first, and the person came second. The idea that a person is a realm unto oneself and is *sovereign* in relation to the community in which one lives is *subversive* from the perspective of the primary rationale of the political and religious history of humanity, involved as it has been in the *building* of civilization. It is only during recent centuries that the notion of individual sovereignty has won significant acceptance at the intellectual level, and it is painfully obvious that, despite such intellectual acceptance accompanying the emergence of modern civilization, the ideal of personal sovereignty has not been fully realized in any nation of the world.

It is nevertheless the case that this ideal is a direct outgrowth of the secret mystery traditions of antiquity, and that the modern notion of individualism was first nurtured within the social fabric of humanity by an underground current of esoteric philosophical schools kept alive through centuries of difficult evolutionary growth in which collective standards of behavior and belief were forcibly imposed within the kingdoms and nations of the world. The central philosophical doctrine that animated those esoteric movements has been that a human being is essentially a *microcosm*, that is, a complete spiritual and material universe unto oneself. The political objective of those movements was to perpetuate that idea in an environment of social authoritarianism, that is, to carry forward in time the doctrine of personal wholeness and freedom within communities that were subjected to the domination of political and religious institutions, the very existences of which were predicated upon the denial of that wholeness and freedom of their subjects. Having overt control of the official dissemination of information, the historically dominant social institutions have been able to formulate political and religious stratagems in such a manner as to deny the realization of personal freedom, not only at the level of direct enforcement of law and canon, but also through the much more pervasive and effective albeit subtle method of *moral indoctrination.*

This being the case, it is no wonder that the very idea of personal independence is bound up with the notion of evil, and the idea of good is bound up with what is professed to benefit the greater community of humanity. That such a patent absurdity (from the standpoint of an actualized humanity) could become so pervasive a belief demonstrates the psychological dissociation that characterizes the preliminary stages of human evolution. The interdependence among humans for physical and emotional well-being tends to complicate this issue and, combined with authoritarian patriarchal domination over the past two-thousand-plus years, has reinforced the idea of the primacy of the group over the individual as a means of rationalizing various forms of oppression among people. There can be no doubt, however, that the evolutionary impetus of humanity has progressed *toward individualism.* This trend may even be associated with the ironclad thermodynamic law of entropy in keeping with Bertrand Russell's observation that the process of entropy "may be described as a tendency toward democracy." The emergence of more overtly democratic forms of government in recent centuries has occurred not so much as a function of the ascendancy of elevated humanitarian ideals as opposed to powerful authoritarian institutions, although this has surely been a major feature of the process, but more as a matter of sheer practical necessity within the context of the entropic disintegration of the world as an energy base available for human utilization. Surely the collapse of the collectivist regime of the Soviet Union bears this out with contemporary relevance and immediacy. A different perspective on the relation of the individual person to collective humanity emerges within the context of the *disintegration* of collective institutions than that which predominated through the course of the growth and development of those institutions.

It is becoming increasingly apparent that humanity is "going to seed"—that is, the bodily structure of civilization as we know it is withering, and the seeds issuing forth from that body in the form of individual personalities and, from a spiritual perspective, individual souls or monads, are becoming psychologically detached from that body so that each person may grow and develop in one's own right and in accordance with one's own law of being *in relation to others*. It is essential to understand that this process is not something we need to strive to make happen, but is rather something that *is happening*, and our strife comes from our realization of and *our resistance against* its occurrence, that is, the neurological *imprinting* of the experience of differentiation. The ethical challenges of the New Aeon are challenges of each person coming to terms with one's uniqueness and individuality. There is a tendency to conspire amongst ourselves to cling to old patterns of dependence and attempt to draw succor from withering social traditions in order to avoid the awesome responsibility of absolute self-determination. We do this in the names of piety, patriotism, loyalty, family, obedience, and, most insidiously, in the name of love. Accordingly, these social institutions are becoming corrupted to the extent that they are employed as means for avoidance of personal responsibility or attempts to constrain the self-expression of others. Understanding this situation inclines one toward agreement with the sublime expression of contemporary truth found in the words: "Do what thou wilt shall be the whole of the Law," and "Love is the law, love under will." Real love, strong love, *under will*, prevails over false love that masks fear of cosmic autonomy and its concomitant feeling of aloneness.

Those who reject this law (with or without direct knowledge of its literal formulation) do so out of unwillingness to self-actualize, and they often invoke the outworn ethos of self-denial as a justification for their own sclerosis, and, more significantly, for their claims upon the lives of those they "love" to compensate for their own moral deficiencies. Naturally, as entropy continues to flow and humanity continues to evolve, severe ethical conflicts arise between those who resonate to and are invigorated by the Law of Freedom, which calls for self-reliance and personal responsibility, and those who would prefer to remain in some form of herd mentality of submission to an exterior source of "authority" in which absolution is presumed to be possible in the forms of vicarious atonement, performance of prescribed rituals, official proclamation, legal acquittal, or whatever form of transcendental personal avoidance one may presume to require. As distasteful and perverted as this conflict becomes it is nonetheless inevitable, and some very strong evidence for the authenticity of *The Book of the Law* is its uncompromising stand against sentimentality which proves to be a puissant weapon of those who, for whatever reason, would remain enslaved by an authoritarian conception of social and personal reality. Indeed, the cause of personal freedom is difficult to uphold in the wake of existing social traditions. Such a stand appears to many to violate the very essence of decency and collective efficacy, but here we are confronted with a characteristic paradox of our times. Although this conundrum constitutes an obstacle to the acceptance of Aleister Crowley's revelation, as more and more people are brought through the inevitable travails of the truth disclosed therein, the realization of its sublimity is growing in time as surely as the illumination of the morning sky.

In coming to this realization, one is able to take more seriously Crowley's claim with regard to *The Book of the Law* as an authentic revelation of spiritual truth from a praeterhuman source that addresses the specific needs of our times as a continuation of the tradition of progressive revelation that has guided the evolutionary progress of humanity from antiquity. In doing so, the initial revulsion to many of its more potent admonitions may be overcome by an increasing appreciation for the necessity of their implementation in the personal struggle for liberation from the doctrines of the past that have since become instruments for the oppression of the human soul. The abandonment of the old doctrines, however, places us in the extremely uncomfortable position of having no exterior referent for the determination of what is right and wrong in the way of personal behavior. This problem may not appear to loom so largely from a theoretical perspective, as we contemplate its implications in our more confident moments of intellectual lucidity and full appreciation for the invisible hand of karmic equilibrium, but as life presents its inevitable existential crises and the choices we must make in our dealings with other people through the course of our daily lives, we become aware of just how much we habitually take refuge in the authoritarian prescriptions of old rather than face the awful feelings of isolation and loss that are often immediate consequences of activating the Law of Freedom.

There is no solution for this problem other than to undergo the ordeals of coming to terms with oneself concerning any issue of personal morality that may be brought into focus by any particular situation. This is one of the main reasons for the general unpopularity of this position in its most poignant formulation. The admonition, "Do what thou wilt shall be the whole of the Law," precludes any form of secure determination of moral truth in objective behavioral terms. It throws one into complete reliance upon one's own subjectivity and sets up a standard of absolute social relativity. This constitutes the primary objection to it. It is argued that there have to be agreed-upon standards of behavior if for no other reason than to provide a working context for human interaction and the administration of civil justice. Indeed, we do need standards. We do need civil laws and moral codes of behavior *as facilitators of the enhancement of human experience and the expansion of human possibilities through interpersonal cooperation.* What is at issue is the recognition of the *primacy of the individual* within the context of such social standards as they obtain within a given society at a given time. Social participation must be wholly voluntary, and social punishment must be executed out of respect for and with direct relevance to the rights of each and every person. These are certainly not very radical ideas *in theory* from the standpoint of modern jurisprudence, but we hardly find them practiced in modern society when it comes to the prerogatives of personal behavior with regard to the most fundamental principle of human freedom, that is, the inherent right to be in control of the use and expression of one's own body. We extol liberty as an ideal, and we have come to institutionalize it ostensibly within a very restrained legal context, but it has yet to be realized as an encompassing social truth. Freedom of sexuality and drug usage, for example, is still conventionally viewed as morally corrupting. We continue to be plagued by legal statutes and social recriminations against victimless "crimes" and contraventions among consenting adults.

This brings us to the more difficult and immediate challenge of evaluating the particulars of contemporary morality in relation to the aeonic transition in postmodern society. How are we to apply the precept of total individual freedom and responsibility to concerns such as murder, rape and other forms of physical abuse, participation in war, the rights of an individual to engage in whatever personal lifestyle one chooses with regard to familial arrangements, sexual activity, and drug usage, the use of private property in ways that adversely effect the environment in which we all must live, a woman's right to have an abortion, the fundamental issue of child rearing and education, the use of public monies to protect corporations from economic forces that work to their disadvantage, the increasing proliferation of violent gang activity in our inner cities and beyond, the virtual and actual disenfranchisement of an ever-growing segment of the population, and the breaching of international political barriers,...? The list goes on and on, and so much of what we hear from the political pundits and religious apologists proves ever less adequate for any proposed resolutions of these difficulties, although we do see an occasional ray of light break through the dark clouds of complacency and oppression.

A well known truth of the matter is that a very well established system of economic advantage is in place for a particular faction of the world community, and that faction has become extremely adept at preserving its advantage through the application of a portion of its resources toward the dissemination of power, information and disinformation. One can hardly find a person on the street who would not acknowledge that this is indeed the way the political affairs of the world are conducted, and yet that same person is very likely to swear by the most fundamental tenets of the system of presumed morality that keeps it that way. Furthermore, the special interests that govern the allocation of resources in this manner are in no way threatened by the exposure of their methodology (such as this one) for the simple reason that talk is cheap and is powerless to persuade in the face of matters of social and personal economic survival, except in the rarest of cases when its effect on the political system as a whole is yet virtually negligible.

To assess morality in terms of economic advantage, however, is a totally spurious endeavor and usually leads to the absurdity of class warfare or what may be called the fallacy of Marxism. Despite the obvious fact of the abuse of wealth and power, there is nothing *inherently* wrong with being wealthy and powerful. Morality and the lack thereof span the full spectrum of economic and political privilege. The good people who happen to be rich and powerful understand this infinitely better than do the bad people who happen to be poor and common. In this regard, the Law of Thelema resolves the whole matter. What is one's True Will? Is one doing it? If so, one is good. If not, one is bad. A person who is doing one's True Will poses no real threat to any other and is oriented toward increasing confidence and purposefulness in the manner that one lives. A person who is not doing one's True Will is prone to disharmonious vacillations, loss of self-control, and various kinds of absurd compulsions that prove injurious to oneself and others. If it is a function of one's True Will to be rich, and one does one's True Will, one will be rich. If it is a function of one's True Will to be poor, and one does one's True Will, one will be poor. One may go from rags to riches or from riches to rags, as did Aleister Crowley. Money or the lack of it is, from a spiritual perspective as it is from a material perspective, purely instrumental. To be rich is simply one possible factor that may or may not contribute to the performance of one's True Will and, if the term "rich" is to have any comparative social significance, it can apply at best to a small minority of any given population. Whatever economic advantages are amassed or perpetuated through failure to actualize one's True Will can only serve to provide material for the fabrication of one's personal self-entrapment within the karmic consequences of one's actions. A laborer who is doing one's True Will is infinitely wealthier than a CEO who isn't. No one defies existence.

What about the victims of crime? Can the fact that one is murdered or raped, directly or in more subtle ways, be attributed to the performance or lack of performance of one's True Will? No more so than any other occurrence. One's faith in the eternal is no less called upon in the New Aeon than it has been in previous times. The difference from the previous aeon is that one is not called upon to sacrifice oneself as an ethical choice and that one is dependent upon no one else's conception of moral or spiritual truth. If one is wronged in the performance of one's True Will, it will work to one's ultimate advantage in the eternal scheme of things and to the detriment of the perpetrator, and this in a more direct and fulfilling manner than was the case in the previous aeon. The spiritual perspective has always been and will always be that the perceived material world forms only a *part* of the full reality of Being. The aim of spirituality is to correctly adjust oneself to the eternal as well as the material realm of experience. The material world provides a source of experience, a place of learning, a laboratory of change and a proving ground. Its spiritual purposes are heterogeneous beyond anyone's ability to fully comprehend. There is no shame in acknowledging this great mystery, only in denying it. One can find no better spiritual counsel for these ethical questions than the Christian admonition: "Be not deceived; God is not mocked: for whatsoever a man soweth, that shall he also reap." [Galatians 6:7]

In order to go to the heart of the consideration of morality, however, we must address the central issue of sexuality. Therein lies the core of the whole matter. The very word "morality" has a decidedly sexual connotation in the vernacular, despite its broader applications. The first thing that commonly comes to mind when one's morality is spoken of is the manner in which one conducts oneself in sexual practices and preferences. This would not be so if in fact sexuality were not central to all issues of morality. In this regard both traditionalists and progressivists are in agreement. The difference pertains to the manner in which each orientation proposes to address this fact. The ethical issues involved in the fundamental dispute over sexuality are extremely subtle and complex, but they can be approached in more or less general terms so as to at least provide a frame of reference to facilitate dialogue on issues that for the most part remain submerged beneath the surface of social intercourse. To begin with, the very idea that sexuality is central to the broader concerns of morality must be qualified. After all, often the most heinous moral violations, such as genocide, murder, theft, and fraud, would appear superficially to have nothing to do with sex. The claim that sexuality is central to morality is therefore subject to the charge of undue preoccupation.

The theoretical basis for this claim is the grounding principle of depth psychology which holds that states of consciousness are driven by libido, that is, sexual energy, also called psychic energy. This idea was introduced into modern psychological theory by Sigmund Freud and has subsequently been expanded upon by other psychologists, including Carl Jung and Wilhelm Reich. The realization of this psycho-physiological truth, however, was one of the central tenets of the ancient vitalistic tradition of mystical philosophy. As were the modern discoveries of evolution and entropy, the discovery of libido was actually a *rediscovery* of a truth with which the priesthoods of antiquity were familiar and from which the dominant institutions of Western civilization have been separated by over two thousand years of religious doctrines that instituted the virtual alienation of humanity from the animating sexual quality of our natural existence. There is currently an intensifying controversy within modern culture concerning this difficulty. The inability thus far to resolve the issue collectively is evidence of how deeply rooted are the ethical conceptions that underlie the belief systems of the respective positions. It has been a major tenet of this book to elucidate a working rationale for the incorporation of *both* of the opposing perspectives involved within the context of the historical evolution of humanity by *uniting* the spiritual and material conceptions of our existence. This rationale will be consummated as we proceed, but in order to do so it is essential first to elucidate the characteristics that distinguish the two basic positions for the purpose of assessing their respective functions in the evolutionary scheme.

From an historical perspective, alienation from sexual spontaneity in Western civilization may be traced to the prohibitions against fornication and adultery by the Jewish religion as a bulwark against paganism. The rite of circumcision must also be considered fundamental to the anti-sexual orientation of Hebrew doctrine. There can be no doubt that circumcision exerted an inhibitory effect upon the expression of genital sexuality within Jewish culture. It must further be acknowledged that such an inhibitory effect was transmitted to both sexes of the progeny of Jewish fathers. From a Tantric perspective, the inhibition of genital sexuality necessarily culminates in the *sublimation* of libido into alternative expressions of non-genital sexuality. Here we encounter a linguistic difficulty in that sexuality tends to be conventionally identified exclusively with genital activity, and this refers back to the previous acknowledgment of possible objections to the hypothesis that all morality is rooted in sexuality. This difficulty is resolved through the realization that psychic energy proceeds from its reservoir pooled at the base of the spinal column and is susceptible to transmutation into alternative forms of expression by its potential for rising through the spinal column and activating various neural centers or *chakras* along the way, culminating, from the standpoint of conventional physiology, in the stimulation of the brain in the cranial region.

The obvious functional objective of the anti-sexual religious orientation of Hebrew tradition was to bring the natural sexual impulse of humanity into submission to a "higher" purpose, that is, mental and spiritual stimulation as opposed to strictly genital gratification. The ultimate fulfillment of this objective is the libidinal illumination of the entire neurostructure of the human organism, and particularly the activation of the quantum level of neural functioning, thus precipitating the realization of divinity, that is, transcendental consciousness, within the context of human perception. The transition, therefore, from the matriarchal vitalistic orientation of the Aeon of Isis to the patriarchal authoritarian orientation of the Aeon of Osiris, the Western focus of which was initiated by the Hebrew tradition, established the evolutionary context within which the temporal (larval) orientation of humanity could be brought to a state of quantum consciousness—that is, *identification* with the eternal aspect of reality as a complement to common physical existence. The negotiation of this transition, however, which has in fact characterized the entire development of the Aeon of Osiris, that is, the Christian-Islamic dispensation for which the Hebrew tradition provided the foundation, has been an extremely difficult, or rather, catastrophic enterprise, which, as suggested in this book and intimated in the works of Aleister Crowley, has yet to be brought to its ultimate consummation. Before contrasting the two opposing moral orientations toward sexuality, therefore, it must be understood that the inhibitory attitude of traditional religion has been *necessary* to the evolutionary process from a dialectical perspective.

The significant effect of the institution of strict lifelong heterosexual monogamy was to secure the role of paternity within society. Biologically, the identity of an infant's mother is not a matter of speculation. There is a visible and inexorable bond between mother and child. Once the seed is planted, however (and usually not for the intended purpose of begetting offspring), the father may become virtually irrelevant to the gestation, birth and subsequent existence of his child. The patriarchal Aeon of Osiris, therefore, codified and substantiated the uniting of the father with the mother in the *responsibility* for directly attending to the survival of their progeny, thus effecting, in principle, a balance between motherhood and fatherhood in the self-generating process of human perpetuity. It had been the instinctive task of the matriarchy to fashion the male gender into a state of fitness for conscious participation in the generative process of humanity. At the inception of the Aeon of Osiris, the time had come for the male gender to emerge from the womb of the matriarchy and share in the responsibility for its own development. This theme reiterates the association of femininity with the eternal and masculinity with the temporal aspects of Being. Thus, Woman (in the generic sense) embodies what is, always has been, and forever will be, and Man (in the generic sense) embodies the temporal process of becoming.

Obviously, the father could not issue forth from the womb of the mother in his fully developed splendor, as it were. Therefore, we see the relegation of the image of the father to a transcendental status and the dual motif of the birth of the son Horus to Isis and his struggle with the materially regressive tendency of masculinity manifested in the form of Set. This conflicting duality came to be codified in the dynamic interaction of the archetypes of Jesus, the Christ Child, and Caesar, the temporal ruler. The institution of monogamy within the Judeo-Christian religious tradition provided the fundamental means for constraining Set to the acknowledgment of the *fact* and the accompanying responsibility of biological fatherhood, however ill-prepared he was for the acceptance of that responsibility. *It is this underlying truth that accounts for the deep moral conviction of the propriety of monogamy.* (The fully actualized human value in this regard, superior to the monogamous ethic, is the responsibility of *all* men and *all* women for *all* children.) There are, however, many less noble motivations for the conviction of the propriety of monogamy that have been bred into civilization through the cultural selection that has resulted from this strongly enforced ethic. Such motivations include possessiveness, jealousy, personal exploitation, guilt, fear of natural instinct and ingrained submission to authority, that is, servility, not to mention the explicit moral sanction for violence unto murder against violators of the taboo, especially when they are women. The implicit understanding of these dynamics, along with the ancient knowledge of the universal principle of entropy, provides a rational basis for the prophecies of the apocalyptic culmination of the patriarchal tradition, that is, the eschatological expectations that characterize patriarchal dogma. Those explicitly formulated expectations are direct evidence of some kind of understanding on the part of the initiators of the patriarchal tradition that it would run its course and ultimately self-destruct in an inevitable planetary conflagration that would be precipitated by the exhaustion of material resources necessary to fuel the insatiable quest for material power resulting from the inhibition of spontaneous libidinal flow within the psychic economy of humanity.

The only possible salvation for physical humanity within this apocalyptic context, as it currently confronts us within our closed planetary environment, lies in the restoration of instinctual sexuality, whereby the psychic economy of the human organism may be relieved of the vacuous quest and the debilitating and destructive compulsions that have resulted from obstruction of the natural flow of libido caused by the imposition of a mandatory and restraining sexual ethic. This debilitated condition is what the pioneering psychologist Wilhelm Reich termed "the emotional plague," which characterizes modern civilization as a consequence of the Judeo-Christian sexual ethos. Reich's work was so threatening to the prevailing values of our civilization that he was castigated by his peers and silenced by the American government. He died in a Federal penitentiary and his books were *burned* by that government in 1957. [*Cosmic Trigger: Final Secret of the Illuminati,* pp. 53, 55] With this perspective in mind, we may contrast the functionality of traditional sexual values with those of an ethos of sexual freedom, whereby the bodily sovereignty of each individual is universally acknowledged and respected such that each individual may pursue libidinal equilibrium in accordance with one's own unique psycho-physiological orientation.

The traditional Judeo-Christian sexual ethos provided a structure within which the destructive passions of the embryonic stage of spiritual development could be managed and directed toward a condition of integral viability, thus facilitating the gestation of a new generation of humankind. This process, however, was made possible only through the sacrifice of the strong to the weak on behalf of that enterprise. A corollary function of this process has been the hyper-exploitation of the inherent potentialities of material existence resulting from the stimulation of the cranial brain by the upwardly directed libido, which has culminated in the development of modern science and the proliferation of technological prowess. This exploitation of Earth's environment constitutes the very utilization of the borrowed material resources that the gestating infant draws from the body of its mother. Herein lies the rationale for the patriarchal inversion of the masculine and feminine roles in relation to earth and sky through the assumption of masculine dominance. This also complements the ego-gratifying strategy of the relinquishment of temporal power to Set as a motivational, as well as a pedagogical evolutionary device. The role of women as sources of sexual pleasure for men and as child bearers has constituted their political disadvantage within the context of patriarchal civilization, and this political situation has contributed significantly to the psychological dissociation that has characterized the Aeon of the Dying God.

An understanding of the functional dynamics of the patriarchal tradition of the Aeon of Osiris clarifies the present need for acceptance of the sexual ethos of the Aeon of Horus upon which we are currently embarking. The emotional development of humanity, ironically both fostered and thwarted by the patriarchal tradition, must be allowed to complement our technological capabilities. Nowhere is the contrast between the moral orientations that characterize the past and present aeons more poignantly and dramatically portrayed than in the prophetic revelation imparted to the world by Aiwass through Aleister Crowley as *The Book of the Law*. We find this contrast characterized in such verses as: "The word of Sin is Restriction: O man! refuse not thy wife, if she will! O lover, if thou wilt, depart! There is no bond that can unite the divided but love: all else is a curse. Accursed! Accursed! be it to the aeons! Hell," [*AL* I:41] and "There is a veil: that veil is black. It is the veil of the modest woman; it is the veil of sorrow, & the pall of death: this is none of me. Tear down that lying spectre of the centuries: veil not your vices in virtuous words: these vices are my service; ye do well, & I will reward you here and hereafter," [*AL* II:52] and "Let Mary inviolate be torn upon wheels:

for her sake let all chaste women be utterly despised among you!"
[*AL* III:55]

These ideas are elaborated more fully in three consecutive verses
of the third chapter of *The Book of the Law* that leave no doubt about
the implications of failure to appreciate the need for abandoning the
sexual ethos of the now-defunct Aeon of Osiris:

> Let the Scarlet Woman beware! If pity and compassion and tender-
> ness visit her heart; if she leave my work to toy with old sweet-
> nesses; then shall my vengeance be known. I will slay me her
> child: I will alienate her heart: I will cast her out from men: as a
> shrinking and despised harlot shall she crawl through dusk wet
> streets, and die cold and an-hungered.
>
> But let her raise herself in pride! Let her follow me in my way!
> Let her work the work of wickedness! Let her kill her heart! Let
> her be loud and adulterous! Let her be covered with jewels, and
> rich garments, and let her be shameless before all men!
>
> Then will I lift her to pinnacles of power: then will I breed from
> her a child mightier than all the kings of the earth. I will fill her
> with joy: with my force shall she see & strike at the worship of Nu:
> she shall achieve Hadit. [*AL* III:43-45]

These powerful admonitions can be elucidated by reflection upon
the event in Egyptian mythology in which Isis freed Set from his
bondage after he had been defeated in battle by Horus. That act was
characteristic of the "compassion" against which women are admon-
ished in the New Aeon. In our present cultural context we find what
has been termed the "battered wife syndrome." Out of fear, but more
significantly "compassion," many women continue to suffer abuse at
the hands of their male companions. Such abuse is often visited as a
consequence of any show of pride or independence by women involved with abusers. This must stop. Good men must be prepared to
take effective action against abusers, but the primary resistance must
be offered by women themselves. A woman has a right to flaunt her
sexuality without fear of reprisal. If a man is aroused unto abuse, he
violates the Law of Freedom and must suffer the consequences.

To achieve Hadit, as may be inferred from the earlier parts of *The
Book of the Law,* means to become spiritually centered and wholly
self-directed, characteristics that were overtly intolerable in women
throughout the patriarchal Aeon of Osiris. The real power of women
as autonomous objects of love and beauty has long been denied them
by the anti-sexual attitudes of the repressive religious doctrines that

were designed to bring Set toward a sense of responsibility for his actions in the world and an ability to control the destructive impulses of his own passions. Such religious doctrines, of course, could not eliminate the fact of natural sexual attraction, and so that attraction became a driving force of hypocrisy and exploitation that came to permeate the very fabric of society, fostering all manner of deeply rooted resentments and animosities that currently account for, among other things, what we refer to as the "battle of the sexes." The only possible way to alleviate this estrangement between the male and female of the species is to throw out the hypocrisy about sexuality and release the pent-up tensions inherited from the formula of the past aeon. There needs to be a rekindling of love through free expression of natural instinct. Naturally, this can only happen in an atmosphere of mutual respect among people, and such respect requires freedom, honesty, and, most emphatically, *protection from abuse.*

One of the greatest impediments to personal freedom that we have inherited from patriarchal tradition, particularity in regard to sexuality, is the institutionalized tolerance of physical abuse that yet characterizes modern civilization. The motivational orientation associated with the archetype of Set still retains his prerogative of grabbing what he wants in the pursuit of alleviating his frustrations and beating up on people he perceives as denying him the gratification of his material desires. This prerogative is exercised at all levels of social edict, from the waging of war for the material resources of Earth to the abuse of corporate power down the chain of command to personal rape and spousal and child abuse. Nothing will improve the collective concerns of humanity until these ethical problems are dealt with fully at the personal level. These matters can be worked out very effectively with ample collective intelligence and will to do so. Our present social institutions are not only logistically incapable of doing for us what we must do for ourselves, but they lack the will to do so despite the political rhetoric of their esteemed colleagues. These institutions are actually the enforcers and beneficiaries of what has been termed "man's inhumanity to man," a phrase itself suggestive of patriarchal bias. This issue dramatically demonstrates the controversy over the relation between the ideals of efficacious government and personal freedom. The telling truth of the matter is that our collective situation is largely governed by, although not limited to, the lowest common denominator of human morality and intelligence which currently leaves much to be desired. This principle being recognized, it should prove a simple matter for the fit to prevail over the unfit, once the habit of relinquishing power to the unregenerate archetypal principle of Set—that is, Caesar run amok—is broken.

There are two developments that together can remedy this situation, one shown to be inevitable and the other visibly beginning to occur throughout the world. The former is the *entropic disintegration* of authoritarian political institutions, and the latter is the *neurological mutation* of humanity toward becoming a species of autonomous individuals. As authoritarianism erodes, and we citizens of the world increasingly stand up for ourselves and our unalienable rights in our relations with each other, a much greater and richer diversity of personal and cultural expression of humanity emerges. The impending crises of overpopulation, ecological damage from increasing high-energy-flow industrial development, and the breakdown of traditional institutions of authority need not obscure the vision of our evolutionary progress as a species. Perspective comes from the realization of *intelligence* and *purpose* as inherent aspects of life, and such realization entails the understanding that even planetary crises of horrific proportions necessarily conform to the requirements of that *purpose* in accordance with formative cosmic evolutionary principles.

Those of us with wills to do so must develop new cultural standards of human interaction based on love and respect for humanity and the process of life, which includes death, and we must be vigilant in the doing. This is the significance of the warrior image as the ruling archetype of the New Aeon. No passive expectation of divine deliverance will do. People must act in the face of adversity. We must struggle for existence in an increasingly challenging environment that will claim many lives as the crisis unfolds. We must liberate the long-repressed torrent of our passions. We must accept the reality of death as an inherent aspect of life and be willing to fight and die for, if necessary, rather than surrender our personal sovereignty. We must integrate our spirituality with our material existence. We must do all these things and more if we want to carry the torch of humanity into the future. The message of *The Book of the Law* is that the world is *ready* for this activation of truth.

As the global evolutionary crisis unfolds, each and every person is challenged to forge one's own course into the New Aeon. The full-blown techno-culture of today's world is the *seed* of future humanity. This seed is visibly breaking, and as it breaks the life within it is surging outward. No one need fear for lack of orientation. Each person, female and male, who would advance the cause of humanity must answer the calling of one's own soul, be driven by the life within, reach out for the objects of one's desire, and fulfill those desires as a warrior with courage and honor. There is nothing else to do. As the old order crumbles, the new order forms. Each person must see one's own way of participation within the context of change. People will work together harmoniously so long as they do not violate each other. Those who violate the Law of Freedom will be put down. Confidence can be found in the fulfillment of greater purpose through the activation of one's True Will. Our humanity will be served by our humanity. We must inspire future generations. We must raise our children well because we *are* our children. We must *rejoice* in our children as we rejoice in ourselves.

There yet remains, however, a major moral issue to be addressed. That is the existence of good and bad people in the world, which is which, and what should be done about such disparity. This matter is addressed from various perspectives throughout the verses of *The Book of the Law*. It is axiomatic that all the serious moral problems in the world are due to people doing bad things. It is also generally true that most people live by a high standard of morality and are not prone to do such bad things to their fellow humans and other life forms as evidenced by what social cohesiveness we enjoy. The fact that there are those among us, however, who are quite willing to knowingly take from our common resources what is not rightfully ours, who are capable of physically abusing others through anger, jealousy, greed, lust, or sheer meanness, and who perpetrate all manner of violence against the natural order of humanity and life on Earth is evidence of a strong current of spiritual immaturity that yet characterizes our species. In some cases it would seem a simple matter to identify those who have relinquished their rights as citizens of humanity by committing such actions. But in many other cases, which ultimately include each of us, there is a shared responsibility for the moral shortcomings of the world.

It is very easy to poke holes in anyone's sanctimonious moralizing on the subject of one's particular notion of acceptable and unacceptable behavior. Even matters of widespread agreement about propriety within a given society can always be seriously disputed. For example, we as Americans feel more or less duty-bound to respect the property rights of others who live within our system of jurisprudence. But that system was superimposed by Europeans upon this continent with no effectual regard for those same principles as they applied to the native population that was displaced accordingly.

Native Americans were simply called savages because they were not practicing Christians versed in the principles of European "enlightenment." How much does each American who has profited from the European conquest of America share in the responsibility for that genocide? Legal strategies are employed daily within our common jurisdiction that have the same effect as armed robbery, and yet, because they are executed in accordance with duly sanctioned legal procedures, they are deemed to be moral and socially beneficial. Private disputes among individuals nearly always involve different conceptions of morality. Nearly every criminal in prison, regardless of how heinous are the crimes that one has committed, will argue either for one's innocence or the moral justification of one's actions.

These circumstances lead inexorably to acceptance of the principle expressed by the words, "Do what thou wilt shall be the whole of the Law," which introduces nothing more nor less than a conscious and honest acknowledgment of the actual state of affairs as it is, has been, and forever shall be. The concept takes on an almost platitudinous tone when expressed negatively, which is to say that no one ought to do anything that violates one's most profound sense of what is morally right. The positive expression, however, emphasizes personal initiative, self-determination and will. Although it is difficult to specify exactly what constitutes goodness in a person in strictly behavioral terms, we all have a definite sense of what it is, and that goodness is hamstrung by the imposition of mandatory codes of behavior. Such codes are aimed ostensibly at the institutionalization of goodness and are therefore only respected by the so-called "good people." The bad people simply take advantage of the codes to evil purpose.

Furthermore, there is no way that goodness can be codified into specific behaviors in the first place. This truth is expressed succinctly in Christian scripture: "Who also hath made us able ministers of the new testament; not of the letter, but of the spirit: for the letter killeth, but the spirit giveth life," [II Corinthians 3:6] and in *The Book of the Law*: "Also reason is a lie; for there is a factor infinite & unknown; & all their words are skew-wise." [*AL* II:32] We lose nothing in the acknowledgment of this truth accept the arbitrary restraint upon our freedom to act exactly as we see fit and to oppose those who exceed their rightful bounds. Yet by the standard inherited from conventional Christianity, the idea of total personal freedom is thought to be the epitome of social delusion and irresponsibility. Such freedom, however, is the only way by which everyone may be held *totally responsible* for their actions. The acknowledgment of freedom *insures* responsibility. The perpetrators of iniquity are well aware of this fact, and they consequently seek ostensibly to resolve social difficulties through increasingly complex and ultimately obfuscating legislation and argumentation.

An important realization follows from the principles of freedom outlined above. We need not be concerned about the identification of evil in general and bad people in particular. It is a common failing and a great moral obstacle to become entangled in the attempt to specify the location of evil. It is only necessary to take action appropriate to any circumstance. The abuse of wealth need only be denied the abuser. The murderer, rapist, or child abuser need only be prevented from repeating such actions, by whatever means necessary including capital punishment. The thief need only be effectively punished according to the mores of his society, etc., etc. Once the hypocrisies of false and sanctimonious moralisms are dispensed with, the evildoers will have no artificial structures to hide behind. Only in an atmosphere of true freedom can the spirit of the Golden Rule be authentically realized.

This difficulty was addressed by the Osirian formula in the Parable of the Tares in which Jesus is reported to have said in response to the question of whether or not the tares, sown in with the wheat by an enemy, should be gathered up: "Nay; lest while ye gather up the tares, ye root up also the wheat with them. Let both grow together until the harvest: and in the time of harvest I will say to the reapers, Gather ye together first the tares, and bind them in bundles to burn them: but gather the wheat into my barn." [Matthew 13:24-30]

This parable not only addresses the profundity of the problem of evil in a universal sense but also suggests the Osirian attitude of restraint from vigilance against wrongdoers as a means of preserving the gestating impetus of humanity. If, as suggested in this book and in the writings of Aleister Crowley, the Aeon of Horus is not only an antithesis to but also a progression from the Aeon of Osiris, then the following passage from *The Book of the Law* may indicate that the time of the harvest is at hand: "Behold! the rituals of the old time are black. Let the evil ones be cast away; let the good ones be purged by the prophet! Then shall this Knowledge go aright." [*AL* II:5] This would seem to imply that it is time for the tares to be separated from the wheat.

Self-actualization appropriate to modern and postmodern understanding requires that individuals must make moral judgments as called upon by circumstance; act accordingly, *and be willing to accept the consequences.* We have only our own understanding and our own individual wills to guide us. Destiny will deal with us accordingly, *both for our acts of commission and for our acts of omission.* The impending world crisis will affect the harvest of the past aeon. Our individual karmas will determine our separate fates in terms of our participation in the future of humanity. "For pure will, unassuaged of purpose, delivered from the lust of result, is every way perfect. The Perfect and the Perfect are one Perfect and not two; nay, are none!" [*AL* I:44-45] By our very existences we are each called upon to play our parts upon the stage of the world, confident that the humanity within us is allied to the humanity beyond us, and that, ultimately, there is no such distinction.

In the second paragraph of the very brief concluding chapter of *The Equinox of the Gods*, entitled "Summary of the Case," the whole of which consists of but seven paragraphs, Aleister Crowley sets forth what may be the most direct and economical statement of the succession of the Aeons to be found in his entire corpus of writings:

> Isis was Liberty; Osiris bondage; but the new Liberty is that of Horus. Osiris conquered her because she did not understand him. Horus avenges both his Father and his Mother. This child Horus is a twin, two in one. Horus and Harpocrates are one, and they are also one with Set or Apophis, the destroyer of Osiris. It is by the destruction of the principle of death that they are born. The establishment of this new Aeon, this new fundamental principle, is the great work now to be accomplished in the world. [p. 134]

The unity of Horus and Set as an archetypal motif for the New Aeon directly poses the most perplexing ethical dilemma with which individuals in today's world must grapple. This suggests that the traditional archetypal champions of good and evil, of righteousness and depravity, of love and hate, can somehow be reconciled through the formula of the New Aeon. The implication, in terms appropriate to Christian dogma, is nothing short of an alliance between God and Satan. How can this be? Does this not suggest a weakening of goodness, a sacrifice of valor, a collaboration with evil? Is all that Horus has fought for in his struggle against Set to be lost in such an unholy merger? It is the inherent resistance to such a mixture of water and oil that currently obstructs our full-fledged entry into the New Aeon.

Such resistance, however, may be dispelled through a simple and obvious rationale.

Set may be identified with sense-oriented ego consciousness, that is, the conscious persona developed in relation to the perception of the common material world of entropic decay. In its pure state (an impossibility in terms of personal wholeness) this conscious ego is devoid of any transcendental perspective whatsoever. The world of material existence is taken as the only reality, and the meaning of all perceived phenomena is interpreted accordingly. The relative dominance and intensity of perceived macroscopic physical reality is such that the conscious ego that must be developed in relation to it, as a matter of sheer survival, constitutes a very agile and tenacious entity fully bent upon the fulfillment of material desires and the self-preservation and aggrandizement of the physical organism. In the initial stages of its formation, this conscious ego *must* utterly disregard moral perspectives because of their apparent irrelevance to and sometimes disregard for physical actualization. Only after the conscious ego is well established can the moral aspects of human existence be assimilated into personal consciousness. Moral codes of behavior are meaningless to infants except as they pertain to the survival value of knowing the behavioral expectations of the giant adults. The concept of stealing, for example, means nothing to a young child who makes no distinctions with regard to ownership. There are only phenomena to be incorporated or repelled by natural instinct. The very circumstances of incarnation absolutely require that the Set aspect of personality be successfully developed and negotiated as the *first order of business* for the early childhood of any human organism. This constitutes the condition of viability in the material world.

At any stage in the life of a person when issues of physical survival become immediate—that is, in any life-threatening situation—the impulse for survival instinctively brings the Set aspect of personality into play. It is generally recognized that one is justified, from both moral and legal standpoints, in taking whatever action necessary, even unto the killing of another person, in the interest of self-preservation or self-defense. A person may also forfeit one's prerogative of self-preservation (in the physical sense) in the enactment of a moral choice within a given situation. That is, one may choose to die in an act of social interaction that affects a desired result, such as the physical survival of a loved one. Such an act would have moral value in relation to its disregard for the physical integrity of the person performing it. In this regard, the distinction must be made between such a *conscious choice* as an act of Self-actualization and the performance of such an act as an ethical requirement, *even if one would otherwise choose not to perform it.* Furthermore, the notion of such a conscious choice may not necessarily entail the loss of one's physical life but rather the sacrifice of one's preferred mode of life, that is, the *manner* in which one desires to live. It is this distinction that characterizes moral behavior respectively in accordance with the Horian Law of Freedom and the Osirian Law of Sacrifice.

The Aeon of the Dying God affected a clear distinction between the existential modes of behavior for both Horus (exemplified by Jesus) and Set (exemplified by Caesar). As a function of his conceptual limitation, Set would invariably opt for continuity within the context of perceived physical reality. As a function of his expanded spiritual perspective, Horus would invariably opt for the sacrifice of his physical being as required to affect spiritual continuity. Each considered the mode of the other to be the essence of human folly. From Set's point of view, the loss of physical existence on the part of Horus appeared to be the relinquishment of effectual power. Horus' point of view, as prescribed within the context of the Aeon of Osiris, was expressed in the Christian teaching:

> Then said Jesus unto his disciples, If any man will come after me, let him deny himself, and take up his cross, and follow me. For whosoever will save his life shall lose it: and whosoever shall lose his life for my sake shall find it. For what is a man profited, if he shall gain the whole world, and lose his own soul? or what shall a man give in exchange for his soul?" [Matthew 16:24-26]

In the Aeon of Osiris, one would find the Horus type on the battlefield, fighting and dying for the good of the nation, while the Set type would remain comfortably ensconced in the seats of political and economic power, enjoying the fruits of victory, including the surplus of women resulting from the mutual destruction of the male Horus types of the competing nations. These role descriptions are, of course, generalizations, and should not be construed to characterize absolute types, but they are not without socio-psychological relevance.

In short, the Aeon of Osiris affected a curse upon both Horus and Set in that Horus was denied material gratification and Set was denied moral gratification by virtue of their respective habitual modes of behavior. Both were functioning in terms of destinies bound by their generational relationship to one another and the absolute requirements of their differing conceptions of reality in accordance with the dualistic Piscean motif. Upon the fulfillment of the objective of the Aeon of Osiris, that is, the attainment of spiritual viability by Set within the conceptual scaffolding predicated upon the realm of perceived material existence, the radical variance of the material and spiritual perspectives can be, and *needs to be*, dispensed with. We are now *required* by the best knowledge available to us to integrate a transcendental conception of reality with the material existence to which we are habituated by our common sensory experience. It is not mere happenstance that twentieth-century physics empirically developed a conception of reality that undermines the traditional notion of inert matter. Even the most skeptical educated mind can no longer deny that we live and invest our being within a transcendental context of multiversal quantum potentiality, despite the fact that it is impossible explicitly to fathom the full range of implications inherent in this scientific discovery. The material perspective of Set and the spiritual perspective of Horus have now become one to the collective mind of humanity. The evolutionary implication of this enigma is that the old Setian perspective of absolute materialism has been rendered nonfunctional. It must be understood that this turn of events constitutes not only a *victory* of Horus over Set through conscious integration of spiritual continuity as a general truth but also a *uniting* of Horus and Set by virtue of that very integration, referred to by Crowley in the above passage as "the destruction of the principle of death."

As far as the distinction between good and bad people is concerned, it is more relevant to address the need for each person to affect the integration of the habitually fractured relation of "matter" and "spirit" *within one's own personality*. Injustices will continue to occur from a social perspective, but increasing material power will accrue to those who are able to expand their consciousness to incorporate transcendental insight into material processes. Concern for one's personal wholeness obviates the need to make moral judgments with regard to the actions of others. If one is called into conflict with another, one needs simply to fight, confident in the realization that in the greater scheme of things right does indeed make might, whatever the superficial outcome may be for any particular skirmish. The integration of "matter" and "spirit" is the upshot of the neurological mutation occurring as a function of our evolution into the New Aeon. This mutation will bestow a distinct tactical advantage to those in whom it is most pronounced. The impending world crisis will affect a significant acceleration of that mutation, particularly in relation to a sharp reduction of population.

The world's present condition of population overload indicates a disproportionate emphasis on material consciousness. A sharp reduction of the population resulting from the depleted energy base available to support human life on the planet will adjust that disproportionate emphasis in favor of transcendental and transpersonal consciousness. The crisis is creating a *need* for moral understanding and fulfillment on the part of those who remain in the world. This shift of consciousness toward transcendental illumination will effect a mutation of the species toward expanded access to the neurostructure of the organism. Questions of morality will become completely subsumed within the context of expanded consciousness among people. Those who have already experienced some measure of this will readily appreciate its mention in the present context. The veil of illusion behind which immoral acts have traditionally been concealed will be penetrated by the heightened sensitivity of human perception that will result from the purging effect of the impending world crisis. The crisis, therefore, despite the tragic toll it will take upon human existence, will prove to be the very means of raising the consciousness of humanity to a level at which the fulfillment of our deepest material and spiritual aspirations may be actualized in accordance with the performance of our True Wills as human beings.

APPENDICES

ASTROLOGICAL SYMBOLS

SIGNS	
♈	ARIES
♉	TAURUS
♊	GEMINI
♋	CANCER
♌	LEO
♍	VIRGO
♎	LIBRA
♏	SCORPIO
♐	SAGITTARIUS
♑	CAPRICORN
♒	AQUARIUS
♓	PISCES

PLANETS	
☉	SOL
☽	LUNA
☿	MERCURY
♀	VENUS
♂	MARS
♃	JUPITER
♄	SATURN
♅	URANUS
♆	NEPTUNE
♇	PLUTO

ADDITIONAL SYMBOLS

☊	NORTH LUNAR NODE
☋	SOUTH LUNAR NODE
⊕	PART OF FORTUNE

QABALAH

Because there are some technical references to Qabalah in the text of this book, it is necessary to provide some basic information about this system of philosophical understanding, particularly as it concerns the tradition of Western magic and mysticism to which Aleister Crowley was heir by virtue of his initiation into the Hermetic Order of the Golden Dawn. That mystery school used Qabalah as the core of its teachings and ceremonial rituals, and Crowley continued to employ it for all of his later work, including the founding of his own Magickal Order.

The very term Qabalah (also known as Cabala, Kabbala, and a host of other alternative spellings) is suggestive of mystery. The colloquial term "cabalistic" is used to connote secretiveness and mysterious species of erudition, and "cabal" refers to a select group of one sort or another with special knowledge, often pertaining to political intrigues and machinations.

The origins of Qabalah are accordingly and appropriately shrouded in mystery. It is known to be a system of Hebrew philosophy purporting to reveal an esoteric interpretation of Jewish scriptures and can be traced through scholarly investigation only as far back as the Middle Ages, however there is a general assumption on the part of practitioners of Qabalistic philosophy that its roots extend into antiquity and beyond. Aleister Crowley offered several accounts of what Qabalah is, including:

> An instrument for interpreting symbols whose meaning has become obscure, forgotten or misunderstood by establishing a necessary connection between the essence of forms, sounds, simple ideas (such as number) and their spiritual, moral, or intellectual equivalents. ...[and] A system of classification of omniform ideas so as to enable the mind to increase its vocabulary of thoughts and facts through organizing and correlating them. [*777 and Other Qabalistic Writings of Aleister Crowley,* p. 125]

Obviously, a thorough study of Qabalah is an extremely involved and complex process that quickly becomes enmeshed in a labyrinth of esoteric terminology and numerical codifications (not to mention the *experiential* development of highly refined mental states). For the purpose of elucidating planetary correspondences referred to in this book, however, it is sufficient to consider some basic ideas associated with the central glyph of Qabalistic philosophy, namely the Tree of Life..

The Tree of Life is a graphic representation of a series of emanations out of "nothingness" whereby progressive levels or degrees of manifestation come into being culminating in the fully manifested material world of ordinary experience. As such, the Tree of Life delineates a schema of cosmic wholeness within what may be understood as an organic or holographic conception of existence such that wholes are contained within parts. The Tree therefore represents wholeness at all levels of manifestation and thus applies to the microcosmic wholeness of an individual human being as well as the macrocosmic wholeness of the conceivable universe. There are ten emanations represented as a succession of "Sephiroth" arranged to depict a complex functional interrelationship among them. Each "Sephira" is therefore associated with a number and occupies a particular place on the Tree. It may be observed that the total configuration suggests the shape of a human body.

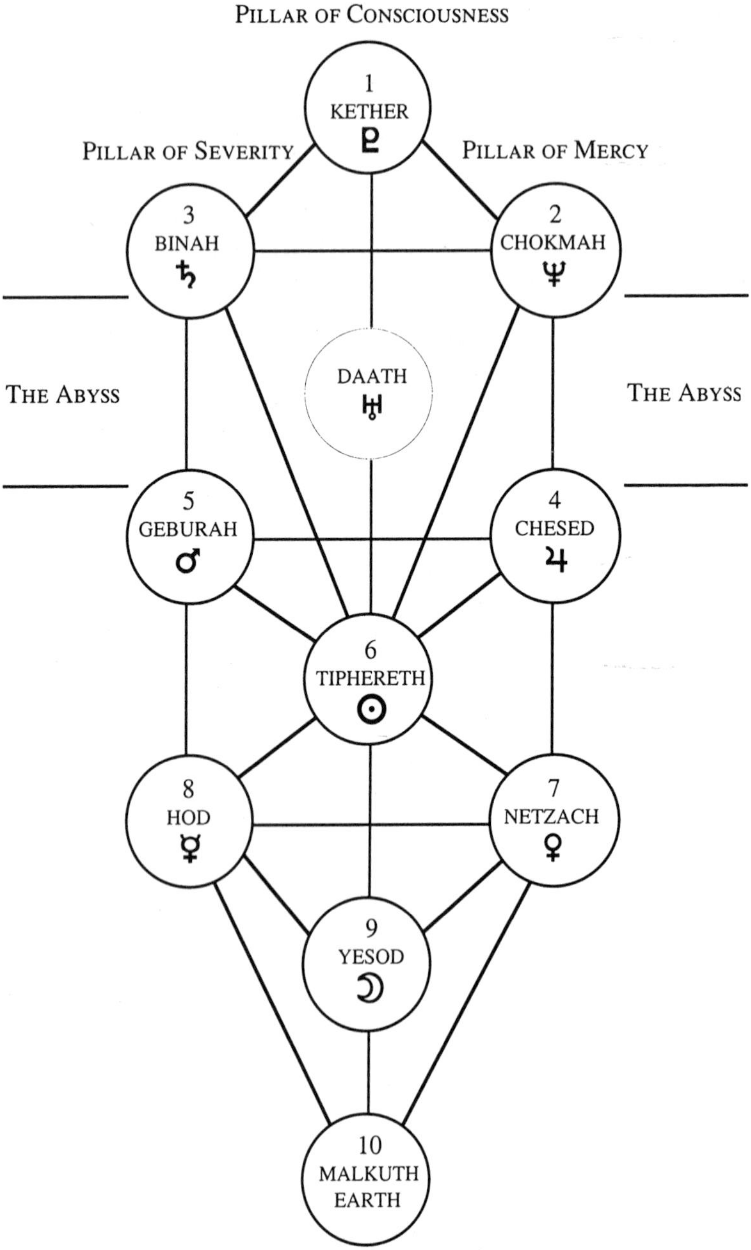

FIGURE 9
The Qabalistic "Tree of Life"
with planetary attributions to the Sephiroth

Each Sephira represents a specialized principle or function in existence that is associated with its corresponding number and a particular planet of the solar system. It is the system of planetary correspondences to the Sephiroth that constitutes the relevance for astrology that applies most specifically to the subject matter of this book. The Sephiroth are also depicted as being connected by an arrangement of twenty-two "paths" that connote particular relationships that obtain among the various Sephiroth. These paths correspond to the twenty-two letters of the Hebrew alphabet and to the twenty-two Trumps of the Major Arcana of the Tarot. The Tree of Life is sometimes depicted with a serpent draped throughout its branches. This symbolism suggests the role of the kundalini force in the activation of ascending levels of cosmic awareness.

A few cursory observations about the fundamental structure of the Tree of Life may suggest its philosophical conception. The upper three Sephiroth constitute what is termed the Supernal Triad, a realm of exalted spiritual truth in which all logical contradictions are resolved into a balanced coherence. The Supernal Triad is separated from the Sephiroth below it by what is termed the Abyss. Below the Abyss, logical contradictions yet engender forms of tension and conflict that characterize the material world. The commonly perceived material world of sensory reality is represented by the tenth Sephira, Malkuth, at the bottom of the Tree. What is sometimes called "the Invisible Sephira," Daath (Knowledge), which is not a Sephira per se, is sometimes represented on the Tree by a broken circle in the center of the Abyss. The Sephiroth are named: 1. Kether (Crown), 2. Chokmah (Wisdom), 3. Binah (Understanding), 4. Chesed (Mercy), 5. Geburah (Severity), 6. Tiphereth (Beauty), 7. Netzach (Victory), 8. Hod (Splendor), 9. Yesod (Foundation), and 10. Malkuth (Kingdom).

The Tree is also divided into three vertical pillars. The left pillar is called the Pillar of Severity which connotes the principle of differentiation and separateness (analysis). The right pillar is called the Pillar of Mercy which connotes the principle of unity and cohesion (synthesis). The middle pillar is called the Pillar of Consciousness which connotes a balanced interaction between the principles of severity and mercy. The sequence of progressive emanations from 1 to 10 follow a zigzag pattern of alternation between the principles of mercy and severity from the top to the bottom of the Tree. This zigzag pattern is called the Lightning Flash and suggests a dialectical

process of cosmic development, from both involutional and evolutionary perspectives.

The system of grades for Crowley's Magickal Order (patterned
after the Golden Dawn system) is structured in accordance with the
Tree of Life in the ascending order of the Sephiroth. The grades are
divided into three groups and are listed in Crowley's official
instructions as follows [*Gems From the Equinox*, p. 15]:

The Order of the S.S.

Ipsissimus	10°	=	1□ [Kether—Pluto]
Magus	9°	=	2□ [Chokmah—Neptune]
Magister Templi	8°	=	3□ [Binah—Saturn]

The Order of the R.C.

Adeptus Exemptus	7°	=	4□ [Chesed—Jupiter]
Adeptus Major	6°	=	5□ [Geburah—Mars]
Adeptus Minor	5°	=	6□ [Tiphereth—Sol]

The Order of the G.D.

Philosophus	4°	=	7□ [Netzach—Venus]
Practicus	3°	=	8□ [Hod—Mercury]
Zelator	2°	=	9□ [Yesod—Luna]
Neophyte	1°	=	10□ [Malkuth—Earth]
Probationer	0°	=	0□

SABIAN SYMBOLS

In chapter 5 of this book a philosophical rationale was developed for the archetypal significance of each of the 360 degrees of the zodiac based upon the morphologically determined ratio of the yearly and daily cycles of temporal existence on Earth and a Platonic conception of Ideal Forms expressed in terms of mathematical relationships. I mentioned there that several systems have been developed in the history of astrology for delineating particular meanings for each of the 360 zodiacal degrees. I have worked with some of those systems, and the one that has proven superior in my practice of astrology, and is also the best known and most widely used in the field of astrology today, is the group of symbols first obtained by Marc Edmund Jones and Elsie Wheeler in 1925. This system was further developed and reformulated by Dane Rudhyar in his monumental book, *An Astrological Mandala: The Cycle of Transformations and Its 360 Symbolic Phases.*

What Jones termed the "Sabian" symbols were obtained through a collaboration between himself and Miss Wheeler in which Jones recorded psychic images "seen" by her corresponding to a random selection of index cards on which the signs and degrees had previously been written on the reverse side. Neither Jones nor Wheeler knew what degree had been selected at the time of each visualization. A full account of the event of obtaining and recording the symbols is presented in Rudhyar's book. This collaborative technique is not unprecedented in the history of occult science. The same basic method was employed by the Elizabethan mathematician Dr. John Dee (who was also the personal astrologer for Queen Elizabeth I) and "psychic" Edward Kelly late in the sixteenth century to obtain the symbolic formulation of what has come to be known as the Enochian System of Magic, further developed by S.L. (MacGregor) Mathers and Aleister Crowley. [*Enochian World of Aleister Crowley: Enochian Sex Magick,* pp. 19-20]

There was some flexibility employed by Jones in working with Miss Wheeler through the process of putting the symbols into words, and Rudhyar has also introduced some alterations of the verbalizations of the symbols, but the integrity of the images has not been compromised by these refinements. A thorough study of Rudhyar's book leaves no doubt as to the authenticity and integrity of his reformulation which leaves the original images virtually intact. An example of such an alteration is Rudhyar's substitution of the symbol for (LEO 3°): "A MIDDLE-AGED WOMAN, HER LONG HAIR FLOWING OVER HER SHOULDERS AND IN A BRALESS YOUTHFUL GARMENT," for the original symbol: "the mature woman having dared to bob her hair." [*An Astrological Mandala,* p. 133] Rudhyar's reformulation obviously suggests to the contemporary reader what the original one would to the reader in 1925.

One of the many beauties of the Sabian symbols for modern investigators is their appropriateness to the common experience of life in the twentieth century. They include images of airplanes, automobiles, chess playing, oil drilling, pugilists, and telephones, etc., as well as traditional and natural imagery that would be appropriate to any historical period, such as birds, trees, volcanoes, graves, and rainbows. Such an amalgamation of modern and traditional imagery provides a vital and relevant context for the contemporary user of the symbols.

The manner in which the Sabian symbols correspond to the morphological conception of astrological interpretation developed in this book is exemplified by the symbolic images for the four Cardinal degrees of the zodiac, that is, the degrees for the morphologically determined equinoxes and solstices—namely the first degrees of the signs: Aries, Cancer, Libra, and Capricorn. Those symbols are recorded in *An Astrological Mandala* as follows:

(ARIES 1°)	A WOMAN JUST RISEN FROM THE SEA. A SEAL IS EMBRACING HER.
(CANCER 1°)	ON A SHIP THE SAILORS LOWER AN OLD FLAG AND RAISE A NEW ONE.
(LIBRA 1°)	IN A COLLECTION OF PERFECT SPECIMENS OF MANY BIOLOGICAL FORMS, A BUTTERFLY DISPLAYS THE BEAUTY OF ITS WINGS, ITS BODY IMPALED BY A FINE DART.
(CAPRICORN 1°)	AN INDIAN CHIEF CLAIMS POWER FROM THE ASSEMBLED TRIBE.

The symbol for Aries 1° is a perfect representation of the emergence of an individualized entity from the "sea" of what may be thought of as Carl Jung's idea of the collective unconscious. Even the reticence appropriate to such a new beginning is suggested by the seal embracing the emerging woman. With regard to this feature Rudhyar observes: "The impulse upward is held back by regressive fear or insecurity; the issue of the conflict depends on the relative strength of the future-ward and the past-ward forces." [*ibid.* p. 50] In the symbol for Cancer 1° we find the sea again represented, but the principal image now is that of a ship—that is, a fully developed, consciously directed entity capable of autonomous, coordinated activity. Furthermore, the sailors lowering an old flag and raising a new one signals the turning point associated with the summer solstice whereby the "day force," although at its most glorious moment in the seasonal cycle, yet by virtue of that fact begins to give way to the tendency toward its decline as the inevitable shift toward the ascendancy of the "night force" occurs. The symbol for Libra 1° of the impaled butterfly suggests the sacrifice of the perfected individualized consciousness in favor of a collective ideal. The symmetry of the butterfly's wing pattern reiterates the equinoctial theme of balanced energy, and the dried wings themselves intimate the falling leaves of autumn with the added subtle implication of transcendent flight. In the symbol for Capricorn 1° the connotation of political power is blatant. The need for the maintenance of collective order appropriate to the winter season is fulfilled through the focused action of political leadership.

Insightful interpretations of each symbol and a thorough-going elucidation of the structural significance of the whole system of Sabian symbols are developed by Rudhyar in *An Astrological Mandala*. The Sabian symbols may be employed to intensify the interpretation of Aleister Crowley's birthchart by applying them within the context of his planetary and lunar nodal placements in terms of their house and sign positions and their dispositions of and aspect relations to one another. These images provide greater insight into the personality of the man and demonstrate the remarkable value of the Sabian symbols for purposes of astrological interpretation.

Following the sequence of the introduction of planetary placements developed in the text of this book, Uranus in Crowley's First House occupies the twentieth degree of Leo. The Sabian symbol for that degree, ZUNI INDIANS PERFORM A RITUAL TO THE SUN, provides additional insight into the nature of Crowley's conscious persona. In addition to and in keeping with his irascible and bombastic nature, he was the founder of a solar religious movement (although its solar characteristic focused on self-actualization as opposed to monotheism, or monism of any type). Saturn in Crowley's Seventh House was placed in the twentieth degree of Aquarius. The Sabian symbol for that degree, A LARGE WHITE DOVE BEARING A MESSAGE, is remarkably appropriate to Crowley's role as a prophet. Here we see symbolized the *objectification* (Seventh House) of the sun-worshipping Uranian First House impulse. It should be recalled in this regard that Crowley's writing of *The Book of the Law,* his major prophetic work, coincided with his first Saturn Return, bringing closure to the extended development of Saturn's first complete transit through his birthchart as delineated in chapter 11. Also, the unusual circumstances under which the book was written and the subsequent difficulty that Crowley initially experienced in coming to identify himself with its message are characteristic of such an extreme objectification.

Crowley's natal Sol was placed in his Fourth House in the twentieth degree of Libra, the Sabian symbol for which is A RABBI PERFORMING HIS DUTIES. This strongly corroborates the spiritual integration of Crowley's personality—that is, his Self, as being rooted (Fourth House) in the religious heritage of the Judeo-Christian tradition. Crowley's use of Qabalah (associated with Judaism) throughout his adult life as the central organizing system for all of his spiritual and philosophical theory and practice aptly confirms the suitability of this symbolic association. Also, the association of his Solar placement in relation to his South Lunar Node (also in Libra) indicates his *karmic inheritance* of this orientation as a basis for his need to *develop* assertiveness by virtue of his North Lunar Nodal placement in Aries as delineated in chapter 7. At this point, it is important to keep in mind that the above three planets, Uranus, Saturn, and Sol, are involved in an exact-degree aspectal interrelation in Crowley's birthchart, which makes of them a tightly configured and intensely focused *system.* The three Sabian symbols for these degrees must therefore be understood to hold a special *archetypal* significance in relation to one another as delineated in chapters 4, 5 and 7.

Venus has a very special significance in Crowley's birthchart for three primary reasons: 1. Its natal conjunction with Sol, 2. Its disposition of Sol, and 3. Its status of final dispositor for *every other factor* in Crowley's birthchart (as delineated in chapter 10). For these reasons, the Sabian symbol for Venus' degree placement in Crowley's birthchart is indicative of a powerful characteristic theme which in effect *permeates* the whole of his personality from the private depths of his subjective experience (Fourth House). That symbol is: (LIBRA 25°): THE SIGHT OF AN AUTUMN LEAF BRINGS TO A PILGRIM THE SUDDEN REVELATION OF THE MYSTERY OF LIFE AND DEATH. The autumn leaf motif is not only appropriate to the Libra placement, but it is also suggestive of the death of the passing aeon, the Aeon of the *Dying* God. The manner in which all of this symbolism coincides with Venus' powerful role in Crowley's birthchart confirms the tendency of his personality to affect the aeonic transition through a profound realization that the old order was disintegrating.

The remaining planet in Crowley's solar gestalt is Mars in his Sixth House occupying the twenty-third degree of Capricorn, the Sabian symbol for which is A SOLDIER RECEIVING TWO AWARDS FOR BRAVERY IN COMBAT. Once again, there is a striking appropriateness for the symbolic image associated with the planetary placement in Crowley's birthchart, Mars being the planet of war. Rudhyar makes a particularly significant observation about this symbol that may be applied to the destiny of Aleister Crowley, especially pertaining to Mars' rulership of his Midheaven:

> The fact that "two" awards are emphasized makes us believe that this may refer subtly to the recognition by the community that, whether he succeeded or failed, an individual who discharged his duty nobly under unusual circumstances is entitled to the respect and appreciation of the collectivity he served so well. [*ibid.*, p. 243]

As a feature of Crowley's natal configuration, this Mars placement may be interpreted to imply that both his "failure" to win the world's approval, which he so fervently sought during his life, and whatever success his legacy may ultimately enjoin were essential to the program of his appointed task. The attitude that he expressed in his final days (explicitly in *Magick Without Tears*) conveys his acceptance of this tragic implication.

A rather interesting opposing pair of images are pictured by the Sabian symbols for Crowley's Lunar Nodal degrees, which complete the placements that comprise his solar gestalt. (The degrees for the angles of Crowley's birthchart cannot be accurately known with confidence, therefore no attempt will be made here to determine them.) His South Lunar Node (indicating his karmic past) is in the eighth degree of Libra in his Third House, very near his *Imum Coeli*

(Fourth House cusp). The Sabian symbol for that degree is A BLAZ-
ING FIREPLACE IN A DESERTED HOME. This is a rather cryptic image.
Why is the fireplace blazing? Who is the fire for? Who built the fire?
There is a striking illogic to the symbol which is suggestive of a
particularly meaningful paradox. In association with the South Lunar
Node, the implication of this symbol would appear to be the inheri-
tance of a core spiritual meaning that has been for the most part lost
to the family of humanity. From this image as a base of operation,
Crowley was challenged to reach unto the heights of new discovery
through his North Lunar Nodal placement in the eighth degree of
Aries in his Ninth House near his Midheaven, the Sabian symbol for
which is A LARGE WOMAN'S HAT WITH STREAMERS BLOWN BY AN
EAST WIND. The east is the source of new beginnings. (East also
reiterates the equinoctial association to Aries.) The large hat implies
protection, which is appropriate to the sensitivity suggested by the
fact that it is a woman's hat. The "east wind" feature of this symbol
is remarkably appropriate for Crowley's spiritual destiny (the very
connotation of the North Lunar Node) n that he would be the vehicle
for the revelation of *The Book of the Law,* in which it is written,
"Abrogate are all rituals, all ordeals, all words and signs. Ra-Hoor-
Khuit hath taken his seat in the East at the Equinox of the Gods;..."
[*AL* I:49] The coming out motif implicit in the bottom to top (that is,
inner to outer) orientation of Crowley's lunar nodal axis is also suggested by the respective degree symbols for the Nodes themselves.

We may begin the application of the Sabian symbols to the interpretation of Crowley's lunar gestalt with the consideration of the
placement of Luna herself. The structural interpretation of that
placement was delineated in chapter 6 to connote a powerful subjective sense of feminine presence as a function of a transcendental
religious perceptual orientation. Luna occupies the twenty-third
degree of Pisces in Crowley's Ninth House, and she rules his Twelfth
House by virtue of Cancer on its cusp. The Sabian symbol for Luna's
degree is A "MATERIALIZING" MEDIUM GIVING A SEANCE. I stated
in chapter 6 that Crowley's lunar placement largely accounted for his
phenomenal proficiency at the practice of ceremonial magic. This
Sabian symbol reinforces that assessment in a powerful way. The
intensity of his perceptual abilities in relation to religious imagery
and an actual piercing of the veil that normally shrouds the spiritual
world from material perception could hardly be more strongly indicated. One of Crowley's great difficulties, attested to by Israel
Regardie who knew him personally, was a natural assumption on his

part that other people shared in his remarkable erudition and perceptual abilities. It is no wonder that he tried to develop techniques for teaching others to see and experience the things that he saw and experienced in keeping with the motto of his own magickal order: "The method of science; the aim of religion." But alas, his remarkable abilities were quite unique and simply cannot be duplicated by others at will.

The four remaining planets in Crowley's lunar gestalt are Neptune and Pluto in intercepted Taurus in his Tenth House, Mercury and Jupiter in intercepted Scorpio in his Fourth House, with Jupiter in opposition to Neptune and Mercury in wide opposition to Pluto. The Sabian symbols for the degrees in which those four planets are placed suggest a host of insights into their functions as components of Crowley's personality, which should be considered within the context of the interpretation presented in chapter 10. The symbol for the degree of Neptune's placement, (TAURUS 3°): NATURAL STEPS LEAD TO A LAWN OF CLOVER IN BLOOM, is appropriate to Neptune's association with the biological realm in general and sexual attraction in particular (clover attracting bees for making honey). The natural steps imply a graded process of attainment appropriate to the discipline of sex magick. On the other hand, Pluto's degree symbol, (TAURUS 24°): AN INDIAN WARRIOR RIDING FIERCELY, HUMAN SCALPS HANGING FROM HIS BELT, implies a trans-biological function (killing) appropriate to Pluto's transcendental connotation as developed in chapter 9 of this book. Here we find the significance of transcendence associated with the warrior attitude appropriate to Crowley's conception of the New Aeon. These powerful transformational agents operated as components of Crowley's *office* (Tenth House)—that is, what he stood for publicly.

The Sabian symbol for the degree of Crowley's Jupiter placement, (SCORPIO 8°): A CALM LAKE BATHED IN MOONLIGHT, suggests both a romantic ideal and a capacity for reflective meditation from deep within his personality (Fourth House). Jupiter's opposition to Neptune in Crowley's birthchart is highlighted by the Sabian symbols for their respective degree placements. Both his expansive romanticism and the powerful sexual current of his inspiration are expressive of the consciousness generating tension of this aspect and its associated symbolism. The Sabian symbol for Mercury's degree in Crowley's birthchart, (SCORPIO 14°): TELEPHONE LINEMEN AT WORK INSTALLING NEW CONNECTIONS, in contrast to Jupiter's degree symbol, portrays active involvement in a highly technical

process. One could hardly imagine a more appropriate image for
Mercury's planetary function. Considered in terms of Mercury's
opposition to Pluto in Crowley's birthchart, we can readily understand his active involvement in working to establish new ways of
thinking, literally rearranging neurological connections in his own
brain and the brains of others to accord with the active ideals appropriate to the conception of the New Aeon of Horus, the Crowned and
Conquering Child.

A concluding observation can be made with regard to the analysis
of the Sabian degree symbols for the planetary and nodal placements
in the birthchart of Aleister Crowley. The phenomenal appropriateness of the images to the respective planetary functions, not only
considered independently but also within the context of his total
planetary configuration, is indicative of a truly remarkable individual. Although it is surely the case that a greater familiarity with the
whole series of Sabian symbols increases one's ability to appreciate
this observation, it should nonetheless prove strikingly apparent to
the reader even as a first encounter with this system of symbols and
how they can be applied to the interpretation of a natal configuration.

REFERENCES

Augustine. *City of God.* Trans. Gerald G. Walsh, et al. Ed. Vernon J. Bourke. New York: Image Books-Doubleday, 1958.

Campbell, Joseph, with Bill Moyers. *The Power of Myth.* Ed. Betty Sue Flowers. New York: Doubleday, 1988.

Crowley, Aleister. *The Book of the Law.* 1938. New York: Samuel Weiser, Inc. 1976.

— *The Confessions of Aleister Crowley: An Autobiography.* Ed. John Symonds and Kenneth Grant. London: Arkana-Penguin, 1989.

— *The Equinox of the Gods.* 1936. Tempe, AZ: New Falcon Publications, 1991.

— *The Law is for All: An Extended Commentary on The Book of the Law.* Ed. Israel Regardie. Tempe, AZ: New Falcon Publications, 1986.

— *Magick Without Tears.* Ed. Israel Regardie. Tempe, AZ: New Falcon Publications, 1991.

Crowley, Aleister, Lon Milo DuQuette, and Christopher S. Hyatt. *Enochian World of Aleister Crowley: Enochian Sex Magic.* Tempe, AZ: New Falcon Publications, 1991.

Davies, P[aul] C.W., and J.R. Brown. *The Ghost in the Atom.* 1986. New York: Cambridge University Press, 1993.

Davies, Paul, and John Gribbin. *The Matter Myth.* New York: Touchstone-Simon & Schuster, 1992.

Gettings, Fred. *The Arkana Dictionary of Astrology.* 1985. New York: Arkana-Penguin, 1990.

Howe, Ellic. *The Magicians of the Golden Dawn.* 1972. New York: Samuel Weiser, Inc., 1978.

James, William. *The Varieties of Religious Experience.* New York: Mentor-New American Library, 1958.

King, Francis. *Crowley on Christ.* 1953. London: The C.W. Daniel Company Ltd., 1974.

Levi, Eliphas. *The Book of Splendours.* 1973. York Beach: Samuel Weiser, Inc., 1984.

New Larousse Encyclopedia of Mythology. Trans. Richard Alsington, and Delano Ames. New York: Crescent Books-Crown, 1968.

Regardie, Israel. *The Eye in the Triangle: An Interpretation of Aleister Crowley.* 1970. Phoenix: Falcon Press, 1982.

—, ed. *Gems From the Equinox: Instructions by Aleister Crowley for His Own Magickal Order.* Phoenix: Falcon Press, 1986.

—, ed. *777 and Other Qabalistic Writings of Aleister Crowley.* 1973. New York: Samuel Weiser, Inc., 1979.

Regardie, Israel, and P.R. Stephensen. *The Legend of Aleister Crowley.* 1930. Phoenix: Falcon Press, 1986.

Rifkin, Jeremy, with Ted Howard. *Entropy: A New World View.* New York: Bantam Books-Viking, 1981.

Roberts, Susan. The Magician of the Golden Dawn: *The Story of Aleister Crowley.* Chicago: Contemporary Books, Inc., 1978.

Rudhyar, Dane. *An Astrological Mandala: The Cycle of Transformations and its 360 Symbolic Phases.* New York: Vintage Books-Random House, 1973.

— *Astrological Signs: The Pulse of Life.* 1943. Boulder: Shambhala, 1978.

— *Astrological Timing: The Transition to the New Age.* 1969. New York: Harper Colophon Books-Harper & Row, 1972.

— *The Lunation Cycle: A Key to the Understanding of Personality.* 1967. Boulder: Shambhala, 1971.

Schulman, Martin. *The Moon's Nodes and Reincarnation.* Karmic Astrology, Vol. I. New York: Samuel Weiser, Inc., 1978.

Sheldrake, Rupert. *A New Science of Life: The Hypothesis of Formative Causation.* Los Angeles: J.P. Tarcher, Inc., 1981.

Suster, Gerald. *The Legacy of the Beast: The Life, Work and Influence of Aleister Crowley.* 1988. York Beach: Samuel Weiser, Inc., 1989.

Thompson, William Irwin. *The Time Falling Bodies Take to Light: Mythology, Sexuality, and the Origins of Culture.* New York: St. Martin's Press, Inc., 1981.

Wilson, Colin. *Aleister Crowley: The Nature of the Beast.* Wellingborough: The Aquarian Press, 1987.

Wilson, Robert Anton. *Cosmic Trigger: Final Secret of the Illuminati.* Tempe, AZ: New Falcon Publications, 1986.

INDEX

THE ACADEMY OF ASTROLOGY

Astrology shows you how the fundamental energies that work in everyone's lives work specifically in *your* life. It shows your uniqueness in relation to the world in terms that everyone else has to deal with also, each in his or her own particular manner. Astrology shows you this in dynamic terms, i.e., not only the basic pattern of your personality, but also the evolving pattern of your personal development in relation to the complex of ever-changing movements of energies in the world.

The Academy of Astrology teaches you how to use astrology in the way it is applied in *Astrology, Aleister & Aeon,* addressing all of the philosophical issues that arise in relation to astrology. Many people hold philosophical positions that are not compatible with astrology. The Academy explores those positions to both resolve any philosophical objections to astrology, and to show the rich philosophical heritage to which astrology has made no mean contribution.

Are you interested in how this technique can be applied to your own birthchart? Do you want to know how to see astrological patterns moving and appearing in the world around you, and how this knowledge can enhance your understanding of life? If so, you may request more information by sending your name and mailing address to:

The Academy of Astrology
5001 E Bonanza Road, Suite 102-423
Las Vegas, NV 89100
U.S.A.